Mrs. Sutherland Orr

**A Handbook to the Works of Robert Browning**

Mrs. Sutherland Orr

**A Handbook to the Works of Robert Browning**

ISBN/EAN: 9783337139117

Printed in Europe, USA, Canada, Australia, Japan

Cover: Foto ©ninafisch / pixelio.de

More available books at **www.hansebooks.com**

# HANDBOOK TO BROWNING'S WORKS.

# A HANDBOOK

## TO THE WORKS OF

# ROBERT BROWNING.

BY

## MRS. SUTHERLAND ORR.

*SIXTH EDITION, REVISED.*

" No pause i' the leading and the light ! "
*The Ring and the Book,* vol. ix. p. 216.

LONDON :
GEORGE BELL & SONS, YORK ST., COVENT GARDEN,
AND NEW YORK.
1892.

CHISWICK PRESS:—C. WHITTINGHAM AND CO., TOOKS COURT,
CHANCERY LANE.

# PREFACE TO THE FIRST EDITION.

THIS book was written at the request of some of the members of the Browning Society, and was originally intended to be a primer. It bears the marks of this intention in its general scheme, and in the almost abrupt brevity which the desired limits of space seemed to impose on its earlier part. But I felt from the first that the spirit of Mr. Browning's work could neither be compressed within the limits, nor adapted to the uses, of a primer, as generally understood ; and the book has naturally shaped itself into a kind of descriptive Index, based partly on the historical order and partly on the natural classification of the various poems. No other plan suggested itself, at the time, for bringing the whole series of these poems at once under the reader's eye : since a description which throughout followed the historical order would have involved both lengthiness and repetition ; while, as I have tried to show, there exists no scheme of natural classification into which the whole series could have been forced. I realize, only now that it is too late, that the arrangement is clumsy and confusing : or at least has become so by the manner in which I have carried it out ; and that even if it justify itself to the mind of my readers, it can never be helpful or attractive to their eye, which had the first right to be considered. That I should have failed in a first attempt, however earnest, to meet the difficulties of such a task, is so natural as to be almost beyond regret, where my credit only is concerned ; but I shall be very sorry if this result of my inexperience detracts from any usefulness which the Handbook might otherwise possess as a guide to Mr. Browning's works. I note also, and with real vexation, some blunders of a more mechanical kind, which I might have been expected to avoid.

I have been indebted for valuable advice to Mr. Furnivall ; and for fruitful suggestion to Mr. Nettleship, whose proposed scheme of classification I have in some degree followed.

A. ORR.

*March 2nd,* 1885.

## PREFACE TO THE SECOND EDITION.

N preparing the Handbook for its second edition, my first endeavour has been to correct, as far as possible, the faults which I acknowledged in my Preface to the first. But even before the time for doing so had arrived, I had convinced myself that where construction or arrangement was concerned, these faults could not be corrected : that I, at least, could discover no more artistic method of compressing into a small space, and to any practical purpose, an even relatively just view of Mr. Browning's work. The altered page-headings will, where they occur, soften away the harshness of the classification, while they remove a distinct anomaly : the discussion of such a poem as " Pauline " under its own title, such a one as " Aristophanes' Apology," under that of a group ; but even this slight improvement rather detracts from than increases what little symmetry my scheme possessed. The other changes which, on my own account, I have been able to make, include the re-writing of some

passages in which the needful condensation had unneces-
sarily mutilated the author's sense ; the completing of
quotation references which through an unforeseen accident had been printed off in an unfinished state ; and the
addition of a few bibliographical facts.  By Mr. Browning's desire, I have corrected two mistakes : the misread-
ing, on my part, of **an** historical allusion in **" The** Statue
and the Bust," and **of a** poetical sentiment **expressed in**
" Pictor Ignotus "—and, by the **insertion of a word or sen-**
tence in the notice of **each,** expanded **or** emphasized the
meaning of several of the minor poems.  I should have
stated in my first Preface, had not the fact appeared to
me self-evident, that I owe to Mr. Browning's kindness
all the additional matter which my own reading could not
supply : such as the index to the Greek names in **" Aris-**
tophanes' Apology," and the Persian in " Ferishtah's
Fancies ;" the notes to " Transcendentalism," and " Pietro
of Abano ;" and that he has allowed me to study in the
original documents the story of " The Ring and the Book."
The two signed notes by which he has enriched the present edition have grown out of recent circumstances.

A. ORR.

*January 11th,* 1886.

## PREFACE TO THE THIRD **EDITION.**

THE present edition of the Handbook includes a
summary **of** Mr. Browning's " Parleyings," which
from the contents of this volume, as well as from
its recent appearance, finds its natural place in a Supplement.

I have added an Index **to the** six volumes of the
" Works," which has been desired for greater facility **of**
reference.

Various corrections and improvements of the nature indicated in the Preface to my second edition have been also made in the book.

A. ORR.

*June 25th*, 1887.


## PREFACE TO THE FIFTH EDITION.

THE deeply painful circumstances in which the Handbook re-appears have compelled me to defer the fulfilment of Mr. Browning's wish, that its quotation references should be adapted to the use of readers of his new edition. They also leave it the poorer by some interesting notes which he more than once promised me for my next reprint; I had never the heart to say to him : "Is it not safer to give them now?"

The correction, p. 149, of the note referring to p. 184 of "Aristophanes' Apology," was lately made by Mr. Browning in the Handbook, pending the time when he could repeat it in his own work. The cancelled footnote on my 353rd page means that he did remove the contradiction of which I spoke.

An open discussion on "Numpholeptos," which took place some months ago, made me aware that my little abstract was less helpful even than its brevity allowed, because I had emphasized the imagery of the poem where it most obscured—or least distinctly illustrated—its idea ; and I re-wrote a few sentences which I now offer in their amended form. A phrase or two in "One Word More" has been altered for the sake of more literal accuracy. No other correction worth specifying has been made in the book.

A. ORR.

*January 7th*, 1890.

## PREFACE TO THE SIXTH EDITION.

THE changes made in the present edition have been almost entirely bibliographical. Their chief object was that indicated in an earlier preface, of bringing the Handbook into correspondence with the latest issue of Mr. Browning's works. I felt reluctant when making them, to entirely sacrifice the convenience of those students of Browning who from necessity, or, as in my own case, from affection, still cling to the earlier editions; and would gladly have retained the old references while inserting the **new.** All however that seemed practical in this direction was to combine the index **of** 1868 with that **of** 1889 in **so far as** they **run** parallel with each other.

A long felt want has been supplied by the addition to the Handbook of a Bibliography of Mr. Browning's works, based on that of Dr. Furnivall, and thoroughly revised by Mr. Dykes Campbell. The bibliographical details scattered throughout the work have also been made more complete.

The time and trouble required for the altered quotation references have been reduced to a minimum by the thoughtful kindness of my friend Miss Fanny Carey of Trent Leigh, Nottingham; who voluntarily, many months ago, prepared for me a list of the new page numbers, leaving them only to be transcribed when the time came. I have also to thank Mr. G. M. Smith for a copy of his general Index to the works.

A. ORR.

*Dec.* 1st, 1891.

# TABLE OF CONTENTS.

## CLASSIFIED GROUPS.

# Contents.

PAGE

# HANDBOOK TO BROWNING'S WORKS.

## GENERAL CHARACTERISTICS.

### THE NATURE OF MR. BROWNING'S GENIUS.

IF we were called upon to describe Mr. Browning's poetic genius in one phrase, we should say it consisted of an almost unlimited power of imagination exerted upon real things ; but we should have to explain that with Mr. Browning the real includes everything which a human being can think or feel, and that he is realistic only in the sense of being never visionary ; he never deals with those vague and incoherent fancies, so attractive to some minds, which we speak of as coming only from the poet's brain. He imagines vividly because he observes keenly and also feels strongly ; and this vividness of his nature puts him in equal sympathy with the real and the ideal—with the seen and the unseen. The one is as living to him as the other.

His treatment of visible and of invisible realities constitutes him respectively a dramatic and a metaphysical poet ; but, as the two kinds of reality are inseparable in human life, so are the corresponding qualities inseparable in Mr. Browning's work. The dramatic activity of his genius always includes the metaphysical. His genius always shows itself as dramatic and metaphysical at the same time.

Mr. Browning's genius is dramatic because it always expresses itself in the forms of real life, in the supposed experiences of men and women. These men and women are usually in a state of mental disturbance or conflict ; indeed, they think much more than they act. But their thinking tends habitually to a practical result ; and it keeps up our sense of their reality by clothing itself always in the most practical and picturesque language which thought can assume. It has been urged that he does not sink himself in his characters as a completely dramatic writer should; and this argument must stand for what it is worth. His personality may in some degree be constructed from his works : it is, I think, generally admitted, that that of Shakespeare cannot ; and in so far as this is the test of a complete dramatist, Mr. Browning fails of being one. He does not sink himself in his men and women, for his sympathy with them is too active to admit of it. He not only describes their different modes of being, but defends them from their own point of view ; and it is natural that he should often select for this treatment characters with which he is already disposed to sympathize. But his women are no less living and no less distinctive than his men ; and he sinks his individuality at all times enough to interest us in the characters which are not akin to his own as much as in those which are. Even if it were otherwise, if his men and women were all variations of himself, as imagined under differences of sex, of age, of training, or of condition, he would still be dramatic in this essential quality, the only one which bears on our contention : that everything which, as a poet, he thinks or feels, comes from him in a dramatic, that is to say, a completely living form.

It is in this way also that his dramatic genius includes

the metaphysical. The abstract, **no** less than the practical questions which shape themselves in his mind, are put before us in the thoughts and words, in the character and conduct of his men and women. This does not mean that human experience solves for him all the questions which it can be made to state, or that everything he believes can be verified by it : for in **that case his mode of** thought would be scientific, and **not** metaphysical ; **it** simply means, that so much of abstract **truth as cannot be** given in a picture of human life, lies outside his philosophy of it. He accepts this residue as the ultimate mystery of what must be called Divine Thought. Thought or spirit is with **him the** ultimate fact of **existence ; the one** thing about which it is **vain to** theorize, **and which we can never** get behind. His gospel would begin, **"In the** beginning **was** the Thought ;" and since he can only conceive this as self-conscious, his "Alpha and Omega" is a Divine intelligence from which all the ideas of the human intellect are derived, and which stamps them as true. These religious conceptions are the meeting-ground of the dramatic and the metaphysical activity of his poetic genius. The two **are** blended in the vision of **a** Supreme Being not to be invested **with** human emotions, **but only** to be reached through them.

**To** show that Mr. Browning is a metaphysical poet, is to show that he is not a metaphysical *thinker*, though he is a thinker whose thought is metaphysical so **far** as principle goes. A metaphysical thinker is always **in** some way or other thinking about *thought;* **and** this is precisely what Mr. Browning has no occasion to do, because he takes its assumptions upon trust. He is a constant analyst of secondary motives and judgments. No modern freethinker could make a larger allowance for what is incidental, personal, and even material in them : we shall see that all his practical philosophy is bound up with this fact. But he has never questioned the origin of our primary or innate ideas, for he has, as I have said, never questioned their truth. It is essential to bear in mind that Mr. Browning is a metaphysical poet, and not a metaphysical thinker, to do justice to the depth and originality of his creative power; for his imagination includes everything which at a given moment a human being can think or feel, and often finds itself, therefore, at some point to which other minds have *reasoned* their way. The coincidence occurs most often with German lines of thought, and it has therefore been concluded that he has studied the works in which they are laid down, or has otherwise moved in the same track; the fact being that he has no bond of union with German philosophers, but the natural tendencies of his own mind. It may be easily ascertained that he did not read their language until late in life; and if what I have said of his mental habits is true, it is equally certain that their methods have been more foreign to him still. He resembles Hegel, Fichte, or Schelling, as the case may be, by the purely creative impulse which has met their thought, and which, if he had lived earlier, might have forestalled it. Mr. Browning's position is that of a fixed centre of thought and feeling. Fifty years ago he was in advance of his age. He stood firm and has allowed the current to overtake him, or even leave him behind. If I may be allowed a comparison: other mental existences suggest the idea of a river, flowing onwards, amidst varying scenes, and in a widening bed, to lose itself in the sea. Mr. Browning's genius appears the sea itself, with its immensity and its limits, its restlessness and its repose, the constant self-balancing of its ebb and flow.

As both dramatic and metaphysical poet, Mr. Browning is inspired by one central doctrine: that while thought is absolute in itself, it is relative or personal to the mind which thinks it; so that no one man can attain the whole truth of any abstract subject, and no other can convict him of having failed to do **so.** And he also believes that since intellectual truth is so largely for each of **us a** matter of personal impression, no language is special enough to convey it. The arguments which he carries on through the mouths of his men and women often represent **even** moral truth as something too subtle, too complex, and too changing, to be definitely expressed ; and if we did not see that he reverences **what is good as** much as he excuses **what is bad, we** might **imagine** that even on this ground **he** considered **no fixed knowledge** to be attainable. These opinions **are, however,** closely bound **up** with his religious beliefs, **and in great** measure explained **by** them. He **is** convinced that uncertainty is essential to the spiritual life ; and his works are saturated by the idea that where uncertainty ceases, stagnation must begin ; that our light **must** be wavering, and our progress tentative, as well as our hopes chequered, and our happiness even devoid of any sense of finality, if the creative intention is not to frustrate itself ; we may not see the path of progress and salvation clearly marked out before **us.** On the other hand, he believes that the circumstances of life are **as much** adapted to the guidance of each separate soul **as if each were the single** object **of** creative care ; and that **therefore while the** individual knows nothing of the Divine scheme, he *is* everything in it.

This faith **in** personality **is** naturally abstruse on the metaphysical side, but it is always picturesque on the dramatic ; for it issues in that love **of** the unusual which is so striking to every reader of Mr. Browning's works ; and we might characterize these in a few words, by saying that they reflect at once the extent of his general sympathies, and his antagonism **to** everything which is general. But the "unusual" which attracts him is not the morbid or the monstrous, for these mean defective life. It is every healthy escape from the conventional and the commonplace, which are also defective life ; and this is why we find in his men and women those vivid, various, and subtly compounded motives and feelings, which make our contact with them a slight, but continuous electric shock.

And since the belief in personality is the belief in human life in its fullest and truest form, it includes the belief in love and self-sacrifice. It may, indeed, be said that while Mr. Browning's judgments are leavened by the one idea, they are steadily coloured by the other ; this again being so evident to his serious readers that I need only indicate it here. But the love of love does more than colour his views of life ; it is an essential element in his theology ; and it converts what would otherwise be a pure Theism into a mystical Christianity which again is limited by his rejection of all dogmatic religious truth. I have already alluded to his belief that, though the Deity is not to be invested with human emotions, He can only be reached through them. Love, according to him, is the necessary channel ; since a colourless Omnipotence is outside the conception as outside the sympathies of man. Christ is a message of Divine love, indispensable and therefore true ; but He is, as such, a spiritual mystery far more than a definable or dogmatic fact. A definite revelation uttered for all men and for all time is denied by the first principles of Mr. Browning's religious belief. What Christianity means for him, and what it does not, we shall also see in his works.

It is almost superfluous to add that Mr. Browning's dramatic sympathies and metaphysical or religious ideas constitute him an optimist. He believes that no experience is wasted, and that all life is good in its way. We also see that his optimism takes the individual and not the race for its test and starting point ; and that he places the tendency to good in a *conscious* creative power which is outside both, and which deals directly with each separate

human soul. But neither must we forget that the creative
purpose, as he conceives it, fulfils itself equally through
good and evil; so that he does not shrink from the contemplation of evil or by any means always seek to ex-
tenuate it. He thinks of it philosophically as a condition
of good, or again, as an excess or a distortion of what is
good; but he can also think of it, in the natural sense, as
a distinct mode of being which a bad man may prefer for
its own sake, as a good man prefers its opposite, and may
defend accordingly. He would gladly admit that the
coarser forms of evil are passing away; and that it is the
creative intention that they should do so. Evil remains
for him nevertheless essential to the variety, and invested
with the dignity of human life; and on no point does he
detach himself so clearly from the humanitarian optimist
who regards evil and its attendant sufferings as a mere
disturbance to life. Even where suffering is not caused by
evil doing, he is helped over it by his individual point of
view; because this prevents his ever regarding it as distinct from the personal compensations which it so often
brings into play. He cannot think of it in the mass;
and here again his theism asserts itself, though in a less
obvious manner.

So much of Mr. Browning's moral influence lies in the
hopeful religious spirit which his works reveal, that it is
important to understand how elastic this is, and what
seeming contradictions it is competent to unite. The
testimony of one poem might otherwise be set against that
of another with confusing results.

Mr. Browning's paternal grandfather was an Englishman of a west country stock;[1] his paternal grandmother a

[1] I stated in my first edition that Mr. Browning was descended from the
"Captain Micaiah Browning" who raised the siege of Derry in 1689 by
springing the boom across Lough Foyle, and perished in the act (the incident being related in Macaulay's "History of England," vol. iv., pp. 244
and 245 of the edition of 1858). I am now told that there is no evidence of
this lineal descent, though there are circumstances which point to some kind

Creole. The maternal grandfather was a German from Hamburg named Wiedemann, an accomplished draughts-man and musician.[1]  The maternal grandmother was completely Scotch.

This pedigree throws a valuable light on the vigour and variety of Mr. Browning's genius; for it shows that on the ground of heredity they are, in great measure, accounted for.  It contains almost the only facts of a biographical nature which can be fitly introduced into the present work.

## HIS CHOICE AND TREATMENT OF SUBJECT.
### VERSIFICATION.

Mr. Browning's choice of subject is determined by his belief that individual feeling and motive are the only true life : hence the only true material of dramatic art. He rejects no incident which admits of development on the side of feeling and motive.  He accepts none which cannot be so developed.  His range of subject covers, therefore, a great deal that is painful, but nothing that is simply repulsive : because the poetry of human life, that is, of individual experience, is absent from nothing which he portrays.

His treatment of his subject is realistic in so far that it is always picturesque.  It raises a distinct image of the person or action he intends to describe ; but the image is, so to speak, always saturated with thought : and I shall later have occasion to notice the false impression of Mr.

of relationship.  Another probable ancestor is Captain ⸺ Browning, who commanded the ship "Holy Ghost," which conveyed Henry V. to France before he fought the battle of Agincourt; and in return for whose services two waves, said to represent waves of the sea, were added to his coat of arms. The same arms were worn by Captain Micaiah Browning, and are so by the present family.

[1] Wiedèmann is the second baptismal name of Mr. Browning's son ; and, in his infantine mouth, it became (we do not exactly guess how), the "Penini," shortened into "Pen," which some ingenious interpreters have derived from the word "Apennine."

Browning's genius which this circumstance creates. Details, which with realists of a narrower kind would give only a physical impression of the scene described, serve in his case to build up its mental impression. They create a mental or emotional atmosphere which makes us vaguely feel the intention of the story as we travel through it, and flashes it upon us as we look back. In "Red Cotton Night-cap Country" (as we shall presently see) he dwells so significantly on the peacefulness of the neighbourhood in which the tragedy has occurred, that we feel in it the quiet which precedes the storm, and which in some measure invites it. In one of the Idyls, "Ivàn Ivànovitch," he begins by describing the axe which will strike off the woman's head, and raising a vague idea of its fitness for any possible use. In another of them, "Martin Relph," the same process is carried on in an opposite manner. We see a mental agony before we know its substantial cause; and we only see the cause as reflected in it. "Ned Bratts," again, conveys in its first lines the sensation of a tremendously hot day in which Nature seems to reel in a kind of riotous stupefaction; and the grotesque tragedy on which the idyl turns, becomes a matter of course. It would be easy to multiply examples.

Mr. Browning's verse is also subordinate to this intellectual theory of poetic art. It is uniformly inspired by the principle that sense should not be sacrificed to sound : and this principle constitutes his chief ground of divergence from other poets. It is a case of divergence— nothing more : since he is too deeply a musician to be indifferent to sound in verse, and since no other poet deserving the name would willingly sacrifice sense to it. But while all agree in admitting that sense and sound in poetry are the natural complement of each other, each will be practically more susceptible to one than to the other, and will unconsciously seek it at the expense of the other. With all his love for music, Mr. Browning is more susceptible to sense than to sound. He values thought more than expression ; matter, more than form ; and, judging him from a strictly poetic point of view, he has lost his balance in this direction, as so many have lost it in the opposite one. He has never ignored beauty, but he has neglected it in the desire for significance. He has never meant to be rugged, but he has become so, in the exercise of strength. He has never intended to be obscure, but he has become so from the condensation of style which was the excess of significance and of strength. Habit grows on us by degrees till its slight invisible links form an iron chain, till it overweights its object, and even ends in crushing it out of sight ; and Mr. Browning has illustrated this natural law. The self-enslavement was the more inevitable in his case that he was not only an earnest worker, but a solitary one. His genius[1] removed him from the first from that sphere of popular sympathy in which the tendency to excess would have been corrected ; and the distance, like the mental habit which created it, was self-increasing.

It is thus that Mr. Browning explains the eccentricities of his style ; and his friends know that beyond the point of explaining, he does not defend them. He has never blamed his public for accusing him of obscurity or ugliness. He has only thought those wrong who taxed him with being wilfully ugly or obscure. He began early to defy public opinion because his best endeavours had failed to conciliate it ; and he would never conciliate it at the expense of what he believed to be the true principles of his art. But his first and greatest failure from a popular point of view was the result of his willingness to accept any judgment, however unfavourable, which coincided with this belief.

"Paracelsus," had recently been published, and declared

---

[1] And—we are bound to admit—the singular literary obtuseness of the England of fifty years ago.

"unintelligible ;" and Mr. Browning was pondering this fact and concluding that he had failed to be intelligible because he had been **too** concise, when an extract from **a** letter of Miss Caroline Fox was forwarded to him by the lady to whom it had been addressed. The writer stated that John Sterling had tried to read the poem **and been** repelled by its *verbosity;* and she ended with **this** question : "*doth he know that Wordsworth will devote a fortnight or more to the discovery of the single word* **that is** *the one fit for his sonnet ?*"

Mr. Browning was not personally acquainted with either John Sterling or Caroline Fox, and what he knew of the former as a poet did not, to his mind, bear out this marked objection to wordiness. Still, he gave the joint criticism all the weight it deserved ; and much more than **it deserved** in the case of Miss Fox, whom he imagined, **from** her self-confident manner, to be a woman of **a** certain age, instead of a girl some years younger than himself ; and often, he tells us, during the period immediately following, he contented himself with two words where he would rather have used ten. The harsh and involved passages in " Sordello," which add so much to the remoteness **of** its thought, were **the first** consequence **of** this lesson. " Pauline " and " Paracelsus " had **been** deeply musical, and the music came back **to** their author's **verse** with the dramas, lyrics, and romances by which " Sordello " was followed. But the dread of being diffuse had doubly rooted itself in his mind, and was to bear fruit again as soon as the more historical or argumentative mood should prevail.

The determination never to sacrifice sense to sound is the secret of whatever repels us in Mr. Browning's verse, and also of whatever attracts. Wherever in it sense keeps company with sound, we have a music far deeper than can arise from mere sound, or even from a flow of real lyric emotion, which has its only counterpart *in* sound. It is in the idea, and of it. It is the brain picture beating itself into words.

The technical rules by which Mr. Browning works, carry out his principle to the fullest extent.

I. He uses the smallest number of words which his meaning allows ; is particularly sparing in adjectives.

II. He uses the largest *relative* number of Saxon (therefore picturesque) words.[1]

III. He uses monosyllabic words wherever this is possible.

IV. He farther condenses his style by abbreviations and omissions, of which some are discarded, but all warranted by authority : " in," " on," and " of," for instance, become " i'," " o'," and " o'." Pronouns, articles, conjunctions, and prepositions are, on the same principle, occasionally left out.

V. He treats consonants as the backbone of the language, and hence, as the essential feature in a rhyme ; and never allows the repetition of a consonant in a rhyme to be modified by a change in the preceding vowel, or by the recurrence of the rhyming syllable in a different word —or the repetition of a consonant in blank verse to create a half-consonance resembling a rhyme : though other poets do not shrink from doing so.[2]

---

[1] A distinguished American philologist, the late George P. Marsh, has declared that he exceeds all other modern English writers in his employment of them.

[2] In "In Memoriam" we have such rhymes as :—

| { now | { curse | { mourn | { good | { light | { report |
| { low | { horse | { turn | { blood | { delight | { port |

In the blank verse of "The Princess," and of "Enoch Arden" such assonances as :—

| { sun | { lost | { whom | { wand |
| { noon | { burst | { seem | { hand. |

| { known | { clipt | { word |
| { down | { kept | { wood, etc. |

I take these instances from the works of so acknowledged a master of verse as Mr. Tennyson, rather than from those of a smaller poet who would be no authority on the subject, because they thus serve to show that the poetic ear may have different kinds as well as degrees of sensibility, and must, in every case, be accepted as, to some extent, a law to itself.

VI. He seldom dilutes his emphasis by double rhymes, reserving these—especially when made up of combined words, and producing **a** grotesque effect—for those **cases** in which the meaning **is** given with **a** modifying colour : a satirical, or self-satirical, intention on the writer's part. Strong instances of **this** occur in **"The** Flight of **the** Duchess," " Christmas Eve," **and** " Pacchiarotto."

VII. He always uses the measure **most** appropriate to his subject, whether **it** be the ten-syllabled blank verse which makes up " The Ring and the Book," the separate dramatic monologues, and nearly **all the** dramas, or the heroic rhymed verse which occurs **in** " Sordello" and " Fifine at the Fair ;" or one of the lyrical measures, of which his slighter poems contain almost, if not quite, every known form.[1]

VIII. **He** takes no liberties with unusual measures ; though he takes any admissible liberty **with** the usual measures, which will interrupt their monotony, and strengthen their effect.

IX. He eschews many vulgarisms or inaccuracies which custom has sanctioned, both in prose and verse, such as, "thou *wert ;*" "better than *them* **all** ;" " he *need* not ;" " he *dare* not." The universal " I *had* better ;" " I *had* rather," is abhorrent to him.[2]

[1] " La Saisiaz," for instance, is written in the same measure as " Locksley Hall," fifteen syllables, divided by a pause, into groups of four trochees, and of three and a half—the last syllable forming the rhyme. It is admirably suited to the sustained and incisive manner in which the argument is carried on. " Ixion," in " Jocoseria," is in alternate hexameter and pentameter, which the author also employs here for the only time ; it imitates the turning of the wheel on which Ixion is bound. " Pheidippides" is in a measure of Mr. Browning's own, composed of dactyls and spondees, each line ending with a half foot or pause. It gives the impression of firm, continuous, and rhythmic motion, and is generally fitted to convey the exalted sentiment and heroic character of the poem.

In his translation of the " Agamemnon," Mr. Browning has used the double ending continuously, so as to reproduce the extended measure of the Greek iambic trimeter.

[2] An objection has been taken to the opinions conveyed in this paragraph,

X. No prosaic turns or tricks of language are ever associated in his verse with a poetic mood.

## The Continuous Character of his Work.

The writer of a handbook to Mr. Browning's poetry must contend with exceptional difficulties, growing out of what I have tried to describe as the unity in variety of Mr. Browning's poetic life. This unity of course impresses itself on his works; and in order to give a systematic survey of them, we must treat as a collection of separate facts what is really a living whole ; and seek to give the impression of that whole by a process of classification which cuts it up alive. Mr. Browning's work is, to all intents and purposes, one group; and though we may divide and

and Mr. Browning's authority has been even, in a manner, invoked against them, I subjoin by his desire the accompanying note. The question of what is, or is not, a vicious locution is not essential to the purposes of the book ; but it is essential that I should not be supposed to have misstated Mr. Browning's views on any point on which I could so easily ascertain them.

"I make use of 'wast' for the second person of the perfect-indicative, and 'wert' for the present-potential, simply to be understood; as I should hardly be if I substituted the latter for the former, and therewith ended my phrase. 'Where wert thou, brother, those three days, had He not raised thee?' means one thing, and 'Where wast thou when He did so?' means another. That there is precedent in plenty for this and many similar locutions ambiguous, or archaic, or vicious, I am well aware, and that, on their authority, I *be* wrong, the illustrious poet *be* right, and you, our critic, *was* and shall continue to be my instructor as to 'every thing that pretty *bin*.' As regards my objection to the slovenly 'I had' for 'I'd,' instead of the proper 'I would,' I shall not venture to supplement what Landor has magisterially spoken on the subject. An adverb adds to, and does not, by its omission, alter into nonsense the verb it qualifies. 'I would rather speak than be silent, better criticize than learn' are forms structurally regular : what meaning is in 'I had speak, had criticize'? Then, I am blamed for preferring the indicative to what I suppose may be the potential mood in the case of 'need' and 'dare'—just that unlucky couple: by all means go on and say 'He need help, he dare me to fight,' and so pair off with 'He need not beg, he dare not reply,' forms which may be expected to pullulate in this morning's newspaper.

"Venice, Oct. 25, 1885."                              "R B."

subdivide **it for** purposes of illustration, the division will be always more or less artificial, and, unless explained away, more or less misleading. We cannot even divide **it** into periods, for **if** the first three poems represent **the** author's intellectual youth, the remainder **are one** long maturity; while even in these the poetic faculty shows itself full-grown. **We** cannot **trace** in it **the** evidence of successive manners like **those of** Raphael, or successive moods like those of Shakespeare; or, if **we** do, this is neutralized by the simple fact that **Mr.** Browning's productive career has been infinitely longer than was Raphael's, and considerably so than Shakespeare's; and that changes which meant the development of a genius in their case, mean the course of a life in his.

And this **is** the central fact of the case. Mr. Browning's work **is** himself. His poetic genius was in **advance of** his general growth, but it has been subject **to** no **other** law. "**The** Ring and the Book" was written at what may be considered the turning-point **of a** human life. It was in some degree a turning-point in **the** author's artistic career: for most of his emotional poems were published before, and most of the argumentative after it; and in this sense his work may be said **to** divide itself into two. But the division is useless for our purpose. The Browning of the second period is the Browning of **the** first, only in a more crystallized form. No true boundary line can be drawn even here.

My endeavour will, therefore, be **to** bring the sense of this real continuity into the divisions which I must impose on Mr. Browning's work; and thus also to infuse something of his life into the meagre statement of contents to which I am forced **to** reduce it. The few words of explanation by which I preface each group may assist this end. **At** the same time I shall resist all temptation to "bring out" what I have indicated as Mr. Browning's leading ideas by headings, capitals, italics, or any other

artificial device whatever ; as in so doing I should destroy
his emphasis and hinder the right reading, besides effacing
the usually dramatic character, of the individual poems.
The impressions I have received from the collective work
will, I trust, be confirmed by it.

# I.

## INTRODUCTORY GROUP.

### "PAULINE," "PARACELSUS," "SORDELLO."

THESE three poems are Mr. Browning's **first**, and they are also, as I have said, the one partial exception to the unity and continuousness of his work; they have, at least, one common characteristic which detaches them from the remainder of it. Each is in its different way the study of a human spirit, too ambitious to submit to the limits of human existence, and which learns humility in its unsuccessful conflict with them  This ambition is of its nature poetic, and seems so much in harmony with Mr. Browning's mind—young and untutored by experience as it then was, full of the consciousness of its own powers as it must have been—that it is difficult not to recognize in it a phase of his own intellectual life.  But if it was so, it is one which he had already outgrown, or lived much more in fancy than in fact.  His sympathy with the ambition of Paracelsus and Sordello is steadily counteracted by his judgment of it ; and **we** are only justified in asserting what is beyond dispute : that these poems represent **an** introductory phase of the author's imagination, one which begins and ends in them.  The mind of his men and women will be exercised on many things, but never again so much upon itself.  The vivid sense of their personality will be less in their minds than in his own.

C

## "PAULINE." (1832.)

This poem is, as its title declares, a fragment of a confession. The speaker is a man, probably still young; and Pauline, the name of the lady who receives the confession, and is supposed to edit it. It is not, however, "fragmentary" in the sense of revealing only a small part of the speaker's life, or of only recording isolated acts, from which the life may be built up. Its fragmentary character lies in this: that, while very explicit as a record of feeling and motive, it is entirely vague in respect to acts. It is an elaborate retrospect of successive mental states, big with the sense of corresponding misdeeds; and pointing among these to some glaring infidelities to Pauline, the man's constant love and friend; but on the whole conveying nothing beyond an impression of youthful excesses, and of an extreme and fantastic self-consciousness which has inspired these excesses, and which now magnifies and distorts them.

An ultra-consciousness of self is in fact the key-note of the whole mental situation. Pauline's lover has been a prey to the spiritual ambition so distinctly illustrated in these three first poems; and, unlike Paracelsus and Sordello, he has given it no outlet in unselfish aims. His life has not been wholly misspent; he is a poet and a student; he has had dreams of human good; he has reverenced great men: and never quite lost the faith in God, and the sense of nearness to Him; and he alleges some of these facts in deprecation of his too harsh verdict upon himself. But his ultimate object has been always the gratification of Self—the ministering to its pleasures and to its powers; and this egotism has become narrower and more consuming, till the thirst for even momentary enjoyment has banished the very belief in higher things. The belief returns, and we leave him at the close of his confession exhausted by the mental fever, **but** released from it—new-born **to a** better life ; though **how** and why this has happened is again **part of** the mystery of the case. " Pauline " is *the* one of Mr. Browning's longer poems of which no intelligible abstract is possible : a circumstance **the** more striking that it is perfectly transparent, **as** well **as** truly poetical, so far as its language is concerned.

The defects and difficulties of " Pauline " are plainly admitted in an editor's note, written **in** French, and signed by this name ; and which, proceeding as it does from the author himself, supplies a valuable comment **on** the work.

" **I** much fear that **my** poor friend will not **be always** perfectly understood **in what** remains to be **read of this** strange fragment, **but** it is less calculated than **any other** part to explain what of its nature can never **be** anything but dream and confusion. I do not know moreover whether in striving at a better connection of certain parts, one would not run the risk of detracting from the only merit to which so singular a production can pretend : that of giving a tolerably precise idea **of the** manner (*genre*) which it can merely indicate. This unpretending opening, this stir of passion, which first increases, and then gradually subsides, these transports of the soul, this sudden return upon himself, and above all, my friend's quite peculiar turn of mind, have made alterations almost impossible. The reasons which he elsewhere asserts, and others still more cogent have secured my indulgence for **this** paper, which otherwise I should have advised him to throw into the fire. I believe none the less in the great principle of all composition—in that principle **of** Shakespeare, of Raphael, and of Beethoven, according to which concentration of ideas is due much more to their conception than to their execution ; I have every reason to fear that the first of these qualities is still foreign to my friend, and I much doubt whether redoubled labour would enable him to acquire the second. It would be best to burn this; but what can I do?"

\*      \*      \*      \*      \*      \*

\*      \*      \*      \*      \*      \*

We might infer from this, as from his subsequent intro-duction, that Mr. Browning disclaimed all that is extra-vagant in the poem, and laid it simply to the charge of the imaginary person it is intended to depict : but that he has also prefaced it with a curious Latin quotation which identifies that person with himself.[1]

"Pauline" did not take its place among the author's collected works till 1868, when the uniform edition of them appeared; and he then introduced it by a preface (to which I have just alluded) in which he declared his unwilling-ness to publish such a boyish production, and gave the reasons which induced him to do so. The poem is boyish, or at all events youthful, in point of conception; and we need not wonder that this intellectual crudeness should have outweighed its finished poetic beauties in its author's mind. It contains however one piece of mental portrai-ture which, with slight modifications, might have stood for Mr. Browning when he re-edited the work, as it clearly did when he wrote it. It begins thus (vol. i. page 14) :

---

[1] The quoted passage is from the works of Cornelius Agrippa, a well-known professor of occult philosophy, and is indeed introductory to a treatise upon it. The writer is quite aware that his work may be scandalizing, hurtful, and even poisonous to narrow minds, but is sure that readers of a superior understanding will get no little good, and plenty of pleasure from it ; and he concludes by claiming indulgence on the score of his youth, in case he should have given even the better judges any cause for offence. For those who read this preface with any previous knowledge of Mr. Browning's life and character, there will be an obvious inference to his own youthful-ness in the exaggerated estimate thus implied of his imaginative sins ; for the tendency of "Pauline" is both religious and moral; and no man has been more innocent than its author, from boyhood up, of tampering with any belief in the black art. His hatred for that "spiritualism," which is its modern equivalent, is indeed matter of history. But the trick he has here played himself may confuse the mind of those who only know him from his works, and for whom his vivid belief in the supernatural may point to a different kind of mysticism.

"I am made up of an intensest life,"

The tribute at page **14** [1] to the saving power **of** imagination is also characteristic of his maturer mind, though expressed in an ambiguous manner. It is interesting to know that in the line (page 26),

"the king
Treading the purple calmly to his death,"

he was thinking of Agamemnon : **as this** shows how **early** his love of classic literature began. The allusion **to** Plato, at pages 19, 20, and 21, largely confirms this impression. The feeling for music asserts itself also **at** page 18, though in a less spiritual form than it assumes **in** his later works. But the most striking piece **of** true biography which "Pauline" contains, **is** its evidence **of the** young writer's affectionate reverence for Shelley, **whom he** idealizes under the name of Sun-treader. **An** invocation **to his** memory occupies three pages, beginning with the ninth ; **it** is renewed **at the** end **of the** poem, and there can be no doubt that the pathetic language in which it is couched came straight from the young poet's own heart. We even fancy that Shelley's influence is visible in the poem itself, which contains a profusion of natural imagery, and some touches **of** naturalistic emotion, not at all **in** keeping with Mr. Browning's picturesque, **but** habitually human genius. The influence, if it existed, passed away with his earliest youth ; not so the admiration and sympathy which it implied ; and this, considering **the** wide difference which separated the two minds, is an interesting fact. [2]

[1] Vol. **i. of the** new uniform edition of 1888-89. This will **be** the one always referred **to.**

[2] The "Andromeda," described as "with" the speaker at pages 29 and 30, is that of Polidoro di Caravaggio, of which Mr. Browning possesses an engraving, which was always before his eyes as he wrote his earlier poems. The original was painted on the wall of a garden attached to the Palazzo Bufalo—or del Bufalo—in Rome. The wall has been pulled down since Mr. Browning was last there.

## "PARACELSUS." (1835.)

"Paracelsus" is a summary of the life, as Mr. Browning conceives it, of this well-known physicist of the sixteenth century; and is divided into five scenes, or groups of scenes, each representing a critical moment in his experience, and reviewing in his own words the circumstances by which it has been prepared. The personages whom it includes are, besides the principal one, Festus and Michal, early friends of Paracelsus, and now man and wife; and the Italian poet Aprile. Michal appears only in the first scene; Aprile in the second or third; but Festus accompanies Paracelsus throughout the drama, in the constant character of judicious, if not profound, adviser, and of tender friend. His personality is sufficiently marked to claim the importance of a type; and as such he stands forth, as contrasted with both Paracelsus and Aprile, and yet a bond of union between them. It is more probable however that he was created for the mere dramatic purpose of giving shape to the confession of Paracelsus, and preserving it from monotony. The story is principally told in a dialogue between them.

The first scene is entitled "Paracelsus aspires;" and takes place at Würzburg between himself, Festus, and Michal, on the eve of his departure from their common home. Both friends begin by opposing his aspirations, and thus lead him to expound and defend them. The aim and spirit of these is the distinguishing feature of the poem. Paracelsus aspires to knowledge: such knowledge as will benefit his fellow-men. He will seek it in the properties of nature, and, as history tells us, he will succeed. But his *aspirations* pass over these isolated discoveries, which he has no idea of connecting into scientific truths: and tend ever towards some final revelation of the secret of life, to flash forth from his own brain when the flesh shall have been subdued, and the imprisoned light of intellect set free. And here Mr. Browning's metaphysical fancy is somewhat at issue with his facts. Paracelsus employed nature in the quest of the supernatural or magical; this is shown by the poem, though in it he begins by repudiating, with all other external aids, the help of the black art. He therefore relied on other kinds of knowledge than that which springs direct from the human mind. The inconsistency however disappears in Mr. Browning's conception of the case, and the metaphysical language which he imputes to Paracelsus in the earlier stages of his career, is not felt to be untrue.

Paracelsus not only aspires to know : he believes it his mission to acquire knowledge ; and he believes also that it is only to be acquired through untried methods, through untaught men : most of all through solitary communion with nature, and at the sacrifice of all human joys. Festus regards this as a delusion, and combats it, in this first scene, with the arguments of common sense ; overshooting the mark just enough to leave his friend the victory. Paracelsus has declared that he appreciates all he is renouncing, but that he has no choice. He knows that the way on which he is about to enter is " trackless ;" but so is the bird's : God will guide him as He guides the bird. And Festus replies that the road to knowledge is *not* trackless. " Mighty marchers" have left their footprints upon it. Nature has not written her secrets in desert places, but in the souls of great men : the " Stagirite,"[1] and the sages who form a glory round him. He urges Paracelsus to learn what they can teach, and then take the torch of wisdom from the exhausted runner's hand, and let his fresh strength continue the race. He warns him against the personal ambition which alloys his unselfish thirst for knowledge ; against the presumption which impels him to serve God (and man)

[1] Aristotle.

```
"     .     .     .     .     apart from such
Appointed channel as he wills shall gather
Imperfect tributes, for that sole obedience
Valued perchance    .    .    .    "    (vol. ii. p. 17.)
```

against the dangers of a course which cuts him adrift from
human love. But Paracelsus has his answer ready.
" The wisdom of the past has done nothing for mankind.
Men have laboured and grown famous : and the evils of
life are unabated : the earth still groans in the blind and
endless struggle with them. Truth comes from within the
human intellect. To KNOW is to have opened a way for
its escape—not a way for its admission. It has often
refused itself to a life of study. It has been born of loiter-
ing idleness. The force which inspires him proves his
mission to be authentic. His own will could not create
such promptings. He dares not set them aside."

The depth of his conviction carries the day, and the
scene ends with these expressive words :—

```
" Par.    .    .    .    .    .
Are there not, Festus, are there not, dear Michal,
Two points in the adventure of the diver,
One—when, a beggar, he prepares to plunge,
One—when, a prince, he rises with his pearl?
Festus, I plunge !
     Fest.              We wait you when you rise !"
```
                                             (vol. ii. p. 38.)

The next two, or indeed three scenes are united under
the title " Paracelsus attains ;" but the attainment is not at
first visible. We find him at Constantinople, in the house
of the Greek conjuror, nine years after his departure from
home. He has not discovered the magical secret which
he came to seek ; and his tone, as he reviews his position,
is full of a bitter and almost despairing sense of failure.
His desultory course has borne scanty and confused results. His powers have been at once overstrained and
frittered away. He is beset by the dread of madness ;
and by the fear, scarcely less intolerable, of a moral ship-
wreck in which even the purity of his motives will disappear.

His thoughts revert sadly **to** his **youth, and** its lost possibilities of love and joy.  At this juncture the poet Aprile **appears,** and unconsciously reveals to him the secret of his unsuccess.  He has sought knowledge at the sacrifice of love ; in so doing he has violated **a** natural law and **is** suffering for **it.**  Knowledge is inseparable from **love in** the scheme of life.  Aprile too has **sinned, but in the** opposite manner ; he has refused to *know.*  He has loved blindly and immoderately, **and retribution has overtaken** him also: for he is dying.  **If the one** existence has **lacked** sustaining warmth, the **other has burned** itself away. Aprile's " Love" is not however restricted to the personal sense of **the** word; it means **the** passion for **beauty, the** impulse to possess **and to create it ;** everything **which belongs to** the life **of** art.  **He represents the æsthetic or** emotional **in** life, **as** Paracelsus represents **the intellectual.  We** see this in the sorrowful confession **of Paracelsus :—**

> " I cannot feed on beauty for the sake
> Of beauty only, nor can drink in balm
> From lovely objects for their loveliness ; "  (vol. ii. **p. 95.**)

and, in the words **already addressed to Aprile (page** 65) :—

> "Are we not halves of one dissevered world,"

Aprile acknowledges his own mistake, in a passage which fully completes the moral of the story, and begins **thus** (page 59) :—

> " Knowing ourselves, our world, our task so great,
> Our time so brief,  .      .      .      .      "

Paracelsus never sees him again, and will speak **of him on a** subsequent occasion as a madman ; but **he** evidently accepts him as a messenger of the truth ; and the message sinks into his soul.

In what is called the third scene, five years more have elapsed ; and Paracelsus is at Bâle, again opening his heart to his old friend.  He is professor at the University.  His

fame extends far beyond it. Outwardly he has "attained."
But the sense of a wasted life, and above all, of moral de-
terioration, is stronger on him than ever, and the tone in
which he expresses it is only calmer than in the previous
soliloquy, because it is more hopeless. He has failed in
his highest aims—and failed doubly : because he has
learned to content himself with low ones. He believes
that he is teaching useful, although fragmentary truths ; that
these may lead to more ; that those who follow him may
stand on his shoulders and be considered great. But the
crowning TRUTH is as far from him as ever; and the mass
of those who crowd his lecture-room do not even come for
what they can learn, but for the vulgar pleasure of seeing
old beliefs subverted, and old methods exposed. He is
humiliated at having declined on to what seems to him a
lower range of knowledge ; still more by the kind of men
with whom it has brought him into contact ; and he sees
himself sinking into a lower depth, in which such praise as
they can give will repay him. His contempt for himself
and them is making him reckless of consequences, and
preparing the way for his disgrace.

In spite however of his failure Paracelsus has done so
much, that Festus is converted ; and ready to justify both
his early belief in his own mission, and the abnormal
means by which he has chosen to carry it out. Their positions are reversed, and he combats his friend's self-abase-
ment as he once combated his too great confidence in
himself. He grieves over what seems to him the depres-
sion of an over-wrought mind, and what he will not regard
as due to any deeper cause. But Paracelsus will take no
comfort ; and when, finally, he denounces the folly of intellectual pretensions, and ends with the pathetic words---in
part the echo of Festus' own :—

> "     .     .     .     .     .     No, no :
> Love, hope, fear, faith—these make humanity ;
> These are its sign and note and character,
> And these I have lost !     .     .     " (vol. ii. p. 109.)

Festus has no answer to give. He parts from Paracelsus perplexed and saddened rather than convinced, but with a dawning consciousness of depths in life, to which his strong but simple soul has no key.

In the fourth scene these depths are more fully and more perplexingly revealed. Two years more have elapsed. Paracelsus has escaped from Bâle, and is at Colmar, once more confessing himself to Festus, and once more said to "aspire." But his aspirations are less easy to understand than formerly, because their aim is less single. The sense of wasted life, Aprile's warnings, some natural rebound against the continued intellectual strain have determined him to strive for a fuller existence, and neglect no opportunity of usefulness or enjoyment. A serious and commendable change would seem to be denoted by the words, "I have tried each way singly : now for both !" (page 121); and again at page 126, where a new-born softness asserts itself. His language has, however, a vein of bitterness, sometimes even of cynicism, which belies the idea of any sustained impulse to good. He is worn in body, weary in mind, fitful and wayward in mood, and just in the condition in which men half impose on others, and half on themselves. He alludes to the habit of drinking as one which he has now contracted ; and he is clearly entering on the period of his greatest excesses, perhaps also of his most strenuous exertions in the cause of knowledge. But his energy is reckless and irregular, and the spirit of the gambler rather than that of the student is in it. He works all night to forget himself by day, gathering up his diminished strength for a lavish expenditure ; and a new misgiving as to the wisdom of his "aspirations" pierces through the assertion that even sickness may lend an aid ; since

> "   .    .    . mind is nothing but disease,
> And natural health is ignorance."      (vol. ii. p. 122.)

We feel that henceforward his path will be all downhill.

Iu the fifth and closing scene, thirteen years later, Paracelsus "attains" again, and for the last time.   He is dying. Festus watches by him in his hospital cell with a very touching tenderness ; and as Paracelsus awakes from a period of lethargy to a delirious remembrance of his past life, he soothes and guides him to an inspired calm in which its true meaning is revealed to him.   The half prophetic death-bed vision includes everything which experience had taught him ; and a great deal which we cannot help thinking only a more modern experience could have taught.   It disclaims all striving after absolute knowledge, and asserts the value of limitation in every energy of life.   The passage in which he describes the faculties of man, and which begins

> "Power—neither put forth blindly, nor controlled
> Calmly by perfect knowledge ;"        (vol. ii. p. 168.)

contains the natural lesson of the speaker's career, supposing him in a condition to receive it.   But it also reflects Mr. Browning's constant ideal of a fruitful and progressive existence ; and the very beautiful monologue of which it forms part is, so far as it goes, his actual confession of faith.   The scientific idea of evolution is here distinctly foreshadowed : though it begins and ends, in Mr. Browning's mind, in the large Theism which was and is the basis of his religious belief.

The poem is followed by an historical appendix, which enables the reader to verify its facts, and judge Mr. Browning's interpretation of them.

## "SORDELLO."   (1840.)

"Sordello" is, like "Paracelsus," the imaginary reconstruction of a real life, in connection with contemporary facts ; but its six "books" present a much more complicated structure.   The historical part of "Paracelsus" is all contained in the one life. In "Sordello" it forms a large **and** moving background, which often disputes our attention with the central figure, and sometimes even absorbs it : projecting itself as it were in an artistic middle distance, in which fact and fancy are blended ; while the mental world through which the hero moves, is in its way, as **rest**less and as crowded as the material. It may save time and trouble to readers of the poem to know something of its historical foundation and poetic motive, before making any great effort to disentangle its various threads ; but it will always be best to read it once without this key : since the story, involved as **it** is, has a sustained dramatic interest which is destroyed by anticipating its course.

The historical personages who take part in it directly and indirectly, are

Ghibellines.

Guelphs.

ECCELINO DA ROMANO **II.**, Surnamed **the Monk :** married, first to Agnes Este ; secondly **to Ade**laide, a Tuscan.

AZZO, LORD OF ESTE (father and son).

RICHARD, COUNT OF **SAN** BONIFACIO (father **and** son).

TAURELLO SALINGUERRA, a soldier, married, first to Retrude, of the family **of** the German Emperor Frederick the Second ; and secondly, in advanced life, to Sofia, fifth daughter of Eccelino the **Monk.**

ADELAIDE, second wife of Eccelino da Romano.

PALMA (properly Cunizza), Eccelino's daughter by Agnes Este.

The poet SORDELLO.

*Historical basis of the Story.*

A Mantuan poet of the name of Sordello is mentioned by Dante in the " Purgatorio," where he is supposed to be recognized as a fellow-townsman by Virgil.

> " Surse ver lui del luogo ove pria stava,
> Dicendo, O Mantovan, Io son Sordello
> Della tua terra : e l' un l' altro abbracciava." [1]

And also in his treatise " De vulgare Eloquentiâ," where he speaks of him as having created the Italian language. These facts are related by Sismondi in his " Italian Re- publics," vol. ii., page 202 ; and the writer refers us for more particulars to his work on the " Literature of Southern Europe." He seems, however, to exhaust the subject when he tells us that the nobility of Sordello's birth, and his intrigue or marriage with Cunizza are attested by con- temporaries ; that a " mysterious obscurity " shrouds his life ; and that his violent death is obscurely indicated by Dante, whose mention of him is now his only title to im- mortality. According to one tradition he was the son of an archer named Elcorte. Another seems to point to him when it imputes a son to Salinguerra as the only offspring of his first marriage, and having died before himself. Mr. Browning accepts the latter hypothesis, whilst he employs both.

The birth of his Sordello, as probably of the real one, coincides with the close of the twelfth century ; and with an active condition of the family feuds which were just merging in the conflict of Guelphs and Ghibellines. The " Biographie Universelle " says :

" The first encounter between the two parties took place at Vicenza towards 1194. Eccelino the Second, who allied himself with the republics of Verona and Padua, was

---

[1] He rose to meet him from the place at which he stood, saying, " Oh Mantuan, I am Sordello of thy land : " and they embraced each other.

exiled from Vicenza himself his whole family and his faction, by a Podesta, his enemy. Before submitting to this sentence, he undertook to defend himself by setting fire to the neighbouring houses ; a great part of the town was burned during the conflict, in which Eccelino was beaten. These were the first scenes of confusion and massacre, which met the eyes of the son of the Lord of Romano, the ferocious Eccelino the Third, born 4th of April, 1194."

In Mr. Browning's version, Adelaide, wife of Eccelino II., is saved with her infant son—this Eccelino the Third —by the devotion of an archer, Elcorte, who perishes in the act. Retrude, wife of Salinguerra, and also present on this occasion, only lives to be conveyed to Adelaide's castle at Goito ; but her new-born child survives ; and Adelaide, dreading his future rivalry with her own, allows his father to think him dead, and brings him up, under the name of Sordello, as her page, declaring him to be Elcorte's son adopted out of gratitude. The "intrigue" between him and Palma (Cunizza) appears in due time as a poetical affinity, strongest on her side, and which determines her to see him restored to his rightful place. Palma's subsequent marriage with Richard, Count of San Bonifacio, serves to justify the idea of an engagement to him, ratified by her father before his retirement from the world, and which she and Salinguerra conspire to break, the one from love of Sordello, the other in the interests of her House. Eccelino's real assumption of the monastic habit after Adelaide's death is represented as in part caused by re- morse—for Salinguerra is his old and faithful ally, and he has connived at the wrong done to him in the conceal- ment of his son ; and his return to the Guelph connexion from which his daughter has sprung, as a general disclaimer of his second wife's views.

The Lombard League also figures in the story, as the consequence of Salinguerra's and Palma's conspiracy

against San Bonifacio ; though it also appears as brought
about by the historic course of events.  Salinguerra, under
cover of military reprisals, has entrapped the Count into
Ferrara, and detained him there, at the moment when he
was expected to meet his lady-love in his own city of
Verona.   Verona prepares to resent this outrage on its
Prince, and with it, the other States which represent
the Guelph cause ; and when Palma—seizing her opportunity—summons Sordello thither in his character of her
minstrel, and reveals to him her projects for him and
for herself, their interview is woven into the historical
picture of a great mediæval city suddenly called to arms.
What Sordello sees when he goes with Palma to Ferrara,
belongs to the history of all mediæval warfare ; and his
sudden and premature death revives the historical tradition though in a new form.  The intermediate details of
his minstrel's career are of course imaginary ; but his
struggle to increase the expressiveness of his mother
tongue again records a fact.

   I have mentioned such accessible authorities as Sismondi and the " Biographie Universelle," because they
*are* accessible : not from any idea that they give the measure of Mr. Browning's knowledge of his subject.   He
prepared himself for writing " Sordello" by studying all
the chronicles of that period of Italian history which the
British Museum supplied ; and we may be sure that every
event he alludes to as historical, is so in spirit, if not in the
letter ; while such details as come under the head of historical curiosities are absolutely true.   He also supplemented his reading by a visit to the places in which the
scenes of the story are laid.

### Its Dramatic Idea.

   The dramatic idea of " Sordello " is that of an imaginative nature, nourished by its own creations, and also consumed by them ; and breaking down in consequence under

the first strain of real conflict and passion. The mysterious Italian poet,—scarcely known but **as** a voice, a mere phantom among living men—was well fitted to illustrate such an idea; he might also perhaps have suggested it. But we know that it was already growing in Mr. Browning's mind ; for Sordello had been foreshadowed in Aprile, though the two are **as** different as their common poetic quality allows. Aprile is consumed by **a** creative passion, which is always akin to love ; Sordello by **an** imaginative fever which has no love in it; and in this respect he presents **a** stronger contrast to Aprile than Paracelsus himself. **As** a poet he may be said **to contain** both **the artist** and the thinker, and therefore to transcend **both ;** and his craving is for neither love nor knowledge, as the foregoing poem represents them, but for that magnitude **of** poetic existence, which means all love and all knowledge, as all beauty and all **power** in itself. **But** he makes the same mistake as Aprile, or at least as Paracelsus, and makes it **in** a greater degree; for he rejects all the human conditions of the poetic life : and strives to live **it, not** in experience or in sympathy, but by **a** pure act of imagination, or as he calls it, of *Will;* and he wears himself out body and soul by a mental strain which proves **as** barren **as** it is continuous. The true joy of living comes home to him at last, and with it the first challenge to self-sacrifice. **Duty** prevails ; but he dies in the conflict, or rather of it.

The intended lesson of the story is distinctly enforced in its last scene, but is patent almost from the first— that the mind must not disclaim the body, nor imagination divorce itself from reality : that the spiritual is bound up **with** the material **in** our earthly **life. All Mr.** Browning's practical philosophy is summed up in this truth, and much of his religion ; for it points **to** the necessity **of** a human manifestation of the Divine Being ; and though Sordello's story contains no explicit reference to Christian doctrine, an unmistakeable Christian sentiment pervades its close. That restless and ambitious spirit had missed its only possible anchorage : the ideal of an intellectual existence at once guided and set free by love.

Mr. Browning has indeed prefaced the poem by saying that in writing it he has laid his chief stress *on the incidents in the development of a soul.* It must be read with reference to this idea ; and I should be bound to give precedence to it over the poetic inspiration of the story if Mr. Browning had practically done so. This is not, however, the case. Sordello's poetic individuality overshadows the moral, and for a time conceals it altogether. The close of his story is distinctly the emerging of a soul from the mists of poetic egotism by which it has been obscured ; and Mr. Browning has meant us from the first to see it struggling through them. But in so doing he has judged Sordello's poetic life as a blind aspiration after the spiritual, while the egotism which he represents as the keynote of his poetic being was in fact the negation of it. The idea was just : that the greatest poet must have in him the making of the largest man. His Sordello is imperial among men for the one moment in which his song is in sympathy with human life ; and Mr. Browning would have made it more consistently so, had he worked out his idea at a later time. But the poem was written at a period in which his artistic judgment was yet inferior to his poetic powers, and the need of ordering his vast material from the reader's, as well as the writer's, point of view— though he states it by implication at the end of the third book—had not thoroughly penetrated his mind.

I venture on this criticism, though it is no part of my task to criticize, because "Sordello" is the one of Mr. Browning's works which still remains to be read ; and even a mistaken criticism may sometimes afford a clue. "Sordello" is not only harder to read than "Paracelsus," but harder than any other of Mr. Browning's works ; its complications of structure being interwoven with diffi-

culties of **a** deeper kind which again react **upon** them.
Enough has been said **to** show that the conception **of**
**the** character is very abstruse on the intellectual **and**
poetic side ; that it presents us with states of thought
and feeling, remote from common experience, and which
**no** language could make entirely clear ; and unfortunately the style is sometimes in itself so obscure that we
cannot judge whether it is the expression **or the** idea
which we fail to grasp. The poem **was** written **under**
the dread of diffuseness which had just **then** taken possession of Mr. Browning's mind, and we **have** sometimes
to struggle through **a** group of sentences out **of** which
he has so laboured **to** squeeze every unnecessary word,
that their grammatical connection is broken up, and
they present **a** compact mass of meaning which **with-**
out previous knowledge it is almost impossible **to con-**
strue. We are also puzzled by an abridged, interjectional,
way of carrying on the historical part **of** the narrative ;
by the author's habit of alluding **to** imaginary or typical
personages in the same tone as **to** real ones ; and **by**
misprints, including errors in punctuation, which will **be**
easily corrected in a later edition, **but** which mar the **pre-**
sent one.

It is only fair to add that he would deprecate the idea
of any excessive labour as bestowed on this, **to his** mind,
immature performance. **It** is for us, not for him, **to** do
justice to it. With all its faults and obscurities, "Sordello" is a great work ; full moreover of pregnant and
beautiful passages which are not affected by them. When
Mr. Browning re-edited "Sordello" in 1863, he considered
the possibility of re-writing it in a more transparent manner ;
but he concluded that the labour would be disproportionate
to the result, and contented himself with summarizing the
contents of each "book" in a continuous heading, which
represents the main thread of the story. It will be useful
to read this carefully.

BOOK THE FIRST.

The story opens at Verona, at the moment of the for-
mation of the Lombard League—a well-known union of
Guelph cities against the Ghibellines in Northern Italy.
Mr. Browning, addressing himself to an imaginary
audience composed of living and dead, describes the city
as it hastens to arms, and the chain of circumstances
through which she has been called upon to do so ; and
draws a curious picture of two political ideals which he
considers respectively those of Ghibelline and Guelph :
the one symbolized by isolated heights, the other by a
continuous level growth ; those again suggesting the
violent disruptions which create imperial power ; these the
peaceful organic processes of democratic life.  The poet
Shelley is desired to withdraw his "pure face" from among
the spectators of this chequered scene ; and Dante is invoked in the name of him whose fame preceded his, and
has been absorbed by it.  A secret chamber in Count
Richard's palace shows Palma and Sordello in earnest
conference with each other.  Then the curtain falls ; and
we are carried back thirty years, and to Goito Castle.

Sordello is there : a refined and beautiful boy ; framed
for all spiritual delights.  As his life is described, it has
neither duties nor occupations ; no concern with the
outer world ; no contact even with that of Adelaide, his
supposed protectress.  He is dreaming away his childhood in the silent gloom of the castle, or the sunny out-
door life of the hills and woods.  He lives in imagination,
blends the idea of his own being with everything he sees ;
and for years is happy in the bare fact of existence.  But
the germ of a fatal spiritual ambition is lurking within
him ; and as he grows into a youth, he hankers after
something which he calls sympathy, but which is really
applause.  He therefore makes a human crowd for him-

self out of carved and tapestried figures, and the few names which penetrate into his solitude, and fancies himself always the greatest personage amongst them. He simulates all manner of heroic performances and of luxurious rest. He is Eccelino, the Emperor's vicar; he is the Emperor himself. He becomes more than this; for his fancy has soared upwards to the power which includes all empire in one—the spiritual power of song. Apollo is its representative. Sordello is he. He has had one glimpse of Palma; she becomes his Daphne; the dream life is at its height.

And now Sordello is a man. He begins to sicken for reality. Vanity and ambition are ripe in him. His egotisms are innocent, but they are absorbing. The soul is as yet dormant.[1]

### BOOK THE SECOND.

The dream-life becomes a partial reality. Sordello's wanderings carry him one day to the walls of Mantua, outside which Palma is holding a "Court of Love." Eglamor sings. His song is incomplete. Sordello feels what is wanting; catches up the thread of the story; and sings it to its proper close.[2] His triumph is absolute. He is installed as Palma's minstrel in Eglamor's place. Eglamor accepts his defeat with touching gentleness, and lies down to die. This poet is meant to embody the limited art, which is an end in itself, and one with the artist's life. Sordello, on the other hand, represents the boundless aspirations which art may subserve, but which

---

[1] The name of Naddo occurs in this book, and will often reappear in the course of the story. This personage is the typical Philistine—the Italian Brown, Jones, or Robinson—and will represent genuine common-sense, or mere popular judgment, as the case may be.

[2] Elys, the subject of this song, is any woman of the then prevailing type of Italian beauty: having fair hair, and a "pear-shaped" face.

must always leave it behind. The parallel will be stated more distinctly later on.

Sordello's first wish is fulfilled. He has found a career which will reconcile his splendid dreams with his real obscurity, and set him, by right of imagination—the true Apolloship—apart from other men. But his true difficulties have yet to begin. It is not enough that he feels himself a transcendent personage. He must make others believe that he is so. Every act of imagination is with him an act of existence, or as Mr. Browning calls it of Will; but this self-asserting was much easier with the imaginary crowd than it can be with the real one. Sordello is soon at cross-purposes with his hearers : for when he sings of human passion, or human prowess, they never dream of identifying him with it ; and when he sings of mere abstract modes of being, they do not understand.

The love of abstract conception is indeed the rock on which he splits. The feelings which are real to us are unreal to him, because they are accidental. What is real to him is the underlying consciousness which according to his view is permanent: the "intensest" self described in "Pauline"—the mind which is spoken of in the fifth "book" of "Sordello" (vol. i. page 236) as nearest to God when emptied of even thought ; and his aim is to put forth all the *qualities* which this absolute existence can assume, and yet be reflected in other men's minds as independent of them. This lands him in struggles not only with his hearers but with himself—for he is unused to expressing what he feels ; and with a language which at best could convey "whole perceptions" like his, in a very meagre form, or a fragmentary one. He still retains the love of real life and adventure which inspired his boyish dreams. There is nothing, as I have said, that he does not wish to *be ;* and now, amidst commonplace human beings, his human desires often take a more simple and natural form. But the poet in him pushes the man aside, and bids him, at all events, wait. He does not know that he is failing through the hopeless disunion of the two. He silences his better humanity, and retains the worst; for he is more and more determined to succeed at whatever cost. Yet failure meets him on every side. He is too large for his public, but he is also too small for it. Every question raised even in talk carries him into the infinite. Every man of his audience has a practical answer ready before he has. Naddo plies him with common sense. " He is to speak to the human heart—he is not to be so philosophical— he is not to seem so clever." Shallow judges pull him to pieces. Shallow rivals strive to sing him down.[1] He loses his grasp of the ideal. He cannot clutch the real. His imagination dries up.

Meanwhile Adelaide has died. Salinguerra, who had joined the Emperor at Naples, is brought back in hot haste by the news that Eccelino has retired to a monas- tery, has disclaimed the policy of his House; and is seal- ing his peace with the Guelph princes by the promised marriage of his sons Eccelino and Alberic with the sisters of Este; and of his daughter Palma with Count Richard of San Bonifacio himself. He is coming to Mantua. Sordello must greet him with his best art. But Sordello shrinks from the trial, and escapes back to Goito, whence Palma has just departed. What his Mantuan life has taught him is thus expressed (vol. i. page 130) :—

> " The Body, the Machine for Acting Will,
> Had been at the commencement proved unfit ;
> That for Demonstrating, Reflecting it,
> Mankind—no fitter: was the Will Itself
> In fault ?"

He is wiser than he was, but his objects remain the same. The sympathies—the moral sense—the soul—are still asleep.

[1] Bocafoli and Plara, mannerists : one of the sensuous school; the other of the pompously pure ; imaginary personages, but to whom we may give real names.

BOOK THE THIRD.

Sordello buries himself once more in the contemplation of nature ; but finds in it only a short-lived peace. The marshy country about Mantua is suddenly converted into water ; and with the shock of this catastrophe comes also the feeling : Nature can do and undo ; her opportunities are endless. With man

> "　.　.　youth once gone is gone :
> Deeds let escape are never to be done." (vol. i. p. 135.)

He has dreamed of love, of revel, and of adventure ; but he has let pass the time when such dreams could be realized ; and worst of all, the sacrifice has been useless. He has sacrificed the man in him to the poet ; and his poetic existence has been impoverished by the act. He has rejected experience that he might *be* his fullest self before living it ; and only *living*, in other words, experience, could have made that self complete. His later years have been paving the way for this discovery ; it bursts on him all at once. He has been under a long strain. The reaction at length has come. He yearns helplessly for the " blisses strong and soft" which he has known he was passing by, but of which the full meaning never reached him until now. He must live yet. The question is, " in what way." And this is unexpectedly answered. Palma sends for him to Verona ; tells him of her step-mother's death—of strange secrets revealed to herself—of the secret influence Sordello has exercised over her life—of a great future awaiting his own, and connecting it with the Emperor's cause. She summons him to accompany her to Ferrara, and hear from Salinguerra's lips what that future is to be.

Sordello has entered on a new phase of existence. He feels that henceforward he is not to *act men*, but to *make them act;* this is how his being is to be fulfilled. It is a

first step in the direction of unselfishness, but not yet into
**it.** The soul is not yet awake.

At this point **of** his narrative Mr. Browning makes **a**
halt, and carries us off to Venice, where he muses **on the**
various questions involved in Sordello's story. The very
act **of** digression leads back to the comparison between
Eglamor and Sordello : between the artist who is one with
his work, and him who is outside and beyond it—between
the completeness of execution which comes of a limited
ideal, and **the** true greatness of those performances which
"can never be more than dreamed." And the case of the
true poet is farther illustrated by that **of** the weather-bound
sailor, who seems to have settled down for life with the
fruits of his adventures, but waits only the faintest sign **of**
a favourable wind to cut his moorings and be off.

Then **comes** a vision of humanity, also in harmony with
the purpose of the poem. **It** takes the form of some frail
and suffering woman, and is addressed by the author with
a tenderness in which we recognize one **of** his constant
ideals of love : the impulse not to worship or to enjoy, but
to comfort and **to** protect. He next considers the problem
of human sorrow and sin, and deprecates the absolute condemnation of the sinner, in language which anticipates that
of "Fifine at the Fair." "Every life has its own law. The
'losel,' the moral outcast, keeps his own conceit **of** truth
though through a maze of lies. Good labours **to** exist
through evil, by means of the very ignorance which sets
each man to tackle it for himself, believing that he alone
can."[1] Mr. Browning rejects at least the *show* of knowledge which gives you a name for what you die of; and
that deepening of ignorance which comes of the perpetual insisting that fountains of knowledge spring everywhere for those who choose to dispense it. "What science
teaches is made useless by the shortness of human existence ; it absorbs all our energy in building up a machine

[1] The belief in personal experience is very strong here.

which we shall have no time to work. All direct truth comes to us from the poet : whether he be of the smaller kind who only see, or the greater, who can tell what they have seen, or the greatest who can make others see it." Corresponding instances follow.[1]

Mr. Browning is aware that one is a poet at his own risk ; and that the poetic chaplet may also prove a sacrificial one. He will still wear it, however, because in his case it means the suffrage of a " patron friend "[2]

> "Whose great verse blares unintermittent on
> Like your own trumpeter at Marathon,—" (vol. i. p. 169.)

He recalls his readers to the " business " of the poem :

> " the fate of such
> As find our common nature—overmuch
> Despised because restricted and unfit
> To bear the burthen they impose on it—
> Cling when they would discard it ; craving strength
> To leap from the allotted world, at length
> They do leap,—flounder on without a term,
> Each a god's germ, doomed to remain a germ
> In unexpanded infancy, unless  . . . ." (pp. 170, 171.)

admits that the story sounds dull ; but suggests the possibility of its containing an agreeable surprise. An amusing anecdote to this effect concludes the chapter.[3]

### BOOK THE FOURTH.

We are now introduced to Taurello Salinguerra : a fine soldier-like figure ; the type of elastic strength in both body and mind. We are told that he possesses the courage of the fighter, the astuteness of the politician, the

[1] The third of these, vol. i. p. 168, is very characteristic of the state of Sordello's, and therefore, at that moment, of his author's mind. The poet who *makes others see* is he who deals with abstractions : who makes the mood do duty for the man.

[2] Walter Savage Landor.

[3] The word " Eyebright " at page 170 stands for Euphrasia its Greek equivalent, and refers to one of Mr. Browning's oldest friends.

knowledge and graces of the man of leisure. **He** has shown himself capable of controlling an Emperor, and of giving precedence to a woman. He is young at sixty, while the son who is half his age, is "lean, outworn and really old." And the crowning difference between him **and Sordello** is this : that while Sordello only draws out other men as a means of displaying himself, he only displays himself sufficiently to draw out other **men.** "His choicest **instruments**" have "surmised him shallow."

He is in his palace **at** Ferrara, musing **over the past— that past** which held the turning-point of his career; which began the feud between himself **and** the **now Guelph** princes, and which naturally merged **him in the Ghibelline** cause. **He** remembers how the fathers of the present Este and San Bonifacio combined to cheat him out of **the** Modenese heiress who was to be his bride—how he retired **to** Sicily, to return with **a** wife of the Emperor's own house —**how** his enemies surprised him at Vicenza. He sees his old comrade Eccelino, **so** passive now, so brave and vigorous then. He sees the town as they fire it together : the rush for the gates : **the** slashing, the hewing, the blood hissing and frying on the iron gloves. His spirit leaps in the returning frenzy of that struggle and flight. **It** sinks again as he thinks of Elcorte—Adelaide's escape—her rescued child ; his own doom in the wife and child who were **not** rescued.

"And now ! he has effaced himself in the interests of the Romano house. Its life has grafted itself on his own ; and to what end? The Emperor is coming. His badge and seal, already in Salinguerra's hands, bestow the title of Imperial Prefect on whosoever assumes the headship of the Ghibellines in the north of Italy ; and Eccelino, its proper chief, recoils ; withdraws even his name from the cause. Who shall wear the badge ? None so fitly as himself, who holds San Bonifacio captive—who has dislocated if not yet broken the Guelph right arm. Yet, is it worth his

while? Shall he fret his remaining years? Shall he rob his
old comrade's son?" He laughs the idea to scorn. . . . .

Sordello has come with Palma to Ferrara. He came to
find the men who were to be the body to his spirit, the
instrument to his will. But he came, expecting that these
would be great. And now he discovers that very few are
great; while behind and beneath, and among them, extends something which has never yet entered his field of
thought : the mass of mankind. The more he looks the
more it grows upon him : this people with the

> "      .      .      .      .    mouths and eyes,
> Petty enjoyments and huge miseries,—"        (vol. i. p. 181.)

and the more he feels that the few are great because the
many are in them—because they are types and representatives of these. Hitherto he has striven to impose himself
on mankind. He now awakes to the joy and duty of
serving it. It is the magnified body which his spirit
needs. And in the new-found knowledge, the new-found
sympathy, his soul springs full-grown into life.

But another check is in store for him. He has taken
for granted that the cause in which he is to be enlisted is
the people's cause. The new soul in him can conceive
nothing less. A first interview with Salinguerra dispels
this dream, and dispels it in such a manner that he leaves
the presence of his unknown father years older and wearier
than when he entered it. He wanders through the city,
mangled by civil war. The effects of Ghibelline vengeance
meet him on every side. Is the Guelph more humane?
He discusses the case with Palma. They weigh deeds with
deeds. " Guelph and Ghibelline are alike unjust and cruel,
alike inveterate enemies of their fellow-men." Who then
represents the people's cause? A sudden answer comes.
A bystander recognizing his minstrel's attire begs Sordello
to sing, and suggests the Roman Tribune Crescentius as
his theme. Rome rises before his mind—the mother

of cities—the great constructive **power** which **weaves** the past into the future ; which represents the continuity of human life. *The reintegration of Rome must typify the triumph of mankind.* But Rome is now the Church ; she is one with the Guelph cause. The Guelph cause is therefore in some sense the true one. Sordello's new-found spiritual and his worldly interests thus range themselves on opposite sides.

### BOOK THE FIFTH.

**The** day draws to its **close.** Sordello has seen **more of** the suffering human beings whom he wishes to serve, and the ideal Rome has collapsed in his imagination like a mocking dream. Nothing can be effected at once. No deed can bridge over the lapse of time which divides the first stage of a great social structure from its completion. Each life may give its touch ; it can give no more ; through the endless generations. The vision of a regenerate humanity, "his last and loveliest," must depart like the rest. Then suddenly **a** voice,

> " . . . . Sordello, **wake !**
> God has conceded two sights to a **man**—
> One, of men's whole work, time's completed plan,
> The other, of the minute's work, man's first
> Step to the plan's completeness : what's dispersed
> Save hope of that supreme step which, descried
> Earliest, was meant still to remain untried
> Only to give you heart to take your own
> Step, and there stay—leaving the rest alone ? " (vol. i. p. 217.)

The facts restate themselves, but from an opposite point of view. No man can give more than his single touch. The whole could not dispense with one of them. The work is infinite, but it is continuous. The later poet weaves into his own song the echoes of the first. "The last of each series of workmen sums up in himself all predecessors," whether he be the type **of** strength like Charle-

magne, or of knowledge like Hildebrand. Strength comes
first in the scheme of life ; it is the joyousness of childhood. Step by step Strength works Knowledge with its
groans and tears. And then, in its turn, Knowledge works
Strength, Knowledge controls Strength, Knowledge
supersedes Strength. It is Knowledge which must prevail
now. May it not be he who at this moment resumes its
whole inheritance—its accumulated opportunities, in himself? He could stand still and dream while he fancied he
stood alone ; but he knows now that he is part of humanity,
and it of him. Goito is left behind ; Ferrara is reached ;
he must do the one thing that is within his grasp.

He must influence Salinguerra. He must interest him
in the cause of knowledge ; which is the people's cause.
With this determination, he proceeds once more to the
appointed presence. His minstrelsy is at first a failure.
He is, as usual, outside his song. He is trying to guide it ;
it is not carrying him away. He is paralysed by the very
consciousness that he is urging the head of the Ghibellines
to become a Guelph. Salinguerra's habitual tact and
good-nature cannot conceal his own sense of the absurdity
of the proposal. Sordello sees in

> "a flash of bitter truth :
> So fantasies could break and fritter youth
> That he had long ago lost earnestness,
> Lost will to work, lost power to even express
> The need of working ! "                    (vol. i. p. 228.)

But he will not be beaten. He tries once more. We see
the blood leap to his brain, the heart into his purpose, as
he challenges Salinguerra to bow before the royalty of
song. He owns himself its unworthy representative :
for he has frittered away his powers. He has identified
himself with existing forms of being, instead of proving his
kingship by a new spiritual birth—by a supreme, as yet
unknown revelation of the power of human will. He has
resigned his function. He is a self-deposed king. He

acknowledges the **man** before him **as** fitter **to** help the world than he is. But this is shame enough. He will **not** see its now elected champion scorn the post **he renounces** on his behalf. And his art is still royal **though he is not.** It is the utterance of the spiritual life : **of the informing** thought—which was **in the** world before deeds **began—** which brought order out of chaos—which **guided deeds** in their due gradation till itself **emerged as SONG : to** react **in** deed ; but **to** need no **help of it ; to be (so we** complete the meaning) as the knowledge **which controls** strength, which supersedes strength.[1]

The walls of the presence-chamber **have fallen away.** Imaginary faces are crowding **around him. He turns to** these. He shows **them** human **life as the poet's mirror** reflects **it : in** its varied masquerade, **in its** mingled good and evil, in **its** steady advance ; **in** the rainbow brightness of its obstructed lights ; the deceptive gloom **of its merely** repeated shadows. **He** enforces in **every tone that con-** tinuity of the plan **of** creation **to** which **the poet alone** holds the clue. Finally, in the name **of the** unlimited truth, the limited opportunity, the **one** duty which **con-** fronts him now, **the** People whose support, in his perfor- mance of it, he may claim for the first time, he forbids **the** Emperor's coming, and invokes Salinguerra's protection for the Guelph cause.

Salinguerra is moved at last, though not in the intended way. He does not yield to Sordello's enthusiasm, but he sees that **it** is worth employing. There is no question of his becoming a Guelph, but why should not Sordello turn Ghibelline? The cause requires **a** youth to "stalk, and bustle, and attitudinize ;" and he clearly thinks this is all **the** youth before him wants to do, whether conscious of **the** fact or not. He thinks the thought aloud. "Palma loves her minstrel ; it is written in her eyes ; let her marry

---

[1] Here, as elsewhere, I give the spirit rather than the letter, or even the exact order of Sordello's words. The necessary condensation requires this.

him. Were she Romano's son instead of his daughter, she could wear the Emperor's badge. Himself fate has doomed to a secondary position. To contend against it is useless." Before he knows what he has done, without really meaning to do it, he has thrown the badge across Sordello's neck, and thus created him Eccelino's successor.

It was a prophetic act. At the moment of its performance

> "    .    .    .    each looked on each :
> Up in the midst a truth grew, without speech." (vol. i. p. 243 )

Palma's moment is come, and she relates the story, as she received it from Adelaide, of Sordello's birth. With blanched lips, and sweat-drops on his face, the old soldier takes the hand of his poet-son, and lays its consecrating touch on his own face and brow. Then, recovering himself, with his mailed arms on Sordello's shoulders, he launches forth in an eager survey of the situation as it may shape itself for both. Palma at last draws him away, and Sordello, exhausted and speechless, is left alone. The two are in a small stone chamber, below the one they have left. Half-drunk with his new emotions, Salinguerra paces the narrow floor. His eyes burn ; his tread strikes sparks from the stone. The future glows before him. He and Sordello combined will break up Hildebrand. They will rebuild Charlemagne ; not in the brute force of earlier days ; but as strength adorned with knowledge, as empire imposing law. Palma listens in satisfied repose ; her task is done.

A stamp is heard overhead.


BOOK THE SIXTH.

Sordello is alone—face to face with his memory, with his conscience, and, as we presently find out, with the greatest temptation he has ever known. The moon is slowly rising ; and just so the light of truth is overflowing his past life, and laying bare its every recess. He sees no fault in this past, except the want of a uniform purpose in which its various moods could have coalesced, the all-embracing sense of existence been translated into **fact** ; but he unconsciously confesses its selfishness, in deciding that this purpose should have been outside him—a remote and uplifting, though sympathetic influence, such as the moon is to the sea. Smaller lives **than his** have attained a higher completeness, because they **have** worked for **an** ideal : because they have had their moon.

"Where then is *his* moon ? What the love, the fear, the motive, in short, that could match the strength, could sway the full tide, of a nature like his ?" He doubts its existence. And **if,** after all, he has been destined **to be a** law to himself, must he not in some sense apply this relative standard to the rest of life ; and may not **the** outward motive be at all times the embodiment of an inner want or law, which only the stronger nature can realize as such ? He has found his purpose. That purpose is the people. "But the people is himself. The desire to help it comes from within. Will he fulfil this **the** better for regarding its suffering part as an outward motive, as something alien to himself, and for which Self must be forsaken ?" In plain words : would he not serve it as well by serving his own interests as by forsaking them ?

This sophistry is so patent that it startles even him ; but it is only silenced to reassert itself in another form. "The Guelph rule would doubtless be the best. But what can he do to promote it ? Attest his belief by refusing the Emperor's badge ? That would be something in the end. But meanwhile, how many sympathies to be broken, how many aversions defied, before the one ideal can be made to prevail. Is not the proceeding too arbitrary ? Would it be justified by the result ? The question is only one of ideas. If the men who supported each opposite cause were wholly good or bad, his course would be clear. But such divisions do not exist. All men are composite. All nature is a blending of good and evil, in which the one is often but a different form of the other. Evil is in fact indispensable ; for it is not only the ground of sympathy, but the active principle of life. Joy means the triumph over obstruction. The suspended effort is death, so far as it goes. Obstruction and effort must begin again and again. The sphere grows larger. It can never be more complete (more satisfying to those who are imprisoned within it). The only gain of existence is to be extracted from its hindrances, by each individual and for himself." The last plea for self-sacrifice is thus removed.

These arguments are often just, even profound ; they might also have been sincere in this special case ; for there was something to be said in favour of accepting the opportunities which offered themselves, and of guiding the course of events, instead of engaging in a probably fruitless opposition to it. But they are not sincere. Sordello is at best deceiving himself, and Mr. Browning intends us to to see this. He is struggling, if unconsciously, to evade the very trials which he thinks so good for other men. His true object soon stands revealed in a first and last effort at compromise. "The people's good is in the future. His is in the present. Can he not speed the one, and yet enjoy the other ?" . . . The present rises up, in its new-found richness, in its undisguised temptation. The joys which lure him become gigantic ; the price of renunciation shrinks to nothing ; and at last, the pent-up passion breaks forth— that passion for life, for sheer life, which inspired his imagination as a boy, which nerved his ambition as a man ; to which his late-found humanities have given voice and shape ; which now gathers itself to a supreme utterance in the grasp of death. "The earthly existence now : the transcendent hereafter, if Fate will. A man's opportunities—a man's powers—a man's self-consciousness of joy and conflict—these things he craves while he may yet possess them."

Then **a** sudden revulsion. "He would drink the very dregs of life! How many have sacrificed it whilst its cup was full, because a better still seemed behind it."

> ".       .       .       . the death I fly, revealed
> So oft a better life this life concealed,
> And which sage, champion, martyr, through each path
> Have hunted fearlessly—   •     •     •     ."
>
> (vol. i. p. 272.)

"But they had **a** belief which he has not. Th*e*y knew what 'masters life.' For him the paramount fact is that of his own being.   .   .   .   ."

This is the last protest of the flesh within him. Sordello is dying, and probably feels that he **is** so ; **and** he lapses into **a** calm contemplation, which reveals to him the last secret of his mistaken career. He already knew that he had ignored the bodily **to** the detriment of his spiritual existence. He **now** feels **that** he has destroyed his **body** by forcing **on it** the exigencies of **the** spirit. He has striven **to** obtain infinite consciousness, infinite enjoyment, from finite powers. He has broken the **law** of life. He has missed (so we interpret **Mr.** Browning's conclusion) the ideal **of** that divine **and** human Love which would have given the freest range to his spirit and yet accepted that law. Eglamor began with love. Will Sordello find it, meeting that gentle spirit on his course?

We know at least that the soul in him has conquered. His stamp upon the floor has brought Palma and Salinguerra to him in anxious haste. They find him dead :

> "Under **his** foot the badge : still, Palma said,
> A triumph lingering in the wide eyes,
> Wider than some spent swimmer's if he spies
> Help from above in his extreme despair,
>
> •     •     •     •     •     ."   (vol. i. p. 279.)

Sordello is buried at Goito Castle, in an old font-tomb in which his mother lies, and beside whose sculptured female forms the child-poet had dreamed his earliest dreams of life and of love. Salinguerra makes peace with the Guelphs, marries a daughter of Eccelino the monk, and effaces himself once for all in the Romano house, leaving its sons Eccelino and Alberic to plague the world at their pleasure, and meet the fate they have deserved. He himself, after varied fortunes, dwindles into a "showy, turbulent soldier," less "astute" than people profess to think : whose qualities even foes admire ; and whose aggressions they punish, but do not much resent. We see him for the last time at the age of eighty, a nominal prisoner in Venice.

The drama is played out. Its actors have vanished from the stage. One only lives on in Mr. Browning's fancy, in the pathos of his modest hopes, and acknowledged, yet scarcely comprehended failure—more human, and therefore more undying than Naddo himself : the poet Eglamor. Sordello he recalls only to dismiss him with less sympathy than we should expect : as ending the ambition for what he could not become, by the well-meant renunciation of what he was born to be ; made a hero of by legends which credited him with doing what his conscience had forbidden him to do ; leaving the world to suffer by his self-sacrifice ; a type of failure more rare and more brilliant than that of Eglamor, yet more full of the irony of life.

In one sense, however, he had lived for a *better thing,* and we are bidden look back, through the feverish years, on a bare-footed rosy child running "higher and higher" up a wintry hillside still crisp with the morning frost,

> "     .     .     . singing all the while
> Some unintelligible words to beat
> The lark, God's poet, swooning at his feet,
> So worsted is he .     .     .     . " (vol. i. p. 288-9.)

The poet in him had failed with the man, but less completely.

## II.

## NON-CLASSIFIED POEMS.

### DRAMAS.

OUR attention is next attracted to Mr. Browning's dramas; for his first tragedy, "Strafford," was published before "Sordello," having been written in an interval of its composition, and his first drama, "Pippa Passes," immediately afterwards. They were published, with the exception of "Strafford," and "In a Balcony," in the "Bells and Pomegranates" series, 1841-1846, together with the "Dramatic Lyrics," and "Dramatic Romances," which will be found distributed under various headings in the course of this volume.

The dramas are :—

"Strafford." 1837.
"Pippa Passes." 1841.
"King Victor and King Charles." 1842.
"The Return of the Druses." 1843.
"A Blot in the 'Scutcheon." 1843.
"Colombe's Birthday." 1844.
"A Soul's Tragedy." 1846.
"Luria." 1846.
"In a Balcony." (A Fragment.) 1853.

The five-act tragedy of "STRAFFORD" turns on the impeachment and condemnation of the man whose name it bears. Its keynote is Strafford's devotion to the King, which Mr. Browning has represented as the constant motive of his life, and also the cause of his death. When the action opens, England is without a Parliament. The question of ship-money is "burning." The Scotch Parliament has just been dissolved, and Charles is determined to subdue the Scots by force. Wentworth has been summoned from Ireland to assist in doing so. He is worn and weary, but the King needs him, and he comes.

He accepts the Scotch war against his better judgment: and next finds himself entrapped by the King's duplicity and selfishness, not only into the command of the expedition to Scotland, but into the appearance of having advised it. Pym has vainly tried to win him back to the popular cause. Lady Carlisle vainly warns him of his danger in subserving the King's designs. No danger can shake his allegiance. He leads the army to the north; is beaten; discovers that the popular party is in league with the Scotch; returns home to impeach it, and finds himself impeached. A Bill of Attainder is passed against him; and Charles, who might prove by one word his innocence of the charges conveyed in it, promises to do so, evades his promise, and finally signs the warrant for Strafford's death. Pym, who loved him best, who trusted him longest, is he who demands the signature.

Lady Carlisle forms a plan for Strafford's escape from the Tower; but it fails at the last moment, and we see him led away to execution. True to the end, he has no thought but for the master who has betrayed him—whose terrible weakness must betray himself—whose fate he sees foreshadowed in his own. He kneels to Pym for the King's life; and, seeing him inexorable, *thanks God that he dies first.* Pym's last speech is a tender farewell to the friend whom he has sacrificed to his country's cause, but whom he trusts soon to meet in the better land, where they will walk together as of old, all sin and all error purged away.

We are told in **the** preface to the first edition of Strafford that the portraits are, so the author thinks, faithful : his "Carlisle," only, being imaginary; and we may add that he regards his conception of her as, in the main, confirmed by a very recent historian of the reign of Charles I. The tragedy was performed in 1837, at Covent Garden Theatre, under the direction of Macready, by whose desire it had been written, and who sustained the **principal** part.

The appearance of "Strafford" coincides so closely with at least the conception of "Sordello" as to afford **a** strong proof of the variety of the author's genius. The evidence is still stronger in "Pippa Passes," in which he leaps directly from his most abstract mode of conception **to** his most picturesque; and, from the prolonged strain **of a** single inward experience, to a quick succession of pictures, in which life is given from a general and external point **of** view. The humour which found little place in the earlier work has abundant scope here; and the descriptive power which was so vividly apparent in all of them, here shows itself for the first time in those touches of local colour which paint without describing. **Mr.** Browning is now fully developed, on the artistic **and** on the practical side of his genius.

Mr. Browning was walking alone, in a wood **near** Dulwich, when the image flashed upon him of some one walking thus alone through life; one apparently too obscure to leave **a** trace of his or her passage, yet exercising **a** lasting though unconscious influence at every step of it; and the image shaped itself into the little silk-winder of Asolo, Felippa, or Pippa.

"PIPPA PASSES" represents the course of one day— Pippa's yearly holiday; and is divided into what is virtually four acts, being the occurrences of "Morning," "Noon," "Evening," and "Night." Pippa rises with the sun, determined to make the best of the bright hours before her ; and she spends them in wandering through the town, singing as she goes, and all the while thinking of its happiest men and women, and fancying herself they. These happy ones are four, each the object of a different love. Ottima, whose aged husband is the owner of the silk mills, has a lover in Sebald.  Phene, betrothed to the French sculptor Jules, will be led this morning to her husband's home.  Luigi (a conspiring patriot) meets his mother at eve in the turret.  The Bishop, blessed by God, will sleep at Asolo to-night.  Which love would she choose?  The lover's?  It gives cause for scandal.  The husband's?  It may not last.  The parent's?  it alone will guard us to the end of life.  God's love?  That is best of all.  It is Monsignore she decides to be.

Ottima and her lover have murdered her husband at his villa on the hillside.  She is the more reckless of the two, and she is striving by the exercise of her attractions to silence Sebald's remorse.  She has succeeded for the moment, when Pippa passes—singing.  Something in her song strikes his conscience like a thunderbolt, and its reviving force awakens Ottima's also.  Both are spiritually saved.

Jules has brought home his bride, and is discovering that some students who owed him a grudge have practised a cruel cheat upon him ; and that the refined woman by whom he fancied himself loved is but an ignorant girl of the lowest class, of whom also his enemies have made a tool.  Her remorse at seeing what man she has deceived disarms his anger, and marks the dawning of a moral sense in her ; and he is dismissing her gently, with all the money he can spare, when Pippa passes—singing.[1]  Something in her song awakens his truer manhood.  Why should he dismiss his wife?  Why cast away

[1] The song professedly refers to Catherine Cornaro, the Venetian Queen of Cyprus, and is the only one in the poem that is based on any fact at all.

a soul which needs him, and which he himself has called
into existence? He does not cast Phene away. Her
salvation and his happiness are secured.

Luigi and his mother are in the turret on' the hillside
above Asolo. He believes it his mission to kill the
Austrian Emperor. She entreats him to desist; and has
nearly conquered his resolution by the mention of the girl
he loves, when Pippa passes—singing. Something in her
song revives his flagging patriotism. He rushes from the
tower, thus escaping the police, who were on his track;
and the virtuous, though mistaken motive, secures his
liberty, and perhaps his life.

Monsignore and his "Intendant" are conferring in the
palace by the Duomo; and the irony of the situation is
now at its height. Pippa's fancy has been aspiring to
three separate existences, which would each in its own
way have been wrecked without her. The divinely-guarded
one which she especially covets is at this moment bent
on her destruction. For she is the child of the brother at
whose death the Bishop has connived, and whose wealth
he is enjoying. She is still in his way, and he is listening
to a plan for removing her also, when Pippa passes—singing. Something in her song stings his conscience or his
humanity to life. He starts up, summons his attendants,
has his former accomplice bound hand and foot, and the
sequel may be guessed.

The scene is varied by groups of students, of poor girls,
and of Austrian policemen, all joking and chatting in
characteristic fashion, and all playing their part in the
story; and also by the appearance of Bluphocks, an
English adventurer and spy, who is in league with the
police for the detection of Luigi, and with the Intendant
for Pippa's ruin; and the saving effect of Pippa's songs is
the more dramatic that it becomes on one occasion the
means of betraying herself. She goes home at sunset,
unconscious of all she has effected and escaped, and

wondering how near she may ever come to touching for good or evil the lives with which her fancy has been identifying her. "So far, perhaps," she says to herself, "that the silk she will wind to-morrow may some day serve to border Ottima's cloak. And if it be only this !"

> "All service ranks the same with God—
> With God, whose puppets, best and worst,
> Are we : there is no last nor first."　　(vol. iii. p. 79.)

These are her last words as she lies down to sleep.

Pippa's songs are not impressive in themselves. They are made so in every case by the condition of her hearer's mind ; and the idea of the story is obvious, besides being partly stated in the heroine's own words. No man is "great" or "small" in the sight of God—each life being in its own way the centre of creation. Nothing should be "great" or "small" in the sight of man ; since it depends on personal feeling, or individual circumstance, whether a given thing will prove one or the other.

"KING VICTOR AND KING CHARLES" is an historical tragedy in two divisions and four parts, of which the time is 1730 and 31, and the place the castle of Rivoli near Turin. The episode which it records may be read in any chronicle of the period ; and Mr. Browning adds a preface, in which he justifies his own view of the characters and motives involved in it. King Victor II. (first King of Sardinia) was sixty-four years old, and had been nominally a ruler from the age of ten, when suddenly (1730) he abdicated in favour of his son Charles. The Queen was dead, and he had privately married a lady of the Court, to whom he had been long attached ; and the desire to acknowledge this union, combined with what seems to have been a premature old age, might sufficiently have explained the abdication ; but Mr. Browning adopts the idea, which for a time found favour, that it had a deeper cause : that the King's intriguing ambition had involved him in many difficulties, and he had devised this plan for eluding them.

Charles has become his father's heir through the death of an older and better loved son. He has been thrust into the shade by the favourite, now Victor's wife, and by the Minister d'Ormea ; his sensitive nature crushed into weakness, his loftiness of purpose never called into play. He seems precisely the person of whom to make at once a screen and a tool. But he has scarcely been crowned when it is evident that he will be neither. He assumes the character of king at the same time as the function ; and by his honesty, courage, and humanity, restores the prosperity of his country, and the honour of his house. He secures even the devotion, interested though it be, of the unscrupulous d'Ormea himself.

Victor, however, is restless in his obscurity ; and by the end of the year is scheming for the recovery of his crown. He presents himself before his son, and demands that it be restored to him ; denouncing what he considers the weakness of King Charles' rule. Charles refuses, gently but firmly, to abandon what has become for him the post of duty ; and King Victor departs, to conspire openly against him. D'Ormea is active in detecting the conspiracy and unveiling it ; and Victor is brought back to the palace, this time a prisoner.

But Charles does not receive him as such. His filial piety is outraged by the unnatural conflict ; and his wife Polixena has vainly tried to convince him that there is a higher because less obvious virtue in resisting than in giving way. He once more acknowledges his father as King. And both he and his wife are soon aware that in doing so, he is only humouring the caprice of a dying man. "*I have no friend in the wide world* is the old King's cry. Give me what I have no power to take from you."

" So few years give it quietly,
My son !  It will drop from me.  See you not ?
A crown's unlike a sword to give away—
That, let a strong hand to a weak hand give !
But crowns should slip from palsied brows to heads
Young as this head :      .      .      . " (vol. iii. p. 162-3.)

Charles places the crown on his father's head. A strange conflict of gratified ambition, of remorseful tenderness, of dreamy regret, stirs the failing spirit. But command and defiance flash out in the old King's last words.

This death on the stage is the only point on which Mr. Browning diverges from historical truth. King Victor lived a year longer, in a modified captivity to which his son had most unwillingly consigned him ; and he is made to suggest this story in the half-insanity of his last moments as one which may be told to the world ; and will give his son the appearance of reigning, while he remains, in secret, King.

"THE RETURN OF THE DRUSES" is a tragedy in five acts, fictitious in plot, but historical in character. The Druses of Lebanon are a compound of several warlike Eastern tribes, owing their religious system to a caliph of Egypt, Hakeem Biamr Allah ; and probably their name to his confessor Darazi, who first attempted to promulgate his doctrine among them ; some also impute to the Druse nation a dash of the blood of the Crusaders. One of their chief religious doctrines was that of divine incarnations. It seems to have originated in the pretension of Hakeem to be himself one ; and as organized by the Persian mystic Hamzi, his Vizier and disciple, it included ten manifestations of this kind, of which Hakeem must have formed the last. Mr. Browning has assumed that in any great national emergency, the miracle would be expected to recur ; and he has here conceived an emergency sufficiently great to call it forth.

The Druses, according to him, have colonized a small

island belonging to the Knights of Rhodes, and become subject to a Prefect appointed by the Order. This Prefect has almost extirpated the Druse sheikhs, and made the remainder of the tribe victims of his cruelty and lust. The cry for rescue and retribution, if not loud, is deep. It finds a passionate response in the soul of Djabal, a son of the last Emir, who escaped as a child from the massacre of his family, and took refuge in Europe; and who now returns, with a matured purpose of patriotic and personal revenge. He has secured an ally in the young Lois de Dreux—an intended Knight of the Order, and son of a Breton Count, whose hospitality he has enjoyed—and induced him to accompany him to the islet, and pass his probation there. This, he considers, will facilitate the murder of the Prefect, which is an essential part of his plan ; and he has obtained the promise of the Venetians, who are hostile to the Knights, to lend their ships for his countrymen's escape as soon as the death of the tyrant shall have set them free.

So far his course is straight. But he has scarcely returned home, when he falls in love with Anael, a Druse girl, whose devotion to her tribe is a religion, and who is determined to marry none but the man who will deliver it ; and he is then seized by an impulse to heighten the act of deliverance by a semblance of more than human power. He declares himself Hakeem, the Divine founder of the sect, again present in human form, and who will again be transformed, or " exalted," so soon as by the slaughter of their tyrant he has set the Druses free. His bride will be exalted with him. The imposture succeeds only too well. " Mystic " as well as " schemer," Djabal, for a moment, deceives even himself ; and when the crisis is at hand, and reason and conscience reassert themselves, the enthusiasm which he has kindled still forces him on. His only refuge is in flight ; and even this proves impossible. He nerves himself, before escaping, to the

Prefect's murder ; and is confronted on the threshold of the Prefect's chamber, by his promised wife, who has herself done the deed.

Anael has loved Djabal, believing him Divine, with what seemed to her too human a love. She felt unworthy to share his exaltation. She has done that which her humanity disclaimed that she might no longer be so. A few moments more, and they both know that the crime has been superfluous. Lois, who also loves Anael, and hopes to win her, has procured from the Chapter of his Order the removal of the tyrant, and been appointed by it in his place ; the day of Druse oppression was already over. But Djabal and Anael are inseparably united. The scorn with which she received his now inevitable confession was intense but momentary. The woman's heart in her revels in its new freedom to cherish and to protect ; and she embraces her lover's shame with a far greater joy than their common triumph could have aroused in her. She is brought forward as the Prefect's murderer in presence of all the personages of the drama ; and falls dead with a cry of " Hakeem " on her lips. Djabal stabs himself on her body, thus " exalting " himself to her. But he has first committed his Druses to the care of Lois, to be led back to their mountain home. He remains Hakeem for them, though branded as an impostor by the rest of the world. Directly, or indirectly, he has done the work of the deliverer.

" A BLOT IN THE 'SCUTCHEON " is a tragedy in three acts, less intricate as well as shorter than those which precede it ; and historical only in the simple motive, the uncompromising action, and the mediæval code of honour, which in some degree fix its date. Mr. Browning places this somewhere in the eighteenth century.

Lord Henry Mertoun has fallen in love with Mildred Tresham. His estates adjoin those of Earl Tresham, her brother and guardian. **He** inherits a noble name, and an unsullied reputation ; **and** need only offer himself to be accepted. But the youthful reverence which he entertains for Lord Tresham makes him shrink from preferring his suit ; and he allows himself and Mildred to drift into a secret intimacy, which begins in all innocence, but does not end so. Then his shyness vanishes. He seeks an interview with the Earl, and obtains his joyful consent to the union. All seems to be going well. But Mildred's awakened womanhood takes the form **of an** overpowering remorse and shame ; **and** these become the indirect cause of the catastrophe.

Gerard, an old retainer of the family, has witnessed Lord Mertoun's nightly **visits to the** castle ; and, amidst **a bitter** conflict of feeling, he tells the Earl what he **has** seen. Tresham summons his sister. He is writhing under the **sense** of outraged family honour ; but **a** still stronger fraternal affection commends the culprit to his mercy. He assists her confession with touching delicacy and tenderness ; shows himself prepared to share her shame, to help her to live it through—to marry her to the man she loves. He insists only upon this, that Mertoun **shall not** be deceived : and that she shall cancel the promise of an interview which she has given him for the following day.

Mildred tacitly owns her guilt, and invokes any punishment **her** brother may adjudge **to** it ; but she will **not** betray her lover by confessing his name, and she will not forbid Mertoun **to** come. The Earl's mind does **not** connect **the** two. No extenuating circumstance suggests itself. **He** has loved his young sister with a chivalrous admiration and trust ; and he **is** one of those men to whom **a** blot in the 'scutcheon is only less terrible than the knowledge that such trust has been misplaced. He is stung to madness by what seems this crowning proof of his sister's depravity ; and by the thought of him who

has thus corrupted her. He surprises Mertoun on the
way to the last stolen visit to his love ; and, before there
has been time for an explanation, challenges and kills him.

The reaction of feeling begins when he perceives that
Mertoun has allowed himself to be killed. Remorse and
sorrow deepen into despair as the dying youth gasps out
the story of his constant love, of his boyish error—of his
manly desire of reparation ; above all, as he reminds his
hearer of the sister whose happiness he has slain ; and
asks if he has done right to set his "thoughtless foot"
upon them both, and say as they perish—

> "  .     .     .     .     .   Had I thought,
> 'All had gone otherwise'  .     .     .     ."
>
> (vol iv. p. 59.)

Mildred is waiting for her lover. The usual signal has
been made : the lighted purple pane of a painted window
sends forth its beckoning gleam. But Mertoun does
not appear; and as the moments pass, a despairing
apathy steals over her, which is only the completed certainty of her doom. She has never believed in the promised happiness. In a strange process of self-consciousness she has realized at once the moral and the natural
consequences of her transgression ; the lost peace of conscience, the lost morning of her love. Her paramount
desire has been for expiation and rest. In one more pang
they are coming. Lord Tresham breaks in on her solitude. His emtpy scabbard shows what he has done. But
she soon sees that reproach is unnecessary, and that Mertoun's death is avenged. It is best so. The cloud has
lifted. The friend and the brother are one in heart again.
She dies because her own heart is broken, but forgiving
her brother, and blessing him. He has taken poison,
and survives her by a few minutes only.

Mildred has a firm friend in her cousin Gwendolen : a
quick-witted, true-hearted woman, the betrothed of Austin
Tresham, who is next heir to the earldom. She alone has

guessed the true state of the case, and, with **the help** of Austin, would have averted the tragedy, **if Lord Tre**sham's precipitate passion had **not** rendered this impossible. These two are in no need **of** their dying kinsman's warning, to remember, **if a** blot should again come in the 'scutcheon, that " vengeance is God's, **not** man's."

This tragedy was performed **in** 1843, **at** Drury Lane Theatre, during the ownership of Macready; in 1848, at "Sadlers Wells," under the direction **of Mr.** Phelps, who had played the part of Lord Tresham **in the** Drury Lane performance.

COLOMBE'S BIRTHDAY **is** a play **in five acts, of which** the scene is the palace at Juliers, the time 16—. Colombe of Ravestein is ostensibly Duchess of Juliers and Cleves; but her title is neutralized by the Salic law under which the Duchy is held; and though the Duke, her late father, has wished to evade it in her behalf, those about her **are** aware that he had no power **to do so, and** that the legal claimant, her cousin, may at any moment assert his rights. This happens on the first anniversary **of** her accession, which is also her birthday.

Prince Berthold is to arrive **in** a few hours. He has sent a letter before him from which Colombe will learn her fate ; and the handful of courtiers **who** have stayed to see the drama out are disputing as **to** who shall deliver it. Valence, an advocate of Cleves, arrives at this juncture, with a petition from his townspeople who are starving ; and is allowed to place it in the Duchess's hands, on condition of presenting the Prince's letter at the same time. He does this in ignorance of its contents ; **he is very** indignant when he knows them ; and the incident naturally constitutes him Colombe's adviser and friend ; while the reverence with which **he** owns himself her subject, also determines her if possible to remain his sovereign.

F

Prince Berthold arrives unprepared for any show of re-sistance ; and is a little startled to find that Colombe defies him, and that one of her courtiers (not choosing to be outdone by Valence) has the courage to tell him so ; but he treats the Duchess and her adviser with all the courtesy of a man whose right is secure ; and Valence, to whom he entrusts his credentials, is soon convinced that it is so.   But he has a far-sighted ambition which keeps him alive to all possible risks : and it occurs to him as wiser to secure the little sovereignty by marrying its heiress than by dispossessing her.   He desires Valence to convey to the young Duchess the offer of his hand.   The offer is worth considering, since as he asserts, it may mean the Empire : to which the Duchy is, in his case, but a necessary stepping-stone ; and Valence, who has loved Colombe since his first glimpse of her at Cleves, a year ago ; who has begun to hope that his affection is returned ; and who knows that the Prince's message is not only a test of her higher nature, but a snare to it, feels nevertheless bound to leave her choice free.   This choice lies clearly between love and power ; for Berthold parades a cynicism half affected, half real ; and on being questioned as to his feeling for the lady, has dismissed the question as irrele-vant.

Valence is, throughout the play, an advocate in the best sense of the word.   As he has pleaded the wrongs of an oppressed people, he sets forth the happiness of a suc-cessful prince—the happiness which the young Duchess is invited to share ; and he departs from all the conven-tionalities of fiction, by showing her the true poetry, not the artificial splendours, of worldly success.   Colombe is almost as grateful as the young Prince could desire, for she assumes that he has fallen in love with her, whether he says so or not ; and here, too, Valence must speak the truth.  "The Prince does not love her."  "How does he know this?"  "He knows it by the insight of one

who does love." Astonished, vaguely pained, Colombe
questions him as to the object of his attachment, and, in
probably **real** ignorance of who it can be, draws **him on**
to a confession. For a moment she is disenchanted. **" So**
much unselfish devotion to turn out merely love ! She
will at all events see Valence's rival."

In the last act **she** discusses the Prince's proposal **with**
himself. He frankly rests it on its advantages for both.
He has much to say in favour of **such an** understanding,
and reminds his listener as she questions and temporizes,
that if he gives no heart he also **asks** none. The courtiers
now see their opportunity. They inform the Prince that
by her late father's will the Duchess forfeits **her** rights **in**
the event of marrying a subject. They point **to such a**
marriage **as** a natural result of the loving **service which**
Valence has this day rendered to her, and **the love which**
is its only fitting reward. And Colombe listening **to the**
just if treacherous praises of this man, **feels no** longer
" sure " that she does " not love him." Valence is summoned ; requested to assert his claim **or to** deny it ; given
**to** understand that the lady's interests demand the latter
course. The manly dignity and exalted tenderness with
which he resigns her convert, as it seems, the doubt into
certainty ; and Colombe takes him on this her birthday
at the sacrifice of " Juliers and the world."

Berthold has a confidant, Melchior, a learned and
thoughtful man, who is affectionately attached **to** the
young prince, and who views with regret the easy worldly
successes which neutralize his higher gifts. Melchior
has also appreciated the genuineness of Colombe's nature,
and conducted the last interview with Valence as one who
desired that loyalty should be attested and love triumph.
He now turns to Berthold with what seems an appeal to
his generosity. But Berthold cannot afford to be generous.
As he reminds the happy bride before him he wants her
duchy much more than she does. He is, however, the

sadder, and perhaps the wiser, for having found this out.

"Colombe's Birthday" was performed in 1853, at the Haymarket Theatre; in 1853 or '54, in the United States, at Boston. The part of Colombe was taken, as had been those of Mildred Tresham and Lady Carlisle, by Miss Helen Faucit, now Lady Martin.

"A SOUL'S TRAGEDY" brings us near to the period of the "Men and Women;" and displays, for the first time in Mr. Browning's work, a situation quite dramatic in itself, but which is nevertheless made by the characters, and imagined for them. It is a story of moral retrogression; but, setting aside its very humorous treatment, it is no "tragedy" for the reader, because he has never believed in that particular "soul," though its proprietor and his friends are justly supposed to do so. The drama is divided into two acts, of which the first represents the "poetry," the second the prose, of a certain Chiappino's life. The scene is Faenza; the time 15—.

Chiappino is best understood by comparison with Luitolfo, his fellow-townsman and friend. Luitolfo has a gentle, genial nature; Chiappino, if we may judge him by his mood at the time of the action, an ill-conditioned one. Luitolfo's gentleness is allied to physical timidity, but his moral courage is always equal to the occasion. Chiappino is a man more of words than of deeds, and wants both the courage and the rectitude which ill-conditioned people often possess. Faenza is governed by a provost from Ravenna. The present provost is a tyrant; and Chiappino has been agitating in a somewhat purposeless manner against him. He has been fined for this several times, and is now sentenced to exile, and confiscation of all his goods.

Luitolfo has helped him until now by paying his fines; but this is an additional grievance to him, for he is in love with Eulalia, the woman whom his friend is going to

marry, and declares that he has only refrained from urging
his own suit, because he was bound by this pecuniary
obligation not to do **so**. He is not too delicate, however,
to depreciate Luitolfo's generosity, and generally run him
down with the woman who is to be his wife; and this is
what he is doing in **the** first scene, under cover **of** taking
leave of her, and while her intended husband **is** inter-
ceding with the provost in his behalf. **A hurried** knock,
which they recognise as Luitolfo's, gives **a** fresh impulse
to his spite; and he begins sneering at the milk-and-
watery manner in which Luitolfo has probably been
pleading his cause, and the **awful** fright in **which** he has
run home, **on** seeing that **the** provost "shrugged his
shoulders" **at** the intercession.

Luitolfo *is* frightened, for his friendship **for Chiappino**
**has been** carrying him away; and **on** finding that entreaties **were** of no use, **he has** struck **at** the provost, and, **as**
he thinks, killed him. **A** crowd which he imagines to **be**
composed **of** the Provost's attendants has followed him
from **the** palace. Torture **stares him** in **the** face; and his
physical sensitiveness has the upper hand again. For a
moment Chiappino becomes a hero; he **is** shamed into
nobleness. He flings his own cloak over Luitolfo, gives
him his passport, hurries him from the house, assumes his
friend's blood-stained garment, and claims his deed. But
he has scarcely done so when he perceives their mistake.
Luitolfo's fears have distorted a friendly crowd into a
hostile one; and the throng which Chiappino has nerved
himself to defy is the populace of Faenza applauding him
**as** its saviour. He postpones **the** duty of undeceiving it
under pretence of the danger being not yet over. The next
step will be to refuse to do **so**. His moral collapse, the
"tragedy" of his "soul," has begun.

In the second act, a month later, this is complete. The
papal legate, Ogniben, has ridden on his mule in to Faenza
to find out what was wanted. "He has not come to punish;

there is no harm done : for the provost was not killed after all.   He has known twenty-three leaders of revolts," and therefore, so we understand, is not disposed to take such persons too seriously.   He has made friends with Chiappino, accepting him in this character, and lured him on with the hope of becoming provost himself ; and Chiappino again rising—or falling—to the situation, has discovered patriotic reasons for accepting the post.   He has outgrown his love, as well as modified his ideas of civic duty ; and he disposes of the obligations of friend-ship, by declaring (to Eulalia) that the blow imputed to him was virtually his, because Luitolfo would fain have avoided striking it, while he would have struck it if he could.    The legate draws him out in a humorous dia-logue ; satirizes his flimsy sophistries under cover of endorsing them, and leads him up to a final self-exposure.

This occurs when he reminds Chiappino in the hearing of the crowd of the private agreement they have come to: that he is to have the title and privileges of Provost on the one hand, and pay implicit obedience to Rome, in the person of her legate, on the other ; but with the now added condition, that if the actual assailant of the late provost is discovered, he shall be dealt with as he deserves.   At which new view of the situation Chiappino is silent ; and Luitolfo, who had missed all the reward of his deed, charac-teristically comes forward to receive its punishment.   The legate orders him to his own house ; advises Chiappino, with a little more joking at his expense, to leave the town for a short time ; takes possession of the key of the pro-vost's palace, to which he does *not* intend to give a new inmate ; bids a cheery goodbye to every one, and rides away as he came.   He has

"known *four* and twenty leaders of revolts."   (vol. iii. p. 302.)

The tragedy of " LURIA " is supposed to be enacted at

some period of the fifteenth century ; being an episode in
the historical struggle between Florence and Pisa. It occupies one day ; and the five acts correspond respectively to
its " Morning," " Noon," " Afternoon," " Evening," and
" Night." The day is that of a long-expected encounter
which is to end the war. The Florentine troops are commanded by the Moorish mercenary Luria. He is en-
camped between the two cities ; and with, or near him, are
his Moorish friend and confidant Husain ; Puccio—the
officer whom he has superseded ; Braccio—Commissary of
the Republic ; his secretary Jacopo, or Lapo ; and a noble
Florentine lady, Domizia.

Luria is a consummate general, a brave fighter, and a
humane man. Every soldier of the army is devoted to
him, and the triumph of the Republic seems secured. But
the men who trust him to win the victory cannot trust him
not to misuse it. They are afraid that his strength will be
turned against themselves so soon as it has disposed of
their foreign foe : and Braccio is on the spot, in order to
watch his movements, to register every deed that can give
the slightest hold for an accusation—in short, to supply
the Signoria with the materials for a trial, which is proceeding step by step with Luria's successful campaign, and
is to crush him the moment this is completed. Every one
but Husain is more or less his enemy. For Lapo is almost
blindly devoted to his chief. Puccio is jealous of the
stranger for whom he has been set aside. Domizia is
making him an instrument of revenge. Her brothers have
been faithful as he is, and condemned as he is to be.
They accepted their sentence because it was the mother-
city who passed it. She encourages Luria to encounter
the same ingratitude, because she believes he will resist
and punish it.

He is not unwarned of his danger. The Pisan general,
Tiburzio, has discovered the conspiracy against him, and
brings him, shortly before the battle, an intercepted letter

from Braccio to the Signoria, in which he is convinced
that he may read his fate. He urges him to open it ; to
desert the perfidious city, and to adopt Pisa's cause. But
Luria's loyalty is unshaken. He tears up the letter in the
presence of Braccio, Puccio, and Domizia : and only when
the battle has been fought and won demands the secret
of its contents. At the word "trial" he is carried away
by a momentary indignation ; but this subsides into a
tender regret that "his Florentines" should have so mis-
judged him ; that he should have given them cause to do
it. He has laboured for their city, not only with the
obedience of a son, but with the devotion of a lover. His
Eastern fancy has been enslaved by her art, her intellect :
by the life of educated thought which so far removed
her from the blind unrest, and the animal strength of
his savage world ; Domizia's attractions have added to
the spell. He has never guarded his love for Florence
against doubt, for he never dreamed that it could be
doubted. He cannot find it in his heart to chastise her
now.

Temptation besets him on every side ; for the armies of
both Florence and Pisa are at his command. Husain and
Domizia urge him on to revenge. Tiburzio entreats him
to give to Pisa the head with which Florence will only
decorate a gateway. Him he thanks and dismisses. To
the others he prepares his answer. Alone for the last
time ; with eyes fixed on the setting sun—his "own
orb" so much nearer to him in his Eastern home, and
which will shine for him there no more—he drains a phial
of poison : the one thing he has brought from his own
land to help him in the possible adversity. Death was to
be his refuge in defeat. He will die on his triumph-day
instead.

They all gather round him once more : Puccio grateful
and devoted ; for he has seen that though discredited
by Florence, Luria was still working for her success—

Tiburzio, who returns from Florence, where he has tendered his submission to Luria's arms, and borne his heartfelt testimony to Luria's honour—Domizia, who has learned from Luria that there are nobler things than retaliation : and now entreats him to forego his vengeance against her city, as she foregoes her own—Braccio, repentant for the wrong done, and beseeching that Luria will not "punish Florence." But they cannot avert the one punishment which that gentle spirit could inflict. He lies dead before them.

"In a Balcony" is a dramatic fragment, equivalent to the third or fourth act, of what might prove a tragedy or a drama, as the author designed. The personages are "Norbert" and "Constance," a young man and woman ; and the "Queen," a woman of a certain age. Constance is a relation and protégée of the Queen—as we imagine, a poor one. She is loved by Norbert ; and he has entered the Queen's service, for the opportunity of wooing and winning her. His diplomatic exertions have been strenuous. They have secured to his royal mistress the possession of a double crown. The "Balcony" echoes with the sound of festivities which are intended to mark the event.

Constance returns Norbert's affection. He thinks the moment come for pleading his and her cause with their sovereign. But Constance entreats him to temporize : either to defer the proposal for her hand, or to make it in so indirect a manner, that the Queen may only see in it a tribute to herself. He has allowed her to think that he served her for her own sake ; she must not be undeceived too roughly. Her heart has starved amidst the show of devotion : its hunger must not be roused by the touch of a living love in which she has no part. A shock of this kind would be painful to her—dangerous to themselves.

Norbert is an honest man, possessed of all the courage of his love : and he finds it hard to believe that the straight-forward course would not be the best ; but he yields to the dictates of feminine wisdom ; and having consented to play a part, plays it with fatal success. The Queen is a more unselfish woman than her young cousin suspects. She has guessed Norbert's love for Constance, and is pre-pared to sanction it ; but her own nature is still only too capable of responding to the faintest touch of affection : and at the seeming declaration that that love is her's, her joy carries all before it. She is married ; but as she de-clares she will dissolve her marriage, merely formal as it has always been ; she will cast convention to the winds, and become Norbert's wife. She opens her heart to Con-stance ; tells her how she has yearned for love, and how she will repay it. Constance knows, as she never knew, what a mystery of pain and passion has been that out-wardly frozen life ; and in a sudden impulse of pity and compunction, she determines that if possible its new happi-ness shall be permanent—its delusions converted into truth.

She meets Norbert again ; makes him talk of his future ; discovers that he only dreams of it as bound up with the political career he has already entered upon ; and though she sees that every vision of this future begins and ends in her, she sees, as justly, that its making or marring is in the Queen's hands. Here is a second motive for self-sacrifice. Norbert has no suspicion of what he has done. The Queen appears before Constance has had time to inform him of it ; and the latter has now no choice but to let him learn it from the Queen's own lips. She draws her on, accordingly, under plea of Norbert's diffidence, to speak of what she believes him to have asked of her, and what she knows to be already granted. She tries to prompt his reply.

But Norbert will not be prompted. He is slow to understand what is expected of him, very indignant when

he does so ; and in terror lest he should still **be misun-**
derstood—in unconsciousness of the torture he **is** inflicting
—he asserts and re-asserts his respect for the one woman,
his absorbing passion for the other. The Queen goes out.
Her looks and silence have been ominous. **The** shadow
of a great dread falls upon the scene. The dance-music
stops. Heavy footsteps are heard approaching. Norbert
and Constance stand awaiting their doom. But they are
united as they have never yet been, and they can defy it ;
for her love has shown itself as capable **of all** sacrifice—
his as above temptation.

Various theories have been formed as **to the kind of**
woman Mr. Browning meant Constance **to be ; but a**
careful and unbiassed reading of the poem **can** leave no
doubt on the subject. He has given her, not the courage
of an exclusively moral nature, but all the self-denial **of a de-**
voted one, growing with the demands which are made
upon it. How single-hearted is **her** attempt **to** sacrifice
Norbert's love, is sufficiently shown by one sentence, addressed to him after his interview with the Queen :

"You were mine.  Now I give myself to you."  (vol. vii. p. 28.)

## "THE RING AND THE BOOK." 1868-69.

From the dramas, we pass naturally to the dramatic
monologues ; poems embodying a lengthened argument or
soliloquy, and to which there is already an approach in the
tragedies themselves. The dramatic monologue repeats
itself in the finest poems of the " Men and Women," and
" Dramatis Personæ ;" and **Mr.** Browning's constructive
power thus remains, as it were, diffused, till it culminates
again in " The Ring and the Book :" at once his greatest
constructive achievement, and the triumph of the monologue form. From this time onwards, the monologue will

be his prevailing mode of expression, but each will often form an independent work. "The Ring and the Book" is thus our next object of interest.

Mr. Browning was strolling one day through a square in Florence, the Piazza San Lorenzo, which is a standing market for old clothes, old furniture, and old curiosities of every kind, when a parchment-covered book attracted his eye, from amidst the artistic or nondescript rubbish of one of the stalls. It was the record of a murder which had taken place in Rome, and bore inside it an inscription which Mr. Browning thus transcribes :—

> "   .   .   . A Roman murder-case:
> Position of the entire criminal cause
> Of Guido Franceschini, nobleman,
> With certain Four the cut-throats in his pay,
> Tried, all five, and found guilty and put to death
> By heading or hanging as befitted ranks,
> At Rome on February Twenty-Two,
> Since our salvation Sixteen Ninety-Eight :
> Wherein it is disputed if, and when,
> Husbands may kill adulterous wives, yet 'scape
> The customary forfeit."                    (vol. viii. p. 6.)

The book proved, on examination, to contain the whole history of the case, as carried on in writing, after the fashion of those days : pleadings and counter-pleadings, the depositions of defendants and witnesses ; manuscript letters announcing the execution of the murderer ; and the "instrument of the Definitive Sentence" which established the perfect innocence of the murdered wife : these various documents having been collected and bound together by some person interested in the trial, possibly the very Cencini, friend of the Franceschini family, to whom the manuscript letters are addressed. Mr. Browning bought the whole for the value of eightpence, and it became the raw material of what appeared four years later as " The Ring and the Book."

This name is explained as follows :—The story of the Franceschini case, as Mr. Browning relates it, forms a circle of evidence to its one central truth ; and this circle was constructed in the manner in which the worker in Etruscan gold prepares the ornamental circlet which will be worn as a ring. The pure metal is too soft to bear hammer or file ; it must be mixed with alloy to gain the necessary power of resistance. The ring once formed and embossed, the alloy is disengaged, and a pure gold ornament remains. Mr. Browning's material was also inadequate to his purpose, though from a different cause. It was too *hard.* It was " pure crude fact," secreted from the fluid being of the men and women whose experience it had formed. In its existing state it would have broken up under the artistic attempt to weld and round it. He supplied an alloy, the alloy of fancy, or—as he also calls it—of one fact more : this fact being the echo of those past existences awakened within his own. He breathed into the dead record the breath of his own life ; and when his ring of evidence had re-formed, first in elastic then in solid strength, here delicately incised, there broadly stamped with human thought and passion, he could cast fancy aside, and bid his readers recognize in what he set before them unadulterated human truth.

All this was not effected at once. The separate scenes of the Franceschini tragedy sprang to life in Mr. Browning's imagination within a few hours of his reading the book. He saw them re-enacted from his terrace at Casa Guidi on a sultry summer night—every place and person projected, as it seemed, against the thundery sky—but his mind did not yet weave them into a whole. The drama lay by him and in him till the unconscious inspiration was complete ; and then, one day in London, he felt what he thus describes :—

> " A spirit laughs and leaps through every limb,
> And lights my eye, and lifts me by the hair,
> Letting me have my will again with these
> .    .    .    .    .    . "  (vol. viii. p. 32.)

and " The Ring and the Book" was born.  All this is
told in an introductory chapter, which bears the title of
the whole work ; and here also Mr. Browning reviews those
broad facts of the Franceschini case which are beyond
dispute, and which constitute, so far as they go, the crude
metal of his ring.  He has worked into this almost every
incident which the chronicle supplies and his book requires no supplement.  But the fragmentary view of its
contents, which I am reduced to giving, can only be held
together by a previous outline of the story.

There lived in Rome in 1679 Pietro and Violante Comparini, an elderly couple of the middle class, fond of show
and good living, and who in spite of a fair income had
run considerably into debt.  They were, indeed, at the
period in question, in receipt of a papal bounty, employed
in the relief of the needy who did not like to beg.  Creditors
were pressing, and only one expedient suggested itself :
they must have a child ; and thus enable themselves to
draw on their capital, now tied up for the benefit of an
unknown heir-at-law.  The wife conceived this plan, and
also carried it out, without taking her husband into her
confidence.  She secured beforehand the infant of a poor
and not very reputable woman, announced her expectation, half miraculous at her past fifty years, and became,
to all appearance, the mother of a girl, the Francesca
Pompilia of the story.

When Pompilia had reached the age of thirteen, there
was also in Rome Count Guido Franceschini, an impoverished nobleman of Arezzo, and the elder of three
brothers, of whom the second, Abate Paolo, and the third,
Canon Girolamo also play some part in the story.  Count
Guido himself belonged to the minor ranks of the priesthood, and had spent his best years in seeking preferment
in it.  Preferment had not come, and the only means of
building up the family fortunes in his own person, was now
a moneyed wife.  He was poor, fifty years old, and per-

sonally unattractive. A contemporary chronicle describes
him as short, thin, and pale, and **with** a projecting nose.
He had nothing to offer but his rank ; but **in** the case of
a very obscure heiress, this might suffice, and such **a one**
seemed to present herself in Pompilia Comparini. **He**
heard **of** her at the local centre of gossip, **the barber's**
shop ; received an exaggerated estimate of **her dowry ;**
and made proposals for her hand ; being supported in his
suit by the Abate Paul. They did not, on their side, under-
state the advantages **of** the connection. They are, indeed,
said to have given as their yearly income, a sum exceeding
their capital, and Violante was soon dazzled into consent-
ing to it. Old Pietro was more **wary.** He made inquiries
as to the state of the Count's fortune, and declined, **under**
plea of his daughter's extreme youth, to think **of him as a**
son-in-law.

Violante pretended submission, secretly led Pompilia to
a church, the **very** church **of San** Lorenzo **in** Lucina,
where four **years later** the murdered bodies **of** all three
were **to be** displayed, and brought her back as Count
Guido's wife. Pietro could only **accept the** accomplished
fact ; and he so far resigned himself **to it, that** he paid
**down** an instalment of his daughter's dowry, **and** made up
the deficiency by transferring to the newly-married couple
all that he actually possessed. This left him no choice
but to live under their roof, and **the** four removed together
to the Franceschini abode at Arezzo. The arrangement
proved disastrous ; and at the end of a few months Pietro
and Violante were glad to return **to** Rome, though with
empty pockets, and **on** money lent them for the journey
by their son-in-law.

We have conflicting testimony **as** to **the** cause of this
rupture. The Governor of Arezzo, writing to the Abate
Paul in Rome, lays all the blame of it on the Comparini,
whom he taxes with vulgar and aggressive behaviour ; and
Mr. Browning readily admits that at the beginning there

may have been faults on their side. But popular judgment, as well as the balance of evidence, were in favour of the opposite view ; and curious details are given by Pompilia and by a servant of the family, a sworn witness on Pompilia's trial, of the petty cruelties and privations to which both parents and child were subjected.

So much, at all events, was clear ; Violante's sin had overtaken her ; and it now occurred to her, apparently for the first time, to cast off its burden by confession. The moment was propitious, for the Pope had proclaimed a jubilee in honour of his eightieth year, and absolution was to be had for the asking. But the Church in this case made conditions. Absolution must be preceded by atonement. Violante must restore to her legal heirs that of which her pretended motherhood had defrauded them. The first step towards this was to reveal the fraud to her husband ; and Pietro lost no time in making use of the revelation. He repudiated Pompilia, and with her all claims on her husband's part. The case was carried into court. The Court decreed a compromise. Pietro appealed from the decree, and the question remained unsettled.

The chief sufferer by these proceedings was Pompilia herself. She already had reason to dread her husband as a tyrant—he to dislike her as a victim ; and his discovery of her base birth, with the threatened loss of the greater part of her dowry, could only result, with such a man, in increased aversion towards her. From this moment his one aim seems to have been to get rid of his wife, but in such a manner as not to forfeit any pecuniary advantage he might still derive from their union. This could only be done by convicting her of infidelity ; and he attacked her so furiously, and so persistently, on the subject of a certain Canon Giuseppe Caponsacchi, whom she barely knew, but whose attentions he declared her to have challenged, that at last she fled from Arezzo, with this very man.

She had appealed for protection against her husband's

violence to the Archbishop and **to the** Governor. She
had striven **to** enlist the aid of his brother-in-law, Conti.
She had implored a priest in confession to write for her to
her parents, and induce them to fetch her away. But the
whole town was in the interest of the Franceschini, or in
dread of them. Her prayers were useless, and Caponsacchi, whom she had heard of as a " resolute man," appeared
her last resource. He was, as she **knew**, contemplating a
journey to Rome; an opportunity **presented** itself for
speaking to him from her window, or **her** balcony; and
she persuaded him, though not without difficulty, **to**
assist her escape, and conduct **her to** her old home. On a
given night she slipped away **from** her husband's **side,**
and joined the Canon where **he** awaited **her with a**
carriage. They travelled day and night **till they reached**
Castelnuovo, a village within four hours **of the journey's**
end. There **they** were compelled to **rest, and there** also
the husband overtook them. **They** were **not** together **at**
the moment; but the fact of the elopement was patent;
and if Franceschini had killed his wife there, in the supposed excitement **of** the discovery, the law might have
dealt leniently with him. But **it** suited him best for **the**
time being to let her live. **He** procured the arrest **of** the
fugitives, and after **a** short confinement on the spot, they
were conveyed to the New Prisons in Rome (Carceri
Nuove) and tried on the charge **of** adultery.

It is impossible not to believe that Count Guido had
been working towards this end. Pompilia's verbal com-
munications with Caponsacchi had been supplemented by
letters, now brought to him in her name, now thrown or
let down from her window as he passed the house. They
were written, **as he** said, on the subject of the flight, and
**as** he also said, he burned them as soon as read, not
doubting their authenticity. But Pompilia declared, on
examination, that she could neither write nor read; and
setting aside all presumption of her veracity, this was

more than probable. The writer of the letters must therefore, have been the Count, or some one employed by him for the purpose. He now completed the intrigue by producing eighteen or twenty more of a very incriminating character, which he declared to have been left by the prisoners at Castelnuovo; and these were not only disclaimed with every appearance of sincerity by both the persons accused, but bore the marks of forgery within themselves.

Pompilia and Caponsacchi answered all the questions addressed to them simply and firmly; and though their statements did not always coincide, these were calculated on the whole to create a moral conviction of their innocence; the facts on which they disagreed being of little weight. But moral conviction was not legal proof; the question of false testimony does not seem to have been even raised; and the Court found itself in a dilemma, which it acknowledged in the following way: it was decreed that for his complicity in "the flight and deviation of Francesca Comparini," and too great intimacy with her, Caponsacchi should be banished for three years to Civita Vecchia; and that Pompilia, on her side, should be relegated, for the time being, to a convent. That is to say: the prisoners were pronounced guilty; and a merely nominal punishment was inflicted upon them.

The records of this trial contain almost everything of biographical or even dramatic interest in the original book. They are, so far as they go, the complete history of the case; and the result of the trial, ambiguous as it was, supplied the only argument on which an even formal defence of the subsequent murder could be based. The substance of these records appears in full in Mr. Browning's work; and his readers can judge for themselves whether the letters which were intended to substantiate Pompilia's guilt, could, even if she had possessed the power of writing, have been written by a woman so young and so uncultured as herself. They will also see that the Count's plot against his wife was still more deeply laid than the above-mentioned circumstances attest.

Count Guido was of course not satisfied. He wanted a divorce; and he continued to sue for it by means of his brother, the Abate Paul, then residing in Rome; but before long he received news which was destined to change his plans. Pompilia was about to become a mother; and in consideration of her state, she had been removed from the convent to her paternal home, where she was still to be ostensibly a prisoner. The Comparini then occupied a small villa outside one of the city gates. A few months later, in this secluded spot, the Countess Franceschini gave birth to a son, whom her parents lost no time in conveying to a place of concealment and safety. The murder took place a fortnight after this event. I give the rest of the story in an almost literal translation from a contemporary narrative, which was published, immediately after the Count's execution, in the form of a pamphlet[1]— the then current substitute for a newspaper.

" Being oppressed by various feelings, and stimulated to revenge, now by honour, now by self-interest, yielding to his wicked thoughts, he (Count Guido) devised a plan for killing his wife and her nominal parents; and having enlisted in his enterprise four other ruffians,"—labourers on his property, "started with them from Arezzo, and on Christmas-eve arrived in Rome, and took up his abode at Ponte Milvio, where there was a villa belonging to his brother, and where he concealed himself with his followers till the fitting moment for the execution of his design had arrived. Having therefore watched from thence all the movements of the Comparini family, he proceeded on Thursday, the 2nd of January, at one o'clock of the night,[2]

---

[1] This pamphlet has supplied Mr. Browning with some of his most curious facts It fell into his hands in London.

[2] The first hour after sunset.

with his companions to the Comparini's house; and having left Biagio Agostinelli and Domenico Gambasini at the gate, he instructed one of the others to knock at the house-door, which was opened to him on his declaring that he brought a letter from Canon Caponsacchi at Civita Vecchia. The wicked Franceschini, supported by two other of his assassins, instantly threw himself on Violante Comparini, who had opened the door, and flung her dead upon the ground. Pompilia, in this extremity, extinguished the light, thinking thus to elude her assassins, and made for the door of a neighbouring blacksmith, crying for help. Seeing Franceschini provided with a lantern, she ran and hid herself under the bed, but being dragged from under it, the unhappy woman was barbarously put to death by twenty-two wounds from the hand of her husband, who, not content with this, dragged her to the feet of Comparini, who, being similarly wounded by another of the assassins, was crying, ' *confession.*' "

" At the noise of this horrible massacre people rushed to the spot; but the villains succeeded in flying, leaving behind, however, in their haste, one his cloak, and Franceschini his cap, which was the means of betraying them. The unfortunate Francesca Pompilia, in spite of all the wounds with which she had been mangled, having implored of the Holy Virgin the grace of being allowed to confess, obtained it, since she was able to survive for a short time and describe the horrible attack. She also related that after the deed, her husband asked the assassin who had helped him to murder her *if she were really dead;* and being assured that she was, quickly rejoined, *let us lose no time, but return to the vineyard;*[1] and so they escaped. Meanwhile the police (Forza) having been called, it arrived with its chief officer (Bargello), and a confessor was soon procured, together with a surgeon,

---

[1] " Villa " is often called " vineyard " or " vigna," on account of the vineyard attached to it.

who devoted himself to the treatment of the unfortunate
girl.

"Monsignore, the Governor, being informed of the
event, immediately despatched Captain Patrizj to arrest
the culprits; but on reaching the vineyard the police
officers discovered that they were no longer there, but had
gone towards the high road an hour before. Patrizj pursued his journey without rest, and having arrived at the
inn, was told by the landlord that Franceschini had insisted upon obtaining horses, which were refused to him
because he was not supplied with the necessary order; and
had proceeded therefore on foot with his companions
towards Baccano. Continuing his march, and taking the
necessary precautions, he arrived at the Merluzza inn,
and there discovered the assassins, who were speedily
arrested, their knives still stained with blood, a hundred
and fifty scudi in coin being also found on Franceschini's
person. The arrest, however, cost Patrizj his life, for he
had heated himself too much, and having received a slight
wound, died in a few days."

"The knife of Franceschini was on the Genoese pattern, and triangular; and was notched at the edge, so that
it could not be withdrawn from the wounded flesh without
lacerating it in such a manner as to render the wound
incurable."

"The criminals being taken to Ponte Milvio, they went
through a first examination at the inn there at the hands
of the notaries and judges sent thither for the purpose,
and the chief points of a confession were obtained from
them."

"When the capture of the delinquents was known in
Rome, a multitude of the people hastened to see them as
they were conveyed bound on horses into the city. It is
related that Franceschini having asked one of the police
officers in the course of the journey *how ever the crime
had been discovered,* and being told *that it had been re-*

*vealed by his wife, whom they had found still living,* was almost stupefied by the intelligence. Towards twenty-three o'clock (the last hour before sunset) they arrived at the prisons. A certain Francesco Pasquini, of Città di Castello, and Allessandro Baldeschi, of the same town, both twenty-two years of age, were the assistants of Guido Franceschini in the murder of the Comparini ; and Gambasini and Agostinelli were those who stood on guard at the gate."

" Meanwhile the corpses of the assassinated Comparini were exposed at San Lorenzo, in Lucina, but so disfigured, and especially Franceschini's wife, by their wounds in the face, that they were no longer recognizable. The unhappy Francesca, after taking the sacrament, forgiving her murderers, under seventeen years of age, and after having made her will, died on the sixth day of the month, which was that of the Epiphany ; and was able to clear herself of all the calumnies which her husband had brought against her. The surprise of the people in seeing these corpses was great, from the atrocity of the deed, which made one really shudder, seeing two septuagenarians and a girl of seventeen so miserably put to death."

" The trial proceeding meanwhile, many papers were drawn up on the subject, bringing forward all the most incriminating circumstances of this horrible massacre ; and others also were written for the defence with much erudition, especially by the advocate of the poor, a certain Monsignor Spreti, which had the effect of postponing the sentence ; also because Baldeschi persisted in denial, though he was tortured with the rope, and twice fainted under it. At last he confessed, and so did the others, who also revealed the fact that they had intended in due time to murder Franceschini himself, and take his money, because he had not kept his promise of paying them the moment they should have left Rome."

" On the twenty-second of February there appeared on

the Piazza del Popolo a large platform **with** a guillotine and two gibbets, on which the culprits **were** to be executed. **Many** stands were constructed for the convenience of those who were curious to witness such **a** terrible act of justice ; and the concourse was **so** great **that some** windows fetched as much **as** six dollars each. **At** eight o'clock Franceschini and his companions were summoned to their death, and having been placed in the **Consorteria,** and there assisted by the Abate Panciatici **and the Cardinal** Acciajuoli, forthwith disposed themselves **to die well.** At twenty o'clock the Company of Death and the **Misericordia** reached the dungeons, and the condemned were **let** down, placed on separate carts, and conveyed **to the place** of execution."

It is farther stated that Franceschini showed **the most** intrepidity and cold blood of them all, and that **he** died with the name of Jesus on his lips. He wore **the same** clothes in which he had committed the crime : a close-fitting garment (*juste-au-corps*) of grey **cloth,** a loose black shirt (*camiciuola*), a goat's hair cloak, **a** white hat, and a cotton **cap.**

The attempt made by him to defraud his accomplices, poor and helpless as they were, has been accepted by Mr. Browning as an indication of character which forbade any lenient interpretation of his previous acts. Pompilia, on the other hand, is absolved, by all the circumstances of her protracted death, from any doubt of her innocence which previous evidence might have raised. Ten different persons attest, not only her denial of any offence against her husband, but, what is of far more value, her Christian gentleness, and absolute maiden modesty, under the sufferings of her last days, and the medical treatment to which they subjected her. Among **the** witnesses are a doctor of theology (Abate Liberato Barberito), the apothecary and his assistant, and a number **of** monks or priests ; the first and most circumstantial deposition being that of an

Augustine, Frà Celestino Angelo di Sant' Anna, and concluding with these words : " I do not say more, for fear of being taxed with partiality.  I know well that God alone can examine the heart.  But I know also that from the abundance of the heart the mouth speaks ; and that my great St. Augustine says : ' As the life was, so is its end.'"

It needed all the evidence in Pompilia's favour to secure the full punishment of her murderer, strengthened, as he was, by social and ecclesiastical position, and by the acknowledged rights of marital jealousy.  We find curious proof of the sympathies which might have prejudiced his wife's cause, in the marginal notes appended to her depositions, and which repeatedly introduce them as lies.

" F. *Lie concerning the arrival at Castelnuovo.*"

" H. *New lies to the effect that she did not receive the lover's letters, and does not know how to write,*" &c., &c.[1]

The significant question, " Whether and when a husband may kill his unfaithful wife," was in the present case not thought to be finally answered, till an appeal had been made from the ecclesiastical tribunal to the Pope himself. It was Innocent XII. who virtually sentenced Count Franceschini and his four accomplices to death.

When Mr. Browning wrote " The Ring and the Book," his mind was made up on the merits of the Franceschini case ; and the unity of purpose which has impressed itself upon his work contributes largely to its power.  But he also knew that contemporary opinion would be divided upon it ; and he has given the divergent views it was certain to create, as constituting a part of its history.  He reminds us that two sets of persons equally acquainted with the facts, equally free from any wish to distort them, might be led into opposite judgments through the mere action of some

---

[1] It is difficult to reconcile this explicit denial of Pompilia's statements with the belief in her implied in her merely nominal punishment : unless we look on it as part of the formal condemnation which circumstances seemed to exact.

impalpable bias in one direction or the. other, while a
third, more critical or more indifferent, would adopt a
compromise between the two ; and he closes his introductory chapter with a tribute to that mystery of human
motive and character which so often renders more conclu-
sive judgments impossible.

> " Action now shrouds, now shows the informing thought ;
> Man, like a glass ball with a spark a-top,
> Out of the magic fire that lurks inside,
> Shows one tint at a time to take the eye
> Which, let a finger touch the silent sleep,
> Shifted a hair's-breadth shoots you dark for bright,
> Suffuses bright with dark, and baffles so
> Your sentence absolute for shine or shade." (vol. viii. p. 55.)

The three forms of opinion here indicated appear in
the three following chapters as the respective utterance
of " HALF-ROME," " THE OTHER HALF-ROME," and
" TERTIUM QUID."

HALF-ROME has an instinctive sympathy with the husband who has been made ridiculous, and the nobleman
who is threatened with an ignominious death ; and is disposed throughout to regard him as more sinned against
than sinning. "Count Guido has been unfortunate in
everything. He is one of those proud and sensitive
men who make few friends, and who meet reverses half-
way. He has waited thirty years for advancement in
the church, is sick of hope deferred, and is on the point
of returning home to end his days, as he thinks, in fru-
gality and peace, when a pretty girl is thrown in his way.
Visions of domestic cheerfulness and comfort rise up
before him. He is entrapped into marriage before he has
had time to consider what he is doing, and discovers
when it is too late that the parents reputed wealthy have
little left but debts ; and that in exchange for their
daughter's dowry, present and prospective, he must
virtually maintain them as well as her."

" He is far from rich, but he makes the best of a bad

bargain—takes the three with him to Arezzo, and lodges them with his mother and his youngest brother, in the old family house. He is repaid with howls of disappointment. Pietro and Violante want splendour and good-living. They haven't married their daughter to a nobleman and gone to live in his palace, to be duller than they were at home, and have less to eat and drink. They abuse the mother, who won't give up her place in the household, and try to sneer the young brother-priest out of his respect for old-fashioned ways. They go back to Rome, trumpeting their wrongs : and, once there, spring a mine upon the luckless Count. They refuse to pay the remainder of Pompilia's dowry, on the ground that she is not their child. Violante Comparini has cheated her husband into accepting a base-born girl as his own, and a well-born gentleman into marrying her, but was ready to have qualms of conscience as soon as it should be convenient to tell the truth ; and now the moment has come."

"Count Guido, left alone with his nameless and penniless wife, still hopes for the best. Pompilia is not guilty of her mock parents' sins. She has been honest enough to take part against them when writing to her brother-in-law in Rome.[1] He and she may still live in peace together. But now the old story begins again—that of the elderly husband and the young wife. Canon Caponsacchi throws comfits at Pompilia in the theatre ; brushes against her in the street ; has constantly occasion to pass under her window, or to talk to some one opposite to it. He, of course, looks up ; Pompilia looks down ; the neighbours say, 'What of that ?' The Count is uncomfortable, but he is only laughed at for his pains ; the fox prowls round the hen-roost undisturbed. He wakes one

---

[1] A letter written in this strain was also produced on the trial ; and Pompilia owned to having written it, but only in the sense of writing over in ink what her husband had traced in pencil—being totally ignorant of its contents.

morning, after a drugged sleep, to find the house ransacked, and Pompilia gone, and everyone able to inform him that she has gone with Caponsacchi, and to Rome. He pursues them, and overtakes them where they have spent the night together. She brazens the matter out, covers her husband with invective, and threatens him with his own sword. He gives both in charge, and follows them to Rome, where he seeks redress from the law. But he does not obtain redress, though the couple's guilt is made as clear as day by a packet of love letters which they had left behind them. They swear that they did not write the letters, and the Court believes them. 'They have done wrong, of course, but there is no proof of crime ;' and they are let off with a mere show of punishment."

" The Count returns to Arezzo to find the whole story known, and himself the laughing-stock of everybody. He is complimented on his patience under his wife's attack—congratulated on having come out of it with a whole skin. He pushes his claim for a divorce on the obvious ground of infidelity ! is met by a counter-claim on the ground of—cruelty ! One exasperating circumstance fellows another. At last he hears of the birth of a child, which will be falsely represented as his heir ; and then the pent-up passion breaks forth, and in one great avenging wave it washes his name clear."

" Yet he gives the guilty one a last chance. He utters the name of Caponsacchi at her door. If she regrets her offence, that name will bar it. It proves a talisman at which the door flies open. The Count and his assistants must be tried for form's sake. But if they are condemned, there is no justice left in Rome. If he had taken his wife's life at the moment of provocation, he would have been praised for the act. But he called in the law to do what he was bound to do for himself ; and the law has assessed his honour at what seemed to be his own price. The vengeance, too long delayed, has been excessive in conse-

quence. It was clumsy into the bargain, since the Canon
has escaped alive. Well, if harm comes, husbands who are
disposed to take the new way instead of the old will
have had a lesson ; and the Count has only himself to
thank."

THE OTHER HALF-ROME is chiefly impressed by the
spectacle of a young wife and mother butchered by her
husband in cold blood : and can only think of her as
having been throughout a victim. It does not absolve
Violante, but it allows something for honest parental feeling in the old couple's desire for a child ; and something
for the good done to this human waif by its adoption into
a decent home. According to this version, it is the Count
and his brother who lay the matrimonial trap, and the
Comparini parents and child who fall into it. " The grim
Guido is at first kept in the background. Abate Paolo
makes the proposal. He is oily and deferential, and flatters
poor foolish Violante, and dazzles her at the same time.
' His elder brother,' he says, ' is longing to escape from
Rome and its pomps and glare. He wants his empty old
palace at Arezzo, and his breezy villa among the vines,'—
and here the emptiness of both is described so as to sound
like wealth. ' Poor Guido ! he is always harping upon
his home. But he wants a wife to take there—a wife not
quite empty-handed, since he is not rich for his rank—but
above all, with a true tender heart and an innocent soul—
one who will be a child to his mother, and fall into his
own ways. Many a parent would be glad to welcome him
as a son-in-law, but report tells him that Violante's
daughter is just the girl he wants.'"

" The marriage takes place. Foolish Pietro is talked
over and strips himself of everything he has. He and his
wife have no choice but to go and live with their son-in-
law and his mother and brother. They meet with nothing
under his roof but starvation, insult, and cruelty, and
return home after a few months, duped and beggared, to

ask hospitality of those whom they **had** once entertained. Violante, overwhelmed by these misfortunes, confesses that Pompilia is not her child, and Pietro proclaims the fact ; not that he wishes to leave Pompilia in **the** lurch, but because he thinks this a sure way of getting her back. —Count Guido is clearly not the man to wish to retain **as** his wife a base-born girl without a **dowry, and whom he** has never loved.—But the case must **be settled by law ;** the law pronounces in Count Guido's **favour so far as the** actual marriage portion is concerned ; and Count Guido clearly lays his plans so as to half-drive and half-tempt his wife into the kind of misconduct **which** will **rid him** of her without prejudicing his right **to** what **she has** brought him."

This half of Rome accepts Pompilia's **story of all that** led to **her** flight, and Caponsacchi's **statement** that **he** assisted in it simply to **save her** life. It thinks the husband's intrigues sufficiently proved **by the fact** that **the** Canon owns to having received letters **which** the wife denies having written, and which must, therefore, have been forged. Count Guido, it declares, has had no wrongs to avenge, and supposing he had wrongs, he has adopted too convenient a mode of avenging them. " He demands protection from the law, and the moment its balance trembles against him he flies out of court, declaring that wounded honour can only be cured by the sword. At all events he has given the law plenty to do : three courts at work for him, and an appeal to the Pope besides. If any law is binding on mankind it is **that** such as he shall be made **an** end of. He is the common enemy of his fellow-men."

TERTIUM QUID sees no reason **for** assuming that the wrong is altogether **on** either side, and reviews the circumstances in such a manner as **to** show that there is probably right on both. He lays stress on the expediency of judging the Comparini by the morals of their class, and

Count Guido by the peculiarities of his own nature ; admits the punishment of the wife and parents to have been excessive, and cannot admit it to have been unprovoked ; does not pretend to decide between the conflicting statements, and does not consider that Pompilia's dying confession throws much light upon them ; seeing that it may be equally true, or false, or neutralized by another reserved for the priest's ear. Does not regard putting the Count to the torture as the right mode of eliciting the truth : because he may be innocent. But declares that if *he* does not deserve to undergo the torture, no one ever did or will. Tertium Quid is sometimes flippant in tone, and his neutral attitude seems chiefly the result of indifference or of caution. He is addressing himself to a Highness and an Excellency, and is careful not to shock the prejudices of either. Still, his statement is the nearest approach to a judicial summing up of which the nature of the work admits.

Mr. Browning now enters on the constructive part of his work. He puts the personages of the drama themselves before us, allowing each to plead his or her own cause. The imaginary occasion is that of Count Guido's trial ; and all the depositions which were made on the previous one are transferred to this. The author has been obliged in every case to build up the character from the evidence, and to re-mould and expand the evidence in conformity with the character. The motive, feeling, and circumstance set forth by each separate speaker are thus in some degree fictitious ; but they are always founded upon fact ; and the literal truth of a vast number of details is self-evident. We first hear :

COUNT GUIDO FRANCESCHINI. He has been caught red-handed from the murder of his wife. His crime is patent. He has himself confessed it under torture. His only hope of reprieve lies in the colour which he may be able to impart to it ; and his speech is cunningly adapted to the nature of the Court, and to the moral and mental constitution of those of whom it is composed. His judges are churchmen : neutral on the subject of marriage ; rather coarsely masculine in their idea of the destiny of women. He does not profess to have entertained any affection for his wife. He derides the idea of having ill-used her, and thinks she might have liked him better if he had done so, instead of threatening her into good behaviour like a naughty child, with hair powder for poison, and a wooden toy for a sword ; has no doubt that, if she had cared to warm his heart, some smouldering embers within it might still have burst into flame ; but admits once for all that there was no question of feeling in the case ; it was a bargain on both sides, and a fair one as far as he was concerned.

Paternity, however, is a condition with which his hearers may be supposed to sympathize ; and he is absolutely eloquent, when he describes the desire he has cherished for a son, and the burning pain which filled him when he knew that it had been defrauded. He tells the story of his wife's intrigue and flight, much as the opinion of Half-Rome has reflected it ; but he laces the question of his child's legitimacy in such a manner as to extract an equal advantage from either view. In either case it was Pompilia's crowning iniquity that she gave birth to a child, and placed it beyond his reach ; and in either case it was the outraged paternal feeling which inspired his act.

The whole monologue is leavened by a spirit of mock deference for religion, for the Church, and for the law which represents the Church. Count Guido is led in from the torture, a mass of mock-patient suffering : wincing as he speaks, but quite in spite of himself—grateful that his pains are not worse—begging his judges not to be too much concerned about him ; " since, thanks to his age and shaken health, a fainting fit soon came to his relief—

indeed, torture itself is a kind of relief from the moral agonies he has undergone." He reminds his judges that the Church was his only mistress for thirty years. He would have served her, he declares, to the end of his life, but that his fidelity had been so long ignored. He trusted to the law—in other words to the Church—to avenge his honour when he ought to have done so himself. She deceived his trust, and still he hoped and endured. When he came to Rome, in his last frenzy of just revenge, he still stayed his hand, because the Feast of the Nativity had begun : it was the period at which the Church enjoins peace and good-will towards men. The face of the heavenly infant looked down upon him ; he prayed that he might not enter into temptation. But the days went by, and the Face withered and waned, and the cross alone confronted him. Then he felt that the hour had come, and he found his way to his wife's retreat.

The door opened to the name of Caponsacchi. His worst fears were thus confirmed. Even so, had he been admitted by Pompilia, weak from her recent sufferings, he might have paused in pity—by Pietro, he might have paused in contempt ; but it was the hag Violante who opened to him : the cheat, the mock-mother, the source of all his wrongs. The impulse to stamp out that one detested life involved all three. And now he triumphs in the deed. He has cast a foul burden from his life. He can look his fellow-men in the face again. Far from admitting that he deserves punishment, he claims the sympathy and the approval of those who have met to judge him : for he has done their work—the work of Divine justice and of natural law. In a final burst of rhetoric he challenges his judges to restore to him his life, his name, his civil rights, and best of all, his son ; and together, he declares, they will rebuild the family honour, and revive the old forgotten tradition of domestic purity and peace. And if one day the son, about to kiss his hand, starts at the marks of violence upon **it, he** will smile and say, " **it** was only an accident—

> "  .    .    .    .    .    .     just a trip
> O' the torture irons in their search for truth,—
> Hardly misfortune, and no fault at all." (vol. ix. **p. 8?.**)

GIUSEPPE CAPONSACCHI next tells his **story.** It includes some details of his earlier life, which throw light on what will follow. He is not a priest from choice. He had interest in the Church, and grew up in **the** expectation of entering it. But when the time came for taking his **vows,** he recoiled from the sacrifice which they involved, **and** yielded only to the Bishop's assurance that **he** need make no sacrifice ; there were two ways of interpreting such vows, and he need not select **the** harder ; **a** man of polish **and** accomplishments was as valuable **to the** Church as **a** scholar or an ascetic. **Her** structure **stood firm, and no** one need now-a-days break his back in the effort to hold her up. Let him **write** his madrigals (he had **a** turn for verse-making) and not become a fixture in his seat in the choir through too close an attendance there. The terms were easy, and Caponsacchi became a priest, no **worse** and no better than he was expected to be ; but with the feelings and purposes of a truer manhood lying dormant within him. These Pompilia was destined to arouse.

He relates that he first saw her **at** the theatre. His attention was attracted by her strange sad beauty : and **a** friend who sat by him, and was a connection **of the** husband's, threw comfits at her to make her return **his** gaze, warning him at the same time to do nothing which could compromise her. He accepted the warning, but could not forget the face. He felt a sudden disgust for the light women and the light pleasures which were alone within his reach, and determined **to** change his mode of life, and leave Arezzo for Rome.

At this juncture a love-letter was brought **to** him. It purported to come from the lady at whom he had flung

the comfits ;[1] offered him her heart, and begged an interview with him. The bearer was a masked woman, who
owned to an equivocal position in Count Guido's household. Caponsacchi saw through the trick, declined the
proposed interview on the ground of his priesthood, and
completed his answer with an allusion to the husband,
which would punish him in the probable case of its passing directly into his hands. The next day the same
messenger appeared with a second letter, reproaching
him for his cruelty ; he answered in the same strain. But
the letters continued, now dropped into his prayer-book,
now flung down to him from a window. At length they
changed their tone. He had been begged to come : he
was now entreated to stay away. The husband, before
absent, had returned : indifferent, had become jealous.
His vengeance was aroused ; and the sooner Caponsacchi
escaped to Rome, the better. This challenge to his
courage had the intended effect. He wrote word that the
street was public if the house was not, and he would be
under the lady's window that evening.

He went. She was standing there, lamp in hand, like
Our Lady of Sorrows on her altar. She vanished, reappeared on a terrace close above his head, and spoke
to him. He had sent her letters, she said, which she
could not read ; but she had been told that they spoke of
love. She thought at first that he must be wicked, and
then she felt that he could not be so wicked as to have
meant what that woman said ; and now that she saw his
face she knew he did not write it. Still, he meant her
well when no one else did. Her need was sore ; he alone
in the world could help her ; she had determined to call to
him. If he had some feverish fancy for what was not
her's to give, he would be cured of it so soon as he knew
all. She told him her story, and entreated him to take

---

[1] Count Guido thought, or affected to think, that these had been thrown
by Caponsacchi.

her to Rome, and consign her **to her** parents' care. He promised, and then his heart misgave him. Would it be right in him? Would **it** be good for **her**? **He** passed two days in a ceaseless internal conflict, and then **determined** to see her once more, but only to comfort and advise.

She stood again awaiting him at her window. Again she spoke, reproaching him for the suspense **she** had undergone. Her manner dispelled all doubt, and he did for **her** what she desired. The journey, which **he describes** in detail, was to him one spontaneous and continued revelation of her purity and truth. Then came **the** trial and his banishment. He **was** compelled to **leave her to** the protection of the law; to the good offices **of the Court** which confronts him now—of the men who, as **he reminds** them, laughed in their sleeve at the young priest's escapade, and at the transparent excuses with which **he** had taxed their credulity,—of the men who, in consideration for his youth, merely sent him **to** disport himself elsewhere, leaving the woman he had striven **to** protect, to the husband who was to murder her.

The news which summons him from Civita Vecchia has fallen on him like a thunderbolt. His being is shaken to its foundations. He strives to contain himself in outward deference to the Court, but a storm of suppressed sorrow and indignation rages beneath all his words: now uttering itself in pitying tender reverence for Pompilia's memory; now in scorn of those who would defame her; now in anger at himself, who is casting suspicion on her innocence by the very passion with which he defends it; now in defiance **of** those who choose to call the passion by the vulgar name of love. He tears up the flimsy calumnies which have been launched against her and himself; flinging them back in short, contemptuous utterances in the teeth of whosoever may believe them; begs his judges to forget his violence; and makes a last attempt to convince himself and them that no selfish desire underlies it Pompilia is dying : he too is dead—to the world. What can she be to him but a dream—a thinker's dream—of a life not consecrated to the Church, but spent, as with her, in one constant domestic revelation of the eternal goodness and truth—a dream from which he will pass content . . . . . ." And here the whole edifice of self-control and self-deception breaks down, and the agonized heart sends forth its cry :—

"O great, just, good God ! Miserable me !" (vol. ix. p. 166.)

The third speaker is POMPILIA. Her evidence is the story of her life. It is given from her deathbed ; and its half-dreamy reminiscences are uttered with the childlike simplicity with which she may have opened her heart to her priest. She is full of strange pathetic wonder at the mystery of existence ; at the manner in which the thing we seem to grasp eludes us, and the seemingly impossible comes to pass. "Husbands are supposed to love their wives and guard them. See how it has been with her! That other man—that friend—they say *he* loves her ; his kindness was all love ! She is a wife and he a priest, and yet they go on saying it ! Her boy, she imagined, would be hers for life : and he is taken from her. He, too, becomes a dream ; and in that dream she sees him grown tall and strong, and tutoring his mother as an imprudent child, for venturing out of the safe street into the lonely house where no help could reach her. It all reminds her of the day when she and a child-friend played at finding each other out in the figures on the tapestry ; and Tisbe recognized her in a tree with a rough trunk for body, and her five fingers blossoming into leaves. Things are, and are not at the same time."

One thing, however, is real amidst the unreality : her joy and pride in finding herself a mother. The event proved that when she left Arezzo the hope of maternity was already dawning upon **her**; and **Mr.** Browning has combined this fact with the latent maternal sentiment of all true women, and read **it** into every impulse of her re-maining life.   She was wretched.   She had vainly sought for help.   She had resigned herself **to** the inevitable. She had lain down at night **with the** old thought—

> " .       .       .       . ' Done, another day !
> How good to sleep and so get nearer death !'—
> When, what, first thing at day-break, pierced the sleep
> With a summons to me?   Up I sprang **alive**,
> Light in me, light without me, everywhere
> Change!"                                         (vol. **ix**. p. 216.)

From this moment, **as** she tells us, everything **was** transformed.   For days, for weeks, Caponsacchi's **name** had been ringing in her ears : in jealous explosions **on her** husband's part ; in corrupting advice on the **part of the** waiting-woman who brought letters supposed **to be** sent to her by him ; in declarations of love which **her** first glance at his **face** told her **he could** not **have** written. This, **too, has** all seemed a grotesquely painful dream.   But when she awoke on the April morning in that bounding **of** the spirit **towards** an unknown joy, **the** name assumed **a** new meaning **for her**, and she said, **"Let** Caponsacchi come."

She remembers little after that, **but the** enfolding ten-derness which secured the fulfilment **of her** hope.   She describes nothing after the "tap" at **the** door, which was the beginning of the end.   She has attained the crown of her woman's existence, and she can bear no resentment towards him whose cruelty embittered, and whose ven-geance **has** cut **it** short.   The motherly heart in her goes out **to the** wicked husband who was **also** once a child, and strives to palliate what he has done.   "He was sinned against as well as sinning.   Her poor parents were blind and unjust in their mode of retaliating upon him.   She was blind and foolish in doing nothing to heal the breach.

Her earthly goods have been a snare to Guido ; she herself was an importunate presence to him. By God's grace he will be the better for having swept her from his path. She thanks him for destroying in her that bodily life which was his to pollute, and for leaving her soul free. Her infant shall have been born of no earthly father. It is the child of its mother's love."

And this love for her child overflows in gratitude to him who saved her for it—a gratitude which is also something more. She has recoiled from the idea of being united to a priest by any bond of earthly affection ; but the knowledge is growing upon her that her bond to Caponsacchi *is* love, though it assumes an ideal character in her innocence, her ignorance, and the exaltation of feeling which denotes her approaching death. She has recalled the incidents of her flight, but only to bear witness to Caponsacchi's virtues : his watchful kindness, his chivalrous courage, the unselfishness which could risk life and honour without thought of reward, the priestly dignity which he never set aside. Her last words contain an invocation to himself which has all the passion of earthly tenderness, and all the solemnity of a prayer. She addresses him as her soldier-saint—as the friend "her only, all her own," who is closest to her now on her final journey ; whose love shall sustain, whose strong hand shall guide her, on the unknown path she is about to tread. She thinks he would not marry if he could. True marriage is in heaven, where there is no making of contracts, with gold on one side, power or youth or beauty on the other, but one is "man and wife at once when the true time is." Would either of them wish the past undone ? Her soul says " No."

> " So, let him wait God's instant men call years ;
> Meantime hold hard by truth and his great soul,
> Do out the duty ! Through such souls alone
> God stooping shows sufficient of His light
> For us i' the dark to rise by. And I rise." (vol. ix. p. 241.)

We have now the written pleadings of two advocates who figure largely in the records of the case ; the one enlisted on the Count's side, the other **on** Pompilia's. They **are**

DOMINUS HYACINTHUS DE ARCHANGELIS (procurator of the poor)

JURIS DOCTOR JOHANNES BAPTISTA BOTTINIUS (fisc, or public prosecutor).

The subject of these pleadings is the possible justification of the crime for which Count Franceschini **is on** trial, but not otherwise the crime itself ; for he has owned **to** its commission ; and though the avowal has been drawn from him by torture, it **is** justly accepted as decisive. **All** the arguments for and against him hinge therefore **on the** evidence of Pompilia's guilt **or** innocence as established by the previous enquiry ; and as we have seen, **the** *formal* result of this enquiry was unfavourable **to her.** The Count obtained his verdict, though the **subsequent** treatment of **the** offenders made it almost nugatory ; and de Archangelis rings the changes on the stock arguments **of** his client's outraged honour, and his **natural** if not legal right to avenge it.

Bottinius, on the other hand, does **not admit** that the husband's honour has been attacked ; but he defends **the** wife's conduct, more by extenuating the acts of which **she** is accused, than by denying them. His denials are generally parenthetic : and imply that the whether **she** did certain things is much less important than the **why** and the how ; and though he professes to present **her as a** pearl of purity, he shows his standard of female purity to be very low.

Mr. Browning might easily have composed **a** more genuine defence from the known facts of the case ; but he represents these quibblings and counter-quibblings as equally beside the mark. The question of the murderer's guilt was being judged on broader grounds ; and the sup-

posed talkers on either side are aware of this. De Archangelis and Bottinius both know that their cleverness will
benefit no one but themselves, and for this reason they are
as much concerned to show how good a case they can
make out of a doubtful one, as to prove that their case is
in itself good. Each is thinking of his opponent, and how
best to parry his attack ; and their arguments are relieved
by a brisk exchange of personalities, in which "de Archangelis" includes his subordinate "Spreti"—"advocate
of the poor"—whose learned contribution to this paper
warfare has probably aroused his jealousy.

Mr. Browning has also displayed the hollowness of the
proceedings by making "de Archangelis" the very opposite
of his saturnine and blood-thirsty client : the last person
we could think of as in sympathy with him. He is a coarse
good-natured paterfamilias, whose ambitions are all centred
on an eight-year-old son, whose birthday it is ; and his
defence of the murder is concocted under frequent inter-
ruptions, from the thought of Cinuncino (little Giacinto, or
Hyacinth), and the fried liver and herbs which are to form
part of his birthday feast. Bottinius is a vain man, occupied only with himself, and regretting nothing so much as
that he may not display his rhetorical powers, by deliver-
ing his speech instead of writing it.

Count Guido, with his accomplices, has been condemned
to death. His friends have appealed from the verdict, on
the ground of his being, though in a minor degree, a priest.
The answer to this appeal rests with the head of the
Church. The next monologue is therefore that of

THE POPE. The reflections here imagined grow out of
a double fact. Innocent the Twelfth refused to shelter
Count Franceschini with his accomplices from the judgment of the law, and thus assumed the responsibility of
his death. He had reached an age at which so heavy a
responsibility could not be otherwise than painful. As Mr.
Browning depicts him, his decision is made From dawn

to dark he has been studying **the** case, piecing together
its fragmentary truths, trying its merits with "true **sweat**
of soul." There is no doubt in his mind that Guido
deserves to die. But he has to nerve himself afresh before
he gives the one stroke of his pen, **the** one **touch to his**
bell, which shall send this **soul** into **eternity; and that is**
what **we see** him doing.

As **he** says **to** himself, he is weighed **down by years.**
He lifts the cares of the whole world on **a** "**loaded branch**"
for which **a** bird's nest were **a** "superfluous **burthen.**"
Yet this strong man **cries** to him for **life**: **and he** alone
has **the** power to grant **it**. How easy **to reprieve!** How
hard to deny to this trembling sinner the moment's respite
which may save his **soul**. He wants precedent **for** such **a**
deed; and he seeks **it in the** records of the **Papacy.** It **is**
from the Popes his predecessors that he must learn how
to dare, to suffer, and—to judge. But these records tell
him how Stephen cursed Formosus; how Romanus and
Theodore reinstated the sanctity of Formosus and cursed
Stephen; and how John reinstated Stephen and cursed
Formosus. They could not all be right. There **is** no
guarantee for infallibility—no test of justice—to be found
here.

How, then, would **he** defend his condemnation **of** Guido
if he himself were now summoned to the judgment-seat?
The question is self-answered: no defence would be
needed; for God sees into the heart. He appraises the
seed of act, which is its motive; not "leafage and
branchage, vulgar eyes admire." The Pope knows that
his motives will stand the scrutiny of God. How, finally,
could he plead his cause with a man like himself: with
the man Antonio Pignatelli, his very self? He must,
once for all, marshal the facts, and let them plead for
him.

Next follows the Pope's version of the story, which
differs from those preceding it, **in** being the summing up

of a spiritual judge, who deals not only with facts but with conditions, and who looks at the thing done, in its special reference to the person who did it. As seen in this light, the blacks of the picture are blacker, the whites, whiter, than they appear from the ordinary point of view. Guido has been doubly wicked because his birth, his breeding, and his connection with the Church, had surrounded him with incitements to good, and with opportunities for it. Pompilia is doubly virtuous because she is a mere "chance-sown," "cleft-nurtured" human weed, owing all her goodness to herself. With Guido, the bad end is secured by the worst means. Not satisfied to murder his wife, he must use a jagged instrument with which to torture her flesh. Not satisfied to torment her in the body, he must imperil her soul by placing desperate temptation in her way. With Pompilia the right virtue is always employed for the good end. She is submissive where only her own life is at stake; brave, when a life within her own calls on her for protection. Guido's accomplices: his brothers, his mother, the four youths who helped him to kill his wife : the Governor, and the Archbishop, who abetted his ill-treatment of her, have alike sinned against their age, their character, or their associations.

Caponsacchi has not been faultless. He has failed somewhat in the dignity of his office, somewhat in its decorum ; his mode of rescuing the oppressed has had too much the character of an escapade. But the more disciplined soldier of the Church would have erred in the opposite direction. The ear which listens only for the voice of authority becomes obtuse to the cry of suffering. The spirit which only moves to command becomes unfit for spontaneous work. Caponsacchi, standing aloof like a man of pleasure, has proved himself the very champion of God, ready to spring into the arena, at the first thud of the false knight's glove upon the ground. He has shown himself possessed of the true courage which does not shrink from temptation, **and does not** succumb to it. Such transgressions as his reflect **rather on the** limits imposed than on the impatience which transgressed them. He must submit to a slight punishment. He must work—be unhappy—bear life. But he ranks **next** in grace **to** Pompilia—the "rose" which the **old** Pope "gathers **for the** breast of God." Of Count Guido's other victims, Pietro and Violante, **the worst** that can **be** said **is this** : they have halted between good and evil ; and, as the way of the world is, suffered through both. The balance of justice once more confirms the Pope's decree.

**Yet at** this very moment his **will** relaxes. **A** sudden **dread is** upon him—a chill such **as comes** with the sudden clouding of a long **clear sky.** The ordeal of a deeper and stranger doubt is yet **to** be faced. He has judged, as he believed, by the light of Divine truth. Has he been mistaken ?

Step by step **he tests** and reconstructs his belief, tracing it back **to** its beginning. God, the Infinite, exists. Man, the atom, comprehends him as the conditions of his intelligence **permit,** but so far truly. Man's mind, like **a convex** glass, reflects him, in **an** image, smaller **or less small,** adequate so far as it goes. **As** revealed **in the** order of nature, God is perfect in intelligence **and in** power ; but not so **in** love ; and there **has** come into the mouths and hearts of men, a tale and miracle of Divine love which makes the evidence of **his** perfection complete. The Pope believes that tale, whether true **in** itself, **or** like man's conception of the infinite, true only for **the** human mind. He accepts **its** enigmas **as a** test of faith : as a sign that life is meant for a training and **a** passage : as a guarantee of our moral growth, and of the good which evil may produce.

Christianity stands firm. And **yet** his heart misgives him ; for it **is** not justified by its results. It is not that the sceptical deny its value : that those bent on earthly

good reject it with open eyes. The surprise and terror is
this : that those who have found the pearl of price—who
have named and known it—will still grovel after the lower
gain. Such the Aretine bishop who sent Pompilia back
to her tormentor ; the friar who refused to save her because he feared the world ; the nuns who at first testified to her purity, and were ready to prove her one of
dishonest life, when they learned that she possessed
riches which by so doing they might confiscate to themselves.

Nor is the fault in humanity at large : for love and faith
have leapt forth profusely in the olden time, at the summons of "unacknowledged," "uncommissioned" powers
of good. Caponsacchi has shown that they do so still.
Before Paul had spoken and Felix heard, Euripides had
pronounced virtue the law of life, and, in his doctrine of
hidden forces, foreshadowed the one God. Euripides felt
his way in the darkness. He, the Pope, walking in the
glare of noon, might ask support of him.[ Where does the
fault lie? It lies in the excess of certainty—in the too
great familiarity with the truth—in that encroachment of
earthly motives on the heavenly, which is begotten by the
security of belief. Between night and noonday there has
been the dawn, with its searching illumination, its thrill
of faith, the rapture of self-sacrifice in which anchorite
and martyr foretasted the joys of heaven. Now Christianity is hard because it has become too easy ; because
of the "ignoble confidence," which will enjoy this world
and yet count upon the next : the "shallow cowardice,"
which renders the old heroism impossible. ]

The Pope is discursive, as is the manner of his age ;
and his reflections have been, hitherto, rather suggested by
the case before him than directly related to it. But he
grasps it again in a burst of prophetic insight which these
very reflections have produced. Heroism has become
impossible,

"Unless  .  .  what whispers me of times to come?
What if it be the mission of that age
My death will usher into life, to shake
This torpor of assurance from our creed?" (vol. **x. p.** 137.)

What **if** earthquake be about **to** try the towers **which** lions dare no longer attack : if man be destined **to live** once more, in the new-born readiness for death ? **Is the** time at hand, when the new faith shall be broken up as the old has been ; when reported truth shall once more be compared with the actual truth—the portrait of the Divine with its reality ? Is not perhaps the Molinist[1] himself thus striving after the higher light ?

The Pope's fancy conjures up the vision of that coming time.  He sees the motley pageant of the Age of Reason pushing the churchly "masque" aside, impatient of **the** slowly-trailing garments, in which he, the last **actor** in it, is passing off the scene.  **He** beholds the trials of **that** transition stage ; **the many** whose crumbling faith **will** land them **on** the lower platform **of** the material life ; **the** few, **who** from habit, will preserve the Christian level ; the fewer still, who, like Pompilia, will do so in the inspired conviction of the truth. He sees two men, or rather types of men, both priests, frankly making the new experiment, and adopting nature as their law.  Under her guidance, one, like Caponsacchi acts, in the main, well ; the other, like Guido Franceschini, wallows in every crime . . . . . The "first effects" of the "new cause" are apparent in those murdering five, and in their victims.

But the old law **is** not yet extinct.  He **(the** Church)

---

[1] The disciple of Michael de Molinos, **not** to **be** confounded with Louis Molina, who is especially known by his attempt to reconcile the theory of grace with that of free will.  Molinos was the founder of an exaggerated Quietism.  He held that the soul could detach itself from the body so as to become indifferent to its action, and therefore non-responsible for it ; and it was natural that all who defied the received laws of conduct, or were suspected of doing so, should be stigmatized as his followers.  Molinism was a favourite bugbear among the orthodox Romanists of Innocent the Twelfth's day.

still occupies the stage, though his departure be close at hand : so, in a last act of allegiance to Him who placed him there, he *smiles with his whole strength once more,*

> " Ending, so far as man may, this offence." (vol. x. p. 141†)

Yet again his arm is stayed. Voices, whether of friend or foe, are sounding in his ear. They reiterate the sophistries which have been enlisted in the Count's defence : the credit of the Church, the proprieties of the domestic hearth ; the educated sense of honour which is stronger than the moral law ; the general relief which will greet the act of mercy. The Pope listens. For one moment we may fancy that he yields. " Pronounce then," the imaginary speakers have said. A swift answer follows :

> " I will, Sirs : but a voice other than your's
> Quickens my spirit    .    .    . " (vol. x. p. 146.)

and the death-warrant goes out.

A favourite theory of Mr. Browning's appears in this soliloquy, for the first time since he stated it in "Sordello," and in a somewhat different form : that of the inadequacy of words to convey the truth. The Pope declares (p. 78) that we need

> " Expect nor question nor reply
> At what we figure as God's judgment-bar !
> None of this vile way by the barren words
> Which, more than any deed, characterize
> Man as made subject to a curse."

and again (p. 79) that

> "    .    .    these filthy rags of speech, this coil
> Of statement, comment, query and response,
> Tatters all too contaminate for use,
> Have no renewing : He, the Truth, is, too,
> The Word."

The scene changes to the prison-cell where Count Guido has received his final sentence of death. Two former friends and fellow-Tuscans, Cardinal Acciajuoli and Abate

Panciatichi, have come to prepare **him** for execution ; but
the one is listening awe-struck to the only kind of confession which they can obtain from him, while the other plies
his beads in a desperate endeavour to exorcise the spiritual
enemy, "ban" the diabolical influences, it is conjuring up.
The speaker is no longer Count Guido Franceschini, but

GUIDO. He is indeed another man than he **was** in **his**
first monologue, for he has thrown off **the mask. His**
tone is at first conciliatory, even entreating: for his hearers
are men **of** his own class, and he hopes to persuade them
to one more intercession in his behalf. But it changes to
one **of** scorn and defiance, **as** the hopelessness **of** his case
lays hold of him, and rises, at the end, to **a** climax of
ferocity which is all but grand.

"Repentance ! if he repent for twelve **hours, will he** die
**the** less on the thirteenth ? He has broken **the** social **law,
and** is about to pay for **it.** What has he to repent of but that
**he has made a** mistake ? Religion ! who of them all believes in it ? Not the Pope himself; for religion enjoins
mercy ; it is meant to temper the harshness of the law :
and he destroys the life which the **law** has given over to
him to save. What man of them all shows by his **acts**
that he believes ; or would be treated otherwise than as a
lunatic if he did ? Let those who will, halt between belief
and unbelief. It has not been in him to **do so.** Give
him the certainty of another world, and he **would have**
lived for it. Owning no such certainty, he has lived for
this one ; he has sought its pleasures and avoided its
pains. Only he has carried the thing too far. The world
has decreed limits to every man's pleasure ; it limits this for
the good **of** all ; and **it** has made unlawful the excess of
pleasure which turns to someone else's pain. He has
exceeded the lawful amount of pleasure, and he pays for
**it** by an extra dose of pain."

"There the matter ends. But his judges want more—a
few edifying lies wherewith to show that he did not die

impenitent, and stop the mouth of anyone who may hint, the day after the execution, that old men are too fond of putting younger ones out of the way. They shall have his confession ; but it must be the truth."

" He killed his wife because he hated her ; because, whether it were her fault or not, she was a stumbling-block in his path. He had been outraged by her aversion, exasperated by her patience, maddened by her never putting herself in the wrong. While her parents were with her, she resisted and clamoured, and then her presence could be endured ; but they were left alone together, and then everything was changed. Day by day, and all day, he was confronted by her automatic obedience, by her dumb despair. She rose up and lay down—she spoke or was silent at his bidding ; neither a loosened hair, nor a crumple in the dress, giving token of resistance ; he might have strangled her without her making a sign. She eloped from him, yet he could not surprise her in the commission of a sin : and he returned from his pursuit of her, ridiculous when he should have been triumphant. He took his revenge at last. And now that he might tell his story and find no one to controvert it—how he came to claim his wife and child, and found no child, but the lover by the wife's side ; was attacked, defended himself, struck right and left, and thus did the deed—she survives, by miracle, to confute him, to condemn him, and worst of all, to forgive him."

" He has been ensnared by his opportunities from first to last. He failed to save himself from retribution, only because he was drunk with the sudden freedom from this hateful load. And Pompilia haunts him still. Her stupid purity will freeze him even in death. It will rob him of his hell—where the fiend in him would burn up in fiery rapture—where some Lucrezia might meet him as his fitting bride—where the wolf-nature frankly glutted would perhaps leave room for some return to human form. For she cannot hate. It would grieve her to know him there; and—if there be a hell—it will be barred to him in consideration for her."

" The Cardinal, the Abate, they too are petrifactions in their way! He may rave another twelve hours, and it will be useless." Yet he makes one more effort to move them. He reminds the Cardinal of the crimes he has committed—of the help he will need when a new Pope is to be elected ; of the possible supporter who may then be in his grave. Then fiercely turning on them both ; " the Cardinal have a chance indeed, when there is an Albano in the case ! The Abate be alive a year hence, with that burning hollow cheek and that hacking cough !—Well, *he* will die bold and honest as he has lived."

At this juncture he becomes aware that the fatal moment has arrived. Steps and lights are on the stairs. The defiant spirit is quenched. " He has laughed and mocked and said no word of all he had to say." In wild terror he pleads for life—bare life. A final vindication of his wife's goodness bursts from him in the words,

> " Abate,—Cardinal,—Christ,—Maria,—God,—
> Pompilia, will you let them murder me ? "  (vol. x. p. 243.)

The concluding part of the work reverses the idea of the first, and is entitled

THE BOOK AND THE RING. It completes the record of the Franceschini case, and gives the concluding touches to the circle of evidence which now assumes its final dramatic form. We have first an account of the execution, conveyed in a gossiping letter from a Venetian gentleman on a visit to Rome, and who reports it as the last news of the week, and the occasion of his having lost a bet. The writer also discusses the Pope's health, the relative merits of his present physician and a former one ; the relative chances of various candidates for the Papacy; and the Pope's possible motives for setting aside " justice, prudence, and esprit de corps," in the manner testified by his recent condemnation of a man of rank. His political likes and dislikes are thrown into the scale, but his predilection for the mob is considered to have turned it. "He allows the people to question him when he takes his walks ; and it is said that some of them asked him, on the occasion of his last, whether the privilege of murder was altogether reserved for noblemen." "The Austrian ambassador had done his best to avert bloodshed, and pleaded hard for the life of one whom, as he urged, he 'may have dined at table with !' and felt so aggrieved by the Pope's answer, that he all but refused to come to the execution, and would barely look at it when he came." Various details follow, some of which my readers already know.

Mr. Browning next speaks of the three manuscript letters bound into the original book ; selects one of these, written by the Count's advocate, de Archangelis, and gives it, first, in its actual contents, and next, in an imaginary postscript which we are to think of as destined for the recipient's private ear. The letter itself is written for the Count's family and friends ; and states, in a tone of solemn regret, that the justifications brought forward by his correspondent arrived too late ; that the Pope thought it inexpedient to postpone the execution, or to accept the plea of youth urged in favour of the four accomplices ; and that they all died that day. It declares that the Count suffered in an exemplary manner, amidst the commiseration and respect of all Rome, and that the honour of his house will lose nothing through the catastrophe.

The supplement is conceived in a very different spirit. The writer laughs at their "pleas" and "proofs," coming, like Pisan help, when the man is already dead—"not that twenty such vindications would have done any good—

"When Somebody's thick head-piece once was bent
On seeing Guido's drop into the bag." (vol. x. p. 256.)

Well, people enjoyed the show, but saw through it all
the same ; and meanwhile his (the writer's) superb defence
goes for nothing ; and though argument is **solid and**
subsists

"While obstinacy and ineptitude
Accompany the owner to his tomb ;" (vol. x. p. 256.)

his hands and his pockets are **empty. Ah well! little**
Cino will gain by it in the long run. **He had been pro-**
mised that if papa couldn't save the **Count's head,** he
should go and see it chopped off : **and** when a patroness
of his joked the child on his defeat, and on Bottini's ruling
the roast, the clever rogue retorted that papa knew better
than to baulk the Pope of his grudge, and could have
argued Bottini's nose off **if** he had chosen. Doesn't the
fop see that he (de Archangelis) **can** drive right **and left**
horses with one hand? The Gomez case shall make **it up**
to him."

The two other **letters** are in **the same** strain **as** the **first.**
Both are written **on the day of the execution. Both** announce it in **a** condoling manner. **Both** allude to **the**
justifications which arrived **too** late : and **in one or** both,
the criminal is spoken of as " poor " Signor Guido. Mr.
Browning has preferred, however, representing the other
side ; and the next which he gives **is,** like Don Hyacinth's
supplement, only such as might have been written. **It is**
supposed to be from Pompilia's advocate Bottinius (or
Bottini), and is in keeping with the spirit of his defence.
**He is** clearly jealous of not having had a worse case to
plead. " He has won," he says. " How **could he** do
otherwise ? with the plain truth on his side, and the **Pope**
ready to steady it on his legs again if he let it drop asleep.
Arcangeli may crow over him, **as** it is, for having been
kept by him **a** month at bay—though even this much was
not his doing ; **the** little dandiprat Spreti was the real
man."

And this is not all. " Of course Rome must have its joke

at the advocate with the case that proved itself : but here is a piece of impertinence he was not prepared for. The barefoot Augustinian, whose report of Pompilia's dying words took all the freshness out of the best points of his defence, has been preaching on the subject ; and the sermon is flying about Rome in print." Next follows an extract from it. The friar warns his hearers not to trust to human powers of discovering the truth. "It is not the long trial which has revealed Pompilia's innocence ; God from time to time puts forth His hand, and He has done so here. But earth is not heaven, nor all truth intended to prevail. One dove returned to the ark. How many were lost in the wave? One woman's purity has been rescued from the world. 'How many chaste and noble sister-fames' have lacked 'the extricating hand?' And we must wait God's time for such truth as is destined to appear. When Christians worshipped in the Catacomb, one man, no worse than the rest, though no less foolish, will have pointed to its mouth, and said, 'Obscene rites are practised in that darkness. The devotees of an execrable creed skulk there out of sight.' Not till the time was ripe, did lightning split the face of the rock, and lay bare a nook—

> "Narrow and short, a corpse's length, no more :
> And by it, in the due receptacle,
> The little rude brown lamp of earthenware,
> The cruse, was meant for flowers, but held the blood,
> The rough-scratched palm-branch, and the legend left
> *Pro Christo.*"    (vol. x. p. 265.)

"And how does human law, in its 'inadequacy' and 'ineptitude' defend the just? How has it attempted to clear Pompilia's fame? By submitting, as its best resource, that wickedness was bred in her flesh and bone. For himself he cannot judge, unless by the assurance of Christ, if he have not lost much by renouncing the world: for he has lost love, and knowledge, and perhaps the means of bringing goodness from its ideal conception into the actual life of man. But the bubble, fame—worldly praise and appreciation—he has done well to set these aside."

"And what is all this preaching," resumes Bottinius, "but **a way** of courting fame? The inflation **of it**! and **the** spite! and the Molinism! As its first pleasant consequence, Gomez, who had intended to appeal from the absurd decision of the Court, declines to ask **the** lawyers for farther help.[1] There **is** an end **of** that job **and its fee.** Nevertheless, his 'blatant brother' shall soon see if law is as inadequate, and advocacy as impotent, **as he** fancies. Providence is this time in their favour. Pompilia **was** consigned to the 'Convertite' (converted ones). She was therefore a sinner. Guido has been judged guilty : but there was **no word as** to the innocence of his wife. The sisterhood claims, therefore, the property which accrued to her through her parents' death, and which she **has** left in trust for her son. Who but himself—the Fisc—shall support the claim, and show the foul-mouthed friar that his dove **was a** raven after all." (He too can drive left **and** right horses on occasion.)

This he actually did. But once more **the Pope intervened:** and Mr. Browning proceeds **to** give the literal substance of the "Instrument" of justification as it lies before him. In this, Pompilia's "perfect fame" is restored, and her representative, Domenico Tighetti, secured against all molestations of her heir and his ward, which the Most Venerable Convent, etc. etc., may commit **or** threaten.

What became of **that** child, Gaetano, as he was called after the new-made saint? Did **he** live **a** true scion of

---

[1] **A** passing allusion is made to this Gomez case in one of the manuscript letters, the writer of which begs Cencini (clearly also an advocate), to send him the papers concerning it. The place it occupies in the thoughts of the two lawyers, as Mr. Browning depicts them, **is** very characteristic of the manner in which his imagination has embraced and vivified every detail of the situation.

the paternal stock, whose heraldic symbols Mr. Browning has described by Count Guido's mouth ?—

> " Or did he love his mother, the base-born,
> And fight i' the ranks, unnoticed by the world?"   (vol. x. p. 277.)

This question Mr. Browning asks himself, but is unable to answer. He concludes his book by telling us its intended lesson, and explaining why he has chosen to present it in this artistic form. The lesson is that which we have already learned from his Pope's thoughts :—

> "  .       .       .       our human speech is naught,
> Our human testimony false, our fame
> And human estimation words and wind."   (vol. x. p. 277.)

Art, with its indirect processes, can alone raise up a living image of that truth which words distort in the stating.

And, lastly, he dedicates the completed work to the "Lyric Love," whose blessing on its performance he has invoked in a memorable passage at the close of his introductory chapter.


## TRANSCRIPTS FROM THE GREEK, WITH

## "ARTEMIS PROLOGIZES."

Another group of works detaches itself from any possible scheme of classification : These are Mr. Browning's transcripts from the Greek.

The "Alkestis" of Euripides, imbedded in the dramatic romance called "Balaustion's Adventure." 1871.

The "Herakles" of Euripides, introduced into "Aristophanes' Apology." 1875.

The "Agamemnon" of Æschylus, published by itself. 1877.

They are even outside my subject because they are literal; and therefore show Mr. Browning as a scholar, but not otherwise as **a** poet than in the technical power and indirect poetic judgments involved in the work. **All** I need say about this **is,** that its literalness detracts in no way from the beauty and transparency of "Alkestis" **or** "Herakles," while it makes "Agamemnon" **very hard to** read; and that **Mr.** Browning has **probably** intended **his** readers **to** draw their own conclusion, **which is so far his,** as to **the** relative quality of the two great classics. **Some** critics contend that a less literal translation **of the** "Agamemnon" would have been not only more pleasing, but more true; but Mr. Browning clearly thought otherwise. Had he not, he would certainly have given his author the benefit of the larger interpretation; **and his** principal motive for this indirect defence of Euripides **would** have disappeared.

Mr. Browning has also given us an original fragment in the classic manner :—

"Artemis Prologizes." ("**Men and** Women,"[1]) published in "Dramatic Lyrics," in 1842.) This was suggested by the "Hippolytos" of Euripides; and destined to become part of a larger poem, which should continue its story. For, according to the legend, Hippolytos having perished through the anger of Aphrodité (Venus), was revived by Artemis (Diana), though only to disappoint her affection by falling in love with one of **her** nymphs, Aricia. Mr. Browning imagines that she has removed him in secret to her own forest retreat, and is nursing him back to life by the help of Asclepios; and the poem is a monologue in which she describes what has passed, from Phædra's self-betrayal to the present time. Hippolytos still lies un-

---

[1] The poems to which I refer as now included in "Men and Women" will be found so in the editions of 1868 and 1888-9; though the redistribution made in 1863 has much curtailed their number.

conscious ; but the power of the great healer has been brought to bear upon him, and the unconsciousness seems only that of sleep.  Artemis is *awaiting the event.*

The ensuing chorus of nymphs, the awakening of Hippolytos, and with it the stir of the new passion within him, had already taken shape in Mr. Browning's mind.  Unfortunately, something put the inspiration to flight, and it did not return.[1]

---

[1] It was in this poem that Mr. Browning first adopted the plan of spelling Greek names in the Greek manner.  He did so, as he tells us in the preface to his "Agamemnon," "innocently enough;" because the change commended itself to his own eye and ear.  He has even assured his friends that if the innovation had been rationally opposed, or simply not accepted, he would probably himself have abandoned it.  But when, years later, in "Balaustion's Adventure," the new spelling became the subject of attacks which all but ignored the existence of the work from any other point of view, the thought of yielding was no longer admissible.  The majority of our best scholars now follow Mr. Browning's example.

# CLASSIFIED GROUPS.

## ARGUMENTATIVE POEMS. SPECIAL PLEADINGS.

**T**HE isolated monologues have a special significance, which **is** almost implied in their form, but
is also distinct from it. Mr. Browning has made
them the vehicle for most of the reasonings **and** reflections which make up so large a part of his imaginative life :
whether presented in his own person, or, as is most often
the case, in that of his men and women. As such, they
are among those of his works which lend themselves to **a**
rough kind of classification; and may be called "argumentative."

They divide themselves into two classes: those in which
the speaker is defending a preconceived judgment, and an
antagonist is implied ; and those in which he is trying to
form a judgment or to accept one : and the supposed
listener, if there be such, is only a confidant. The first
kind of argument or discussion is carried on—apparently
—as much for victory as for truth ; and employs the
weapons of satire, or the tactics **of** special-pleading, as
the case demands. The second is an often pathetic and
always single-minded endeavour **to** get at the truth.

Those monologues in which the human spirit is represented as communing with itself, contain some of Mr. Browning's noblest dramatic work; but those in which the militant attitude is more pronounced throw the strongest light on what I have indicated as his distinctive intellectual quality: the rejection of all general and dogmatic points of view. His casuistic utterances are often only a vindication of the personal, and therefore indefinite quality of human truth; and their apparent trifling with it is often only the seeking after a larger truth, in which all seeming contradictions are resolved. It was inevitable, however, that this mental quality should play into the hands of his dramatic imagination, and be sometimes carried away by it; so that when he means to tell us what a given person under given circumstances would be justified in saying, he sometimes finds himself including in the statement something which the given person so situated would be only likely to say.

The first of these classes, or groups, which we may distinguish as SPECIAL PLEADINGS, contains poems very different in length, and in literary character; and to avoid the appearance of confusion, I shall reverse the order of their publication, and place the most important first:—

"Aristophanes' Apology;[1] or The Last Adventure of Balaustion." (1875.)

"Fifine at the Fair." (1872.)

"Prince Hohenstiel-Schwangau, Saviour of Society." (1871.)

"Bishop Blougram's Apology" (Men and Women). (1855.)

---

[1] The classification of this poem is open to the obvious objection that it is not a monologue; but a dialogue or alternation of monologues, in which the second speaker, Balaustion (who is also the narrator), is, for the time being, as real as the first. Its conception is, however, expressed in the first title; and the arguments and descriptions which Balaustion supplies only contribute to the vividness with which Aristophanes and his defence are brought before us. "Aristophanes' Apology" is identical in spirit with the other poems of this group.

" Mr. Sludge, the Medium." (Dramatis Personæ.)
(1864.)

"ARISTOPHANES' APOLOGY" is, as its second title shows,
a sequel to " Balaustion's Adventure" (1871). Both turn
on the historical fact that Euripides was reverenced far
more by the non-Athenian Greeks than by the Athenians;
and both contain a transcript from him. But the interest
of " Aristophanes' Apology" is independent of its
" Herakles," while that of " Balaustion's Adventure" is
altogether bound up with its Alkestis; and in so far as
the "adventure" places Balaustion herself before us, it
will be best treated as an introduction to her appearance
in the later and more important work.

Balaustion is a Rhodian girl, brought up in a worship
for Euripides, which does not, however, exclude the appreciation of other great Greek poets. The Peloponnesian
War has entered on its second stage. The Athenian fleet
has been defeated at Syracuse. And Rhodes, resenting
this disgrace, has determined to take part against Athens,
and join the Peloponnesian league. But Balaustion will not
forsake the mother-city, the life and light of her whole
known world ; and she persuades her kinsmen to migrate
with her to it, and, with her, to share its fate. They accordingly take ship at Kaunus, a Carian sea-port belonging
to Rhodes. But the wind turns them from their course,
and when it abates, they find themselves in strange waters,
pursued by a pirate bark. They fly before it towards what
they hope will prove a friendly shore—Balaustion hearten-
ing the rowers by a song from Æschylus, which was sung
at the battle of Salamis—and run straight into the hostile
harbour of Syracuse, where shelter is denied them.

The captain pleads in vain that they are Kaunians, subjects of Rhodes, and that Rhodes is henceforward on
Sparta's side. " Kaunian the ship may be : but Athenians
are on board. All Athens echoed in that song from

Æschylus which has been ringing across the sea. The voyagers may retire unhurt. But if ten pirate ships were pursuing them, they should not bring those memories of Salamis to the Athenian captives whom the defeat of Nicias has left in Syracusan hands." The case is desperate. The Rhodians turn to go.

Suddenly a voice cries, "Wait. Do they know any verses from Euripides?" "More than that, they answer, Balaustion can recite a whole play—that strangest, saddest, sweetest song—the 'Alkestis.' It does honour to Herakles, their god. Let them place her on the steps of their temple of Herakles, and she will recite it there." The Rhodians are brought in, amidst joyous loving laughter, among shouts of "Herakles" and "Euripides." The recital takes place;[1] it is repeated a second day and a third; and Balaustion and her kinsmen are dismissed with good words and wishes, for, as she declares :

> ".   .   . Greeks are Greeks, and hearts are hearts,
> And poetry is power,    .    .    ."        (vol. xi. p. 14)

The story of Alkestis scarcely needs repeating. Apollo had incurred the anger of Jupiter by avenging the death of his son Æsculapius on the Cyclops whose thunder-bolt had slain him ; and been condemned to play the part of a common mortal, and serve Admetus, King of Thessaly, as herdsman. The kind treatment of Admetus had made him his friend : and Apollo had deceived the Fate sisters into promising that whenever the king's life should become their due, they would renounce it on condition of some other person dying in his stead. When the play opens, the fatal moment has come. Alkestis, wife of Admetus, has offered herself to save him ; and Admetus, though he does so with a heavy heart, has been weak enough to

---

[1] This incident is founded on fact. It is related in Plutarch's Lives, that after the defeat of Nicias, all those of the captives who could recite something from Euripides were kindly treated by the Syracusans.

accept the sacrifice. Death enters the palace, from which even Apollo can no longer turn him away.

But just as Alkestis has breathed her last, Herakles appears; and his great cheery voice is heard on the threshold of the house of mourning, inquiring if the master be within. Admetus suppresses all signs of emotion, that he may receive him as hospitality demands; and Herakles, hearing what has happened from a servant of the house, is moved to gratitude and pity. He wrestles with Death; conquers him; and brings back Alkestis into her husband's presence, veiled, and in the guise of a second companion. Admetus will at first neither touch nor look at her. He has promised his dying wife to give her no successor; and her memory is even dearer to him than she herself has been. The god however reasons, persuades, and insists; and at length, very reluctantly, Admetus gives his hand to the stranger, whom he is then told to unveil. Herakles has delayed the recognition, that Alkestis might be enabled to probe her husband's fidelity, and convince herself that sorrow had made him worthier of her.

Balaustion half recites the play, half describes it, " as she has seen it at Kameiros this very year," occasionally compressing an unimportant scene, but always closely adhering to the original. She knows that she is open to the reproach of describing more than the masked faces of the actors could allow her to see; but she meets it in these words :—

> "What's poetry except a power that makes?
> And, speaking to one sense, inspires the rest,
> Pressing them all into its service;"   (vol. xi. pp. 17-18.)

The whole work is a vindication of the power of poetry, as exerted in itself, and as reproduced in those who have received its fruits (pages 110, 111); and Balaustion herself displays it in this secondary form, by suggesting a version of the story of Alkestis, more subtly, if less simply, beautiful than the original. She makes *Love* the conqueror of Death. According to her, the music made by Apollo among Admetus's flocks has tamed every selfish passion in the King's soul ; and when the time comes for his wife to die, he refuses the sacrifice. "Zeus has decreed that their two lives shall be one ; and if they must be severed, he must go who was the body, not she, who was the soul, of their joint existence." But Alkestis declares that the reality of that existence lies not in her but in him, and she bids him look at her once more before his decision is made. In this look, her soul enters into his ; and, thus subduing him, she expires. But when she reaches the nether world she is rejected as a deceiver. "The death she brings to it is a mockery, since it doubles the life she has left behind." Proserpine sends her back to her husband's side ; and the "lost eyes" re-open beneath his gaze, while it still embraces her.

Apollo smiles sadly at the ingenuousness of mortals, who thus imagine that the chain of eternal circumstance could snap in one human life ; at their blindness to those seeds of pity and tenderness which the crushed promise of human happiness sets free. Yet he seems to think they lose nothing by either. "They do well to value their little hour. They do well to treasure the warm heart's blood, of which no outpouring could tinge the paleness or fill the blank of eternity, the power of love which transforms their earthly homes, their

> .      .      .  hopes and fears, so blind and yet so sweet
> With death about them."                                    (p. 115.)
> .      .      .            ! ¦      .      .      .

"Balaustion" means wild pomegranate flower ; and the girl has been so called on account of her lyric gifts. She recalls the pomegranate tree, because its leaves are cooling to the brow, its seed and blossom grateful to the sense, and because the nightingale is never distant from it. She will keep the name for life—so she tells **her** friends—and with it a better thing which her songs have gained her. One youth came daily to the temple-steps at Syracuse to hear her. He was at her side at Athens when she landed. They will be married at this next full moon.

"Alkestis" failed "to get the prize" when its author was competing with Sophocles. "But Euripides has had his reward : in the sympathies which he **has** stirred ; in the genius which he has inspired. His crown came direct from Zeus."

We need not name the poetess whom Mr. **Browning** quotes at the close **of** this poem. The painter **so** generously eulogized is F. Leighton.

When we meet Balaustion again, **in** "Aristophanes' Apology," many things have happened. She has seen her poet in his retirement (this was mentioned in her "adventure"), kissed his hand, and received from it, together with other gifts, his tragedy of Herakles. Euripides has died ; Athens has fallen ; and Balaustion, with her memories in her heart, and her husband, Euthykles, by her side, is speeding back towards Rhodes. She is deeply shocked by the fate of her adoptive city, to which her fancy pays a tribute of impassioned reverence, too **poetic** to be given in any but Mr. Browning's words. **Yet** she has a growing belief that that fate was just. Sea and air and the blue expanse of heaven are full of suggestion of that spirit-life, with its larger struggles or its universal peace, which is above the world's crowd and noise. And she determines that sorrow for what is fleeting shall not gnaw at her heart.

But in order to overcome the sorrow, she must loosen it from her. The tragedy she has witnessed must enact itself once more for Euthykles and her, he writing as she dictates. It will have for prologue a second adventure of her own, which he also has witnessed ; and this adventure will constitute the book. It is prefaced in its turn by a backward glance at the circumstances, (so different from the present) in which she related the first.

It was the night on which Athens received the news that Euripides was dead : Euthykles had brought this home to her from the theatre. They were pondering it gravely, but not sadly, for their poet was now at rest, in the companionship of Æschylus, safe from the petty spites which had frothed and fretted about his life. He had lived and worked, to the end, true to his own standard of right, heedless of the reproach that he was a man-hater and a recluse, without regard for civic duty, and with no object but his art. He had left it to Sophocles to play poet and commander at the same time, and be laughed at for the result. He had first taken the prize of " Contemplation " in his all but a hundred plays ; then, grasping the one hand offered him which held a heart, had shown at the court of Archelaus of Macedon whether or not the power of active usefulness was in him. His last notes of music had also been struck for that one friend.

Even Athens did him justice now. The reaction had set in ; one would have his statue erected in the theatre ; another would have him buried in the Piræus ; etc. etc. Not so Euthykles and Balaustion. His statue was in their hearts. Their concern was not with his mortal vesture, but with the liberated soul, which now watched over their world. They would hail this, they said, in the words of his own song, his " Herakles."

The reading was about to begin, when suddenly there was torch-light—a burst of comic singing—and a knocking at the door ; Bacchus bade them open ; they delayed. Then a name was uttered, of " authoritative " sound, of " immense significance ; " and the door was opened to— Aristophanes. He was returning from the performance of his " Thesmophoriazusae,"[1] last year a failure, but this

---

[1] The name signifies celebration of the festival of the Thesmophoria. This was held by women only, in honour of Ceres and Proserpine.

time, thanks to some new and audacious touches, a brilliant success. His chorus trooped before him—himself no more sober than was his wont—crowned, triumphant, and drunk ; a group of flute-boys and dancing-girls making up the scene. All these, however, slunk away before Balaustion's glance, Aristophanes alone confronting **her. And,** as she declares, it was " no ignoble presence." **For the** broad brow, the flushed cheek, the commanding features, the defiant attitude, all betokened **a** mind, wantoning among the lower passions, but yet master of them.

He addresses Balaustion **in a tone** of mock deference ; banters her on her poetic name, her dignified mien, and the manner in which she has scared his chorus **and its** followers away ; " not indeed that that matters, since **the** archon's economy and the world's squeamishness **will soon** abolish it altogether."[1] Then struck by a passing thought, he stands grave, silent—another man in short—awaiting what she has to say.

**In** this **sober** moment, Balaustion welcomes him **to her** house. She welcomes him as the Good Genius : as genius of the kindly, though purifying humour, which, like summer lighting, illumines, but does not destroy. She knows and implies that he is not only this. **But** she greets the light, no matter to what darkness it be allied. She reverences the god who forms one half **of** him, so long as the monster which constitutes the other, remains out of sight ; a poetic myth **is** made to illustrate this feeling. The gravity, however, is short-lived. The lower self in Aristophanes springs up again, and his " apology " begins.

"Aristophanes' APOLOGY " is a defence of comedy, as understood and practised by himself : that is, as a broad

[1] The chorus of each new play was supplied to its author by the Government, when considered worth the outlay. Sketches of this and other plays alluded to in the course of the work may be read in the first volume of Mahaffy's " History of Classical Greek Literature."

**K**

expression of the natural life, and a broad satire upon those who directly or indirectly condemn it. It is addressed to Euripides in the person of his disciple. It is at the same time an attack upon him ; and in either capacity it covers a great deal of ground. For the dispute does not lie simply between comedy and tragedy—which latter, with the old tragedians, was often only the naturalism of comedy on a larger scale—but between naturalism and humanity, as more advanced thinkers understood it ; between the old ideas of human and divine conveyed by tragedy and comedy alike, and the new ones which Euripides, the friend of Socrates, had imported into them ; and the question at issue involved, therefore, not only art and morals, but the entire philosophy of life. The "Apology" derives farther interest and significance from the varied emotions by which it is inspired. The speaker (as is the case in "Fifine at the Fair") is answering not only his opponent, but his own conscience. How the conscience of Aristophanes has been aroused he presently tells : first struggling a little with the false shame which the experience has left behind. This is the scene which he describes.

A festive supper had followed the successful play. Jollity was at its height. The cup was being crowned to Aristophanes as the "Triumphant," when a knock came to the door : and there entered no "asker of questions," no casual passer-by, but the pale, majestic, heavily-draped figure of Sophocles himself. Slowly, solemnly, and with bent head, he passed up the hall, between two ranks of spectators as silent as himself ; raised his eyes as he confronted the priest,[1] and announced to him, that since Euripides was "dead to-day," and as a fitting spectacle for the god, his chorus would appear at the greater feast,

---

[1] The plays were performed at the lesser and greater festivals of Bacchus ; this, the Lenaia, being the smaller one. Hence, the presence of priest as well as archon at the ensuing banquet

next month, clothed in black and ungarlanded. Then silently, and amidst silence, he passed out again.

This, then, was the purport of the important news which was known to have arrived in port, but which **every one** had interpreted in his own way. Euripides **was** no more ! But neither the news nor he who brought it could create more than a momentary stupor ; and the tipsy fun soon renewed itself, at the expense of the living tragedian and the dead. Aristophanes alone remained grave. The value **of** the man whom he had aspersed and ridiculed stood out before him summed **up** by the **hand of** Death. He recalled the failure which **had marked** the now hope- less limitation of his own genius, and those **last** words addressed to him by Euripides which brought **home its** lesson.[1] The archon, "Master of the Feast," judging that its "glow" was "extinct," **had risen to** conclude **it by** crowning the parting cup. He had crowned **it with** judicious reserve to the " Good Genius ;" and Strattis (the comic poet) had burst forth in an eulogium of the Comic Muse which claimed the title of Good Genius for her— when yielding **to** this new and over-mastering impulse, he (Aristophanes) checked the coming applause, and demanded that the Tragic Muse and her ministrant Euri- pides should receive the libation instead ; justifying the demand by a noble and pathetic tribute to the memory of the dead poet, and to the great humanities which only the *tragic* poet can represent.

But he found no response. **The** listeners mistook **his** seriousness for satire, and broke out afresh at the excel- lence of such a joke ; and recovering his presence of mind as quickly as he had lost it, he changed his tone, thanked

---

[1] The failure here alluded to is his Ploutos or Plutus—an inoffensive but tame comedy written when Aristophanes was advanced in years, and of which the ill-success has been imputed to this fact. Mr. Browning, however, treats it as a proof that the author's ingrained habit of coarse fun had unfitted him for the more serious treatment of human life.

those alike who had laughed with him, and who had wept with the "Lord of Tears;" and desired that the cup be consecrated to that genius of complex poetry which is tragedy and comedy in one.   It was sacrilege, he declared, to part these two ; for to do so was to hack at the Hermai [1] —to outrage the ideal union of the intellectual and the sensuous life in man.  And from this new vantage-ground he launched another bolt at Euripides, whose coldness, he asserted, had belied this union, and made him guilty of a crime inexpiable in the sight of the gods.

Yet he could not dismiss him from his thoughts.   He wanted to go over the old ground with him, and put himself in the right.   Balaustion and her husband were in a manner representatives of the dead tragedian.   That was why he had come.   He was not sure that he expressed, or at the moment even felt, all that he had just repeated. "Drunk he was with the good Thasian, and drunk he probably had been."   Nevertheless, the impulse he had thus obeyed sprang perhaps from some real, if hitherto undiscovered depths in his soul.

Up to this moment his defence has been carried on in a disjointed manner, and consists rather in defying attack than in resisting it : the defiant mood being only another aspect of the perturbed condition which has brought him to Balaustion's door.   It finds its natural starting-point in the coarse treatment of things and persons which his "Thesmophoriazusae," with its "monkeying" of Euripides,[2] has so recently displayed.  But he reminds Balaustion that the art of comedy is young.   It is only three generations since Susarion gave it birth.  (He explains this more fully later on.)   It began when he and his companions daubed their faces with wine lees, mounted a cart,

---

[1] Figures placed above the entrance of Athenian houses, and symbolizing the double life. It was held as sacrilege to deface them, as had been recently and mysteriously done.

[2] Introducing him into the play, as in the disguise of a disreputable woman.

and drove by night through the villages : crying from house
to house, how this man starved his labourers, that other
kissed his neighbour's wife, and so on. The first comedian
battered with big stones. He, Aristophanes, is at the
stage of the wooden club which he has taken pains to
plane smooth, and inlay with shining studs. The mere
polished steel will be for his successors.

"And is he approaching the age of steel?" Balaustion
asks, well knowing that he is not. "His play failed last
year. Was his triumph to-night due to a gentler tone?
Is he teaching mankind that brute blows are not human
fighting, still less the expression of godlike power; and
that ignorance and folly are convicted by their opposites,
not by themselves ? "

" Not he, indeed," he replies ; " he improves on his art :
he does not turn it topsy-turvy. *He* does not work on
abstractions. *His* power is not that of the recluse. He
wants human beings with their approbation and their
sympathy, and his Athens, to be pleased in her own way.
He leaves the rest to Euripides. Real life is the grist to
*his* mill. It is clear enough, however, that the times are
against him. Every year more restrictions ; Euripides
with his priggishness ; Socrates with his books and his
moonshine, and his supercilious ways : never resenting
his (Aristophanes') fun, nor seeming even to notice it,[1]
not condescending to take exception to any but the
'tragedians ;' as if he, the author of the 'Birds,' was a
mere comic poet !" Then follows a tirade on the variety of
his subjects; their depth, their significance, and the mawk-
ishness and pedantry which they are intended to confute.

" Drunk ! yes, he owns that he is." This in answer to
a look from Balaustion, which has rebuked a too hazar-
dous joke—" Drink is the proper inspiration. How else

---

[1] Aristophanes' comedy of the "Clouds" was written especially at
Socrates, who stood up unconcernedly in the theatre that the many strangers
present might understand what was intended.

was he beaten in the 'Clouds,' his masterpiece, but that his opponent had inspired himself with drink, and he this time had not?[1] Purity! he has learned what that is worth "—With more in the same strain. Now, however, that his adventure is told, the tumult of feeling in some degree subsides, and the more serious aspects of the apology will come into play.

Balaustion and her husband, seeing the sober mood return, once more welcome "the glory of Aristophanes" to their house, and bid him on his side share in their solemnity, and commemorate Euripides with them. This calls his attention to the portrait of the dead poet ; those implements of his work which were his tokens of friendship to Balaustion ; the papyrus leaf inscribed with the Herakles itself ; and he cannot resist a sneer at this again unsuccessful play. His hostess rebukes him grandly for completing the long outrage on the living man by this petty attack on his "supreme calm ;" and as supreme calmness means death, he begins musing on the immunities which death confers, and their injustice. "Give him only time and he will pulverize his opponents ; *he* will show them whether this work of his is unintelligible, or that other will not live. But let them die ; and they slink out of his reach with their malice, stupidity, and ignorance, while survivors croak 'respect the dead' over the hole in which they are laid. At all events, he retorts on them when he can—unwisely perhaps, since those he flings mud at are only immortalized by the process. Euripides knew better than to follow his example."

Again Balaustion has her answer. "He has volleyed mud at Euripides himself while pretending to defend the same cause : the cause of art, of knowledge, of justice,

---

[1] Mr. Mahaffy's description of the "Clouds" contains an account of this defeat, which sets forth the amusing conceit and sophistry of Aristophanes' explanation of it. He alludes here to the prevailing custom of several dramatic writers competing for a prize.

and of truth';" and she makes his cheek burn by reminding him of what petty and what ignoble witticisms that
mud was made up. At last he begins in real earnest.
"Balaustion, he understands, condemns comedy both in
theory and in practice, from the calm and rational heights
to which she, with her tragic friend, **has attained. Here**
are his arguments in its favour."

"It claims respect as an institution, because **as such it**
is coeval with liberty—born of the feast **of** Bacchus, **and**
therefore of the good gifts of the earth—a **mode of** telling
truth without punishment, and of chastising without **doing**
harm. It claims respect **by** its advance **from simple**
objects to more composite, from plain thumping to more
searching modes of attack. The **men** who **once** exposed
wrong-doing by shouting it before **the wrong-doer's** door,
now expose it by representing its various **forms. The**
comic poets denounce not only the thief, **the fool,** the
miser, but the advocates of war, **the** flatterers **of the** populace, the sophists who set up Whirligig[1] **in** the place **of**
Zeus, the thin-blooded tragedian in league with the
sophists, who preaches against the flesh. Where facts are
insufficient he has recourse to fancy, and exaggerates the
wronged truth the **more** strongly to enforce **it** (here
follows a characteristic illustration.) To those **who** call
Saperdion the Empousa, he shows her **in a** Kimberic
robe;[2] in other words, he exposes her charms more fully
than she does it herself, the better to convict those who
malign them."

And here lies his grudge against Euripides. Euripides
is one of those who call Saperdion a monster—who slander
the world of sense with its beauties and its enjoyments,

---

[1] Whirligig is a parody of the word "vortex." Vortex itself is used in
derision of Socrates, who is represented in the "Clouds" as setting up this
non-rational force in the place of Zeus—the clouds themselves being subordinate divinities.

[2] Saperdion was a famous Hetaira, the Empousa, a mythological monster.
Kimberic or Cimberic means transparent.

or who contemptuously set it aside. " Born on the day of Salamis—when heroes walked the earth ; and gods were reverenced and not discussed—when Greeks guarded their home with its abundant joys, and left barbarian lands to their own starvation—he has lived to belie every tradition of that triumphant time. He has joined himself with a band of starved teachers and reformers to cut its very foundations away. He exalts death over life, misery over happiness ; or, if he admits happiness, it is as an empty name."

" Moreover, he reasons away the gods ; for they are, according to him, only forms of nature. Zeus *is* the atmosphere. Poseidon *is* the sea. Necessity rules the universe. Duty, once the will of the gods, is now a voice within ourselves bidding us renounce pleasure, and giving us no inducement to do so."

" He reasons away morality, for he shows there is neither right nor wrong, neither 'yours' nor 'mine,' nor natural privilege, nor natural subjection, that may not be argued equally for or against. 'Why be in such a hurry to pay one's debt, to attend one's mother, to bring a given sacrifice ?'"

" He reasons away social order, for he declares the slave as good as his master, woman equal to man, and even the people competent to govern itself. 'Why should not the tanner, the lampseller, or the mealman, who knows his own business so well, know that of the State too ?'"

"He ignores the function of poetry, which is to see beauty, and to create it : for he places utility above grace, truth above all beauty. He drags human squalor on to the scene because he recognizes its existence. The world of the poet's fancy, that world into which he was born, does not exist for him. He spoils his art as well as his life, carving back to bull what another had carved into a sphinx."

"How are such proceedings to be dealt with ? They

appeal to the mob. **The mob is not** to be swayed by polished arguments **or** incidental hints. **We** don't scare sparrows with a Zeus' head, though the eagle may recognize it as his lord's. A big Priapus is the figure required."

"And this," so Aristophanes resumes his defence, "comedy supplies. Comedy is **the** fit instrument of popular conviction : and the wilder, the more effective : since **it** is the worship of life, of the originative power **of** nature ; and since that power has lawlessness for its apparent **law.** Even Euripides, with his shirkings and his superiority, has **been** obliged to pay tribute **to the** real. He could not shake it off all at once. **He** tacked a Satyric play to **some** five **of** his fifty trilogies : and if this **was grim** enough at first, he threw **off** the mask in Alkestis, showing how one could be indecent in **a** decent way."[1]

For the reasons **above** given, which he farther expands and illustrates, Aristophanes chooses the " meaner muse " for his exponent. " And who, after all, is **the** worse for it ? Does he strangle **the** enemies **of** the **truth ?** No. **He** simply doses them with comedy, *i.e.* with words. Those who offend **in** words **he** pays back **in** them, exaggerating a little, but only so as to emphasize what he means ; just as love and hate use each other's terms, because those proper to themselves have grown unmeaning from constant use. And what is the ground of difference between Balaustion and himself ? Slender enough, in all probability, as he could show her, if they were discussing the question for themselves alone. As **it** is, Euripides has attacked him in the sight of the mob. His defence is addressed to it : he uses the arguments it can understand. It does not follow that they convey **a** literal statement of his own views. Euripides is not the only man who is **free** from

---

[1] A pure libel on this play, which is noted **for** its novel and successful attempt to represent humour without indecency. Aristophanes here alludes to the prevailing custom of concluding every group of three tragedies with a play in which the chorus consisted of Satyrs : a custom which Euripides broke through.

superstition. He too on occasion can show up the gods ; " and he describes the manner in which he will do this in his next play. All that is serious in the Apology is given in the concluding passage. " Whomever else he is hard upon, he will level nothing worse than a harmless parody at Sophocles, for he has no grudge against him :—

> ' He founds no anti-school, upsets no faith,
>  But, living, lets live,'          (vol. xiii. p. 110.)

And all his, Aristophanes', teaching is this :—

> '   .    .    .    .    .     accept the old,
>  Contest the strange ! acknowledge work that's done,
>  Misdoubt men who have still their work to do !'     (p. 111.)

He has summed up his case. Euripides must own himself beaten. If Balaustion will not admit the defeat, let her summon her rosy strength, and do her worst against his opponent."

Balaustion pauses for a moment before relating her answer to this challenge : and gives us to understand that, in thus relieving her memory, she is reproducing not only this special experience, but a great deal of what she habitually thinks and feels ; thus silencing any sense of the improbable, which so lengthened an argument accurately remembered, might create in the reader's mind.

Her tone is at first deprecating. " It is not for her, a mere mouse, to argue on a footing of equality with a forest monarch like himself. It is not for her to criticize the means by which his genius may attain its ends. She does not forget that the poet-class is that essentially which labours in the cause of human good. She does not forget that she is a woman, who may recoil from methods which a man is justified in employing. Lastly, she is a foreigner, and as such may blame many things simply because she does not understand them. She may yet have to learn that the tree stands firm at root, though its boughs dip and dance before the wind. She may yet have to learn that those who witness his **plays** have been **previously** braced to receive the good and reject the evil in them, like the freshly-bathed hand which passes unhurt through flame. She may judge fālsely from what she sees."

" But," she continues,[1] " let us imagine a remote future, and **a** far-away place—say the Cassiterides[2]—and men and women, lonely and ignorant—strangers **in very deed** —but with feelings similar **to our** own. **Let us** suppose that some work of Zeuxis or Pheidias **has been** trans- ported to their shores, and **that** they **are compelled to** acknowledge its excellence from its own point **of view—its** colouring true to nature, though not to their own type—its unveiled forms decorous, though not conforming **to their** own standard of decorum. Might **they not still, and** justly, tax it **on** its own ground **with some flaw or incon**- gruity, which proved the artist to have been human ? **And** may not **a** stranger, judging you in **the same way,** recog- nize in you one part of peccant humanity, poet **'three** parts divine' though you be?"

" You declare comedy to **be a** prescriptive rite, **coeval** in its birth with liberty. But the great days of Greek national life had been reached when comedy began. You declare also that you have refined on the early practice, and imported poetry into it. Comedy is therefore, as you defend it, not only a new invention, but your own. And, finally, you declare your practice of it inspired by a fixed purpose. You must stand or fall by the degree in which this purpose has been attained."

" You would, by means of comedy, discredit **war. Do** you stand alone in this endeavour?" And she quotes a beautiful passage from ' Cresphontes,' a play written by Euripides for the same end. " And how, respectively, have you sought your end? Euripides, by appealing to the

---

[1] The inverted commas include here, as elsewhere in the Apology, only the very condensed substance of Mr. Browning's words.

[2] Tin-islands. Scilly Islands, loosely speaking, Great Britain.

nobler feelings which are outraged by war; you, by expatiating on the animal enjoyments which accompany peace. The 'Lysistrata' is your equivalent for 'Cresphontes.' Do you imagine that its obscene allurements will promote the cause of peace? Not till heroes have become mean voluptuaries, and Cleonymos,[1] whom you yourself have derided, becomes their type."

"You would discredit vice and error, hypocrisy, sophistry and untruth. You expose the one in all its seductions, and the other in grotesque exaggerations, which are themselves a lie; showing yourself the worst of sophists —one who plays false to his own soul."

"You would improve on former methods of comedy. You have returned to its lowest form. For you profess to strike at folly, not at him who commits it: yet your tactics are precisely to belabour every act or opinion of which you disapprove, in the form of some one man. You pride yourself, in fact, on giving personal blows, instead of general and theoretical admonitions; and even here you seem incapable of hitting fair; you libel where you cannot honestly convict, and do not care how ignoble or how irrelevant the libel may be. Does the poet deserve criticism as such? Does he write bad verse, does he inculcate foul deeds? The cry is, 'he cannot read or write;' 'he is extravagant in buying fish;' 'he allows someone to help him with his verse, and make love to his wife in return;' 'his uncle deals in crockery;' 'his mother sold herbs' (one of his pet taunts against Euripides); 'he is a housebreaker, a footpad, or, worst of all, a stranger;'" —a term of contempt which, as Balaustion reminds him, has been repeatedly bestowed upon himself.

"What have you done," she continues, "beyond devoting the gold of your genius to work, which dross, in the person of a dozen predecessors or contemporaries,

---

[1] A demagogue of bad character attacked by Aristophanes; a big fellow and great coward.

has produced as well. Pun and parody, satire and invective, quaintness of fancy, and elegance, have each had its representative as successful **as you. Your life-work, until** this moment, has been the record of **a genius** increasingly untrue to its better self. Such satire as yours, however well intended, could advance no honest cause. Its exaggerations make it useless for either praise or **blame.** Its uselessness is proved by the result : your jokes **have re-**coiled upon yourself. The statues still stand which **your** mud has stained; the lightning **flash of truth can alone** destroy them. War still continues, **in** spite of the seductions with which you have invested peace. **Such improvements as are** in progress take an opposite direction to that which you prescribe. Public sense and decency **are only** bent on cleansing your sty."

And now her tone changes. " Has Euripides **succeeded** any better? None can say ; for he spoke **to a dim** future above and beyond the crowd. If he **fail, you two will** be fellows in adversity ; **and,** meanwhile, **I am** convinced that your wish unites **with his to waft the** white sail on its way.[1] Your nature, too, is kingly." She concludes with a tribute to the " Poet's Power," which **is** one with creative law, above and behind all potencies **of** heaven **and** earth; and to that inherent royalty of truth, in which alone she could venture to approach one so great as he. He too, as poet, must reign by truth, if he assert his proper sway.

> " Nor, even so, had boldness nerved my tongue,
> But that the other king stands suddenly
> In all the grand investiture of death,
> Bowing your knee beside my lowly head—
> Equals one moment ! "                 (vol. xiii. p. 144.)

Then she bids him "arise and go." Both have **done** homage to Euripides.

---

[1] White was the Greek colour of victory. This passage, not easily paraphrased, is a poetic recognition of the latent sympathy of Aristophanes with the good cause.

" Not so," he replies; "their discussion is not at an end. She has defended Euripides obliquely by attacking himself. Let her do it in a more direct fashion." This leads up to what seems to her the best defence possible: that reading of the " Herakles" which the entrance of Aristophanes had suspended. Its closing lines set Aristophanes musing. The chorus has said:

> " The greatest of all our friends of yore,
> We have lost for evermore !"                    (p. 231.)

" Who," he asks, " has been Athens' best friend? He who attracted her by the charm of his art, or he who repelled her by its severity?" He answers this by describing the relative positions of himself and Euripides in an image suggested by the popular game of Cottabos.[1] " The one was fixed within his 'globe;' the other adapted himself to its rotations. Euripides received his views of life through a single aperture, the one channel of ' High ' and ' Right.' Aristophanes has welcomed also the opposite impressions of ' Low' and ' Wrong,' and reproduced all in their turn. Some poet of the future, born perhaps in those Cassiterides, may defy the mechanics of the case, and place himself in such a position as to see high and low at once— be Tragic and Comic at the same time. But he meanwhile has been Athens' best friend—her wisest also—since he has not challenged failure by attempting what he could not perform. He has not risked the fate of Thamyris, who was punished for having striven with the higher powers, as if his vision had been equal to their own."[2] And he recites a fragment of song, which Mr. Browning unfortunately has not completed, describing the fiery rap-

---

[1] A game said to be of Sicilian origin and played in many ways. Details of it may be found in Becker's "Charikles," vol. ii.

[2] Thamyris of Thrace, said to have been blinded by the Muses for contending with them in song. The incident is given in the " Iliad," and was treated again by Sophocles, as Aristophanes also relates.

ture in which that poet marched, all unconscious, **to his**
doom. Some laughing promise and prophecy ensues, **and**
Aristophanes departs, in the 'rose-streaked morning grey,'
bidding the couple farewell till **the** coming year.

That year has come **and** gone. Sophocles **has died**:
and Aristophanes **has** attained his final triumph in the
"Frogs"—a play flashing with every variety of his genius
—as softly musical in the mystics' chorus **as** croaking **in**
that of the frogs—in which Bacchus himself is ridiculed,
and Euripides is more coarsely handled **than** ever. And
once more the voice of Euripides has interposed between
the Athenians and their doom.[2] When Ægos Potamos
had been fought, and Athens **was** in Spartan hands,
Euthykles flung the "choric flower" of the "Electra" **in**
the face of the foe, and

> " . . . because Greeks are Greeks, though Sparté's brood,
> And hearts are hearts, though in Lusandros' breast,
> And poetry is power,    .    .    . '     (p. 253.)

**the** city itself was spared. But when tragedy ceased,
comedy was allowed its work, and it danced **away the**
Piræan bulwarks, which were demolished, by Lysander's
command, to the sound of the flute.

And now Euthykles and Balaustion are nearing Rhodes.
Their master lies buried in the land to which they have
bidden farewell ; but the winds and waves of their island
home bear witness to his immortality : for theirs seems the
voice of nature, re-echoing the cry, "There **are no** gods,
**no** gods !" his prophetic, if unconscious, tribute to the One
God, "who saves" him.

Balaustion has no genuine historic personality. She is
simply what Mr. Browning's purpose required : a large-
souled woman, who could be supposed to echo his appreciation of these two opposite forms of genius, and express
his judgments upon them. But the Euripides she de-

---

[2] This also is historical.

picts is entirely constructed from his works; while her
portrait of Aristophanes shows him not only as his works
reflect, but as contemporary criticism represented him;
he is one of the most vivid of Mr. Browning's characters.
The two transcripts from Euripides seem enough to prove
that that poet was far more human than Aristophanes
professed to think; but the belief of Aristophanes in
the practical asceticism of his rival was in some degree
justified by popular opinion, if not in itself just; and we
can understand his feeling at once rebuked and irritated
by a contempt for the natural life which carried with it so
much religious and social change.  Aristophanes was a
believer in the value of conservative ideas, though not
himself a slave to them.  He was also a great poet,
though often very false to his poetic self.  Such a man
might easily fancy that one like Euripides was untrue to
the poetry, because untrue to the joyousness of existence;
and that he shook even the foundations of morality by
reasoning away the religious conceptions which were
bound up with natural joys.  The impression we receive
from Aristophanes' Apology is that he is defending something which he believes to be true, though conscious of
defending it by sophistical arguments, and of having enforced it by very doubtful deeds; and we also feel that
from his point of view, and saving his apparent incon-
sistencies, Mr. Browning is in sympathy with him.  At
the same time, Balaustion's rejoinder is unanswerable, as
it is meant to be; and the double monologue distinguishes
itself from others of the same group, by being not only
more dramatic and more emotional, but also more con-
clusive; it is the only one of them in which the question
raised is not, in some degree, left open.

The poem bristles with local allusions and illustrations
which puzzle the non-classical reader.  I add an explana-
tory index to some names of things and persons which
have not occurred in my brief outline of it.

Vol. xiii. **p. 4.** *Koré.* (Virgin.) Name given to Per-
sephoneé. **In** Latin, Proserpina.

P. 6. *Dikast* and *Heliast.* Dicast = Judge, Heliast =
Juryman, in Athens.

P. 7. 1. *Kordax-step.* 2. *Propulaia.* (Propylaia.) **1.**
An indecent dance. **2.** Gateway of the Acropolis. **3.**
*Pnux.* (Pnyx.) 4. *Bema.* 3. Place for **the** Popular
Assembly. 4. Place whence speeches were made.

P. 8 *Makaria.* Heroine in a play **of** Euripides, **who**
killed herself for her country's sake.

**P. 10.** 1. *Milesian smart-place.* **2.** *Phrunikos.* **(Phry-**
nicus.) 1. The painful remembrance of the capture **of**
Miletus. **2. A** dramatic poet, who made this capture the
subject of a tragedy, "which, when performed (493), **so**
painfully wrung the feelings of the Athenian audience
that they burst into tears in the theatre, and **the** poet was
condemned **to** pay **a** fine of 1,000 drachmai, **as** having
recalled **to** them their own misfortunes." [1] **He is** derided
by Aristophanes in the "Frogs" for his method of introducing his characters.

**P. 12.** *Amphitheos, Deity, and Dung.* A character in
the Acharnians of Aristophanes—"not **a god, and yet**
immortal."

P. 14. 1. *Diaulos.* 2. *Stade.* 1. A double line of the
Race-course. 2. The *Stadium*, on reaching which, the
runner went back again.

P. 16. *City of Gapers.* Nickname of Athens, from the
curiosity of its inhabitants.

P. 17. *Koppa-marked.* Race-horses of the best breed
were marked with the old letter Koppa.

**P. 18.** *Comic Platon.* The comic writer of that name :
author of plays and poems, *not* THE Plato.

P. 21. *Salabaccho.* Name of a courtesan.

P. 30. *Cheek-band.* Band worn by trumpeters to support the checks. *Cuckoo-apple.* Fruit so-called = fool-making food. *Threttanelo, Neblaretai.* Imitative sounds : 1. Of a harp-string. 2. Of any joyous cry. *Three-days' salt-fish slice.* Allowance of a soldier on an expedition. (It was supposed that at the end of this time he could forage for himself.)

P. 31. *Goat's breakfast and other abuse.* Indecent allusions, to be fancied, not explained.

P. 32. *Sham Ambassadors.* Characters in the Acharnians. *Kudathenian.* Famous Athenian. *Pandionid.* Descendant of Pandion, King of Athens. *Goat-Song.* Tragœdia—Tradegy. It was called goat-song because a goat-skin, probably filled with wine, was once given as a prize for it. The expression occurs in Shelley.

P. 33. *Willow-Wicker Flask.* Nickname of the poet it is applied to, a toper.

P. 36. *Lyric Shell or Tragic Barbiton.* Lesser and larger lyre.

P. 38. *Sousarion.* Susarion of Megara, inventor of Attic comedy. *Chionides.* His successor.

P. 39. *Little-in-the-Fields.* The Dionysian Feast ; a lesser one than the City Dionysia.

P. 40. *Ameipsias.* A comic poet, contemporary with Aristophanes, whose two best plays he beat.

P. 42. *Iostephanos.* "Violet-crowned," name of Athens. *Kleophon.* A demagogue of bad character, attacked by Aristophanes as profligate, and an enemy of peace. *Kleonumos.* A similar character ; also a big fellow, and great coward.

P. 43. *Telekleides.* Old comic poet, on the same side as Aristophanes. *Mullos and Euetes.* Comic poets who revived the art of comedy in Athens after Susarion.

P. 44. *Morucheides.* Son of Morychus—like his father, a comic poet and a glutton. *Sourakosios.* Another comic poet.

P. 46. *Trilophos.* Wearer **of** three crests **on** his helmet.

P. 47. *Ruppapai.* Word used by the crew in rowing—hence, the crew itself.

P. 49. *Free dinner in the Prutaneion.* (Prytaneion.) Such was accorded to certain privileged persons. *Ariph_rades.* A man of infamous character, singer to the harp : persistently attacked by Aristophanes. *Karkinos.* Comic actor : had famous dancing sons.

P. 50. *Exomis.* A woman's garment. ***Parachoregema.*** Subordinate chorus, which sings in the absence of the principal one. *Aristullos.* Bad character satirized by Aristophanes, and used in one of his plays **as** a travesty of Plato. This incident, and Plato's amused indifference, **are** mentioned at p. 137 **of** the Apology.

P. 51. *Murrhine, Akalantis.* **Female** names in the Thesmophoriazusae. *New Kalligeneia.* **Name** given to Ceres, meaning, "bearer of lovely **children.**" *The Toxotes.* A Syrian archer **in the** "Thesmophoriazusae." *The Great King's Eye.* Mock name given to **an** ambassador from Persia in **the** Acharnians. *Kompolakuthes.* Bully-boaster : with a play on the name of Lamachus.

P. 52. *Silphion.* A plant used as **a** relish. ***Kleon-Clapper.*** Corrector of Kleon.

P. 54. *Trugaios.* Epithet of Bacchus, "vintager ;" here name of a person in the comedy of "Peace." *Story of Simonides.* Simonides, **the** lyric poet, sang an ode to his patron, Scopas, **at** a feast ; and as he had introduced into it the praises of Castor and Pollux, Scopas declared that he would only pay his own half-share of the ode, and the Demi-gods might pay the remainder. Presently it was announced to Simonides that **two** youths desired to see him outside the palace ; on going there he found nobody, but meanwhile the palace fell in, killing his patron. Thus was he *paid.*

P. 58. *Maketis.* Capital of Macedonia.

P. 60. *Lamachos.* General who fell at the siege of Syracuse; satirized by Aristophanes as a brave, but boastful man.

P. 67. *Sophroniskos' Son.* Socrates.

P. 74. *Kephisophon.* Actor, and friend of Euripides; enviously reported to help him in writing his plays.

P. 79. *Palaistra.* A wrestling-school, or place of exercise.

P. 82. *San.* Letter distinguishing race-horses. *Thearion's Meal-Tub Politics.* Politics of Thearion the baker. *Pisthetarios.* Character in the " Birds," alias " Mr. Persuasive." *Strephsiades.* Character in the " Clouds."

P. 83. *Rocky ones.* Epithet given to the Athenians.

P. 85. *Promachos.* Champion.

P. 86. *The Boulé.* State Council. *Prodikos.* Prodicus. A Sophist, satirized in the "Birds" and "Clouds."

P. 87. *Choes.* Festival at Athens. "The Pitchers."

P. 89. *Plataian help.* The Plataeans sent a thousand well appointed warriors to help at Marathon. The term stands for *timely* help.

P. 94. *Plethron square.* 100 feet square.

P. 98. *Palaistra tool.* Tool used at the Palaistra, or wrestling school : in this case the strigil.

P. 99. *Phales. Iacchos.* Two epithets of Bacchus— the former indecent.

P. 112. *Kinesias.* According to Aristophanes, a bad profligate lyric poet, notable for his leanness.

P. 113. *Rattei.* Like " Neblaretai," an imitative or gibberish word expressing joyous excitement. *Aristonumos. Sannurion.* Two comic poets, the latter ridiculed by Aristophanes for his leanness.

P. 124. *Parabasis.* Movement of the chorus, wherein the Coryphœus came forward and spoke in the poet's name.

P. 128.  *Skiadeion.*  Sunshade.  Parasol.

P. 129.  *Theoria. Opora.*  Characters in the Eirené or "Peace:" the first personifying games, spectacles, sights; the second, plenty, fruitful autumn, and so on.

**P.** 133.  *Philokleon.*  Lover of Kleon. (Cleon.) *Bdelukleon.*  Reviler of Kleon.

P. 135.  *Logeion.*  Front **of the** stage **occupied by the** actors.

P. 137.  *Kukloboros-roaring.*  Roaring like the torrent Cycloborus (in Attica).

P. 140.  *Konnos.*  The play by Ameipsias which beat the "Clouds." *Euthumenes.*  One who refused **the** pay of the comic writers, while he tripled that of those who attended at the Assembly. *Argurrhios.* **As** before. *Kinesias.* **As** before.

P. 144.  *Triballos.*  A supposed *country* **and** clownish god.

P. 172.  *Propula.*  (Propyla.)  Gateway to **the Acro-**polis.

P. 248.  *Elaphebolion month.*  The "Stag-striking" month.

P. 249.  *Bakis prophecy.*  Foolish prophecies attributed to one Bacis, rife at that time; a collective name for all such.

P. 255.  *Kommos.*  **General weeping—by the** chorus and an actor.

## "FIFINE AT THE FAIR."

" Fifine at the Fair " is a defence of inconstancy, or of the right of experiment in love ; and is addressed by a husband to his wife, whose supposed and very natural comments the monologue reflects. The speaker's implied name of Don Juan sufficiently tells us what we are meant to think of his arguments ; and they also convict themselves by landing him in an act of immorality, which brings its own punishment. This character is nevertheless a standing puzzle to Mr. Browning's readers, because that which he condemns in it, and that which he does not, are not to be distinguished from each other. It is impossible to see where Mr. Browning ends and where Don Juan begins. The reasoning is scarcely ever that of a heartless or profligate person, though it very often betrays an unconsciously selfish one. It treats love as an education still more than as a pleasure ; and if it lowers the standard of love, or defends too free an indulgence in it, it does so by asserting what is true for imaginative persons, though not for the commonplace: that whatever stirs even a sensuous admiration appeals also to the artistic, the moral, and even the religious nature. Its obvious sophistries are mixed up with the profoundest truths, and the speaker's tone has often the tenderness of one who, with all his inconstancy, has loved deeply and long. We can only solve the problem by referring to the circumstances in which the idea of the poem arose.

Mr. Browning was, with his family, at Pornic many years ago, and there saw the gipsy who is the original of Fifine. His fancy was evidently sent roaming, by her audacity, her strength—the contrast which she presented to the more

spiritual types of womanhood ; and this contrast even-
tually found expression in a poetic theory of life, in which
these opposite types and their corresponding modes of
attraction became the necessary complement of each .
other.   As he laid down the theory, Mr. Browning would
be speaking in his own person.   But he would turn into
someone else in the act of working it out —for it insensibly
carried with it a plea for yielding to those opposite attractions, not only successively, but at the same time ;  and a
modified Don Juan would grow up under his pen, thinking in some degree his thoughts, using in some degree his
language, and only standing out as a distinctive character
at the end of the poem.   The higher type of womanhood
must appear in the story, at the same time as the lower
which is represented by Fifine ;  and Mr. Browning would
instinctively clothe it in the form which first suggested or
emphasized the contrast.   He would soon, however, feel
that the vision was desecrated by the part it was called
upon to play.   He would disguise or ward it off when
possible : now addressing Elvire by her husband's mouth,
in the terms of an ideal companionship, now again reducing her to the level of an every-day injured wife ; and when
the dramatic Don Juan was about to throw off the mask,
the flickering wifely personality would be extinguished
altogether, and the unfaithful husband left face to face
with the mere phantom of conscience which, in one sense,
Elvire is always felt to be.   This is what actually occurs ;
and only from this point of view can we account for the
perpetual encroaching of the imaginary on the real, the
real on the imaginary, which characterizes the work.

A fanciful prologue, "Amphibian," strikes its key-note.
The writer imagines himself floating on the sea, pleasantly
conscious of his bodily existence, yet feeling unfettered by
it. A strange beautiful butterfly floats past him in the air ;
her radiant wings can be only those of a soul ; and it
strikes him that while the waves are his property, and the

air is hers, hers is true freedom, his only the mimicry of it. He sees little to regret in this, since imagination is as good as reality ; and Heaven itself can only be made up of such things as poets dream. Yet he knows that his swimming seems but a foolish compromise between the flight to which he cannot attain, and the more grovelling mode of being which he has no real wish to renounce ; and he wonders whether she, the already released, who is upborne by those sunlit wings, does not look down with pity and wonder upon him. So also will Elvire, though less dispassionately, watch the intellectual vagaries of her Don Juan, which embrace the heavens, but are always centred in earth. This prologue is preceded by a quotation from Molière's "Don Juan," in which Elvire satirically prescribes to her lover the kind of self-defence—or something not unlike it—which Mr. Browning's hero will adopt.

Don Juan invites his wife to walk with him through the fair : and as he points out its sights to her, he expatiates on the pleasures of vagrancy, and declares that the red pennon waving on the top of the principal booth sends an answering thrill of restlessness through his own frame. He then passes to a glowing eulogium on the charms of the dark-skinned rope-dancer, Fifine, who forms part of the itinerant show.

Elvire gives tokens of perturbation, and her husband frankly owns that as far as Fifine is concerned, he cannot defend his taste : he can scarcely account for it. " Beautiful she is, in her feminine grace and strength, set forth by her boyish dress ; but with probably no more feeling than a sprite, and no more conscience than a flower. It is likely enough that her antecedents have been execrable, and that her life is in harmony with them." Still, he does not wish it supposed that he admires a body without a soul : and he tries to convince himself that Fifine, after all, is not quite without one. "There is no grain of sand

on the sea-shore which may not, once in a century, be the
first to flash back the rising sun ; there can be no human
spirit which does not in the course of its existence **greet**
the Divine light with one answering ray."

**But no** heavenly spark can be detected in Fifine ; **and**
he is reduced to seeking a virtue for her, a justification
for himself, in that very fact.  If she has **no virtue, she**
also pretends **to** none.  If she gives nothing to **society,**
she asks nothing of it.  His fancy raises up a procession
of such women as the world has crowned : **a Helen, a**
Cleopatra, some Christian saint ; **he bids Elvire see her-**
self as part of it—as the true Helen, who, according to the
legend, never quitted Greece, contemplated her own phantom within the walls of Troy—and be satisfied that she is
" best " of all.  " All alike are wanting in one grace **which**
Fifine possesses : that of self-effacement.  Helen and Cleopatra demand unquestioning homage for their **own mental**
as well as bodily charms ; the saint demands it for the principle she sets forth.  His love demands that he shall see
into her heart ; his wife that he shall believe the impossible
as regards her own powers of devotion.  Fifine says, ' You
come to look at my outside, my foreign face and figure
my outlandish limbs.  Pay for the sight **if** it has pleased
you, and give me credit for nothing beyond what you see.'
So simply honest an appeal must touch his heart."

Don Juan well knows what his wife thinks of all this,
and he says it for her.  " Fifine attracts him for **no** such
out of the way reason.  Her charm is that she is something new, and something which does not belong **to** him.
He is the soul of inconstancy ; and if he had the sun **for**
his own, he would hanker after other light, were it that of
a tallow-candle or a squib."  But he assures her that this
reasoning is unsound, and his amusing himself with a
lower thing does not prove that **he** has become indifferent
to the higher.  He shows this by reminding her of a picture of Raphael's, which he was mad to possess ; which

now that he possesses it, he often neglects for a picture-book of Doré's ; but which, if threatened with destruction, he would save at the sacrifice of a million Dorés, perhaps of his own life. And now he turns back to her phantom self, as present in his own mind ; describes it in terms of exquisite grace and purity ; and declares hers the one face which fits into his heart, and makes whole what would be half without it.

Elvire is conciliated ; but her husband will not leave well alone. He has established her full claim to his admiration : but he is going to prove that so far as her physical charms are concerned, she owes it to his very attachment : "for those charms are not attested by her looking-glass. He discovers them by the eye of love—in other words—by the artist soul within him."

All beauty, Don Juan farther explains, is in the imagination of him who feels it, be he lover or artist ; be the beauty he descries the attribute of a living face, of a portrait, or of some special arrangement of sound. The feeling is inspired by its outward objects, but it cannot be retraced to them. It is a fancy created by fact, as flame by fuel ; no more identical with it. The fancy is not on that account a delusion. It is the vision of ideal truth : the recognition by an inner sense of that which does not exist for the outer. That is why hearts choose each other by help of the face, and why they choose so diversely. The eye of love, which again is the eye of art, reads soul into the features, however incomplete their expression of it may be. It reconstructs the ideal type which nature has failed to carry out.

He illustrates this by means of three faces roughly sketched in the sand. At first sight they are grotesque and unmeaning. Yet a few more strokes of the broken pipe which is serving him as a pencil, will give to two of these a predominating expression ; convert the third into a likeness of Elvire.

" These completing touches represent the artist's action upon life. By this method Don Juan has been enabled, on a former occasion, to complete a work of high art. A block of marble had come into his possession, half shaped **by** the hand of Michael Angelo.

" .    .    . One hand,—the Master's,—smoothed and scraped
That mass, he hammered on and hewed at, till he hurled
Life out of death, and left a challenge : for the world,
Death still,—    .    .    .    .    . "  (vol. **xi.** p. 260.)

Not death to him : for as he gazed **on** the rough-hewn block, a form emerged upon his mental sight—a form which he interpreted as that of the goddess Eidotheé.[1] And as his soul received it from that of the dead master, his hand carried it out."

Mr. Browning's whole theory of artistic perception **is** contained in the foregoing lines ; but **he** proceeds **to** enforce it in another **way.** " The life thus evoked **from** death, the beauty from ugliness, is the gain **of** each special soul —its permanent conquest over matter. The mode of effecting this is the special secret of every soul ; and this Don Juan defines as its chemic secret, the law of **its** affinities, the law of its actions and reactions. Where **one, he** says, lights force, another draws forth pity ; where one finds food for self-indulgence, another acquires strength for self-sacrifice. One blows life's ashes into rose-coloured flame, another into less heavenly hues. Love will have reached its height when the secret of each soul has become the knowledge of all ; and the many-coloured rays of individual experience are fused in the white light **of** universal truth."

Here again Don Juan imagines a retort. Elvire makes short work of his poetic theories, and declares that this professed interest in souls is a mere pretext for the grati-

[1] Eidotheé or Eidothea, is the daughter of Proteus—the old man of the sea. A legend concerning her is found in the 4th book of the Odyssey.

fication of sense. "Whom in heaven's name is he trying to take in?" He entreats music to take his part.
" It alone can pierce the mists of falsehood which intervene
between the soul and truth. And now, as they stroll home-
wards in the light of the setting sun, all things seem
charged with those deeper harmonies—with those vital
truths of existence which words are powerless to convey.
Elvire, however, has no soul for music, and her husband
must have recourse to words."

The case between them may, he thinks, be stated in this
question, "How do we rise from falseness into truth?" "We
do so after the fashion of the swimmer who brings his
nostrils to the level of the upper air, but leaves the rest of
his body under water—by the act of self-immersion in the
very element from which we wish to escape. Truth is
to the aspiring soul as the upper air to the swimmer : the
breath of life. But if the swimmer attempts to free his
head and arms, he goes under more completely than
before. If the soul strives to escape from the grosser
atmosphere into the higher, she shares the same fate. Her
truthward yearnings plunge her only deeper into falsehood.
Body and soul must alike surrender themselves to an element in which they cannot breathe, for this element can
alone sustain them. But through the act of plunging we
float up again, with a deeper disgust at the briny taste we
have brought back ; with a deeper faith in the life above,
and a deeper confidence in ourselves, whom the coarser
element has proved unable to submerge."

" Suppose again, that as we paddle with our hands under
water, we grasp at something which seems a soul. The
piece of falsity slips through our fingers, but by the mechanical reaction just described, it sends us upwards into
the realm of truth. This is precisely what Fifine has
done. Of the earth earthy as she is, she has driven you
and me into the realms of abstract truth. We have thus
no right to despise her " This discourse is interrupted

by a contemptuous allusion **to a** passage in " Childe
Harold," (fourth canto), in which the human intelligence is
challenged to humble itself before the ocean.

Elvire is still dissatisfied.   The suspicious fact remains,
that whatever experience her husband desires to gain, it is
always a woman who must supply it.   This he frankly
admits ; and he gives his reason.   " Women lend **them-**
selves to experiment ; men do not.   Men are egotists, **and**
absorb whatever comes in their way.   Women, whether
Fifines **or** Elvires, allow themselves to **be absorbed.**   **You**
master men only by reducing yourself to their level.   **You**
captivate women by showing yourself at your best.   **Their**
power of hero-worship **is** illustrated by the **act of the**
dolphin, ' True woman creature,' which bore **the ship-**
wrecked Arion **to the** Corinthian **coast.**   Men **are not only**
wanting in true love : their best powers are **called forth**
by hate.   They resemble **the** vine, first ' stung ' into '**fer-**
tility' by the browsing **goat,** which nibbled away **its** ten-
drils, and gained the ' indignant wine' **by** the process.   **In**
their feminine characteristics Elvire stands far higher
than Fifine ; **but** Fifine is for that **very** reason more useful
as a means **of** education ; for Elvire **may** be trusted im-
plicitly ; Fifine teaches one to take care **of** himself.   **They**
are to each other as the strong ship and the little rotten
bark."   This comparison is suggested by a boatman whom
they lately saw adventurously pushing his way through
shoal and sandbank because he would not wait for the tide.

Don Juan begs leave to speak one word more in defence
of Fifine and her masquerading tribe ; it will recall his
early eulogium on her frankness.   " All men are actors :
but these alone do **not** deceive.   **All** you are expected
to applaud in them is the excellence **of the** avowed
sham."

Don Juan has thus developed **his** theory that soul is
attainable through flesh, truth through falsehood, the real
through what only seems ; and, as he thinks, justified the

conclusion that a man's spiritual life is advanced by every experience, moral or immoral, which comes in his way. He now relates a dream by which, as he says, those abstract reflections have been in part inspired; in reality, it continues, and in some degree refutes them. The dream came to him this morning when he had played himself to sleep with Schumann's Carnival; having chosen this piece because his brain was burdened with many thoughts and fancies which, better than any other, it would enable him to work off; and as he tells this, he enlarges on the faculty of music to register, as well as express, every passing emotion of the human soul. He notes also the constant recurrence of the same old themes, and the caprice of taste which strives as constantly to convert them into something new.

The dream carries him to Venice, and he awakes, in fancy, on some pinnacle above St. Mark's Square, overlooking the Carnival. Here his power of artistic divination—alias of human sympathy, is called into play; for the men and women below him all wear the semblance of some human deformity, of some animal type, or of some grotesque embodiment of human feeling or passion. He throws himself into their midst, and these monstrosities disappear. The human asserts itself; the brute-like becomes softened away; what imperfection remains creates pity rather than disgust. He finds that by shifting his point of view, he can see even necessary qualities in what otherwise struck him as faults.

Another change takes place: one felt more easily than defined; and he becomes aware that he is looking not on Venice, but on the world, and that what seemed her Carnival is in reality the masquerade of life. The change goes on. Halls and temples are transformed beneath his gaze. The systems which they represent: religions, philosophies, moralities, and theories of art, collapse before him, re-form and collapse again. He sees that the deepest truth can only build on sand, though itself is stationed on a rock ; and can only assert its substance in the often changing forms of error. The vision seems to declare that change is the Law of Life.

" Not so," it was about to say. " That law is permanence." The scene has resembled the forming and reforming, the blending and melting asunder of a pile of sunset clouds. Like these, when the sun has set, it is subsiding into a fixed repose, a stern and colourless uniformity. Temple, tower, and dwelling-house assume the form of one solitary granite pile, a Druid monument. This monument, as Mr. Browning describes it,[1] consists really of two, so standing or lying as to form part of each other. The one cross-shaped is supposed to have been sepulchral, or in some other way sacred to death. The latter, on which he mainly dwells, was until lately, the centre of a rude nature-worship, and is therefore consecrated to life. It symbolizes life in its most active and most perennial form. It means the force which aspires to heaven, and the strength which is rooted in the earth. It means that impulse of all being towards something outside itself, which is constant amidst all change, uniform amidst all variety. It means the last word of the scheme of creation, and therefore also the first. It repeats and concludes the utterance already sounding in the spectator's ear :—

> "  .     .     . ' All's change, but permanence as well.'
> —Grave note whence—list aloft !—harmonics sound, that mean :
> Truth inside, and outside, truth also ; and between
> Each, falsehood that is change, as truth is permanence.
> The individual soul works through the shows of sense,
> (Which, ever proving false, still promise to be true)
> Up to an outer soul as individual too;
> And, through the fleeting, lives to die into the fixed,
> And reach at length 'God, man, or both together mixed,'"[2]   (p. 332.

.     .     .     .     .     .     .     .

---

[1] There is such a monument at Pornic.
[2] These words are taken from a line in the Prometheus of Æschylus.

The condition of this monument, its history, the conjectures to which it has given rise, are described in a humorous spirit which belies its mystic significance; but that significance is imbedded in the very conception of the poem, and distinctly expressed in the author's subsequent words. The words which I have just quoted contain the whole philosophy of " Fifine at the Fair " as viewed on its metaphysical side. They declare the changing relations of the soul to some fixed eternal truth foreshadowed in the impulses of sense. They are the burden of Don Juan's argument even when he is defending what is wrong. They are the constantly recurring keynote of what the author has meant to say.

Don Juan draws also a new and more moral lesson from this final vision of his dream. " Inconstancy is not justified by natural law, for it means unripeness of soul. The ripe soul evolves the Infinite from a fixed point. It finds the many in the one. Elvire is the *one* who includes the *many.* Elvire is the ocean : while Fifine is but the foamflake which the ocean can multiply at pleasure. Elvire shall henceforth suffice to him."

But here, as elsewhere, he makes a great mistake : that of confusing nature with the individual man. Her instability supplied him with no excuse for being inconstant, and her permanence gives him no motive for constancy ; and he proves this in another moment by breaking bounds no longer in word only, but in deed. It turns out that he had put gold as well as silver into Fifine's tambourine. The result, intended or not, has been a letter slipped into his hand. He claims five minutes to go and " clear the matter up ; " exceeds the time, and on returning finds his punishment in an empty home.

This at least, we seem intended to infer. For Elvire has already startled him by assuming the likeness of a phantom, and he gives her leave, in case he breaks his word, to vanish away altogether. The story ends here ;

but its epilogue " The Householder" depicts a widowed
husband, grotesquely miserable, fetched home by his departed wife ; and his identity with **Don** Juan seems unmistakable.    This scene is more humorous than pathetic,
**as** befits the dramatic **spirit** of the poem ; but the most
serious purport and most comprehensive meaning **of**
" Fifine at the Fair" **are** summed up in its closing words.
The " householder" **is** composing his epitaph, and his
wife thus concludes **it :** " Love is **all,** and Death **is**
nought."


## " PRINCE HOHENSTIEL-SCHWANGAU,
## SAVIOUR **OF** SOCIETY."

" Prince Hohenstiel-Schwangau **"** is a defence **of the**
doctrine of expediency : and the monologue is supposed
**to** be carried on by the late Emperor of the French, under
this feigned name.    Louis Napoleon is musing over past
and present, and blending them with each other in a
waking dream.  He seems in exile again.  But the events of
his reign are all, or **for** the most part behind him, and
they have earned for him the title **of** " inscrutable."    A
young lady of an adventurous type has crossed his path,
in the appropriate region **of** Leicester Square.    Some
adroit flattery on her side has disposed him to confidence,
and he is proving to her, over tea and cigars, that he is not
so " inscrutable" after all ; or, if he be, that the key to the
enigma **is a** simple one.    " This wearer of crinoline seems
destined to play Œdipus to the Sphinx he is supposed to
be ; **" or** better still, as he gallantly adds, the " Lais " for
whose sake he will unveil the mystery unasked.    The
situation he thus assumes is not dignified ; but as Mr.
Browning probably felt, his choice of a *confidante* suits

M

the nature of what he has to tell, as well as the circumstances in which he tells it.  Politically, he has lived from
hand to mouth.  So in a different way has she.  A very
trifling incident enables him to illustrate his confession,
which will proceed without interruption on the listener's
part.

They are sitting at a table with writing materials upon
it.  Among these lies a piece of waste-paper.  Prince
Hohenstiel descries upon it two blots, takes up a pen, and
draws a line from one to the other.  This simple, half-
mechanical act is, as he declares, a type of his whole life;
it contains the word of the enigma.  His constant principle
has been : not to strive at creating anything new ; not to
risk marring what already existed ; but to adapt what he
found half made and to continue it.  In other words, he
has been a sustainer or "saviour," not a reformer of
society.

Many pages are devoted to the statement and vindication of this fact, and they contain everything that can be
said, from a religious or practical point of view, in favour
of taking the world as we find it.  Prince Hohenstiel's
first argument is : that he has not the genius of a reformer,
and it is a man's first duty to his Creator to do that only
which he can do best ; his second : that sweeping reforms
are in themselves opposed to the creative plan, because
they sacrifice everything to one leading idea, and aim at
reducing to one pattern those human activities which God
has intended to be multiform ; the third and strongest :
that the scheme of existence with all its apparent evils is
God's work, and no man can improve upon it.  There
have been, he admits, revolutions in the moral as well as
the physical world ;  and inspired reformers, who were
born to carry them on ; but these men are rare and portentous as the physical agencies to which they correspond,
and whether " dervish (desert-spectre), swordsman, saint,
lawgiver," or "lyrist," appear only when the time is ripe

for them. Meanwhile, the great machine advances by means of the minute springs, the revolving wheel-work, of individual lives. Let each of these be content with its limited sphere. God is with each and all.

And Prince Hohenstiel has another and still stronger reason for not desiring to tamper with the existing order of things. He finds it good. He loves existence as he knows it, with its mysteries and its beauties ; its complex causes and incalculable effects ; the good it extracts from evil ; the virtue it evolves from suffering. He reveres that Temple of God's own building, from which deploys the ever varying procession of human life. If the temple be intricate in its internal construction, if its architectural fancies impede our passage ; if they make us stumble or even fall ; his invariable advice is this : " Throw light on the stumbling-blocks ; fix your torch above them at such points as the architect approves. But do not burn them away." He considers himself therefore, not a very great man, but a useful one : one possessing on a small scale the patience of an Atlas, if not the showy courage of a Hercules : one whose small achievements pave the way for the great ones.

Thus far the imaginary speaker so resembles Mr. Browning himself, that we forget for the moment that we are not dealing with him ; and his vicarious testimony to the value of human life lands him, at page 145, in a personal protest against the folly which under cover of poetry seeks to run it down. He lashes out against the " bard " who can rave about inanimate nature as something greater than man ; and who talks of the "unutterable" impressions conveyed by the ocean, as greater than the intelligence and sympathy, the definite thoughts and feelings which *can* be uttered. The lines from " Childe Harold " which will be satirized in " Fifine at the Fair " are clearly haunting him here. But we shall now pass on to more historic ground.

It is a natural result of these opinions that Prince Hohenstiel-Schwangau regards life as the one boon which contains every other ; and that the material prosperity of his people has been the first object by which his "sustaining" policy was inspired. He does not deny that even within the limits thus imposed, some choice of cause or system seemed open to him. " It seemed open to him to choose between religion and free-thought, between monarchy and government by the people : and to throw his energies entirely into one scale or the other, instead of weighting one and the other by turns. It could justly have been urged that the simpler aim is included in the more complex, and that he would promote the interests of his subjects by serving them from the wider, rather than from the narrower point of view."

" But what is true in theory is not always so in practice. He has loved a cause, and believed in it—the cause of united Italy ; and so long as he was free to express sympathy with this—so long, his critics say, as he was a mere voice, with air to float in, and no obstacle to bar his way —he expressed it from the bottom of his soul. But with the power to act—with the firm ground wheron to act— came also the responsibilities of action : the circumstance by which it must be controlled. He saw the wants of his people ; the eyes which craved light alone, and the mouths which craved only bread. He felt that the ideal must yield to the real, the remote to what was near ; and the work of Italian deliverance remained incomplete. It was his very devotion to the one principle which brought the reproach of vacillation upon him."

" He broke faith with his people too "—so his critics continue—" for he supplied food to their bodies ; but withheld the promised liberties of speech and writing which would have brought nourishment to their souls."

And again he answers that he gave them what they wanted most. He gave them that which would enable them to acquire freedom of soul, **and without** which such freedom would have been useless.

He concedes something, however, **to** reformers **by** declaring, as his final excuse, that he **would not have** thus yielded **to** circumstances if the average **life of** man were a hundred years instead of twenty; for, given suffi- cient time, all adverse circumstance may be overcome. "The body dies if it be thwarted. Mind—in other **words,** intellectual truth—triumphs through opposition. **Envy,** hatred, and stupidity, are to it as the rocks which obstruct the descending stream, and toss it in jewelled spray above the chasm by which it **is** confined. Abstract thinkers have therefore their rights also; and it is well that those, in some respects, greater and better men than **he, who** are engaged in the improvement **of the** world, should **find** success enough **to** justify their **hopes;** failure enough **to** impose caution on **their** endeavours."

The Prince confesses once for **all,** that **since** improve- ment is so necessarily limited; since **the higher** life is incompatible with life in the flesh : he **is** content **to wait** for the higher life and make the **best he** can of the **lower.** But if anyone declares that this quiescent attitude means indolence or sleep, his judgment is on a par with that which was once passed on the famous statue of the Lao- coon. Some artist had covered the accessories of the group, and left only the contorted central figure, with nothing to explain its contortions. One **man** said as **he** looked upon it,

> ". . . I think the gesture strives
> Against some obstacle we cannot **see.**" (p. 172.)

Every other spectator pronounced the "gesture" a yawn.

Prince Hohenstiel gives us a second proof that he is not without belief in the ideal. He accepts the doctrine of evolution : though not in its scientific sense. He likes the idea of having felt his way up to humanity **(as he** now feels his way in it) through progressive forms of existence; he being always himself, and nowise the thing he dwelt in. He likes to account in this manner for the feeling of kinship which attracts him to all created things. It also completes his vision of mankind as fining off at the summit into isolated peaks, but held together at the base by its common natural life; and thus confirms him in the impression that the personal needs and mutual obligations of the natural life are paramount.

As he concludes this part of his harangue, an amused consciousness steals over him that he has been washing himself very white; and that his self-defence has been principally self-praise—at least, to his listener's ears. So he proceeds to show that his arguments were just, by showing how easily, being blamed for the one course of action, he might have been no less censured for the opposite. He imagines that his life has been written by some romancing historian of the Thiers and Victor Hugo type; and that in this version, practical wisdom, or SAGACITY, is made to suggest everything which he has really done, while he unwisely obeys the dictates of ideal virtue and does everything which he did not.

Hohenstiel-Schwangau (France) had made him her head-servant: president of the assembly which she had elected to serve her; and he knew that his fellow-servants were working for their own ends, while he alone was faithful to his bond. He, doubtless, had his dreams, conjured up by SAGACITY, of pouncing upon the unfaithful ones, denouncing them to his mistress, the State, and begging her to allow him to do their work as well as his own, till such time as the danger was past, and her desire for a more popular government could be fulfilled. But in so doing he would have deceived her, and he chose the truth. He knew that he had no right to substitute himself for the multitude, his knowledge for their ignorance, his will for theirs; since wise and foolish were alike of God's creating, and each had his own place and purpose in the general scheme. (Here and through the following pages, 176-7, the real and **the** imaginary Prince appear merged into each other.) He performed **his** strict duty, and left things to their natural course.

His position grew worse and worse. **His** fellow-servants made no secret of their plans—to **be** carried **into** execution when his time of service should have expired, **and his** controlling hand been removed from them. Each had his own mine of tyranny—whether Popedom, Socialism, or other—which he meant to spring on the people fancying itself free. The Head Servant was silent. They took fright **at** his silence. "It meant mischief." **"It** meant counterplot." **"It** meant some stroke of **State."** "He must be braved and bullied. His re-election must **be prevented; the** sword **of** office must **be wrested** from **his** grasp."

At length his time expired, and *then* he acted **and spoke.** He made no "stroke of State." **He** stepped down from his eminence; laid his authority in the people's hand; proved to it its danger, and proposed that Hohenstiel-Schwangau should give him the needful authority for protecting her. The proposal was unanimously accepted; and **he** justified his own judgment and that of his country by chastising every disturber **of** the public peace, and reducing alike knaves and fools to silence and submission. But now SAGACITY found fault : "he had not taken the evil in time; he might have nipped it in the bud, and saved life and liberty by so doing : he had waited till it was full grown, and the cost in life and liberty had been enormous." He replied that he had been checked by his allegiance to the law ; and that rather than strain the law, however slightly, he was bound **to** see it broken.

And so, the record continues, **he** worked and acted to the end. He had received his authority from the people ; he governed first for them. (Here again, and at the following page 184, we seem to recognize the real Hohenstiel or Louis Napoleon, rather than the imaginary.)   He walked reverently—superstitiously, if spectators will—in the path marked out for him, ever fearing to imperil what was good in the existing order of things ; but casting all fear aside when an obvious evil cried out for correction. Hohenstiel-Schwangau—herself a republic—had attacked the liberties of Rome, and destroyed them with siege and slaughter.   On his accession to power, he found this "infamy triumphant."

SAGACITY suggested that he should leave it untouched. "It was no work of his ; he was not answerable for its existence.   It had its political advantages for his own country."

But he would not hear of such a course.   There was a canker in the body politic, requiring to be cut out ; and he cut it out : though the patient roared, the wound bled, and the operator was abused by friend and foe.

"Why so rough and precipitate?" again SAGACITY interposed, "though the right were on your side?  Why not temporize, persuade, even threaten, before coming to blows?"

"Yes," was the reply, "and see the evil strengthen while you look on."

SAGACITY defended her advice on larger grounds ; and here too he was at issue with her.   Hohenstiel-Schwangau had a passion for fighting.  She would fight for anything, or for nothing, merely to show that she knew how.   Give her a year's peace after any war, and she was once more ready for the fray.   Prince Hohenstiel and SAGACITY both agreed that this evil temper must be destroyed ; but SAGACITY advised him to undermine—Prince Hohenstiel chose to combat it.

SAGACITY said, " Here is an interval of peace.   Prolong it, make it delightful ; but do so under cover of intending to cut it short.   If you would induce a fierce mountain

tribe to come down from its fortress and settle in the
plain, you do not bid it destroy the fortress. You bid it
enjoy life in the city, and remember that it runs no risk in
doing so, because it has its fortress to fall back upon at the
first hint of danger. And the time will come when it can
hear with equanimity that the fortress has gone to ruin,
and that fighting is no longer in fashion. The mountain
tribe will have learned to love the fatness of the valley,
while thinking of those mother ribs of its mountain fast-
ness which are ever waiting to prop up its life. Just so
put a wooden sword into the hand of the Hohenstieler,
and let him brag of war, learning meanwhile the value of
peace."

" Not so," the Prince replied ; "my people shall not be
cheated into virtue. Truth is the one good thing. I
will tell them the truth. I will tell them that war, for
war's sake, is damnable; that glory at its best is shame,
since its image is a gilded bubble which a resolute hand
might prick, but the breath of a foolish multitude buoys
up beyond its reach." " And what," he asked, "is the glory,
what the greatness, which this foolish nation seeks? That
of making every other small ; not that of holding its place
among others which are themselves great. Shall such a
thing be possible as that the nation which earth loves best
—a people so aspiring, so endowed; so magnetic in its
attraction for its fellow-men—shall think its primacy endangered because another selects a ruler it has not patro-
nized, or chooses to sell steel untaxed ? "

" But this does not mean that Hohenstiel is to relinquish
the power of war. The aggressiveness which is damnable
in herself is to be condemned in others, and to be punished
in them. Therefore, for the sake of Austria who sins, of
Italy who suffers, of Hohenstiel-Schwangau who has a
duty to perform, the war which SAGACITY deprecates must
be waged, and Austria smitten till Italy is free."

"At least," rejoins SAGACITY, "you secure some reward

from the country you have freed ; say, the cession of Nice
and Savoy ; something to satisfy those at home who doubt
the market-value of right and truth."

" No," is the reply, "you may preach that to Metternich
and remain with him." And so the Prince worked on ; determined that neither fear, nor treachery, nor much less
blundering, on his part, should imperil the precarious
balance of the world's life.

Once more, and for the last time, SAGACITY lifts up her
voice. " You were the fittest man to rule.  Give solidity
to your life's work by leaving a fit successor to carry it on.
Secure yourself this successor in a son.  The world is
open to you for the choice of your bride."

And again the ideal Prince retorts on the suggestion.
" The fit successor is not secured in this way.  All ex-
perience proves it.  The spark of genius is dropped where
God will.  It may find hereditary (hence accumulated)
faculties ready to be ignited.  It may fire the barren rock."
And, changing the metaphor,

> " .     .     .     . The seed o' the apple-tree
> Brings forth another tree which bears a crab :
> 'Tis the great gardener grafts the excellence
> On wildings where he will."          (p. 203.)

He ends by calling up the vision of an Italian wayside
temple, in which, as the legend declares, succession was
carried on after a very different principle. Each successive
high priest has become so by murdering his predecessor,
his qualification being found in that simple fact ; or in the
qualities of cunning or courage of which it has been the
test.[1]

And now the dream is lived through, and Prince
Hohenstiel-Schwangau awakens in his own palace : not

[1] Mr. Browning desires me to say that he has been wrong in associating
this custom with the little temple by the river Clitumnus which he describes
from personal knowledge. That to which the tradition refers stood by the
lake of Nemi.

much better pleased with his own plain speaking than
with the imaginary heroics of Messrs. Hugo and Thiers.
"One's case is so much stronger before it is put into
words. Motives which seem sufficient in the semi-dark-
ness of one's own consciousness, are so feeble in the light
of day. When we reason with ourselves, we subordinate
outward claims without appearing to do so : since the
necessity of making the best of life for our own sake
supplies unconsciously to ourselves the point of view from
which all our reasonings proceed. When forced to think
aloud, we stoop to what is probably an untruth. We say
that our motives were—what they should have been ;
what perhaps we have fancied them to be."

These closing pages convey the author's comment on
Prince Hohenstiel's defence. They present it, in his well-
known manner, as what such a man might be tempted to
say ; rather than what this particular man was justified
in saying. But he takes the Prince's part in the lines
beginning,

> " Alack, one lies oneself
> Even in the stating that one's end was truth," (p. 209.)

for they farther declare that though we aim at truth, our
words cannot always be trusted to hit it. The best
cannon ever rifled will sometimes deflect. Words do this
also. We recognize the conviction of the inadequacy of
language which was so forcibly expressed in the Pope's
soliloquy in "The Ring and the Book," but in what seems
a more defined form.

## "BISHOP BLOUGRAM'S APOLOGY."

"Bishop Blougram's Apology" is a defence of religious conformity in those cases in which the doctrines to which we conform exceed our powers of belief, but are not throughout opposed to them; its point of view being that of a Roman Catholic churchman, who has secured his preferment by this kind of compromise. It is addressed to a semi-freethinker, who is supposed to have declared that a man who could thus identify himself with Romish superstitions must be despised as either knave or fool; and Bishop Blougram has undertaken to prove that he is not to be thus despised; and least of all by the person before him.

The argument is therefore special-pleading in the full sense of the word; and it is clear from a kind of editor's note with which the poem concludes, that we are meant to take it as such. But it is supposed to lie in the nature of the man who utters, as also in the circumstance in which it is uttered: for Bishop Blougram was suggested by Cardinal Wiseman;[1] and the literary hack, Gigadibs, is the kind of critic by whom a Cardinal Wiseman is most likely to be assailed: a man young, shallow, and untried; unused to any but paper warfare; blind to the deeper issues of both conformity and dissent, and as much alive to the distinction of dining in a bishop's palace as Bishop Blougram himself. The monologue is spoken on such an occasion, and includes everything which Mr. Gigadibs says, or might say, on his own side of the question. We must therefore treat it as a conversation.

Mr. Gigadibs' reasoning resolves itself into this: "*he* does not believe in dogmas, and he says so. The Bishop cannot believe in them, but does not say so. He is true

[1] The Cardinal himself reviewed this poem, not disapprovingly, in a catholic publication of the time.

to his own convictions : the Bishop is not true to his."
And the Bishop's defence is as follows.

" Mr. Gigadibs aims at living his own life : in other
words, the ideal life.   And this means that he is living no
life at all.   For a man, in order to live, must make the best
of the world he is born in ; he must adapt himself to its
capabilities as a cabin-passenger to those of his cabin.   He
must not load himself with moral and intellectual fittings
which the ship cannot carry, and which will therefore
have to be thrown overboard.   He (the Bishop) has
chosen to live a real life ; and has equipped himself
accordingly."

" And, supposing he displays what Mr. Gigadibs considers the courage of his convictions, and flings his dogmas
overboard,—what will he have gained ?  Simply that his
uncertainty has changed sides.  Believing, he had shocks
of unbelief.   Disbelieving, he will have shocks of belief
(note a fine passage, vol. iv. p. 245) : since no certainty
in these matters is possible."

" But," says Gigadibs ; " on that principle, your belief is
worth no more than my unbelief."

" Yes," replies the Bishop, " it is worth much more in
practice, if no more in theory.  Life cannot be carried on
by negations.   Least of all will religious negations be
tolerated by those we live with.  And the more definite the
religion affirmed, the better will the purposes of life be
advanced by it." .

" Not those of a noble life," argues Gigadibs, " nor in
the judgment of the best men.  You are debasing your
standard by living for the many fools who cannot see
through you, instead of the wiser few who can."

To which the Bishop replies that he lives according to
the nature which God has given him, and which is not so
ignoble after all ; and that he succeeds with wise men as
well as with fools, because they do not see through him
either : because their judgment is kept in constant sus-

pension as to whether he can believe what he professes or cannot; whether, in short, he is a knave or a fool. The proposition is vividly illustrated; and a few more obvious sophistries complete this portion of the argument.

Gigadibs still harps upon the fact that conformity cannot do the work of belief; and the Bishop now changes his ground. "He conforms to Christianity in the *wish* that it may be true; and he thinks that this wish has all the value of belief, and brings him as near to it as the Creator intends. The human mind cannot bear the full light of truth; and it is only in the struggle with doubt and error that its spiritual powers can be developed." He concedes, in short, that he is much more in earnest than he appeared; and the concession is confirmed when he goes on to declare that we live by our instincts and not by our beliefs. This is proved—he alleges—by such a man as Gigadibs, who has no warrant in his belief for living a moral life, and does so because his instincts compel it. Just so the Bishop's instincts compel a believing life. They demand for him a living, self-proving God (here the doctrine of expediency re-asserts itself), and they tell him that the good things which his position confers are the gift of that God, and intended by Him for his enjoyment. "You," he adds, "who live for something which never is, but always is *to be*, are like a traveller, who casts off, in every country he passes through, the covering that will be too warm for him in the next; and is comfortable nowhen and nowhere."

One of his latest arguments is the best. Gigadibs has said: "If you must hold a dogmatic faith, at all events reform it. Prune its excrescences away."

"And where," he retorts, "am I to stop, when once that process has begun? I put my knife to the *liquefaction*,[1]

---

[1] This refers to the popular Neapolitan belief that a crystallized drop of the blood of the patron saint, Januarius, is miraculously liquefied on given occasions.

and end, **like** Fichte, by slashing at God Himself. And meanwhile, we have to control a **mass** of ignorant persons whose obedience is linked to the farthest end of the chain (to **the** first superstition which I **am** called upon **to lop** off). We have here again a question of making **the** best of our cabin-fittings, the best of the opportunities which life places to our hand." In conclusion, he **draws a con-**temptuous picture of the obscure and inconsequent **exis-**tence which Gigadibs accepts, **as** the apostle without genius and without enthusiasm, of **what** is, if **it be one at** all, **a** *non-working* truth.

Gigadibs is silenced, and, as it proves, impressed ; **but** the Bishop is too clever to **be** very proud of his victory ; for he knows it has been **a** personal, much more than **a** real one. His strength has lain chiefly in the assumption (which only the entire monologue **can** justify **or even con-**vey) that his opponent would change places **with him if** he could ; and **he** knows that in arguing **from** this point of view he has been only half sincere. His reasonings have been good enough for the occasion. **That is** the best he can say for them.

## MR. SLUDGE, **THE MEDIUM.**

" Sludge, the Medium," is intended **to** show that even so ignoble a person **as** a sham medium may **have** some-thing to say in his own defence ; and so far as argument goes, Sludge defends himself successfully on two separate lines. But in the one case he excuses his imposture : in the other, **he** in great measure disproves it. **And** this second part of the monologue has **been** construed by some readers into a genuine plea for the theory and practice of " spiritualism." Nothing, however, could be more opposed **to** the general tenour of Mr. Browning's work. He is simply showing us what such a man might say in his own behalf, supposing that the credulity of others had tempted him into a cheat, or that his own credulity had made him a self-deceiver ; or, what was equally possible, in even the present case, that both processes had gone on at the same time. The amount of abstract truth which the monologue is intended to convey is in itself small, and more diluted with exaggeration and falsehood than in any other poem of this group.

Sludge has been found cheating in the house of his principal patron and dupe. The raps indicating the presence of a departed mother have been distinctly traced to the medium's toes. There is no lying himself out of it this time, so he offers to confess, on condition that the means of leaving the country are secured to him. There is a little bargaining on this subject, and he then begins :—

" He never meant to cheat. It is the gentlefolk who have teased him into doing it ; they *would* be taken in. If a poor boy like him tells a lie about money, or anything else in which they are 'up,' they are ready enough to thrash it out of him ; but when it is something out of their way, like saying : he has had a vision—he has seen a ghost— it's ' Oh, how curious ! Tell us all about it. Sit down, my boy. Don't be frightened, &c. &c. ;' and so they lead him on. Presently he is obliged to invent. They have found out he is a medium. A medium he has got to be. ' Couldn't you hear this? Didn't you see that? Try again. Other mediums have done it, perhaps you may.' And, of course, the next night he sees and hears what is expected of him."

" He gets well into his work. He sees visions ; peeps into the glass ball ; makes spirits write and rap, and the rest of it. There is nothing to stop him. If he mixes up Bacon and Cromwell, it only proves that they are both trying to speak through him at once. If he makes Locke talk gibberish, and Beethoven play the Shakers' hymn, and a dozen other such things : ' Oh ! the spirits are using him and suiting themselves out of his stock.' When he guesses right, it shows his truth. When he doesn't, it shows his honesty. A hit is good and a miss is better. When he boggles outright, ' he **is** confused with the **phe-nomena.'** And when this has gone on for weeks, **and he** has been clothed and cosseted, and his patrons **have** staked their penetration upon him ; **how** is he to turn round and say he has been cheating all **the time?** '**I** should like to see you do it !' **It** isn't that he wouldn't often have liked to be in the gutter again !"

This amusing account is diversified with expressions of Sludge's hearty contempt for all the men and women he has imposed **upon :** above all, for their absurd fancy that any scrap of unexpected information must **have come to** him in a supernatural way. "As **if a** man could hold his nose out of doors, and **one** smut out of the millions not stick **to it ;** sit still for a whole day, and one **atom of news** not drift into his ear !" This idea recurs in various forms.

Well ! he owns that he has cheated ; and now that he has done so, he is not at all sure that it *was* all cheating, that there wasn't something real in **it** after all. "We are all taught to believe that there **is** another world ; and the Bible shows that men have had dealings with it. We are told this can't happen now, because we are under another **law.** But I don't believe we are under another law. Some men 'see' and others don't, that's the only difference. I see a sign and **a** message in everything that happens to **me ;** but I take a small message where you **want a** big one. I am the servant who comes at a tap of his master's knuckle on the wall ; you are the servant who only comes when the bell rings. **Of** course I mistake the sign sometimes. But what does that matter if I sometimes don't mistake? You say : one fact doesn't establish a system.

You are like the Indian who picked up a scrap of gold, and never dug for more. You pick up one sparkling fact, and let it go again. I pick up one such, then another and another, and let go the dirt which makes up the rest of life."

Sludge combats the probable objection that the heavenly powers are too great, and he is too small for the kind of services he expects of them. Everything, he delares, serves a small purpose as well as a great one. Moreover, nothing nowadays *is* small. It is at all events the lesser things and not the greater which are spoken of with awe. The simple creature which is only a sac is the nearest to the creative power ; and since also man's filial relation to the Creator is that most insisted on, the more familiar and confiding attitude is the right one.

He lastly declares and illustrates his view that many a truth may stagnate for want of a lie to set it going, and thinks it likely enough that God allows him to imagine he is wielding a sham power, because he would die of fright if he knew it was a real one. He adds one or two somewhat irrelevant items to his defence ; then finding his patron unconvinced, discharges on him a volley of abuse, and decides to try his luck elsewhere. " There must be plenty more fools in other parts of the world."

## ARGUMENTATIVE POEMS CONTINUED.
### (REFLECTIONS.)

To the second class of these poems, which are of the nature of reflections, belong—taking them in the order of their importance :—

" Christmas-Eve and Easter-Day." (1850.)
" La Saisiaz." (1878.)
" Cleon." (" Men and Women.") (1855.)

"An Epistle containing the strange medical experience of Karshish, the Arab physician." (" Men and Women.") (1855.)

"Caliban upon Setebos ; or Natural Theology in the Island." (Dramatis Personæ.) (1864.)

CHRISTMAS-EVE AND EASTER-DAY are two distinct poems, printed under this one head : and each describing a spiritual experience appropriate to the day, and lived through in a vision of Christ. This vision presents itself to the reader as a probable or obvious hallucination, or even a simple dream ; but its utterances are more or less dogmatic ; they contain much which is in harmony with Mr. Browning's known views ; and it is difficult at first sight to regard them in either case as proceeding from an imaginary person who is only feeling his way to the truth. This, however, they prove themselves to be.

The first poem is a narrative. Its various scenes are enacted on a stormy Christmas Eve ; and it opens with a humorous description of a little dissenting chapel, supposed to stand at the edge of a common ; and of the various types of squalid but self-satisfied humanity which find their spiritual pasture within its walls. The narrator has just "burst out" of it. He never meant to go in. But the rain had forced him to take shelter in its porch, as evening service was about to begin : and the defiant looks of the elect as they pushed past him one by one, had impelled him to assert his rights as a Christian, and push in too. The stupid ranting irreverence of the pastor, and the snuffling satisfaction of the flock, were soon, however, too much for him, and in a very short time he was again —where we find him—out in the fresh night air.

Free from the constraint of the chapel, he takes a more tolerant view of what he has seen and heard there. He gives the preacher credit for having said a great deal that was true, and in the manner most convincing to the already convinced who were assembled to hear him.   For his own part, he declares, Nature is his church, as she has been his teacher ; and he surrenders himself with a joyful sense of relief to the religious influences of the solitude and the night : his heart glowing with the consciousness of the unseen Love which everywhere appeals to him in the visible power of the Creator.   Suddenly a mighty spectacle unfolds itself.   The rain and wind have ceased. The barricade of cloud which veiled the moon's passage up the western sky has sunk riven at her feet.   She herself shines forth in unbroken radiance, and a double lunar rainbow, in all its spectral grandeur, spans the vault of heaven.   There is a sense as of a heavenly presence about to emerge upon the arc.   Then the rapture overflows the spectator's brain, and the Master, arrayed in a serpentining garment, appears in the path before him.

But the Face is averted.   " Has he despised the friends of Christ ? and is this his punishment ? "   He prostrates himself before Him ; grasps the hem of the garment ; entreats forgiveness for what was only due to the reverence of his love, to his desire that his Lord should be worshipped in all spiritual beauty and truth.

The Face turns towards him in a flood of light.   The vesture encloses him in its folds, and he is borne onwards till he finds himself at Rome, and in front of St. Peter's Church.   He sees the interior without entering.   It swarms with worshippers, packed into it as in the hollow of a hive. All there is breathless expectation, ecstatic awe ; for the mystery of the mass is in process of consummation, and in another moment the tinkling of the silver bell will announce to the prostrate crowd the actual presence of their Lord ; will open to them the vision of the coming heavenly day.   Here, too, is faith, though obscured in a different manner.   Here, too, is *love :* the love which in bygone days hurled intellect from its throne, and trampled on the glories of ancient art—which instructed its votaries to feel blindly for its new **and** all-sufficient life, as does the babe for its mother's breast—which consecrates **even** now the deepest workings **of** the heart and mind **to the** service of God. And Christ enters the Basilica, into which, after a momentary doubt, he himself follows Him.

They float onwards again, and again he is left alone but for the hem of the garment ; for Christ has entered **the** lecture-hall of a rationalistic German professor, and into this He will not bid His disciple follow Him ; **but the in-** terior of the building is open, as before, to the disciple's mental sight. The lecturer is refreshing his hearers' **con-** victions by an inquiry into the origin of the Christian Myth and the foundation of fact on which it rests ; **and he** arrives at the conclusion that Christ was a man, but whose work proved Him **all** but Divine ; His Gospel **quite other** than those who heard **it** believed, **but in value nearly the** same.

The spectator begins musing **on** the anomalies of **this** view. "Christ, only **a** man, is to be reverenced as some- thing more. On what ground ?—The ground of intellect ? —Yet he teaches us only what a hundred **others** have taught, without claiming to be worshipped on account of it—The ground of goodness ?—But goodness is due from each man to his fellows ; it is no title to sovereignty over them." And he thus sums up his own conviction. " He may be called a *saint* who best teaches us to keep our lives pure ; he a *poet* whose insight dims that of his fellow-men. He is no less than this, though guided by an instinct no higher than that of the bat ; no more, though inspired by God. All gifts are from God, and no multiplying of gifts can convert the creature into the Creator. Between Him who created goodness, and made it binding on the conscience of man : and him who reduces it **to a** system, of which the merits may be judged by man : **lies** the interval which separates Nature, who decrees the circulation of the blood, from the observer Harvey, who discovered it. One man is

Christ, another Pilate ; beyond their dust is the Divinity of God."

" And the ' God-function' with regard to virtue was first to impress its truths on every human breast ; and secondly, to give a motive for carrying them out ; and this motive could be given only by one, who, being life's Lord, died for the sake of men. Whoever conceives this love, and takes this proof to his heart, has found a new motive, and has also gained a truth."

But Christ lingers within the hall " Is there something after all in that lecture which finds an echo in the Christian soul ? Yes, even there. There is the ghost of love, if nothing more, in the utterance of that virgin-minded man, with the 'wan, pure look,' and the frail life burning itself away in the striving after truth. For his critical tests have reduced the pearl of price to ashes, and yet left it, in his judgment, a pearl ; and he bids his followers gather up their faith as an almost perfect whole ; go home and venerate the myth on which he has experimented, adore the man whom he has proved to be one. And if his learning itself be loveless, it may claim our respect when a tricksy demon has let it loose on the Epistles of St. Paul, as it claims' our gratitude when expended on secular things. It is at least better than the ignorance which hates the word of God, if it cannot wholly accept it ; while these, his disciples, who renounce the earth, and chain up the natural man on a warrant no more divine than this, are by so much better than he who at this moment judges them. Let them carry the doctrine by which they think themselves carried, as does the child his toy-horse. He will not deride nor disturb them."

The subject of these experiences has reached a state of restful indifference. " He will adhere to his own belief, and be tolerant towards his neighbour's : since the two only differ as do two different refractions of a single ray of light. He will study, instead of criticizing, the different creeds which are fused into one before the universal Father's throne."

But this is not the lesson he has been intended to learn. The storm, breaking out afresh, catches up and dashes him to the ground, while the vesture, which he had let slip during his last musings, recedes swiftly from his sight. Then he knows that there is one "way," and he knows also that he may find it ; and in this new conviction he regains his hold of the garment, and at one bound has re-entered the little chapel, which he seems never indeed to have left. The sermon is ending, and he has heard it all. He still appreciates its faults of matter and manner ; but he no longer rejects the draught of living water, because it comes to him with some taste of earth. What the draught can do is evidenced by those wrecks of humanity which are finding renewal there. There his choice shall rest ; for, nowhere else, so he seems to conclude, is the message of Love so simply and so directly conveyed.

A great part of the narrative is written in a humorous tone, which shows itself, not only in thought and word, but in a jolting measure, and even grotesque rhymes. The speaker desires it to be understood that he is not the less in earnest for this apparent "levity ;" and the levity is quite consistent with religious seriousness in such a person as the poem depicts. But, as I have shown, it is alone enough to prove that the author is not depicting himself. The poem reflects him more or less truly in the doctrine of Divine Love, the belief in personal guidance, and the half-contemptuous admiration with which the speaker regards those who will mortify the flesh in obedience to a Christ-*man.* But it belies the evidence of his whole work when, as in Section XVII., it represents moral truth as either innate to the human spirit, or directly revealed to it ; and we shall presently notice a still greater dis-crepancy which it shares with its companion poem.[1]

[1] The " Iketides " (Suppliants), mentioned in Section XVIII., is a Tragedy

"*Easter-Day*"[2] deals with the deeper issues of scepticism and faith; and opens with a dialogue in which the two opposite positions are maintained. Both speakers start from the belief in God, and the understanding that Christianity is unproved; but the one accepts it in faith: the other regards it as, for the time being, negatived.

The man of faith begins by exclaiming, how hard it is to be (practically) a Christian; and how disproportionate to our endeavour is our success in becoming so. The sceptic replies that to his mind the only difficulty is belief. " Let the least of God's commands be proved authentic: and only an idiot would shrink from martyrdom itself, with the certain bliss that would reward it." The man of faith, who is clearly the greater pessimist of the two, thinks the world too full of suffering to be placed, by any knowledge, beyond the reach of faith—beyond the necessity of being taken upon trust. And his adversary concedes that absolute knowledge would—where it was applicable—destroy its own end. In social life, for instance, it would do away with all those acts of faith, those instinctive judgments and feelings, which are the essence *of* life. But he thinks one may fairly desire a better touchstone for the purposes of God than human judgment or feeling; and that, if we cannot know them with scientific certainty, one must wish the balance of probability to lie clearly on one side.

The man of faith is of opinion that this much of proof exists for everyone who chooses to seek it. " The burning question is how we are to shape our lives. For himself he is impelled to follow the Christian precept, and renounce the world." The sceptic denies that God demands such a sacrifice, and sees only man's ingratitude in the impression

by Æschylus, the earliest extant: and of which the text is especially incomplete: hence, halting, and " maimed."

  [2] This poem, like " Aristophanes' Apology," belongs in spirit more than in form to its particular group. Each contains a dialogue, and in the present case we have a defence, though not a specious one, of the judgment attained.

that **He** does so. The man of faith admits that it would **be** hard to have made the sacrifice, and be rewarded only by death ; while the many unbelievers who have virtually made it for one or other of the hobbies which he describes, have at least its success **to** repay them. But **even so, he** continues, he **would** have chosen the better part ; for he would have chosen Hope,—the hope which **aspires to a** loftier end. " His opponent, it is **true,** hopes **also ; but** *his* hopes are blind. They **are not those** of **St. Paul, but** those which, according **to** Æschylus, **the** Titan gave to men, to spice therewith the meal of life, and prevent their devouring it in too bitter haste ; **and if** hope—or faith—is meant to be something more than a relish . . . . !"

**The** opponent protests against this attack upon **the** " trusting ease " of **his** existence, and declares that his interlocutor **is not** doing as he **would be done by.** Where-upon the first speaker relates something which befell him on the Easter-Eve **of** three years ago, and which startled him out of precisely such **a** condition.

He was crossing the common, lately spoken **of by their** friend, and musing **on** life and the last judgment : when the following question occured to him : what would be his case if he died and were judged at that **very** moment ? " From childhood," he continues, "I have always insisted on know-ing the worst ; and I now plunged straight into the recesses of my conscience, prepared for what spectre might **be** hidden there. But all I encountered was *common sense*, which did its best to assure me that I had nothing to fear : that, considering all the difficulties of life, I had kept my course through it **as** straight, and advanced as rapidly as could be expected." (More reflections, half serious **half** playful ensue.) "Suddenly I threw back my head, and saw the midnight sky on fire. It was a *sea* of fire, now writhing and surging ; now sucked back into the darkness, now overflowing it till **its** rays poured downwards on to the earth. I felt that the Judgment Day had come. I felt also, in that supreme moment of consciousness, that I had chosen the world, and must take my stand upon the choice. I defended it with the courage of despair. 'God had framed me to appreciate the beauties of life ; I could not put the cup untasted aside ; He had not plainly commanded me to do so ; He knew how I had struggled to resign myself to leaving it half full ; Hell could be no just punishment for such a mood as that.'"

"Another burst of fire. A brief ecstasy which confounded earth and heaven. Then ashes everywhere. And amid the wreck—like the smoke pillared over Sodom—mantled in darkness as in a magnific pall which turned to grey the blackness of the night—pity mingled with judgment in the intense meditation in which his gaze was fixed—HE stood before me. I fell helpless at His feet. He spoke :

'The judgment is past ; dispensed to every man as though he alone were its object. *Thy* sin has been the love of earth. Thou hast preferred the finite to the infinite—the fleshly joys to the spiritual. Be this choice thy punishment. Thou art shut out from the heaven of spirit. The earth is thine for ever.'"

"My first impulse was one of delighted gratitude. 'All the wonders—the treasures of the natural world, are *mine ?*'"

"'Thine,' the Vision replied, 'if such shows suffice thee ; if thou wilt exchange eternity for the equivalent of a single rose, flung to thee over the barrier of that Eden from which thou art for ever excluded.'"

"'Not so,' I answered. 'If the beauties of nature are thus deceptive, my choice shall be with Art—art which imparts to nature the value of human life. I will seek man's impress in statuary, in painting. . . . .'"

"'Obtain that,' the Vision again rebuked me, 'the one form with its single act, the one face with its single look : the failure and the shame of all true artists who felt the whole while they could only reproduce the part.'"

And again the Vision expatiates on the limited nature of the earthly existence—the limited horizon which reduces man to the condition of the lizard pent up **in a** chamber in the rock—the destined shattering of the prison wall which will quicken the stagnant sense to the impressions of a hitherto unknown world—the spiritual **hunger** with which the saints, content in their earthly prison, still hail the certainty of deliverance.

" ' Let me grasp at Mind,' I then entreated,—' whirl enraptured through its various spheres. Yet **no. I know** what thou wilt say. Mind, too, is **of** the earth ; **and all** its higher inspirations proceed from another **world—are** recognized as doing so by those who receive them. I will catch no more at broken reeds. I will relinquish the world, and take **Love** for **my** portion. I will love **on,** though love too may deceive me, remembering its **consolations** in the past, struggling for its rewards **in the** future.' "

" ' AT LAST,' the Vision exclaimed, ' **thou** choosest LOVE. And hast thou not seen that the mightiness of **Love** was curled inextricably about the power and the beauty which attached thee to the world—that through them it has vainly striven to clasp thee? Abide by thy choice. Take the show for the name's sake. Reject the reality as manifested in Him who created, and then died for thee. Reject that Tale, **as** more fitly invented by the sons of Cain—as proving too much love on the part of God.' "

" Terrified and despairing, I cowered before Him, imploring the remission of the sentence, praying that the old life might be restored to me, with its trials, its limitations ; but with their accompanying hope that it might lead to the life everlasting."

" When I ' lived ' again, the plain was silvered over with dew ; the dawn had broken."

Looking back on this experience, the narrator is disposed to regard it as having been a dream. It has nevertheless been a turning-point in his existence ; for it has taught him to hear in every blessing which attaches him to the earth, a voice which bids him renounce it. And though he still finds it hard to be a Christian, and is often discouraged by the fact, he welcomes his consciousness of this : since it proves that he is not spiritually stagnating— not cut off from the hope of heaven.

Mr. Browning is, for the time being, outside the discussion. His own feelings might equally have dictated some of the arguments on either side ; and although he silences the second speaker, he does not mean to prove him in the wrong. He is at one with the first speaker, when he suggests that certainty in matters of belief is no more to be desired than to be attained ; but that personage regards uncertainty as justifying presumptions of a dogmatic kind ; while its value to Mr. Browning lies precisely in its right to exclude them. And, again ; while the value of spiritual conflict is largely emphasized in his works, he disagrees with the man of faith in " Easter-Day " as with the dogmatic believer in " Christmas-Eve," as to the manner in which it is to be carried on. According to these the spirit fights against life : according to him it fights in, and by means of, its opportunities. From his point of view human experience is an education : from theirs it is a snare.

So much of personal truth as these poems contain will be found re-stated in " La Saisiaz," written twenty-eight years later, and which impresses on it the seal of maturer thought and more direct expression.

" LA SAISIAZ " (Savoyard for " The Sun ") is the name of a villa among the mountains near Geneva, where Mr. Browning, with his sister and a friend of many years' standing, spent part of the summer of 1877. The poem so christened is addressed to this friend, and was inspired by her death : which took place with appalling suddenness

while they were there together. The shock **of the** event
re-opened the great questions which had long before been
solved by Mr. Browning's mind : **and** within sight of **the**
new-made grave, he re-laid the foundations of his faith,
that there is another life for the soul.

The argument is marked by a strong **sense of** the personal and therefore relative character **of human** experience and knowledge. It accepts **the** "subjective
synthesis" **of** some non-theistic thinkers, though exclud-
ing, of course, the negations on which this **rests ;** and its
greater maturity **is** shown **by the** philosophic form in
which the author's old religious doctrine of personal **(or**
subjective) truth has **been re-cast.** He assumes here, it is
true, that God and the soul exist. He considers **their**
existence as given, in the double fact that there **is** something in **us** which **thinks or perceives,**[1] and something
outside and beyond **us, which is** perceived by **it** ; and this
subject and object, which he names **the** Soul and God, are
**to** him beyond the necessity **of farther proof,** because
beyond the reach of it. He might therefore challenge for
his conclusions something more **than** an optional belief.
He guards himself, nevertheless, against imposing **the**
verdict of his **own** experience on **any** other man : **and**
both the question and the answer into which the **poem**
resolves itself begin for his own spirit and end so.

Mr. Browning knows himself **a** single point **in** the
creative series **of** effect and cause : at the same moment
one and the other : all behind and before him a blank.
Or, more helpless still, he **is** the rush, floated by a current,
**of** which the whence and whither **are** independent **of** it,
**and** which may land it to strike root again, or cast it
ashore a wreck. He asks himself, as he **is** whirled on
his "brief, blind voyage" down **the** stream of life, which
of these fates it has in store for him. Knowing this, that
God and the soul exist—no less than this, and no more—

---

[1] We recognize the *cogito ergo sum* of Descartes.

he asks himself whether he is justified in believing that, because his present existence is beyond a doubt, its renewal is beyond doubt also : that the current, which has brought him thus far, will land him, not in destruction, but in another life.

"Everything," he declares, "in my experience—and I speak only of my own—testifies to the incompleteness of life, nay, even to its preponderating unhappiness. The strong body is found allied to a stunted soul. The soaring soul is chained by bodily weakness to the ground. Help turns to hindrance, or discloses itself too late in what we have taken for such. Every sweet brings its bitter, every light its shade ; love is cut short by death :"—

> "I must say—or choke in silence—' Howsoever came my fate,
> Sorrow did and joy did nowise,—life well-weighed,—preponderate.'
> By necessity ordained thus ?  I shall bear as best I can ;
> By a cause all-good, all-wise, all-potent ?  No, as I am man !
> Such were God : and was it goodness that the good within my range
> Or had evil in admixture or grew evil's self by change ?
> Wisdom—that becoming wise meant making slow and sure advance
> From a knowledge proved in error to acknowledged ignorance ?
> Power ? 'tis just the main assumption reason most revolts at !  power
> Unavailing for bestowment on its creature of an hour,
> Man, of so much proper action rightly aimed and reaching aim,
> So much passion,—no defect there, no excess, but still the same,—
> As what constitutes existence, pure perfection bright as brief
> For yon worm, man's fellow-creature, on yon happier world—its leaf !
> No, as I am man, I mourn the poverty I must impute :
> Goodness, wisdom, power, all bounded, each a human attribute !"
>
> (vol. xiv. p. 183.)

"If we regard this life as final, we must relinquish our conception of the power of God : for His work is then open to human judgment, in the light of which it yields only imperfect results."

"But let us once assume that our present state is one of probation, intended by God as such : and every difficulty is solved.  Evil is no longer a mark of failure in the execution of the Divine Scheme : it becomes essential to it ; my experience indeed represents it as such.  I cannot conceive **evil as** abolished without abrogation of the laws of life. For it is not only bound up with all the good of life ; it is often its vehicle. Gain **is** enhanced by recent loss. Ignorance places us nearest to knowledge. Beauty is most precious, truth most potent, where ugliness and falsehood prevail **; and** what but the loss of Love **teaches us** what its true value has been ?"

" May I then accept the conclusion that this life will be supplemented by a better one ?"

Mr. Browning initiates his final inquiry by declaring that he will accept only the testimony of fact. He **rejects** surmise, he seeks no answer in the beauties or **in the** voices of nature ; none in the minds **of** his fellow-men ; **none** even in **the** depths **of his** sentient **self** with its **" aspiration "** and "reminiscence :" its plausible assurances **that God** would **be "** unjust," **and** man " wronged," if **a second life** were **not granted** to us.

**And here** he seems **for a** moment **to** deny, **what he has** elsewhere stated, and **everywhere** implied, **in the** poem : that his **own** spirit **must be** to him, despite **its isolation and** weakness, the one messenger **of** Divine truth.

But he is only saying **the** same thing in **a** different **way.** He rejects the spontaneous **utterance of his own** spirit ; but relies on its conclusions. He rejects **it** as pleader ; but constitutes it judge. And this distinction is carried out in a dialogue, in which Fancy speaks for the sponta- neous self ; Reason for the judicial—the one making its *thrusts,* and the other *parrying* them. The question at issue has, however, slightly shifted its ground ; and we find ourselves asking : not, " is the Soul immortal ?" but " what would be the consequence to life of its being proved so ?"

FANCY. " The **soul** exists after death. I accept the surmise as certainty : and would see **it** put to use during life."

REASON. **" The** ' use ' of it will **be** that the wise man will die at once : since death, in the absence of any supernatural law to the contrary, must be clear gain. The soul must fare better when it has ceased to be thwarted by the body; and we have no reason to suppose that the obstructions which have their purpose in this life would be renewed in a future one. Are we happy? death rescues our happiness from its otherwise certain decay. Are we sad? death cures the sadness. Is life simply for us a weary compromise between hope and fear, between failure and attainment? death is still the deliverer. It must come some day. Why not invoke it in a painless form when the first cloud appears upon our sky?"

FANCY. "Then I concede this much: the certainty of the future life shall be saddled with the injunction to live out the present, or accept a proportionate penalty."

REASON. "In that case the wise man will live. But whether the part he chooses in it be that of actor or of looker-on, he will endure his life with indifference. Relying on the promises of the future, he will take success or failure as it comes, and accept ignorance as a matter of course."

FANCY. "I concede more still. Man shall not only be compelled to live: he shall know the value of life. He shall know that every moment he spends in it is gain or loss for the life to come—that every act he performs involves reward or punishment in it."

REASON. "Then you abolish good and evil in their relation to man; for you abolish freedom of choice. No man is good because he obeys a law so obvious and so stringent as to leave him no choice; and such would be the moral law, if punishment were *demonstrated* as following upon the breach of it; reward on its fulfilment. Man is free, in his present state, to choose between good and evil—free therefore to be good; because he may believe, but has no demonstrated *certainty*, that his future welfare depends on it."

It is thus made clear that only in man's present state of

limited knowledge is a life of probation conceivable ; while only on the hypothesis that this life is one of probation, can that of a future existence be maintained. Mr. Browning ends where he began, with a *hope*, which is practically a *belief*, because to his mind the only thinkable approach to it.

A vivid description of **the** scenes amidst which the tragedy took place accompanies this discussion.

"CLEON" is a protest against the inadequacy of the earthly life ; and the writer is supposed to be one of those Greek poets or thinkers to whom St. Paul alludes, in a line quoted from Aratus in the Acts, and which stands at **the** head of **the** poem. Cleon believes in Zeus under **the** attributes of the one God ; but **he** sees nothing in his belief **to** warrant the hope of immortality ; and his love of life is so intense and so untiring that this fact is very grievous to him.

He is stating his case to **an** imaginary king—Protus—**his** patron and friend ; whose convictions are much the same as his own, but who thinks him in some degree removed from the common lot : since his achievements in philosophy and in art must procure him not only a more perfect existence, but in one sense a more lasting one. Cleon protests against this idea.

" He has," he admits, " done all which the King imputes **to** him. If he has not been a Homer, a Pheidias, or **a** Terpander, his creative sympathies have united all three ; and in thus passing from the simple to the complex, he has obeyed the law of progress, though at the risk perhaps of appearing a smaller man."

" But his life has not been the more perfect on that account. Perfection exists only in those more mechanical grades of being, in which joy is unconscious, but also self-sufficing. To grow in consciousness is to grow in the capability and in the desire **for joy** ; to decline rather

O

than advance, in the physical power of attaining it. Man's soul expands ; his ' physical recipiency ' remains for ever bounded."

" Nor are his works a source of life to him either now or for the future.   The conception of youth and strength and wisdom is not its reality : the knowing (and depicting) what joy is, is not the possession of it.   And the surviving of his work, when he himself is dead, is but a mockery the more."

It is all so horrible that he sometimes imagines another life, as unlimited in capability, as this in the desire, for joy, and dreams that Zeus has revealed it.   " But he has not revealed it, and therefore it will not be."   St. Paul is preaching at this very time, and Protus sends a letter to be forwarded to him ; but Cleon does not admit that knowledge can reside in a "barbarian Jew ; " and gently rebukes his royal friend for inclining to such doctrine, which, as he has gathered from one who heard it, "can oe held by no sane man."

Cleon constantly uses the word soul as antithesis to body : but he uses it in its ancient rather than its modern sense, as expressing the sentient life, not the spiritual ; and this perhaps explains the anomaly of his believing that it is independent of the lower physical powers, and yet not destined to survive them.

The EPISTLE of Karshish is addressed to a certain Abib, the writer's master in the science of medicine.   It is written from Bethany ; and the "strange medical experience" of which it treats, is the *case* of Lazarus, whom Karshish has seen there.   Lazarus, as he relates, has been the subject of a prolonged epileptic trance, and his reason impaired by a too sudden awakening from it.   He labours under the fixed idea that he was raised from the dead ; and that the Nazarene physician at whose command he rose (and who has since perished in a popular tumult) was no other than God : who for love's sake had taken human form, and workèd and died for men. Karshish regards the madness **of** this idea as beyond rational doubt : but he is perplexed and haunted by its consistency : by the manner in which this supposed vision of the Heavenly life has transformed, even inverted **the** man's judgment of earthly things. He combats the impression as best **he** can : recounts his scientific discoveries—the new plants, minerals, sicknesses, or cures to which his travels in Judea have introduced **him; half** apologizes for his digression from these more important matters; tries to excuse the hold which Lazárus has taken upon him by the circumstances in which they met ; and breaks out at last in this agitated appeal to Abib and the truth :—

> "The very God ! think, Abib ; dost thou think
> So, the All-Great, were the All-Loving too—
> .    .    .    .    .    .    .    .
> The madman saith He said so : **it is** strange."
>                                   (vol. iv. **p. 198.**)

**The** solitary sage alluded to is of course imaginary. **Like the** doubtful messenger to whom the letter will be entrusted, he helps to mark the incidental character with which Karshish strives to invest his "experience."

"CALIBAN UPON SETEBOS" carries us into an opposite sphere of thought. It has for its text these words from Psalm 50 : *Thou thoughtest that I was altogether such an one as thyself :* and is the picture of an acute but half savage mind, building up the Deity on its own pattern. Caliban is much exercised by the government of the world, and by the probable nature of its ruler ; and he has filched an hour from his tasks, on a summer noon, when Prospero and Miranda are taking his diligence upon trust, **to** go and sprawl **full** length in the mud of some cave, and talk the problem **out.** The attitude is described, as his reflections are carried on, in his own words ; but he speaks as children do, in the third person.

Caliban worships Setebos, god of the Patagonians, as did his mother before him ; but her creed was the higher of the two, because it included what his does not : the idea of a future life.   He differs from her also in a more original way.   For she held that a greater power than Setebos had made the world, leaving Setebos merely to "vex" it ; while he contends that whoever made the world and its weakness, did so for the pleasure of vexing it himself; and that this greater power, the "Quiet," if it really exists, is above pain or pleasure, and had no motive for such a proceeding.

Setebos is thus, according to Caliban, a secondary divinity.   He may have been created by the Quiet, or may have driven it off the field ; but in either case his position is the same.   He is one step nearer to the human nature which he cannot assume.   He lives in the moon, Caliban thinks, and dislikes its "cold," while he cannot escape from it.   To relieve his discomfort, half in impatience half in sport, he has made human beings ; thus giving himself the pleasure of seeing others do what he cannot, and of mocking them as his playthings at the same time.

This theory of creation is derived from Caliban's own experience.   In like manner, when he has got drunk on fermented fruits, and feels he would like to fly, he pinches up a clay bird, and sends it into the air ;  and if its leg snaps off, and it entreats him to stop the smarting, or make the leg grow again, he may give it two more, or he may break off the remaining one ; just to show the thing that he can do with it what he likes.

He also presumes that Setebos is envious, because *he* is so ; as for instance : it he made a pipe to catch birds with, and the pipe boasted : "*I* catch the birds.  *I* make a cry which my maker can't make unless he blows through me," he would smash it on the spot.

For the rest he imagines that Setebos, like himself, is

neither kind **nor** cruel, **but** simply acts on all possible occasions as his fancy prompts him. The one thing which would arouse his own hostility, **and** therefore that **of** Setebos, **would** be that any creature should think he **is** ever prompted by anything else ; **or** that his adopting **a** certain course one day would be **a** reason for following **it on** the next.

Guided by these analogies—which he illustrates **with** much quaintness and variety—Caliban humours Setebos, always pretending to be envious of him, and never allowing himself to seem too happy. He moans in the sunlight, gets under holes to laugh, **and** only ventures **to** think aloud, **when** out **of** sight **and** hearing, as **he is at the** present **moment.** Thus sheltered, however, he makes too free with his tongue. He risks **the** expression of a hope that old age, or the Quiet, will some day make an end of his Creator, whom he loves none the better for being so like himself. **And in** another moment he is crouching in abject fear : for an awful thunderstorm has broken out. "That raven scudding away 'has told him all.'"

"Lo ! 'Lieth flat and loveth Setebos !" (vol. vii. p. 161.)

and will do anything to please him so that he escape this time.

The most impressive **of the** dramatic monologues, "A Death in the Desert," detaches itself from this double group. It **is** contemplative in tone, but inspired by a formed conviction, and, dramatically at least, by an instructive purpose ; and thus becomes the centre of another small division of Mr. Browning's poems, which for want of **a** less ugly and hackneyed word we may call "didactic."

## DIDACTIC POEMS.

The poems contained in this group are, taking them in the order of their importance,

"A Death in the Desert." Dramatis Personæ. 1864.

"Rabbi Ben Ezra." Dramatis Personæ. 1864.

"Deaf and Dumb : a group by Woolner." Dramatis Personæ. 1864.

"The Statue and the Bust." Dramatic Romances. Published in "Men and Women." 1855.

"A DEATH IN THE DESERT" is the record of an imaginary last scene in the life of St. John. It is conceived in perfect harmony with the facts of the case : the great age which the Evangelist attained : the mystery which shrouded his death : the persecutions which had overtaken the Church : the heresies which already threatened to disturb it ; but Mr. Browning has given to St. John a foreknowledge of that age of philosophic doubt in which its very foundations would be shaken ; and has made him the exponent of his own belief—already hinted in "Easter Eve" and "Bishop Blougram :" to be fully set forth in "The Ring and the Book" and "La Saisiaz"—that such doubt is ordained for the maturer mind, as the test of faith, and its preserver.

The supposed last words of the Evangelist, and the circumstances in which they were spoken, are reported by loving simplicity as by one who heard them, and who puts forward this evidence of St. John's death against the current belief that he lingers yet upon earth. The account, first spoken, then written, has passed apparently from hand to hand, as one disciple after the other died the martyr's death ; and we find the MS. in the possession of an unnamed person, and prefaced by him with a descriptive note, in which religious reverence and bibliographical interest are touchingly blended with each other.

St. John is dying in the desert, concealed in an inmost chamber of the rock. Four grown disciples and a boy are with him. He lies as if in sleep. But, as the end approaches, faint signs of consciousness appear about the mouth and eyes, and the patient and loving ministrations of those about him nurse the flickering vital spark into a flame.

St. John returns to life, feeling, as it were, the retreating soul forced back upon the ashes of his brain, and taxing the flesh to one supreme exertion. But he lives again in a far off time when "John" is dead, and there is no one left who *saw*. And he lives in a sense as of decrepit age, seeking a "foot-hold through a blank profound;" grasping at facts which snap beneath his touch; in strange lands, and among people yet unborn, who ask,

"Was John at all, and did he say he saw?" (vol. vii. p. 128.)

and will believe nothing till the proof be proved.

This prophetic self-consciousness does not, however, displace the memory of his former self. John knows himself the man who *heard* and *saw*—receiving the words of Christ from His own mouth, and enduring those glories of apocalyptic vision which he marvels that he could bear, and live; seeing truths already plain grow of their own strength: and those he guessed as points expanding into stars. And the life-long faith regains its active power as the doubting future takes shape before him; as he sees its children

"    .    .    . stand conversing, each new face
Either in fields, of yellow summer eves,
On islets yet unnamed amid the sea;
Or pace for shelter 'neath a portico
Out of the crowd in some enormous town
Where now the larks sing in a solitude;

Or muse upon blank heaps of stone and sand
Idly conjectured to be Ephesus :
.    .    .    .    .    . " (vol. vii. p. 134.)

and he hears them questioning truths of deeper import than those of his own life and work.

The subsequent monologue is an earnest endeavour to answer those questionings, which he sets forth, in order that he may do so ; his eloquence being perhaps the more pathetic, that in the depth of his own conviction—in his loving desire to impart it—he assumes a great deal of what he tries to prove. "He has *seen* it all—the miracle of that life and death ; the need, and yet the transiency, of death and sin ; the constant presence of the Divine love ; those things which not only *were* to him, but *are*. And he is called upon to prove it to those who *cannot see :* whose spirit is darkened by the veil of fleshly strength, while his own lies all but bare to the contact of the Heavenly light. He must needs be as an optic-glass, bringing those things before them, not in confusing nearness, but at the right historic distance from the eye."

"Life," he admits, "is given to us that we may learn the truth. But the soul does not learn from it as the flesh does. For the flesh has little time to stay, and must gain its lesson once and for all. Man needs no second proof of the worth of fire : once found, he would not part with it for gold. But the highest spiritual certainty is not like our conviction of a bodily fact ; and though we know the worth of Christ as we know the preciousness of fire, we may not in like manner grasp this truth, acknowledging it in our lives. He—John—in whose sight his Lord had been transfigured, had walked upon the waters, and raised the dead to life : *he, too,* forsook Him when the 'noise' and 'torchlight,' and the 'sudden Roman faces,' and the 'violent hands' were upon them. . . . ."

The doubter, he imagines, will argue thus, taking "John's" Gospel for his starting-point :—

(*a*) "Your story is proved inaccurate, if **not** untrue. The doctrine which rests upon **it** is therefore unproved, except in so far as it is attested by the human heart. And this proof again is invalid. For the doctrine is that of Divine love ; and we, who believe in love, because we ourselves possess it, may read it into a record in which **it has** no place. Man, in his mental infancy, read his **own** emotions and his own will into the forces of nature, as **he** clothed their supposed personal existence in his **own** face and form. But his growing understanding discarded the idea of these material gods. It now replaces the idea of the one Divine intelligence by that of universal law. God is proved **to us as** law—'named,' but 'not **known.**' A divinity, which we **can** recognize by like attributes to our **own, is** disproved **by** them."

(*b*) "And granting that there is truth in your teaching : why is this allowed **to** mislead us? Why **are** we left **to** hit or miss the truth, according **as our** insight is weak or strong, instead of being plainly told this thing *was*, or it *was **not?*** Does 'John' proceed with us as did the heathen bard, who drew a fictitious picture of the manner in which fire had been given to man ; and left his readers to discover that the fact was not the fable itself, but only contained in **it** ?"

And John replies :

(*a*) "Man is made for progress, and receives therefore, step by step, such spiritual assistance as is proportionate to his strength. The testimony of miracles is granted when it is needed to assist faith. **It** is withdrawn so soon as **it** would compel it. He who rejects God's love **in** Christ because he has learned the need **of** love, is as **the** lamp which overswims with oil, the stomach which flags from excess of food : his mind is being starved by the very abundance of what was meant to nourish it. Man was spiritually living, when he shrank appalled from the spectacle of Nature, and needed to be assured that there was a might beyond *its* might.   But when he says, 'Since Might is everywhere, there is no need of Will;' though he knows from his own experience how Might may combine with Will, then is he spiritually dead.   And man is spiritually living, when he asks if there be love

"Behind the will and might, as real as they?" (vol. vii. p. 140.)

But when he reasons : since love is everywhere, and we love and would be loved, we make the love which we recognize as Christ : and Christ was *not;* then is he spiritually dead.   For the loss which comes through gain is death, and the sole death."

(*b*) The second objection he answers by reverting to his first statement.   "Man is made for progress.   He could not progress if his doubtings were at once changed to certainties, and all he struggles for at once found.   He must yearn for truth, and grasp at error as a 'midway help' to it.   He must learn and unlearn.   He must creep from fancies on to fact ; and correct to-day's facts by the light of to-morrow's knowledge.   He must be as the sculptor, who evokes a life-like form from a lump of clay, ever seeing the reality in a series of false presentments ; attaining it through them.   God alone makes the live shape at a jet."

The tenderness which has underlain even John's remonstrances culminates in his closing words.   "If there be a greater woe than this (the doubt) which he has lived to see, may he," he says, "be 'absent,' though it were for another hundred years, plucking the blind ones from the abyss."

"But he was dead." (vol. vii. p. 146.)

The record has a postscript, written not by the same person, but in his name, confronting the opinions of St. John with those of Cerinthus, his noted opponent in belief, into whose hands the MS. is also supposed to have fallen.

It is chiefly interesting as heightening **the historical effect** of the poem.[1]

" RABBI BEN EZRA " is the expression of a religious philosophy which, being, from another point of view, Mr. Browning's own, has much in common with that which he has imputed to St. John ; and, as "A Death in **the** Desert" only gave **the** words which the Evangelist might **have** spoken, so is " Rabbi Ben Ezra " only the possible **utter**ance of that pious and learned Jew.  But the Christian doctrine of the one poem brings into strong relief the pure Theism of the other ; and the religious imagination in "Rabbi Ben Ezra" is strongly touched with the gorgeous and solemn realism which distinguishes the Old Testament from the **New.**

**The** most striking feature of Rabbi Ben Ezra's **philo**sophy is his estimate of age.  According to him the soul is eternal, but it completes the first stage of its experience in the earthly life ; and the climax of the earthly life is attained, not in the middle **of** it, but **at its close.**  Age is therefore **a** period, not only **of rest,** but of fruition.

" Spiritual conflict **is** appropriate **to** youth.  It is well that youth should sigh for the impossible, and, if needs be, blunder in the endeavour to improve what is.  He would be a brute whose body could keep pace with his soul.  The highest test of man's bodily powers is the distance to which **they** can project **the** soul on **the** way which it must travel alone."

" But life in the flesh is good, showering gifts alike on sense and brain.  It is right that at some period of its

---

[1] **The** narrator, **in** a parenthetic statement, imputes a doctrine to St. John, which is an unconscious approach on Mr. Browning's part to the "animism" of **some ancient and** mediæval philosophies.  It carries the idea of the Trinity into the individual life, by subjecting this to three souls, the lowest of which reigns over the body, and is that which "Does :" the second and third being respectively that which " Knows" and "Is."  The reference to **the** " glossa of Theotypas " is part of the fiction.

existence man's heart should beat in unison with it ; that having seen God's power in the scheme of creation, he should also see the perfectness of His love ; that he should thank Him for his manhood, for the power conferred on him to live and learn.  And this boon must be granted by age, which gathers in the inheritance of youth."

"The inheritance is not one of earthly wisdom.  Man learns to know the right and the good, but he does not learn how outwardly to apply the knowledge ; for human judgments are formed to differ, and there is no one who can arbitrate between them.  Man's failure or success must be sought in the unseen life—not in that which he has done, but in that which he has aspired to do."

"Nothing dies or changes which has truly BEEN.  The flight of time is but the spinning of the potter's wheel to which we are as clay.  This fleeting circumstance is but the machinery which stamps the soul (that vessel moulded for the Great Master's hand).  And its latest impress is the best : though the base of the cup be adorned with laughing loves, while skull-like images constitute its rim."

> "Look not thou down but up !
> To uses of a cup,
> The festal board, lamp's flash and trumpet's-peal,
> The new wine's foaming flow,
> The Master's lips a-glow !
> Thou, heaven's consummate cup, what needst thou
>     with earth's wheel?"
>
> (vol. vii. p. 119.)

"DEAF AND DUMB" conveys, in a single stanza, the crowning lesson of the life of Paracelsus, and indeed of every human life : for the sculptured figures to which it refers have supplied the poet with an example of the "glory" which may "arise" from "defect," the power from limitation.  It needs, he says, the obstructing prism to set free the rainbow hues of the sunbeam.  Only dumbness can give to love the full eloquence of the eyes ; only

deafness can impress love's yearnings on the movements
of neck and face.

"THE STATUE AND THE BUST" is a warning against
infirmity of purpose. Its lesson is embodied in a picturesque story, in which fact and fiction are combined.

In the piazza of the SS. Annunziata at Florence is an
equestrian statue of the Grand Duke Ferdinand the First,
representing him as riding away from the church, and
with his head turned in the direction of the once Riccardi Palace, which occupies a corner of the square.
Tradition asserts that he loved a lady whom her husband's
jealousy kept a prisoner there, and whom he could only
see **at** her window ; and that **he** avenged his **love** by
placing himself in effigy where his glance could **always**
dwell upon her.

**In** Mr. Browning's expanded version, the love is returned, and the lovers determine **to fly** together. But
each day brings fresh motives **for** postponing the flight,
and each day they exchange glances **with** each other—he
passing by on his horse, she looking down from her
window—and comfort themselves with the thought **of** the
morrow. And as the days slip by, their love grows cooler,
and they learn to be content with expectation. They
realize at **last** that the love has been a dream, and that
they have spent their youth in dreaming it ;' apd in order
that the dream may continue, and the memory of their
lost youth be preserved, they cause, he his statue to be
cast, she her bust to be moulded, and each placed in the
attitude in which they have daily looked upon each other.
They feel the irony of the proceeding, though they find
satisfaction in it. Their image will do all that the reality
has done.

**Mr.** Browning blames these lovers for not carrying out
their intention, whether or not **it** could be pronounced
a good one. "Man should carry his best energies into

the game of life, whether the stake he is playing for be good or bad—a reality or a sham. As a test of energy, the one has no value above the other."

He leaves the " bust " in the region of fancy, by stating that it no longer exists. But he tells us that it was executed in " della Robbia" ware, specimens of which, still, at the time he wrote, adorned the outer cornice of the palace. The statue is one of the finest works of John of Bologna.

The partial darkening of the Via Larga by the over-hanging mass of the Riccardi (formerly Medici) Palace[1] is figuratively connected in the poem with the "crime" of two of its inmates : the "murder," by Cosimo dei Medici and his (grand) son Lorenzo, of the liberties of the Floren-tine Republic.

The smallness of this group, and its chiefly dramatic character, show how little direct teaching Mr. Browning's works contain. There is, however, direct instructiveness in another and larger group, which has too much in com-mon with all three foregoing to be included in either, and will be best indicated by the term "critical." In certain re-spects, indeed, this applies to several, perhaps to most, of those which I have placed under other heads ; and I use it rather to denote a lighter tone and more incidental treatment, than any radical difference of subject or in-tention.

---

[1] The present Riccardi palace in the Via Larga was built by Cosmo dei Medici in 1430 ; and remained in the possession of the Medici till 1639, when it was sold to Marchese Riccardi. The original Riccardi palace in the Piazza S. S. Annunziata is now (since 1870) Palazzo Antinori.

In my first edition, the "crime" is wrongly interpreted as the murder of Alexander, Duke of Florence, in 1536 ; and the confusion, I regret to find, increased by a wrong figure (8 for 5), which has slipped into the date.

## CRITICAL POEMS.

"Old Pictures in Florence." ⎫ Dramatic Lyrics.
"Respectability." ⎪ Published in " Men
"Popularity." ⎬ a n d  **Wome n.**
"Master Hugues of Saxe-gotha." ⎭ 1855.
"A Light Woman." Dramatic Romances. **Published**
in " Men and Women." 1855.

"Transcendentalism." (" Men and Women.") 1855.

"How it Strikes **a Contemporary.**" (" Men **and**
Women.") 1855.

" Dîs aliter Visum ; **or,** Le Byron de nos Jours." **("Dra-**
matis Personæ.") 1864.

" At the **Mermaid.**" ⎫
" House." ⎪
" Shop." ⎬ " Pacchiarotto, and other
" Pisgah Sights," **I. and II.** ⎪ Poems." 1876.
" Bifurcation." ⎪
" Epilogue." ⎭

The first and fourth of these are significant from the insight they give into Mr. Browning's conception of art.
We must allow, in reading them, for the dramatic and
therefore temporary mood in which they were written, and
deduct certain utterances which seem inconsistent with
**the** breadth of the author's views. But they reflect him
truly in this essential fact, that he considers art as subordinate to life, and only valuable in so far as it expresses
it. This means, not that his standard is realistic : but
that it is entirely human ; it could scarcely **be** otherwise
in a mind so devoted to the study **of** human life ; but these
very poems display also, on Mr. Browning's part, a loving
familiarity with the works of painters, sculptors, and
musicians, and a practical understanding of them, which

might easily have resulted in a partial acceptance of artistic standards as such, and of the policy of art for art; and it is only through the breadth and strength of his dramatic genius, that artistic sympathies in themselves so strong could be subjected to it.

In music, this position appears at first sight to be reversed; for Mr. Browning rejects the dramatic theory which would convert it into a direct expression of human thought.    Here, however, the poet in him comes into play.   He leaves the plastic arts to express what may be both felt and thought; and calls on music to express what may be felt but not thought.   In this sense he accepts it as an independent science subject to its own ideals and to its own laws.   But this only means that, in his opinion, the relation of music to human life is different from that of plastic art : the one revealing the unknown, while the other embodies what is known.

"OLD PICTURES IN FLORENCE" is a fanciful monologue, spoken as by one who is looking down upon Florence, through her magical atmosphere, from a villa on the neighbouring heights.   The sight of her Campanile brings Giotto to his mind; and with Giotto comes a vision of all the dead Old Masters who mingle in spirit with her living men.   He sees them each haunting the scene of his former labours in church or chapter-room, cloister or crypt; and he sees them grieving over the decay of their works, as these fade and moulder under the hand of time.   He is also conscious that they do not grieve for themselves.   Earthly praise or neglect cannot touch them more.   But they have had a lesson to teach; and so long as the world has not learnt the lesson, their souls may not rest in heaven.

"Greek art had *its* lesson to teach, and it taught it.   It reasserted the dignity of the human form.   It re-stated *the truth* of the soul which informs the body, and the body which expresses it. Men saw in its creations their own qualities carried to perfection, and were content to know that such perfection **was** possible, **and to** renounce the hope of attaining it. In this experience the first stage was progress ; the second was stagnation. Progress began again, when men looked on these images of themselves and said : "we are not inferior **to** these. We are greater than they. For what has come to perfection perishes, **and** we are imperfect because eternity is before us ; because we were made to *grow*." The soul which has eternity within its grasp cannot express itself in a single glance ; nor can its consciousness be petrified into an unchanging sorrow or joy. **The** painters **who** set aside Greek art undertook to vindicate **the** activity of **the soul.** They made its hopes and **fears** shine through the flesh, though the flesh they shone through **were frayed** and **torn by the** process. This **was the** work which they **had to do ;** and which remains undone, while men speak of them as " Old Master" this, and " Early " the other, and do not dream that " Old **"** and " New" are fellows : "that all **are** links in **the** chain of the one progressive **art** life ; **the** one spiritual revelation."

The speaker now relapses into the playful mood which his more serious reflections have scarcely interrupted. He thinks of the removable paintings which lie hidden in cloister or church, and which a sympathizing purchaser might rescue from decay ; and he reproaches those melancholy ghosts for not guiding such purchasers to them. **He,** for instance, does not aspire **to** the works of the very great ; but a number of lesser lights, whose name and quality he recites, might, he thinks, have lent themselves to **the** fulfilment of his artistic desires ;[1] and he declares himself particularly hurt by the conduct of his old friend Giotto, who has allowed some picture he had been hunt-

[1] Mr. Browning possesses or possessed pictures by all the artists mentioned in this connection.

ing through every church in Florence to fall into other hands. He concludes with an invocation to a future time when the Grand Duke will have been pitched across the Alps, when art and the Republic will revive together, and when Giotto's Campanile will be completed—which glorious consummation, though he may not live to see, he considers himself the first to predict.

Mr. Browning alludes, in the course of this monologue, to the two opposite theories of human probation : one confining it to this life, the other extending it through a series of future existences ; and without pronouncing on their relative truth, he owns himself in sympathy with the former. He is tired and likes to think of rest. The sentiment is, however, not in harmony with his general views, and belongs to the dramatic aspect of the poem.[1]

MASTER HUGUES OF SAXE GOTHA, also a monologue, is christened after an imaginary composer ; and consists of a running comment on one of his fugues, as performed by the organist of some unnamed church. The latter has just played it through : the scored brow and deep-set eyes of Master Hugues fixed on him, as he fancied, from the shade ; and he now imagines he hears him say, " You have done justice to the notes of my piece, but you must grasp its meaning to understand where my merit lies ; " so he plays the fugue again, listening for the meaning, and reading it as out of a book. From this literary or dramatic point of view, the

---

[1] (Verses 26, 27, 28.) "Bigordi" is the family name of Domenico, called "Ghirlandajo," from the family trade of wreath-making. "Sandro' stands for Alessandro Botticelli. "Lippino" was son of Fra Lippo Lippi. Mr. Browning alludes to him as "wronged," because others were credited with some of his best work. "Lorenzo Monaco" (the monk) was a contemporary, or nearly so, of Fra Angelico, but more severe in manner. "Pollajolo" was both painter and sculptor. "Margheritone of Arezzo" was one of the earlier Old Masters, and died, as Vasari states, "infastidito" (deeply annoyed), by the success of Giotto and the "new school." Hence the funeral garb in which Mr. Browning depicts him.

impression received is as follows. Some one lays down a proposition, unimportant in itself, and not justly open to either praise or blame. Nevertheless a second person re-torts on it, a third interposes, a fourth rejoins, and a fifth thrusts his nose into the matter. The five are fully launched into a quarrel. The quarrel grows broader and deeper. Number one restates his case somewhat differently. Number two takes it up on its new ground. Argument is followed by vociferation and abuse ; a momentary self-restraint by a fresh outbreak of self-assertion. All tempers come into play, all modes of attack are employed, from pounding with a crowbar to pricking with a pin. And where all this time is music ? Where is the gold of truth ? Spun over and blackened by the tissue of jangling sounds, as is the ceiling of the old church by cobwebs.

> "Is it your moral of Life ?
> Such a web, simple and subtle,
> Weave we on earth here in impotent strife,
> Backward and forward each throwing his shuttle,
> Death ending all with a knife ?" (vol. vi. p. 202.)

The organist admires Master Hugues, and approaches his creations with an open mind ; but he cannot help feeling that this mode of composition represents the tor-tuousness of existence, and that its "truth" spreads golden above and about us, whether we accept her or not. He ends by bidding Master Hugues and the five speakers clear the arena ; and leave him to "unstop the full organ," and "blare out," in the "mode Palestrina," what another musician has had to say.

This scene in an organ loft has many humorous touches which would in any case forbid our taking it too seriously ; and we must no more think of Mr. Browning as indifferent to the possible merits of a fugue than as indifferent to the beauties of a Greek statue. But the dramatic situation has in this, as in the foregoing case, a strong basis of personal truth.

Two more of these poems show **the irony of circum-stance** as embodied in popular opinion.

"POPULARITY" is an expression of admiring tender-ness for some person whom the supposed speaker knows and loves as a poet, though it is the coming, not the pre-sent age, which will bow to him as such. But the main idea of the poem is set forth in a comparison. The speaker "sees" his friend in the character of an ancient fisherman landing the Murex-fish on the Tyrian shore. "The 'murex' contains a dye of miraculous beauty; and this once extracted and bottled, Hobbs, Nobbs, and Co. may trade in it and feast; but the poet who (figuratively) brought the murex to land, and created its value, may, as Keats probably did, eat porridge all his life."

"HOW IT STRIKES A CONTEMPORARY" describes a poet whose personality was not ignored, but mistaken; and the irony of circumstance is displayed both in the extent of this mistake, and the colour which circumstance has given to it. This poet is a mysterious personage, who constantly wanders through the city, seeing everything without appearing to use his eyes. His clothing, though old and worn, has been of the fashion of the Court. He writes long letters, which are obviously addressed to "our Lord the King," and "which, no doubt, have had to do with the disappearance of A., and the fate of B." He can be, people think, no other than a *spy*. A spy, we must admit, might proceed in much the same manner. Mr. Browning does, however, full justice to the excesses of popular imagination, once directed into a given channel, in the parallel touches which depict the portentous luxury in which the spy is supposed to live: the poor though decent garret in which the poet dies.

"TRANSCENDENTALISM" is addressed to a young poet,

who **is** accused of presenting his ideas "naked," instead
of draping them, in poetic fashion, in sights and sounds :
**in other** words, of talking across his harp instead of singing to it. He acts on the supposition that, **if** the young
want imagery, older men want rational thoughts. And his
critic is declaring this a mistake. "Youth, indeed, would
be wasted in studying the transcendental Jacob Boehme
for the deeper meaning of things which life gives it to see
and feel ; but when youth is past, we need all the more to
be made to see and feel. It is not a thinker like Boehme
who will compensate us for the lost summer of **our life** ;
but a magician like John of Halberstadt, who can, at **any**
moment, conjure roses up."[1]

There is a strong vein of humour in the argument, **which**
gives the impression of being consciously overstated. **It**
is neverthess a genuine piece of criticism.

"AT THE MERMAID" and the "EPILOGUE" deal with
public opinion in its general estimate of poets and poetry ;
and they expose its fallacies in **a** combative spirit, which
would exclude them from a more rigorous definition of
the term "critical." In the first **of** these Mr. Browning
speaks under the mask of Shakespeare, and gives vent to

---

[1] The "magic" symbolized is that of genuine poetry ; but the magician,
or "mage," is an historical person ; and the special feat imputed to him was
recorded of other magicians in the Middle Ages, if not of himself.

"Johannes Teutonicus, a canon of Halberstadt in Germany, after he had
performed a number of prestigious feats almost incredible, **was** transported
by the Devil in the likeness of a black horse, and was both seen and heard
upon one and the same Christmas day to say Mass in Halberstadt, in
Mayntz, and in Cologne " (" Heywood's Hierarchy," bk. iv., p. 253).

The "prestigious feat" of causing flowers to appear in winter was a
common one. "In the year 876, the Emperor Lewis then reigning, there
**was** one Zedechias, by religion a Jew, by profession a physician, but indeed
a magician. In the midst of winter, in the Emperor's palace, he suddenly
caused **a** most pleasant and delightful garden to appear, with all sorts of
trees, plants, herbs, and flowers, together with the singing of all sorts of birds,
to be seen and heard." (Delrio, " Disquisitio Magicæ," bk. i., chap. iv., and
elsewhere ; and many other authorities.)

the natural irritation of any great dramatist who sees his various characters identified with himself. He repudiates the idea that the writings of a dramatic poet reveal him as a man, however voluminous they may be ; and on this ground he even rejects the transcendent title to fame which his contemporaries have adjudged to him. They know him in his work. They cannot, he says, know him in his *life*. He has never given them the opportunity of doing so. He has allowed no one to slip inside his soul, and " label " and " catalogue " what he found there.

This is truer for Shakespeare than for Mr. Browning, who has often addressed his public with comparative directness, and would be grieved to have it thought that in the long course of his writings he has never spoken from his heart. He would also be the first to admit that, in the course of his writings, the poet must, indirectly, reveal the man. But he has too often had to defend himself against the impression that whatever he wrote as a poet must directly reflect him as a man. He has too often had to repeat, that poetry is an art which " *makes*," not one which merely *records;* and that the feelings it conveys are no more necessarily supplied by direct experience than are its facts by the Cyclopædia. And with the usual deduction for the dramatic mood, we may accept the retort as genuine.

I have departed in the case of this poem from the mere statement of contents, which is all that my plan admits of, or my readers usually can desire : because it expresses an indifference to general sympathy which belies the author's feeling in the matter. Mr. Browning speaks equally for himself and Shakespeare, when he derides another idea which he considers to be popular : that the fit condition of the poet is melancholy. " I," he declares, " have found life joyous, and I speak of it as such. Let those do otherwise who have wasted its opportunities, or been less richly endowed with them."

The " Epilogue " is **a** criticism on critics, and is spoken distinctly by Mr. Browning himself. **He** takes for his text **a line** from Mrs. Browning :[1]

"The poets pour us wine,"

and denounces those consumers of the wine of poetry, who expect it to combine strength and sweetness in **an impossible** degree. Body and bouquet, **he** affirms, may **be** found on the label of a bottle, but not in the **vat** from which the bottle was filled. " Mighty " **and** " mellow " may be born at once ; but the **one is** for now, **the other** only for after-time. The earth, **he** declares, is **his vineyard** ; his grape, the loves, the hates, and the thoughts of man ; his wine, what these have made it. Bouquet may, he admits, be artificially given. Flowers grow everywhere which will supplement **the** flavour of the grape **;** and his **life** holds flowers of memory, which blossom **with** every spring. But **he** denies that **his brew would** be **the** more popular if **he** stripped his meadow **to** make **it so.** How much do his public drink **of** that which they profess to approve ? They declare Shakespeare and Milton **fit** beverage for man and boy. " Look into their cellars, and see how many barrels are unbroached of the one brand, what drippings content them of the **other.** He **will be** true to his task, and to Him who set it."

"Wine, pulse in might from me !
It may never emerge in must from vat,
Never fill cask nor furnish can,
Never end sweet, which strong began—
God's gift to gladden the heart of man ;
   But spirit's at proof, I promise that !
No sparing of juice spoils what should be
   Fit brewage—mine for me."

(vol. xiv. p. 148.)

At the 18th stanza the figure is changed, and Mr. Browning speaks of his work (by implication) as a stretch

---

[1] " Wine of Cyprus." The quotation heading the poem qualifies it as "wine for the superiors in age and station."

of country which is moor above and mine below; and in which men will find—what they dig for.

"HOUSE." is written in much the same spirit as "At the Mermaid." It reminds us that the whole front of a dwelling must come down before the life within it can be gauged by the vulgar eye ; however we may fancy that this or that poetic utterance has unlocked the door— that it opens to a "sonnet-key."[1]

"SHOP" is a criticism on those writers, poets or other-wise, who are so disproportionately absorbed by the mate-rial cares of existence as to place the good of literature in its money-making power ; and depicts such in the cha-racter of the shopman who makes the shop his home, instead of leaving it for some mansion or villa as soon as business hours are past. "The flesh must live, but why should not the spirit have its dues also?"

"RESPECTABILITY" is a comment on the price paid for social position. A pair of lovers have been enjoying a harmless escapade ; and one remarks to the other that, if their relation had been recognized by the world, they might have wasted their youth in the midst of proprieties which they would never have learned the danger and the pleasure of infringing. The situation is barely sketched in ; but the sentiment of the poem is well marked, and connects it with the foregoing group.

"A LIGHT WOMAN," "DÎS ALITER VISUM," and "BIFURCATION" raise questions of conduct.
A man desires to extricate his friend from the toils of "A LIGHT WOMAN ;" and to this end he courts her him-self. He is older and more renowned than her present victim, and trusts to her vanity to ensure his success.

---

[1] Such as Wordsworth assumed to have been in use with Shakespeare.

But his attentions arouse in her something more. He discovers too late that he has won her heart. He can only cast it away, and a question therefore arises: he knows how he appears to his friend ; he knows how **he** will appear to the woman whom his friend loved ; "how does he appear to himself?" In other words, **did the** end for which he has acted justify the means employed ? He doubts it.

" DÎS ALITER VISUM" records the verdict of **later days** on a decision which recommended itself **at the time :** that is, to the person who formed it. A man and **woman** are attracted towards each **other,** though she **is** young and unformed ; he, old in years and in experience ; and he is, **or seems** to **be,** on the point of offering her **his hand.** But **caution** checks the **impulse.** They drift asunder. He forms a connection with an opera-dancer. She makes a loveless marriage. **Ten** years **later** they meet again ; and she reminds him of what passed between **them,** and taxes him with the ruin **of** four souls. He has thought only of the drawbacks **to** *present* enjoyment, which the unequal union would have involved ; he never thought or cared how its bitter-sweetness might quicken the striving for eternity.

This criticism reflects the woman's point of view, and was probably intended **to** justify it. It does not follow that the author would not, in another dramatic mood, have justified the man, in his more practical estimate **of** the situation. Mr. Browning's poetic self is, however, expressed in the woman's belief : that everything which disturbs the equal balance of human life gives a vital impulse to the soul. The stereotyped completeness of the lower existences supplies him here also with a warning.

The title of " BIFURCATION " refers to two paths in life, followed respectively by two lovers whom circumstances divide. The case is not unusual. The woman sacrifices love to duty, and expects her lover to content himself with her choice. Why not, she thinks? She will be constant to him; they will be united in the life to come. And meanwhile, she is choosing what for her is the smoother and safer path, while for him it is full of stumbling-blocks. Love's guidance is refused him, and he falls. Which of these two has been the sinner: he who sinned unwillingly, or she who caused the sin? We feel that Mr. Browning condemns the apparent saint.

" PISGAH SIGHTS. I." depicts life as it may *seem* to one who is leaving it; who is, as it were, "looking over the ball." As seen from this position, Good and Evil are reconciled, and even prove themselves indispensable to each other. The seer becomes aware that it is unwise to strive against the mixed nature of existence; vain to speculate on its cause. But the knowledge is bitter-sweet, for it comes too late.

" PISGAH SIGHTS. II." is a view of life as it *might* be, if the knowledge just described did not come too late; and shows that according to Mr. Browning's philosophy it would be no life at all. The speaker declares that if he had to live again, he would take everything as he found it. He would neither dive nor soar; he would strive neither to teach nor to reform. He would keep to the soft and shady paths; learn by quiet observation; and allow men of all kinds to pass him by, while he remained a fixture. He would gain the benefit of the distance with those below and above him, since he would be magnified for the one class, while seen from a softening point of view by the other. And so also he would admire the distant brightness, "the mightiness yonder," the more for keeping his own place. If seen too closely, *the star might prove a glow-worm.*

## EMOTIONAL POEMS.

### LOVE.

Those of Mr. Browning's poems **which are directly** prompted by thought have their counterpart **in a large** number which are specially inspired **by emotion ; and** must be noticed as such.   But this group will **perhaps be** the most artificial of all ; for while thought is **with him** often uncoloured by feeling, he seldom expresses feeling as detached from thought.  **The** majority, for instance, of his love poems **are** introduced by the title **"dramatic,"** and describe love as bound up with such varieties **of life** and character, that questions **of life** and character are necessarily raised **by them ;** the emotion thus conveyed being really more intense, because **more** individual, than could be given in any purely **lyric** effusion not warmed by the poet's own life.   Some **few,** however, are genuine lyrics, whether regarded as personal utterances or not ; and in the case of **two** or three of these, the personal utterance is unmistakable.

Under the head of LYRICAL LOVE POEMS must be placed " One Word More," to E. B. B. (" Men and Women." 1855.)

" Prospice." (" Dramatis Personæ." 1864.)

" Numpholeptos."
" Prologue."        } " Pacchiarotto and other Poems."
" Natural Magic."    }     1876.
" Magical Nature."   }
" Introduction.       } " The **Two** Poets **of** Croisic."
**" A** Tale."          }    1878.

" ONE WORD MORE " is a message of love, as direct

as it is beautiful ; but as such it also expresses an idea
which makes it a fitting object of study.   Most men and
women lay their highest gift at the feet of him or of her
they love, and with it such honour as the world may render
it.   They value both, as making them more worthy of those
they love, and for their sake rejoice in the possession.
Mr. Browning feels otherwise.   According to him the gifts
by which we are known to the world have lost gracious-
ness through its contact.   Their exercise is marred by
its remembered churlishness and ingratitude.     Every
artist, he declares, longs "once" and for "one only,"
to utter himself in a language distinct from his art ; to
"gain" in this manner, "the man's joy," while escaping
"the artist's sorrow."   So Raphael, the painter, wrote a
volume of sonnets to be seen only by one.   Dante, poet
of the "Inferno," drew an angel in memory of the one (of
Beatrice).   He—Mr. Browning—has only his verse to offer.
But as the fresco painter steals a camel's hair brush to paint
flowerets on his lady's missal—as he who blows through
bronze may also breathe through silver for the purpose
of a serenade, so may *he* lend his talent to a different use.
He has completed his volume of "Men" and "Women."
He dedicates it to her to whom this poem is addressed.
But his special offering to her is not the book itself, in
which he speaks with the mouth of fifty other persons,
but the word of dedication—the "One Word More"—in
which he speaks to her from his own.   The dramatic turns
lyric poet for the *one only.*

And what he says of himself, he in some degree thinks
of her.   The moon, he reminds her, presents always the
same surface to the world : whether new-born, waxing, or
waning ; whether, as they late saw her, radiant above the
hills of Florence ; or, as she now appears to them, palely
hurrying to her death over London house-tops.   But for
the "moonstruck mortal" she holds another side, glorious
or terrible as the case may be—unknown alike to herds-

man and huntsman, philosopher and poet, among the rest
of mankind. **So** she, who is his **moon** of poets, has also
her world's side, which he can see and praise with the rest ;

> " **But the best is** when I glide from out them,
> Cross a step or two of dubious twilight,
> Come out on the other side, the novel
> Silent silver lights and darks undreamed of,
> Where I hush and bless myself with silence." **(vol. iv. p.** 305.)

" PROSPICE " (look forward) is a challenge to spiritual
conflict, exultant with the certainty of victory, glowing with
the prospective joy of re-union with one whom death has
sent before. We cannot doubt that this poem, like the
preceding, came from the depths of the poet's own heart.

" NUMPHOLEPTOS " (caught by a nymph) is passionately
earnest in tone, and must **rank as** lyrical in spite of the
dramatic, at least fantastic, circumstance **in which the**
feeling is clothed. It **is** the almost despairing **cry of a**
human love, devoted to a being of superhuman **purity ; and**
who does not reject the love, but accepts it **on an** impossible condition : that the lover shall complete himself as a
**man by** acquiring the fullest knowledge **of life,** and shall
emerge unsullied from its experiences. This woman, more
**or** less than mortal, belongs rather to the "fairyland of
science " than to the realm of mythology. She stands, in
passionless repose, at the starting-point of the various
paths of earthly existence. These radiate from her, many-
hued with passion and adventure, **as** light rays **scattered**
by **a** prism ; and, in **the** mocking hopes with which **she**
invests their course, she seems herself the cold white
light, of which their glow is born, **and** into which it will
also die. She bids her worshipper travel down each
red and yellow ray, bathe in its hues, and return to her
"jewelled," but not smirched ; and each time he returns,
not jewelled, but smirched; always **to** appear monstrous in
her sight ; always to be dismissed with the same sad smile :

so pitying that it promises love, so fixed that it bars its possibility. He rebels at last, but the rebellion is momentary. He renews his hopeless quest.

"PROLOGUE" is a fanciful expression of the ideas of impediment visible and invisible, which may be raised by the aspect of a brick wall; such a one, perhaps, as projects at a right angle to the window of Mr. Browning's study, and was before him when he wrote.

"NATURAL MAGIC" attests the power of love to bring, as by enchantment, summer with its warmth and blossoms, into a barren life.

"MAGICAL NATURE" is a tribute to the beauty of countenance which proceeds from the soul, and has therefore a charmed existence defying the hand of time.

The INTRODUCTION to the "TWO POETS OF CROISIC," (reprinted under the title of "Apparitions,") recalls the sentiment of "Natural Magic." The "TALE" with which it concludes is inspired by the same feeling. Its circumstance is ancient, and the reader is allowed to imagine that it exists in Latin or Greek; but it is simply a poetic and profound illustration of what love can do always and everywhere. A famous poet was singing to his lyre. One of its strings snapped. The melody would have been lost, had not a cricket (properly, cicada) flown on to the lyre and chirped the missing note. The note, thus sounded, was more beautiful than as produced by the instrument itself, and, to the song's end, the cricket remained to do the work of the broken string. The poet, in his gratitude, had a statue of himself made with the lyre in his hand, and the cricket perched on the point of it. They were thus immortalized together: she, whom he had enthroned, he, whom she had crowned.

Love is the cricket which repairs **the** broken harmonies of life.

The dramatic setting of the majority of the Love poems serves, as I have said, to bring out the vitality of **Mr.** Browning's conception of love ; and though anything like labelling a poet's work brings with it a sense **of** anomaly, we shall only carry out the spirit **of** this particular group by connecting each member of **it with** the condition of thought or feeling it is made **to** illustrate.

It will be seen that the dramatic Lyrics **and** Dramatic Romances, which supply so many of the poems of the following and other groups, had been largely recruited from the first collection of " Men and Women ;" having first, in **several** instances, contributed to that work.

## DRAMATIC LOVE POEMS.

" Cristina." (Love as the special gain of life.) " Dramatic Lyrics." 1842.

" Evelyn Hope." (Love as conquering Time.) " Dramatic Lyrics." Published in " Men and Women." 1855.

" Love among the Ruins." (Love as the one lasting reality.) " Dramatic Lyrics." Published in " Men and Women." 1855.

" A Lover's Quarrel." (Love as the great harmony which triumphs over smaller discords.) " Dramatic Lyrics." Published in " Men and Women." 1855.

" By the Fireside." (Love in its ideal maturity.) " Dramatic Lyrics." Published in " Men and Women." 1855.

" Any Wife to any Husband." (Love in its ideal of constancy.) " Dramatic Lyrics." Published in " Men and Women." 1855.

" Two in the Campagna." (Love as an unsatisfied yearning.) " Dramatic Lyrics." Published in " Men and Women." 1855.

"Love in a Life." (Love as indomitable purpose.) "Dramatic Lyrics." Published in "Men and Women." 1855.

"Life in a Love." (Love as indomitable purpose.) "Dramatic Lyrics." Published in "Men and Women." 1855.

"The Lost Mistress." (Love as the completeness of self-surrender.) "Dramatic Lyrics." 1842.

"A Woman's last Word." (Love as the completeness of self-surrender.) "Dramatic Lyrics." Published in "Men and Women." 1855.

"A Serenade at the Villa." (Love as the completeness of self-surrender.) "Dramatic Lyrics." Published in "Men and Women." 1855.

"One Way of Love." (Love as the completeness of self-surrender.) "Dramatic Lyrics." Published in "Men and Women." 1855.

"Rudel to the Lady of Tripoli." (Love as the completeness of self-surrender.) "Men and Women." Published in "Dramatic Lyrics." 1842.

"In Three Days." (Love as the intensity of expectant hope.) "Dramatic Lyrics." Published in "Men and Women." 1855.

"In a Gondola." (Love as the intensity of a precarious joy.) "Dramatic Romances." Published in "Dramatic Lyrics." 1842.

"Porphyria's Lover." (Love as the tyranny of spiritual appropriation.) "Dramatic Romances." Published in "Dramatic Lyrics." 1842.

"James Lee's Wife." (Love as saddened by the presentiment and the consciousness of change.) "Dramatis Personæ." 1864

"The Worst of it." (Love as the completeness of self-effacement.) "Dramatis Personnæ." 1864.

"Too Late." (Love as the sense of a loss which

death has rendered irrevocable.) " Dramatis Personæ."
1864.

The two first of these are inspired by the belief **in the**
distinctness and continuity of the soul's life ; and represent
**love** as a condition of the soul with which positive experience has very little to do ; but **in** all the others it is
treated as part of this experience, and subject for the
time being to its laws. The situation sketched—for **it** is
nothing more—in " CRISTINA" **is** that **of a** man and
woman whom a glance has united, and who both have recognized in this union the predestined object **of** their life.
The knowledge has only flashed on the woman's mind, to
be extinguished by worldly ambitions and worldly honours;
and for her, therefore, the union remains barren. But the
existence of the man **is** enriched and perfected by it. She
has spiritually lost him, but *he* has gained *her;* for though
**she** has drifted away from him, he retains **her** soul. (This
poetical paradox is the strong point of the poem.) **It is**
henceforth his mission to test their blended powers; and
when that has been accomplished, he will have done, he
says, with this world.

" EVELYN HOPE " is the utterance of a love which has
missed its fruition in this life, but confidently anticipates
it for a life to come. The beloved is a young girl. The
lover is three times her age, and was a stranger to her ;
she is lying dead. But God, he is convinced, creates love
**to** reward love : and no matter what worlds must be tra-
versed, what lives lived, what knowledge gained or lost,
before that moment is reached, Evelyn Hope will, in the
end, be given to him.

" LOVE AMONG THE RUINS" depicts a pastoral solitude
in which are buried the remains of an ancient city, fabulous in magnificence and in strength. A ruined turret

Q

marks the site of a mighty tower, from which the king of
that city overlooked his domains, or, with his court, watched
the racing chariots as they encircled it in their course. In
that turret, in the evening grey, amidst the tinkling of the
sheep, a yellow-haired maiden is waiting for him she
loves ; and as they bury sight and speech in each other's
arms, he bids the human heart shut in the centuries, with
their triumphs and their follies, their glories and their sins,
for " Love is best."

" A LOVER'S QUARREL " describes, not the quarrel
itself, but the impression it leaves on him who has un-
wittingly provoked it : one of amazement as well as
sorrow, that such a thing could have occurred.   The
speaker, apostrophizing his absent love, reminds her how
happy they have been together, with no society but their
own ; no pleasures but those of sympathy ; no amusements
but those which their common fancy supplied ; and he asks
her if it be possible that so perfect a union can be destroyed by a hasty word with which his deeper self has
had nothing to do. He believes this so little that he is sure
she will, in some way, come back to him ; and then they
will part no more.

A vein of playfulness runs through this monologue,
which represents the lovers before their quarrel as more
like children enjoying a long holiday, than a man and a
woman sharing the responsibilities of life. It conveys,
nevertheless, a truth deeply rooted in the author's mind :
that the foundation of a real love can never be shaken.

" BY THE FIRESIDE " is a retrospect, in which the
speaker is carried from middle-age to youth, and from his,
probably English, fireside to the little Alpine gorge in
which he confessed his love ; and he summons the wife
who received and sanctioned the avowal to share with
him the joy of its remembrance. He describes the scene

of his declaration, the conflict of feeling which its risks involved, the generous frankness **with** which she cut the conflict short. He dwells on **the** blessings which their union has brought **to** him, and which make his youth seem barren by the richness of his maturer years ; and he asks her if there exist another woman, with whom he could thus have retraced the descending path of life, **and** found nothing to regret in what he had left behind. He declares that their mutual love has been for **him** that crisis **in the** life of the soul to which **all** experience tends—the pre-destined test of its quality. It is his title to honour as well as his guarantee of everlasting joy.

The subtler realities of life and love are reflected throughout the poem in picturesque impressions often no less subtle, and the whole is dramatic, *i.e.*, imaginary, as far as conception goes ; but the obvious genuineness **of** the sentiment is confirmed by the allusion to the " perfect wife " who,

> " Reading by firelight, that great brow
> And the spirit-small hand propping it," **(vol. vi. p. 132.)**

is known to all of us.

" ANY WIFE TO ANY HUSBAND" might be the lament of any woman about to die, who believes that her husband will remain true to her in heart, but will lack courage to be so in his life. She anticipates the excuses he will offer for seeking temporary solace in the society of **other** women ; but these all, to her mind, resolve themselves into **a** confession **of** weakness ; and it grieves her that such a confession should proceed from one, in all other respects, so much stronger than she. "Were she the sur-vivor, it would be so easy to her to **be** faithful to the end ! " Her grief is unselfish. The wrong she apprehends will be done to his spiritual dignity far more than to his love for her, though with a touch of feminine inconsistency she identifies the two ; and she cannot resign herself to the idea that he whose earthly trial is "three parts" overcome will break down under this final test. She accepts it, however, as the inevitable.

"Two in the Campagna." The sentiment of this poem can only be rendered in its concluding words :

> "Infinite passion, and the pain
> Of finite hearts that yearn."   (vol. vi. p. 153.)

For its pain is that of a heart both restless and weary : ever seeking to grasp the Infinite in the finite, and ever eluded by it. The sufferer is a man. He longs to rest in the affection of a woman who loves him, and whom he also loves ; but whenever their union seems complete, his soul is spirited away, and he is adrift again. He asks the meaning of it all—where the fault lies, if fault there be ; he begs her to help him to discover it. The Campagna is around them, with its "endless fleece of feathery grasses," its "everlasting wash of air ;" its wide suggestions of passion and of peace. The clue to the enigma seems to glance across him, in the form of a gossamer thread. He traces it from point to point, by the objects on which it rests. But just as he calls his love to help him to hold it fast, it breaks off, and floats into the invisible. His doom is endless change. The tired, tantalized spirit must accept it.

"Love in a Life" represents the lover as inhabiting the same house with his unseen love ; and pursuing her in it ceaselessly from room to room, always catching the flutter of her retreating presence, always sure that the next moment he will overtake her.

"Life in a Love" might be the utterance of the same person, when he has grasped the fact that the loved one is determined to elude him. She may baffle his pursuit, but he will never desist from it, though it absorb his whole life.

"THE LOST MISTRESS" is the farewell expression of a discarded love which has accepted the conditions of friendship. Its tone is full of manly self-restraint and of patient sadness.

"A WOMAN'S LAST WORD" is **one of** moral and intellectual self-surrender. She has been contending with her husband, and been silenced by the feeling, not that the truth is on his side, but that it was not worth the pain of such a contention. What, she seems to ask herself, is the value of truth, when it is false to her Divinity; or knowledge, when it costs her **her** Eden? She begs him **whom** she worships **as** well as loves, to mould her **to** himself; but she begs also the privilege of a few tears—a last tribute, perhaps, to her sacrificed conscience, and her lost liberty.

"A SERENADE AT THE VILLA" has a tinge **of** melancholy humour, which makes it the more pathetic. A lover has been serenading the lady of his affections through a sultry night, in which Earth seemed to **turn** painfully in her sleep, and the silent darkness was unbroken, except by an occasional flash of lightning, and a few drops of thundery rain. He wishes his music may have told her that whenever life is dark or difficult there will be one near to help and guide her : one whose patience will never tire, and who will serve her best when there are none **to** witness his devotion. But her villa looks **very** dark ; its closed windows **are** very obdurate. The gate ground its teeth as it let him pass. And he fears she only said **to** herself, that if the silence of a thundery night was oppressive, such noise was a worse infliction.

"ONE WAY OF LOVE." This lover has strewn the

roses of a month's gathering on his lady's path, only for
the chance of her seeing them : as he has conquered the
difficulties of the lute, only for the chance of her liking its
sound ; thrown his whole life into a love, which is hers to
accept or reject. She cares for none of these things. So
the roses may lie, the lute-string break. The lover can
still say, " Blest is he who wins her."

" RUDEL TO THE LADY OF TRIPOLI" is a pathetic declaration, in which the lover compares himself to a sun-
flower, and proclaims it as his badge. The French poet
Rudel loves the "Lady of Tripoli ;"[1] and she is dear to
him as is the sun to that foolish flower, which by constant
contemplation has grown into its very resemblance. And
he bids a pilgrim tell her that, as bees bask on the sun-
flower, men are attracted by his song ; but, as the sun-
flower looks ever towards the sun, so does he, disregarding
men's applause, look towards the East, and her.

" IN THREE DAYS " is a note of joyful expectation, and
doubtless a pure lyric, though classed as dramatic-
lyrical. The lover will see his love in three days ; and his
complex sense of the delay, as meaning both *all* this
time, and *only* this, is leavened by the joyful consciousness
that the reunion will be as absolute as the union has been.
He knows that life is full of chance and change. The
possibilities of three days are a great deal to encounter,
very little to have escaped. Unsuspected dangers may
lurk in the coming year. But—he will see her in three
days ; and in that thought he can laugh all misgiving and
all fear to scorn.

" IN A GONDOLA" is a love scene, beginning with a serenade from a gondola, and continued by the two lovers in
it, after the Venetian fashion of the olden time. They are

---

[1] This is told in the tales of the Troubadours.

escaping, as they think, the vigilance of a certain **"Three"**
—one of whom we may conjecture to be the lady's husband
or father—and **have** already regained **her home, and fixed**
the signal for to-morrow's meeting, **when the** lover **is** surprised and stabbed. As they glide through the canals **of**
the city, by its dark or illuminated palaces, **each** concealing perhaps some drama of love or crime—the sense of
danger never absent from them,—the tense emotion re-
lieves itself in playful though impassioned fancies, in
which the man and the woman vie with each other. But
when the blow has fallen, the light tone gives way, on the
lover's side, to one **of** solemn joy **in** the happiness which
has been realized.

> " . . . . The Three, **I do not scorn**
> **To death,** because they never lived : **but I**
> **Have** lived indeed, and so—(yet one more kiss)—can die ! "
>
> **(vol. v. p. 77.)**

" PORPHYRIA'S LOVER " is an episode **which, with one**
**of the** poems **of** " Men and Women," " Johannes Agricola
in Meditation," first appeared under the **head of** " Mad-
house Cells." [1] Porphyria is deeply attached to her
" lover," but has not courage to break the ties of an artificial world, and give herself to him ; and when one night
love prevails, and she proves it by **a** voluntary act of
devotion, he murders her in the act, that her nobler and
purer self may be preserved. Such **a** crime might be
committed in a momentary aberration, **or** even intense
excitement, of feeling. It is characterized here by a
matter-of-fact simplicity, which **is** its sign of madness.
The distinction, however, is subtle ; and we can easily
guess why this and its companion poem did not retain

---

[1] Published, simultaneously, in Mr. Fox's " Monthly Repository." The
song in " Pippa Passes " beginning " A king lived long ago," and the verses
introduced in " James Lee's Wife," were also first published in this Magazine,
edited by the generous and very earliest encourager of Mr. Browning's
boyish attempts at poetry.

their title. A madness which is fit for dramatic treatment is not sufficiently removed from sanity.

"JAMES LEE'S WIFE" is the study of a female character developed by circumstances, and also impressing itself on them; the circumstances being those of an unfortunate marriage, in which the love has been mutual, but the constancy is all on the woman's side. "James Lee" is (as we understand) a man of shallow nature, whose wife's earnestness repels him when its novelty has ceased to charm. The "Wife" is keenly alive to his change of feeling towards her : and even anticipates it, in melancholy forebodings which probably hasten its course.

## I.

### JAMES LEE'S WIFE SPEAKS AT THE WINDOW.

Love carries already the seed of doubt. The wife addresses her husband, who is approaching from outside, in words of anxious tenderness. The season is changing ; coming winter is in the air. Will his love change too?

## II.

### BY THE FIRESIDE.

The note of apprehension deepens. The fire they are sitting by is supplied by ship-wood. It suggests the dangers of the sea, the sailor's longing for land and home. "But the life in port has its dangers too. There are worms which gnaw the ship in harbour, as the heart in sleep. Did some woman before her, in this very house perhaps, begin love's voyage full sail, and then suddenly see the ship's planks start, and hell open beneath the man she loves?"

## III.

### IN THE DOORWAY.

She remonstrates with her **fear**. Winter **is drawing** nearer : nature becoming cold and bare. But they two have all the necessaries of life, and love besides. **The** human spirit (the **spirit of** love) was meant by **God to** resist change, to put its life into the **darkness and the** cold. **It** should fear neither.

## IV.

### ALONG THE BEACH.

**The** fear has **become a certainty. The wife** reasons with **her** husband **as they** walk **together. "** He wanted her love, **and she gave it** to him. **He has it, and yet is** not content. Why **so ?** She is **not** blind **to his** faults, but she does not love him the less for **them. She has** taken him as he was, with the good seed **in him and the** bad, waiting patiently for the good **to** bring its harvest ; enduring patiently when the harvest failed. Whether praise-**worthy** or blameworthy, he has been **her** world !"

" That is what condemns her in his eyes : she loves too well ; **she** watches too patiently. His nature is impatient of bondage. Such devotion as hers is a bond."

## V.

### ON THE CLIFF.

She reflects on **the** power of love. **A** cricket **and a** butterfly settle down before her : **one** on a piece of burnt-**up** turf, one on the dark flat surface of a rock which the receding tide has left bare. The barren surfaces are transfigured by their brightness. Just so will love settle on the low or barren in life, and transform it.

## VI.

### READING A BOOK UNDER THE CLIFF.

She has reached the transition stage between struggle and resignation. She accepts change and its disappointments as the law of life. We discover this in her comment on the book in question, from which some verses are introduced.[1] The author apostrophizes a moaning wind which appeals to him as a voice of woe more eloquent than any which is given to animal or man : and asks it what form of suffering, mental or bodily, its sighs are trying to convey. James Lee's wife regards the mood here expressed as characteristic of a youthful spirit, disposed to enlarge upon the evils of existence by its overweening consciousness of power to understand, strength to escape or overcome them. Such a one, she says, can only learn by sad experience what the wind in its moaning means : that subtle change which arrests the course of happiness, as the same wind, stirring however softly in a summer dawn, may annul the promise of its beauty.

> " Nothing can be as it has been before ;
> Better, so call it, only not the same.
> To draw one beauty into our hearts' core,
> And keep it changeless ! such our claim ;
> So answered,—Never more !"

She who has learnt it, can only ask herself if this old world-sorrow be cause for rejoicing through the onward impulse ever forced upon the soul ; if it be sent to us in probation. She cannot answer. God alone knows. The fully realized significance of such death in life gives an unutterable pathos to her concluding words.

[1] These verses were written when Mr. Browning was twenty-three.

# VII.

### AMONG THE ROCKS.

She accepts disappointment as also a purifier of love. A sunny autumn morning is exercising its genial influence, and the courage of self-effacement awakens in her. As earth blesses her smallest creatures with her smile, so should love devote itself to those less worthy beings who may be ennobled by it. Its **rewards** must be **sought in** heaven.

# VIII.

### BESIDE THE DRAWING-BOARD.

She accepts the duties **of life as an** equivalent **for its** happiness, *i.e.*, for **the** happiness **of love.** She has **been** drawing from the cast of **a** hand—enraptured with its delicate beauty—thinking how **the** rapture must **have** risen into love in the artist who **saw** it living ; when **the** coarse (laborious) hand **of** a little peasant girl reminds her that life, whether beautiful or not, is the artist's noblest study ; and that, as the uses of a hand are independent of its beauty and will survive it, life with its obligations will survive love. "She has been **a** fool **to** think she must be loved or die."

# IX.

### ON DECK.

**She** makes the final sacrifice **to** her husband's happiness, and leaves him. But in so doing she pays **a** last tribute to the omnipotence of love. She knows there is nothing in her that will claim a place in his remembrance. She knows also that if he had loved her, it might be otherwise. Love could have transformed her in his sight as it has transfigured him in hers. Their positions might

even have been reversed. If one touch of such a love as
hers could ever come to her in a thought of his, he might
turn into a being as ill-favoured as herself. She would
neither know nor care, since joy would have killed her.

We learn from the two last monologues, especially the
last, that James Lee's wife was a plain woman. This
may throw some light on the situation.

"THE WORST OF IT" is the cry of anguish of a man
whose wife has been false to him, and who sees in her
transgression only the injury she has inflicted on herself,
and his own indirect part in its infliction. The strain of
suppressed personal suffering betrays itself in his very endeavour to prove that he has not been wronged : that it
was his fault, not hers, if his love maddened her, and the
vows by which he had bound her were such as she could
not keep. But the burden of his lament—"the worst of
it" all—is, that her purity was once his salvation, her past
kindness has for ever glorified his life ; that she is dishonoured, and through him, and that no gratitude of his,
no power of his, can rescue her from that dishonour. In
his passionate tenderness he strives to pacify her conscience, and again, as earnestly to arouse it. "Her
account is not with him who absolves her, but with the
world which does not ; with her endangered womanhood,
her jeopardized hope of Heaven." He implores her for
her own sake to return to virtue though not to him. For
himself he renounces her even in Paradise. He "will pass
nor turn" his "face" if they meet there.

The pathos of "TOO LATE" is all conveyed in its title.
The loved woman is dead. She was the wife of another
man than he who mourns for her. But so long as there
was life there was hope. The lover might, he feels,
have learned to compromise with the obstacles to his
happiness. Some shock of circumstance might have

rolled them away. **If** the loved one spurned him once, he had of late been earning her friendship. She might **in** time **have** discovered that the so-called poet whom **she had** preferred to him was a mere lay-figure **whom her** fancy had draped. But all this is at an end. Hope **and** opportunity are alike gone. He remains to condemn his own quiescence in what was perhaps not inevitable ; **in** what proved no more for her happiness than **for his. The** husband is probably writing her epitaph.

"Too Late" expresses an attachment **as** individual as it is complete. "Edith" **was not** considered a beauty. She was not one even in her **lover's** eyes. This fact, and the manner in which he shows **it, give a** characteristic force to the situation.

## EMOTIONAL POEMS (CONTINUED).

### RELIGIOUS, ARTISTIC, AND EXPRESSIVE OF THE FIERCER EMOTIONS.

The emotions which, after that of love, are most strongly represented in Mr. Browning's works are the RELIGIOUS and the ARTISTIC : emotions closely allied in every nature in which they happen to co-exist, and which are so in their proper degree in Mr. Browning's ; the proof of this being that two poems which I have placed in the Artistic group almost equally fit into the Religious. But the religious poems impress us more by their beauty than by their number, if we limit it to those which are directly inspired by this particular emotion. Religious questions have occupied, **as** we have seen, some of Mr. Browning's most important reflective poems. Religious belief forms the undercurrent of many of the emotional poems. And it was natural therefore, that religious feeling should not often lay hold of him in a more exclusive form.    It does so only in three cases ; those of

"Saul." ("Dramatic Lyrics." Published in part in "Dramatic Romances and Lyrics," 1845 ; wholly, in Men and Women," 1855.)

"Epilogue." (" Dramatis Personæ." 1864.)

"Fears and Scruples." ("Pacchiarotto and other Poems." 1876.)

The religious sentiment in "SAUL." anticipates Christianity. It begins with the expression of an exalted human tenderness, and ends in a prophetic vision of Divine Love, as manifested in Christ.  The speaker is David.  He has been sent into the presence of Saul to sing and play to him ; for Saul is in the agony of that recurring spiritual conflict from which only David's song can deliver him ; and when the boy-shepherd has crept his way into the darkness of the tent, he sees the monarch with arms outstretched against its poles, dumb, sightless, and stark, like the serpent in the solitude of the forest awaiting its transformation.

David tells his story, re-enacting the scene which it describes, in strong, simple, picturesque words which rise naturally into the language of prophecy.  He tells how first he tried the influence of pastoral tunes : those which call the sheep back to the pen, and stir the sense of insect and bird ; how he passed to the song of the reapers—their challenge to mutual help and fellowship ; to the warrior's march ; the burial and marriage chants ; the chorus of the Levites advancing towards the altar ; and how at this moment Saul sent forth a groan, though the lights which leapt from the jewels of his turban were his only sign of motion.  Then—the tale continues—David changes his theme. He sings of the goodness of human life, as attested by the joyousness of youth, the gratitude of old age.  He sings of labour and success, of hope and fulfilment, of high ambitions and of great deeds ; of the great king in whom are

centred all the gifts and the powers of human nature—of
Saul himself. And at these words the tense body relaxes,
the arms cross themselves on the breast. But the eyes
of Saul still gaze vacantly before him, without consciousness of life, without desire for it.

David's song has poured forth the full cup of material
existence; he has yet to infuse into it that draught of
"Soul Wine" which shall make it desirable. In a fresh
burst of inspiration, he challenges his hearer to follow him
beyond the grave. "The tree is known by its fruits; life
by its results. Life, like the palm **fruit, must** be crushed
before its wine can **flow.** Saul **will die.** But his passion
and his power will thrill the generations to come. His
achievements will live in the hearts of his people; for whom
their **record,** though covering **the whole** face **of** a rock,
will still **seem** incomplete." And as the "Soul Wine"
works, as the vision of this earthly immortality unfolds
itself before the sufferer's sight, he becomes a king again.
The old attitude and expression **assert** themselves. **The**
hand is gently laid on the young singer's forehead; **the eyes**
fix themselves in **grave** scrutiny upon **him.**

Then the **heart of** David goes **out to the** suffering
monarch in filial, pitying tenderness; and **he** yearns to
give him more than this present life—a new life equal to it
in goodness, and which shall be everlasting.

And the yearning converts itself into prophecy. "What
he, as man, **can** desire for his fellow-man, God will surely
give. What **he** would suffer for those he loves, surely
God would suffer. Human nature **in its** power of love
would otherwise outstrip the Divine. He cries for the
weakness to be engrafted upon strength, the human to be
manifested in the Divine. And exulting in the consciousness that his cry is answered, he hails the advent of Christ.
He bids Saul "see" that a Face like his who now speaks
to him awaits him at the threshold of an eternal life; that
a Hand like his hand opens to him its gates.

David's prophecy has rung through the universe ; and
as he seeks his home in the darkness, unseen "cohorts"
press everywhere upon him. A tumultuous expectation
is filling earth and hell and heaven. The Hand guides
him through the tumult. He sees it die out in the birth
of the young day. But the hushed voices of nature attest
the new dispensation. The seal of the new promise is on
the face of the earth.

The EPILOGUE is spoken by three different persons, and
embodies as many phases of the religious life. The
"FIRST SPEAKER, *as David*," represents the old Testament Theism, with its solemn celebrations, its pompous
worship, and the strong material faith which bowed down
the thousands as one man, before the visible glory of the
Lord.

The "SECOND SPEAKER, *as Renan*" represents nine-
teenth-century scepticism, and the longing of the heart for
the old belief which scientific reason has dispelled. This
belief is symbolized by a "Face" which once looked down
from heights of glory upon men; by a star which shone
down upon them in responsive life and love. The face
has vanished into darkness. The star, gradually receding,
has lost itself in the multitude of the lesser lights of
heaven. And centuries roll past while the forsaken
watchers vainly question the heavenly vault for the sign
of love no longer visible there.

This lament assumes that Theism, having grown into
Christianity, must disappear with it ; and the pathetic
sense of bereavement gives way to shuddering awe, as the
farther significance of the sceptical position reveals itself.
*Man* becomes the summit of creation ; the sole successor
to the vacant throne of God.

The "THIRD SPEAKER," Mr. Browning himself, cor-
rects both the material faith of the Old Testament, and
the scientific doubt of the nineteenth century, by the idea

of a more mystical and individual intercourse between **God**
and man. Observers have noted in the Arctic Seas that
the whole field of waters seem constantly hastening towards some central point of rock, **to** envelope it in their
playfulness and their force ; **in** the blackness they have
borrowed from the nether world, or the radiance they have
caught from heaven ; then tearing **it** up by the **roots, to**
sweep onwards towards another peak, and make *it* their
centre for the time being. So do **the** forces of life and
nature circle round the individual man, doing in each the
work of experience, reproducing for each the Divine Face
which is inspired by the spirit of creation. And, as the
speaker declares, he needs no " Temple," because the world
is that. Nor, as **he** implies, needs he look beyond the
range of his own being for the lost Divinity.

> " That one Face, far from vanish, rather grows,
> **Or** decomposes but to recompose,
> Become my universe that feels and knows !" (vol. vii. p. 255 )

" FEARS AND SCRUPLES " illustrates this personal religion **in** an opposite manner. **It** is the expression of **a**
tender and very simple religious feeling, saddened by the
obscurity which surrounds its object, and still more by the
impossibility of proving to other minds that this object is
a real one. It is described as the devotion to an unseen
friend, known only by his letters and reported deeds, but
whom one loves as by instinct, believes in without testimony, and trusts to as accepting the allegiance **of** the
smaller being, and sure sooner or later to acknowledge it.
**In** the present case the days are going by. No sign of
acknowledgment has been given. Sceptics assure the
believer that his faith rests on letters which were forged,
on actions which others equally have performed ; he can
only yearn for some word or token which would enable
him to shut their mouth. But when some one hints that
the friend is only concealing himself to test his power of

R

vision, and will punish him if he does not see ; and another objects that this would prove the friend a monster ; he crushes the objector with a word : "and what if the friend be GOD?"

The next group is fuller and still more characteristic : for it displays the love of Art in its special conditions, and, at the same time, in its union with all the general human instincts in which artistic emotion can be merged. We find it in its relation to the general love of life in

"Fra Lippo Lippi." ("Men and Women." 1855.)

In its relation to the spiritual sense of existence in

"Abt Vogler." ("Dramatis Personæ." 1864.)

As a transformation of human tenderness in

"Pictor Ignotus." ("Men and Women." Published in "Dramatic Romances and Lyrics." 1845.)

In its directly sensuous effects in

"The Bishop orders his Tomb at Saint Praxed's Church." ("Men and Women." Published as "The Tomb at Saint Praxed's" in "Dramatic Romances and Lyrics." 1845.)[1]

In its associative power in

"A Toccata of Galuppi's." ("Dramatic Lyrics." Published in "Men and Women." 1855.)

In its representative power in

"The Guardian-Angel : a Picture at Fano." ("Dramatic Lyrics." Published in "Men and Women." 1855.)

"Eurydice to Orpheus : a Picture by Leighton." ("Dramatis Personæ." 1864.)

"A Face." ("Dramatis Personæ." 1864.)

"FRA LIPPO LIPPI" is a lively monologue, supposed to be uttered by that friar himself, on the occasion of a night frolic in which he has been surprised. Cosmo dei Medici had locked him up in one room of the palace till some pictures he was painting for him should be finished ;[2] and on this particular night he has found the confinement

---

[1] First in "Hood's Magazine."

[2] Two of these are now in the National Gallery ; one presented to it by Sir Charles Eastlake, the other after his death by Lady Eastlake.

intolerable. He has whipped **his** bed clothes **into** a rope, scrambled **down from** his window, **and run after** a girlish **face** which laughingly invited him from **the** street ; and **was** about to return **from** the equivocal neighbourhood into which the fun had led him, when his monkish **dress** caught the attention of the guard, and he was captured **and** called to account. He proceeds **to** give a sketch of his life and opinions, which supplies a fair excuse for the escapade. **The** facts he relates **are**, including **this** one, historical.

Fra Lippo Lippi **had** no vocation for the priesthood. **He was** enticed into a Carmelite convent when **a** half-starved orphan of eight years old, ready to subscribe to any arrangement which promised him enough to eat. There he developed an extraordinary talent for drawing ; and **the** Prior, glad to turn it to account, gave him the cloisters and the church to **paint**. But the rising artist had received his earliest inspirations in **the streets**. **His** first practice had been gained in scrawling faces in his copybooks, and expanding the notes of his musical texts **into** figures **with arms** and legs. **His** conceptions **were not sufficiently** spiritual to satisfy the Prior's ideal **of** Christian **art**. The men and women he painted **were all** true to life. The simpler brethren were delighted as they recognized each familar type. But **the** authorities looked grave at so much obtruding of the flesh ; and the Prior clearly laid down his theory that painting was meant to inspire religious thoughts, and not to stifle them ; and must therefore show no more of the human **body than** was needed **to** image forth **the soul**.

**Fra** Lippo Lippi comments freely and quaintly on the absurdity of showing soul by means of bodies so ill-painted that no one can bear to dwell upon them, as on the fallacy involved in all contempt for the earthly life. "He will never believe that the world, with all **its** life and beauty, **is** an unmeaning blank. He is sure, 'it means intensely and means good.' **He is** sure, too, that to reproduce **what**

is beautiful in it is the mission of Art. If anyone objects, that the world being God's work, Art cannot improve on it, and the painter will best leave it alone : he answers that some things are the better for being painted ; because, as we are made, we love them best when we see them so. The artist has lent his mind for us to see with. That is what Art means ; what God wills in giving it to us."

Nevertheless (he continues) he rubbed out his men and women ; and though now, with a Medici for his patron, he may paint as he likes, the old schooling sticks to him.[1] And he works away at his saints, till something comes to remind him that life is not a dream, and he kicks the traces, as he has done now. He ends with a half-joking promise to make the Church a gainer through his mis-conduct (supposing that the secret has been kept from her), by a beautiful picture which he will paint by way of atonement.

This picture, which he describes very humorously, is that of the Coronation of the Virgin, now in the "Belle Arti" at Florence.[2]

ABT VOGLER is depicted at the moment when this com-poser of the last century has "been extemporizing on the musical instrument of his invention." His emotion has not yet subsided ; and it is that of the inspired musician, to whom harmonized sound is as the opening of a heavenly world. His touch upon the keys has been as potent to charm, as the utterance of that NAME which summoned into Solomon's presence the creatures of Earth, Heaven, and Hell, and made them subservient to his will. And the "slaves of the sound," whom he has conjured up, have

---

[1] Mr. Browning thus skilfully accounts for the discrepancy between the coarseness of his life and the refined beauty of much of his work.

[2] The painter spoken of as "hulking Tom" is the celebrated one known as "Masaccio" (Tommasaccio), who learned in the convent from Lippo Lippi, and has been wrongly supposed to be his teacher. He is also one of those who were credited with the work of Lippino, Lippo Lippi's son.

built him **a** palace more evanescent than Solomon's, but, **as** he describes it, far more beautiful. They have laid **its** foundations below the earth. They have carried its transparent walls up to the sky. They have tipped each summit with meteoric fire. As earth strove upwards towards Heaven, Heaven, in this enchanted structure, has yearned downwards towards **the** earth. The great Dead **came** back; and those conceived for a happier future **walked** before their time. New births of life and splendour united far and near; **the** past, **the** present, and the to-come.

The vision has disappeared with the sounds which called it forth, and the musician feels sorrowfully that it cannot be recalled: for the effect was incommensurate with the cause; they had nothing in common with each other. We can trace the processes of painting and verse; we can explain their results. Art, however triumphant, is subject to natural laws. But that which frames out of three notes of music "not a fourth sound, but a star" is the Will, which is above law.

And, therefore, **so** Abt Vogler **consoles** himself, the music persists, though **it** has passed from **the** sense of him who called it forth: for it is an echo of the eternal life; a pledge **of** the reality of every imagined good—of the continuance of whatever good has existed. Human passion and aspiration are music sent up to Heaven, to be continued and completed there. The secret of the scheme of creation is in the musician's hands.

Having recognized this, Abt Vogler can subside, proudly and patiently, on the common chord—the commonplace realities, of life.

" PICTOR IGNOTUS" (Florence, 15—), is the answer of an unknown painter to the praise which he hears lavished on another man. He admits its justice, but declares that he too could have deserved it; and his words have all the bitterness of a suppressed longing which an unexpected

touch has set free. He, too, has dreamed of fame ; and
felt no limits to his power of attaining it.  But he saw, by
some flash of intuition, that it must be bought by the dishonour of his works ; that, in order to bring him fame,
they must descend into the market, they must pass from
hand to hand ; they must endure the shallowness of their
purchasers' comments, share in the pettiness of their lives.
He has remained obscure, that his creations might be
guarded against this sacrilege. " He paints Madonnas and
saints in the twilight stillness of the cloister and the aisle ;
and if his heart saddens at the endless repetition of the
one heavenward gaze, at least no merchant traffics in what
he loves. There, where his pictures have been born,
mouldering in the dampness of the wall, blackening in the
smoke of the altar, amidst a silence broken only by prayer,
they may ' gently ' and ' surely ' die." He asks himself,
as he again subsides into mournful resignation, whether
the applause of men may not be neutralized at its best
by the ignoble circumstances which it entails.

"THE BISHOP ORDERS HIS TOMB AT SAINT PRAXED'S
CHURCH " (Rome, 15—) displays the artistic emotion in its
least moral form : the love of the merely beautiful as such ;
and it shows also how this may be degraded : by connecting it in the mind of the given person, with the passion for
luxury, and the pride and jealousies of possession. The
Bishop is at the point of death. His sons (nominally
nephews) are about him ; and he is urging on them anxious
and minute directions for the tomb they are to place for
him in St. Praxed's church.

This tomb, as the Bishop has planned it, is a miracle of
costliness and beauty ; for it is to secure him a double
end : the indulgence of his own tastes, and the humiliation
of a former rival who lies modestly buried in the same
church. In the delirium of his weakness, these motives,
which we imagine always prominent, assume the strength

of mania. His limbs are already stiff; he feels himself growing into his own monument; and his fancy revels in the sensations which **will** combine **the** calm of **death** with **the** consciousness of **sepulchral** magnificence. He pleads, **as for** dear life, with **those who are** to inherit his **wealth, and** who may at their pleasure fulfil his last wishes or disregard them : that he may have jasper for his tomb —basalt (black antique) for its slab—the rosiest marble for **its** columns—the richest design **for its bronze frieze !** A certain **ball** of lapis-lazuli (such as **never yet was** seen) is to "poise" between his knees ; **and he** gasps forth the secret of **how** he saved this **from the** burning **of** his church, **and** buried **it out** of sight **in a vineyard,** as if he were staking his **very life on the** revelation.

But in his heart he knows that his entreaties are useless : that his sons will keep all they can ; and the tone of entreaty is dashed with all the petulance of foreseen **disappointment.** Weakness prevails at last. He resigns himself to the inevitable ; blesses his undutiful sons ; and dismisses them.

Other strongly **dramatic details** complete **the** picture.[1]

"A TOCCATA **OF GALUPPI'S**" is a fantastic little vision **of bygone** Venice, evoked by **the** music of **an** old Venetian **master, and** filling us with the sense of a joyous ephemeral existence, in which the glow of life is already struck by the shuddering chill of annihilation. This sense is created by the sounds, as Mr. Browning describes them : **and** their directly expressive power must stand **for** what it **is** worth. Still, the supposed effect is mainly **that** of association ; **and the** listener's fancy the medium through which it acts.

"A FACE" describes **a** beautiful head and throat **in its** pictorial details—those which painting might reproduce.

---

[1] The Bishop's tomb is entirely fictitious ; but something which is made to stand for it is now shown to credulous sight-seers in St. Praxed's Church.

"THE GUARDIAN-ANGEL" and "EURYDICE TO ORPHEUS" describe each an actual picture in the emotions it expresses or conveys.

The former represents an angel, standing with outstretched wings by a little child. The child is half kneeling on a kind of pedestal, while the angel joins its hands in prayer : its gaze directed upward towards the sky, from which cherubs are looking down. The picture was painted by Guercino, and is now in the church of St. Augustine, at Fano, on the Italian coast. Mr. Browning relates to an absent friend (who appears in the "Dramatic Romances" as Waring) how he saw it in the company of his own "angel ;" and how it occurred to him to develop into a poem one of the thoughts which the picture had "struck out." The thought resolves itself into a feeling : the yearning for guidance and protection. The poet dreams himself in the place of that praying child. The angel wings cover his head : the angel hands upon his eyes press back the excess of thought which has made his brain too big. He feels how thankfully those eyes would rest on the "gracious face" instead of looking to the opening sky beyond it ; and how purely beautiful the world would seem when that healing touch had been upon them.

The second was painted by F. Leighton. It represents Orpheus leading Eurydice away from the infernal regions, but with an implied variation on the story of her subsequent return to them. She was restored to Orpheus on the condition of his not looking at her till they had reached the upper world ; and, as the legend goes, the condition proved too hard for him to fulfil. But the face of Leighton's Eurydice wears an intensity of longing which seems to challenge the forbidden look, and make her responsible for it. The poem thus interprets the expression, and translates it into words.

the wife, confronting him at the same moment, **bade** him kill her, but spare the man she loved. He did not kill her —then : for she had turned his love into contempt. **He** despised her too much to inflict even a lesser punishment, which should compromise the dignity, or disturb the outward calmness, of his life. But from that moment their union was a form ; and while he worked as those do who have something to forget, and she shared **the** position which his labours procured for him, an impassable, if unseen, gulf lay between them.

Three years had passed, when suddenly, one night, the wife begged to speak with her husband alone. Her **request** was granted ; and then the truth broke forth. She loved—had loved—no one but him ; but she was jealous of his devotion to the State. She imagined herself second to it in his affections ; and it was the jealousy **in** her which had made her strive to arouse it in him. That other man had been nothing to her but a tool. Her secret, **she now** knew, **was** killing her. Conscience **forbade** her **to** elude her punishment by **death.** She therefore spoke.

" Would she write this ? " he asked ; and **he** dictated to her the confession she had just made, in the terms most humiliating to him who was intended to hear it.

" Could she but write it in her blood ! " This, too, was possible. He put into her hand a dainty Eastern weapon, one prick **of** which, he said, would draw so much blood as was required. It did more than this, for it was poisoned. But, before she died, she knew that her explanation had raised her husband's contempt into hatred, and that the revenge of which she was now found worthy had quenched the hatred in forgiveness.

" She lies as erst beloved " (the narrative concludes) " in the church of him who hears this confession ; whom his grate conceals as little as that cloak once did—whom vengeance overtakes **at** last."

The poisoned dagger, which was the instrument of re-venge—the pledge of forgiveness—is spoken of as part of a collection preserved in the so-called study, which was the scene of the interview ; and the speaker dwells at some length on the impression of deadly purpose com-bined with loving artistic care, which their varied form and fantastic richness convey. This collection is actually in Mr. Browning's possession ; and he values it, perhaps, for the reason he imputes to its imagined owner : that those who are accustomed to the slower processes of thought, like to play with the suggestions of prompt (if murderous) action ; as the soldier, tired of wielding the sword, will play with paper and pen.

## HISTORICAL POEMS, OR POEMS FOUNDED ON FACT.

Many of Mr. Browning's poems are-founded on fact, whether historical, or merely of known occurrence ; but few of them can be classed by their historic quality, be-cause it is seldom their most important. In " Prince Hohenstiel-Schwangau," for instance, we have a chapter in recent history : but we only read it as an abstract dis-cussion, to which a chapter in history has given rise ; and in " Pacchiarotto, and how he worked in Distemper," and " Filippo Baldinucci on the Privilege of Burial" (published in the same volume), we find two incidents, each of them true, and each full of historic significance ; but which owe all their vitality to the critical and humorous spirit, in which Mr. Browning has described them. The small list of poems which are historical more than anything else, might be recruited from the Dramatic Idyls ; but, for various reasons, this publication must stand alone ; and even here, it is often difficult to disengage the actual fact, from the imaginary conditions in which it appears.  Our present group is therefore reduced to—

"Red Cotton Night-Cap Country ; **or, Turf** and Towers." (1873.)

"The Inn Album." (1875.)

"The Two Poets of Croisic." (1878.)

"Cenciaja." (" Pacchiarotto, and other Poems." 1876.)

We may also place here, as it is historical in character, "The Heretic's Tragedy ; a Middle Age Interlude" ("Dramatic Romances." Published in "Men and Women." 1855.)

The real-life drama which Mr. Browning has reproduced under the title of " RED COTTON NIGHT-CAP COUNTRY," was enacted partly in Paris, partly in a retired corner of Normandy, where he spent the late summer of 1872 ; and ended in a trial which had been only a fortnight closed, when he supposes himself to be relating it.  His whole story is true, except that in it which reality itself must have left to the imagination.  Only the names of persons and places are fictitious.[1]

The principal actor in this drama, Léonce Miranda, was son and heir to a wealthy Spanish jeweller in the Place Vendôme.  He was southern by temperament as by descent ; but a dash of the more mercantile Parisian spirit had come to him from his French mother ; and while keenly susceptible to the incitements of both religious and earthly passion, he began life with the deliberate purpose of striking a compromise between them.  At an early age he determined to live for this world now, and for the other when he was older ; and in the meantime to be moderate in his enjoyments.  In conformity with this plan he ran riot on Sunday ; but worked diligently during the rest of the week.  He bestowed his

---

[1] These were correctly given in the MS., and appeared so in the first proofs of the book ; but were changed from considerations of prudence.

fancy on five women at once; but represented himself,
when in their company, as a poor artist or musician, and
wasted no money upon them.

One day, however, he fell in love. The object of his
affections, Clara Mulhausen, or, as she first calls herself, "de Millefleurs," was an adventuress; but she did
not at first allow him to find this out; and when he did
so, her hold upon him had become too strong to be affected
by the discovery. A succession of circumstances, which
Mr. Browning describes, first cemented the bond, then
destroyed its secrecy; and since Clara had a husband,
and the position could not be legalized, Léonce Miranda
had no choice but to accept the social interdict, and with
her retire from Paris. He placed a substitute in the business, which had devolved on him through his father's
death; and the pair took up their abode at Clairvaux,
an ancient priory, which the father had bought. Here
Miranda built and improved; indulged his amateur pro-
pensities for painting and music; remained devoted to his
love, and was rewarded by her devotion. For five years
they were very happy.

The first interruption to their happiness was a summons
to Miranda, from his mother in Paris, to come and answer
for his excessive expenditure. The immorality of his life
she had condoned (a curious proof of this is given), for she
hoped it would be its own cure. But "his architectural
freaks, above all, a Belvedere which he had constructed in
his grounds, were a reckless waste of substance which she
could not witness without displeasure." She had immense
influence with her son; and he took her rebuke so much
to heart, that he only left her to fling himself into the
Seine. He was brought out alive; but lay for a month at
death's door, and made no progress towards recovery till
he had been restored to Clara's care; and Clara was painfully winning him back to health, when the telegraphic
wires flashed a second summons upon him. His presence

was again demanded in the maternal home. "The business was urgent. Its nature he would learn on arrival."

He hastened to his mother's house, to find her a corpse —laid out with all the ghastly ceremonial which Catholic fancy could devise—and to be told that his misconduct had killed her. The tribe of cousins, who had planned the *coup de théâtre*, were there to enjoy its result. This did not fail them. Miranda fainted away. As soon as consciousness returned, he made his act of atonement. He foreswore the illegal bond. He willed away his fortune to his kinsfolk; and would retain of it, from that moment, only a pittance for himself, and the means of honourable subsistence for Clara. They were to meet in the same house a week later, to arrange in what manner that sinful woman should be acquainted with the facts.

The day came. The cousins arrived. Miranda did not appear. He had broken down at the funeral in a fresh outburst of frenzied grief; but from this he had had time to recover. Someone peeped into his room. There he stood, by a blazing fire, a small empty coffer by his side, engaged in reading some letters which he had taken from it. Whose they were, and what the reading had told him, was quickly shown. He replaced them in the box, plunged this in the fire; and reiterating the words, "Burn, burn and purify my past!" held it there till both his hands had been consumed; no sign of pain escaping him. He was dragged away by main force, protesting against this hindrance to his salvation. "He was not yet purified. SHE was not yet burned out of him." In his bed he raved and struggled against the image which again rose before his eyes, which again grew and formed itself in his flesh.

The delirium was followed by three months of exhaustion. The moment the sick man could "totter" out of his room, he found his way to her whom he had abjured, and who was in Paris calmly awaiting his return to her. She came back with him. He introduced her to his kinsmen. " It was all right," he said ; " Clara would henceforth be—his brother; he would still fulfil his bond." From this, however, he departed, in so far as not to content himself with a pittance. He sold his business to the " cousinry," and, as they considered, on hard terms. He and Clara then returned to Clairvaux.

And now, as Mr. Browning interprets the situation, his experience had entered on a new phase. He had tested the equal strength of the earthly and the heavenly powers, and he knew that he could elude neither, and that neither could be postponed to the other. He no longer strove to compromise between these opposing realities, but threw his whole being into the struggle to unite them. He adhered to his unlawful love. His acts of piety and charity became grotesque in their excessiveness. (Of these again particulars are given.) Two years went by ; and then, one April morning, Miranda climbed his Belvedere, and was found, soon after, dead, on the turf below. There seemed no question of accident. The third attempt at suicide had succeeded.

On this fact, however, Mr. Browning puts a construction of his own. He asserts the poet's privilege of seeing into the man's mind; and makes him think before us in a long and impassioned soliloquy, which sets forth the hidden motive of his deed. As Mr. Browning conceives him, he did not mean to kill himself. He did so in a final, irresistible impulse to manifest his faith, and to test the foundations of it. It has had for its object, not the spiritual truths of Christianity, but its miraculous powers; and these powers have of late been symbolized to his mind by the Virgin of the Ravissante.[1] The conflict of despotisms has thus been waged between the natural woman and the supernatural : each a monarch in her way. As he looks from his tower towards the Church of

---

[1] A feigned name for one of the three wonder-working images which are worshipped in France.

the Ravissante, he apostrophizes **her** who is enthroned there.

He imagines her to have reproached him for his divided allegiance; and asserts, in answer, that he has been subject to her all his life. " He could not part with his soul's treasure. But he has, for her sake, lavished his earthly goods, burned away his flesh. If his sacrifice has **been** incomplete, it was because another power, mysterious **and** unnamed, but yet as absolute as she, had cast its spells about him. He would have resisted the Enchantress, if she, the Despot, had made a sign. But what token has he ever received, of her acceptance, her approbation ? She exacts from her servants the surrender of both body and soul; the least deficiency in the offering neutralizes its sum. And what does she give in exchange for body and soul ? Promises ? Is a man to starve while the life-apple is withheld from him, if even husks are within **his** reach ? Miracles ? Will she make **a** finger grow on **his** maimed hand ? Would he **not** be called a **madman if he** expected it ?"

And yet he believes. He summons **her** to justify **his** belief. He claims of her a genuine miracle—a miracle of power, which will silence scepticism, and re-establish the royalty of the Church—a miracle of mercy, which will wipe away the past; reconcile duty and love; give Clara into his hands as his pure and lawful wife. " She is to carry him through the air to the space before her church as she was herself conveyed there . . . ." Then come the leap and the catastrophe.

He had by a second will bequeathed all his possessions to the Church, reserving in them a life-interest for his virtual wife ; and when the cousinry swooped down on what they thought their prey, Madame Mulhausen could receive them and their condolences with the indignant scorn which their greed and cruelty deserved. They disputed the will on the alleged plea of the testator's insanity. The trial was interrupted by the events of 1870, but finally settled in the lady's favour ; the verdict being uncompromising as to her moral, as well as legal claim to the inheritance.

Mr. Browning had lately stood outside the grounds of Clairvaux, and seen its lady pass. She was insignificant in face and expression ; and he was reduced to account-. ing for the power she had exercised, by that very fact. She seemed a blank surface, on which a man could inscribe, or fancy he was inscribing, himself; and it is a matter of fact that, whether from strength of will, or from the absence of it, she presented such a surface to her lover's hand. She humoured his every inclination, complied with his every wish. And because she did no more than this, and also no less, Mr. Browning pronounces her far from the best of women, but by no means one of the worst. The two had, after all, up to a certain point, redeemed each other.

The title of the book arose as follows. The narrative is addressed (as the volume is dedicated) to Miss Annie Thackeray; and its supposed occasion is that of a meeting which took place at St. Rambert—actually St. Aubin —between her and Mr. Browning, in the summer of 1872. She had laughingly called the district " White Cotton Night-Cap Country," from its sleepy appearance, and the universal white cap of even its male inhabitants. Mr. Browning, being acquainted with the tragedy of Clairvaux, thought " *Red* Cotton Night-Cap Country " would be a more appropriate name; and adopted it for his story, as Miss Thackeray had adopted hers for one which she promised to write. But he represents himself as playing at first with the idea ; and as leading the listener's mind, from the suggestions of white night-caps to those of the red one: and from the outward calmness of the neighbouring country, to the tragic possibilities which that calmness conceals.

**The** supplementary heading, "Turf and Towers," must have been inspired by the literal facts of the case; but it supplies an analogy for the contrasted influences which fought for Miranda's soul. The "tower" represents the militant or religious life. The "turf," the self-indulgent; and the figure appears and reappears at every stage of the man's career. The attempt at compromise is symbolized by a pavilion: a structure aping solidity, but only planted on the turf. The final attempt at union is spoken of as an underground passage connecting the two, and by which the fortress may be entered instead of scaled. The difficulty of making one's way through life amidst the ruins of old beliefs and the fanciful overgrowth in which time has clothed them; the equal danger of destroying too much and clearing away too little; also find their place in the allegory.

The possible friend and adviser, to whom Miranda is referred at vol. xii. p. 122, was M. Joseph Milsand, who always at that time passed the bathing season at St. Aubin.[1]

[1] Mr. Browning allows me to give the true names of the persons and places concerned in the story.

"THE INN ALBUM" is a tragedy in eight parts or
scenes: the dialogue interspersed with description; and
carried on by four persons not named. It is chiefly enacted in the parlour of a country inn; and the Inn
"Album," in spite of its grotesque or prosaic character,
becomes an important instrument in it.

Four years before the tragedy occurred—so we learn
from the dialogue—a gentlemanly adventurer of uncertain
age had won and abused the affections of a motherless
girl, whom he thought too simple to resent the treachery.
He was mistaken in this; for her nature was as proud as
it was confiding; and her indignation when she learned

that he had **not** intended marriage was such as to surprise
him into offering it. She rejected the offer with contempt.
He went his way, mortified and embittered. A month
later she had buried herself in **a** secluded and squalid
village, as wife of the old, poor, overworked, and hopelessly
narrow-minded clergyman, whose cure it was. She ab-
stained, however, for his own sake, from making any painful disclosures to her husband ; and **the** daily and hourly
expiation brought **no** peace with it ; **for she** remained in
her deceiver's power.

Three years went **by.** The elderly adventurer then fell
in with a young, wealthy, and inexperienced man, who had
loved the same woman, and whose honourable addresses
had **been** declined for his **sake ;** and he acquired **over**
this **youth an** influence almost **as** strong as that which
he had exercised over the young girl. He found **him**
grieving **over** his disappointment, and undertook **to**
teach him how to forget it ; became **his** master **in the**
art of dissipation ; helped to empty his pockets **while he**
filled his own ; and finally induced him to **form a merce-**
nary engagement **to a** cousin **whom he** did not love.
When the story opens, the young man has come to visit
his bride-elect in her country home ; **and his** Mephis-
topheles has followed him, under a transparent pretext, to
secure a last chance of winning money from him at cards.
The presence of the latter is to be a secret, because he is
too ill-famed a personage to be admitted into the lady's
house ; so they have arrived on the eve of the appointed
day, and put up at a village inn on the outskirts **of the**
cousin's estate. There they have spent the night in play.
There also the luck has turned ; and the usual winner has
lost ten thousand pounds. His friend insists on cancelling
the debt. He affects to scout **the** idea. "The money
shall, by some means or other, be paid."

The discussion is renewed with the same result, **as** they
loiter near the station, at which the younger will presently

make a feint of arriving ; and for the first time he asks the elder why, with such abilities as his, he has made no mark in life. The latter replies that he found and lost his opportunity four years ago, in a woman, who, he feels more and more, would have quickened his energies to better ends. He then, with tolerable frankness, relates his story. The younger follows with his own. But, for a reason which explains itself at the time, the connection between the two escapes them.

The woman herself next appears on the scene, and with her, the girl cousin. They are friends of old ; and the married one has emerged from her seclusion at the entreaty of the betrothed, to pass judgment on her intended husband. The young girl is not satisfied with her own feeling towards him whom she has promised to marry ; though she has no misgiving as to his sentiments towards her. She is to bring him for inspection to the inn. And the friend, entering its parlour alone, is confronted by her former lover, who has temporarily returned there.

A stormy dialogue ensues. She denounces him as the destroyer, ever lying in wait for her soul. He taunts her with the malignant hatred with which for years past from the height of her own prosperity she has been weighing down his. She retorts in a powerful description of the love with which he once inspired her, of the living death in which she has been expiating her mistake. And as he listens, the old feeling in him revives, and he kneels to her, imploring that she will break her bonds, and secure their joint happiness by flying with him. She sees nothing, however, in this, but a second attempt to ensnare her ; and is repulsing the entreaty with the scorn which she believes it to deserve, when the younger man bursts merrily into the room. A wave of angry pain passes over him as he recognizes the heroine of his own romance, and hastily infers from the circumstances in which he finds her, that he has been the victim of a double deception. The truth gradually shapes itself in his mind ; but meanwhile the older man has grasped the situation, and determined to make capital of it—to avenge his rebuff and to rid himself of his debt at the same time. He begs the lady to leave the room for a few moments, handing her, for her entertainment, the inn "album," over which he and his friend were exchanging jokes a few hours ago ; and in which he has, at this moment, inscribed some lines. The purport of these is that this young man loves her ; and that unless she responds to his advances, the secret of her past life shall be revealed to her husband.

Alone with the younger man, he exhausts himself in coarse libels against the woman, of whom that morning only he was speaking, as the lost opportunity of his life ; bids him ask of her what he desires, and have it ; and calls on him to admit, that in preserving him from marrying her, and placing her nevertheless at his disposal, he will have earned his gratitude, and paid the value of the ten thousand pounds.

When the woman returns, the album in her hand, the calm of death is upon her. She has lived prepared for this emergency, provided also with the means of escaping from it. But she will not die without entreating her young admirer to shake off, before it is too late, the evil influence to which both, though in different ways, have succumbed ; and her dignity, her kindness, the instinctive reverence, and now chivalrous pity, with which she has inspired him carry all before them. He renews his declaration ; implores her to accept him as her husband, if she is free— her friend if she is not ; her husband even if the relation she is living in be something less than marriage ; to exact any delay, to impose any probation, so that in the end she accepts him.

She replies by putting her hand into his, *to remain there*, as she says, *till death shall part them*. The older man, who has just re-entered the room, congratulates them on

having arrived at so sensible an understanding. The
woman, now very pale, contrives to point to the fatal
entry in the album which she still grasps ; and asks her
friend—after quoting the writer's words—how, but in her
own way, the mouth of such a one could have been stopped.

"So," exclaims the youth. And he flies at the man's
throat, and strangles him.

She has only time to thank her deliverer ; to tell him
why his devotion is unavailing—to provide for his safety
by writing in the album from which he has torn the
fatal page, that he has slain a man who would have outraged her : and that her last breath is spent in blessing him.

A merry voice is heard ; and the young, light-hearted
girl comes all unconscious to the scene of the tragedy.
The curtain falls before she has entered upon it.

The betrayal of the lady, the transaction of which she
becomes the subject, and her consequent suicide, are
taken from an episode in English high life, which occurred
in the present century.

"THE TWO POETS OF CROISIC" is an extract from the
history of two writers of verse, whose respective works
obtained from circumstances a brilliant but short-lived
renown. It forms part of a reminiscence, supposed to be
conjured up by a wood fire near which the narrator, with
his wife, is sitting. The fire, as he describes it, is made
of ship-wood : for it burns in all the beautiful colours which
denote the presence of metallic substances and salts ; and
as his fancy reconstructs the ship, it also raises the vision
of a distant coast well known to his companion and to himself. He sees Le Croisic—the little town it is—the poor
village it was [1]—with its storm-tossed sea—its sandy strip

[1] Le Croisic is in the Loire Inférieure, at the south-east corner of Brittany.
It has now a good bathing establishment, and is much frequented by French
people ; but sardine-fishing and the crystallizing of sea-salt are still its
standing occupations.

of land, good only for the production of salt—its solitary
Menhir, which recalls, and in some degree perpetuates, the
wild life and the barbarous Druid worship of old Breton
times.[1] And in the bright-hued flames, which leap up and
vanish before his bodily eyes, he sees also the two ephemeral reputations which flashed forth and expired there.

René Gentilhomme, born 1610, was a rhymer, as his
father had been before him. He became page to the
Prince of Condé, and occupied his spare time by writing
complimentary verse. One day, as he was hammering at
an ode, a violent storm broke out ; and the lightning shat-
tered a ducal crown in marble which stood on a pedestal
in the room in which he sat. Condé was regarded as future
King of France : for Louis XIII. was childless, and his
brother Gaston believed to be so ; in consideration of this
fact, men called him "Duke." René took the incident as
an omen, and turned his ode into a prophecy which he de-
livered to his master as the utterance of God. "The Prince's
hopes were at an end : a Dauphin would be born in the
ensuing year." A Dauphin was born ; and René, who had
at first been terrified at his own boldness, received the title
of Royal Poet, and the honours due to a seer. But he
wrote little or no more ; and he and the tiny volume
which composed his works soon disappeared from sight.

The narrator, however, judges that this oblivion may
not have been unsought, since one who had believed himself the object of a direct message from God, would have
little taste for intercourse with his fellow men ; and he
suspends his story for a moment to ask himself how such
a one would bear the weight of his experience ; and how
far the knowledge conveyed by it might be true. He decides (as we should expect) that a direct Revelation is forbidden by the laws of life ; but that life is full of indirect
messages from the unseen world ; that all our "simulated

---

[1] The details of this worship as carried on in the island opposite Le Croisic,
and which Mr. Browning describes, are mentioned by Strabo.

thunder-claps ; " all our "counterfeited truths," all those
glimpses of beauty which startle while they elude the soul,
are messages of this kind : darts shot from the spirit world,
which rebound as they touch, yet sting us to the consciousness of its existence. And so René Gentilhomme had had
a true revelation, in what reminded him that there are
things higher than rhyming and its rewards.

Paul Desforges Maillard was born nearly a century
later, and wrote society verses till the age of thirty, when
the desire for wider fame took possession of him. He
competed for a prize which the Academy had offered to
the poet who should best commemorate the progress made
by the art of navigation during the last reign. His poem
was returned. It was offered, through the agency of a
friend, to a paper called "The Mercury." The editor, La
Roque, praised the work in florid terms, but said he dared
not offend the Academy ; he, too, returned the MS.
Paul, mistaking the polite fiction for truth, wrote back an
angry tirade against the editor's cowardice ; and the latter,
retorting in as frank a fashion, told the writer that his poem
was execrable, and that it was only consideration for his
feelings which had hitherto prevented his hearing so.

At this juncture Paul's sister interposed. He was wrong,
she declared, to proceed in such a point-blank manner.
In cases like these, it was only wile which conquered. He
must resume his incognito, and try, this time, the effect of
a feminine disguise. She picked out and copied the
feeblest of his songs or sonnets, and sent it to La Roque,
as from a girl-novice who humbly sued for his literary
protection. She was known by another name than her
brother's (Mr. Browning explains why) ; the travesty was
therefore complete. The poem was accepted ; then another and another. The lady's fame grew. La Roque
made her, by letter, a declaration of love. Voltaire also
placed himself at her feet.

Paul now refused to efface himself any longer. The

clever sister urged in vain that it was her petticoats which had conquered, and not his verse. He went to Paris to claim his honours, and introduce himself as the admired poetess to La Roque and Voltaire. Voltaire bitterly resented the joke; La Roque affected to enjoy it; but nevertheless advised its perpetrator to get out of Paris as fast as possible. The trick had answered for once. It would not be wise to repeat it. Again Paul disregarded his sister's advice, and reprinted the poems in his own name. "They had been praised and more than praised. The world could not eat its own printed words!"

He discovered, however, that the world *could* eat its words; or, at least, forget them. The only fame—the speaker adds—which a great man cannot destroy, is that which he has had no hand in making. Paul's light, with his sister's, went out as did that of his predecessor.

Mr. Browning gives, in conclusion, a test by which the relative merit of any two real poets may be gauged. *The greater is he who leads the happier life.* To be a poet is to see and feel. To see and feel is to suffer. His is the truest poetic existence who enslaves his sufferings, and makes their strength his own. He who yokes them to his chariot shall win the race.[1]

"CENCIAJA" signifies matter relating to the "Cenci;"[2] and the poem describes an incident extraneous to the "Cenci" tragedy, but which strongly influenced its course. This incident was the murder of the widowed Marchesa

---

[1] The story of Paul Desforges Maillard forms the subject of a famous play, Piron's "Métromanie."

[2] It is also, and perhaps chiefly, in this case, a pun on the meaning of the plural noun "cenci," "rags," or "old rags." The cry of this, frequent in Rome, was at first mistaken by Shelley for a voice urging him to go on with his play. Mr. Browning has used it to indicate the comparative unimportance of his contribution to the Cenci story. The quoted Italian proverb means something to the same effect: that every trifle will press in for notice among worthier matters.

dell' Oriolo, by her younger son, Paolo Santa Croce, who thus avenged her refusal to invest him with his elder brother's rights. He escaped the hands of justice, though only to perish in some other disastrous way. But the matricide had been committed on the very day which closed the trial of the Cenci family for the assassination of its Head ; and it sealed Beatrice's fate. Her sentence seemed about to be remitted. The Pope now declared that she must die.

> .    .    .    .    " Paolo Santo Croce
> Murdered his mother also yestereve,
> And he is fled : she shall not flee at least ! "
>
> (vol. xiv. p. 104.)

The elder son of the Marchesa, Onofrio Marchese dell' Oriolo, was arrested on the strength of an ambiguous scrap of writing, which appeared to implicate him in his brother's guilt ; and subjected in prison to such a daily and day-long examination on the subject of this letter, that his mind gave way, and the desired avowal was extracted from him. He confessed to having implied, under reserves and conditions which practically neutralized the confession, his assent to his mother's death. He was beheaded accordingly ; and the Governor of Rome, Taverna, who had conducted the inquisition, was rewarded by a Cardinal's hat. Other motives were, however, involved in the proceeding than the Pope's quickened zeal for justice. He had entrusted the case to his nephew, Cardinal Aldobrandini ; and it was known that the Cardinal and the Marchese had courted the same lady, and the latter unwisely flaunted the possession of a ring which was his pledge of victory.

This story, with other details which I have not space to give, was taken from a contemporary Italian chronicle, of which some lines are literally transcribed.

The heretic of " THE HERETIC'S TRAGEDY " was

Jacques du Bourg-Molay, last Grand Master of the Order of Knights Templars, and against whom preposterous accusations had been brought. This "Jacques," whom the speaker erroneously calls "John," and **who** might stand for any victim of middle-age fanaticism, was burned in Paris in 1314; and the "Interlude," we are told, "would seem to be a reminiscence of this event, as distorted **by** two centuries of refraction from Flemish brain **to brain."** The scene is carried on by **one** singer, **in a succession of** verses, and by a chorus which **takes up the last and most** significant words of each verse; the organ accompanying in **a** plagal cadence,[1] which completes **its** effect. **The** chant is preceded by an admonition from the abbot, which lays down its text **: that** God **is** unchanging, and **His justice** as infinite as His mercy; and singer and chorus both denounce **the** impious heresy of "John:" who admitted only the love, and sinned the "Unknown Sin," **in** his confidence in it. How the logs are fired; **how the** victim roasts; amidst what hideous and fantastic torments **the** damned soul "flares forth into the **dark"** is quaintly and powerfully described.

## ROMANTIC POEMS.

The prevalence of thought in Mr. Browning's poetry has created in many minds an impression that he is more a thinker than a poet : that his poems not only are each inspired by some leading idea, but have grown up in subservience to it; and those who hold this view both do him injustice as a poet, and underrate, however unconsciously, the intellectual value of what his work conveys. For in a

---

[1] That of the Gregorian chant: a cadence concluding on the dominant instead of the key-note.

poet's imagination, the thought and the thing—the idea and its image—grow up at the same time ; each being a different aspect of the other.[1]  He sees, therefore, the truths of Nature, as Nature herself gives them ; while the thinker, who conceives an idea first, and finds an illustration for it afterwards, gives truth only as it presents itself to the human mind—in a more definite, but much narrower form.    Mr. Browning often *treats* his subject as a pure thinker might, but he has always *conceived* it as a poet ; he has always seen in one flash, everything, whether moral or physical, visible or invisible, which the given situation could contain.[2]    This fact may be recognized in many of the smaller poems, which, for that reason, I shall find it impossible to class ; but it is best displayed in a couple of longer ones, which I have placed under the head "Romantic."   They are distinct from the majority of the "Dramatic Romances," although included in them.    For with these the word "romantic" denotes an imaginary experience, which may be frankly supernatural, as in "The Boy and the Angel ;" or only improbable, as in "Mesmerism ;" or semi-historical and local, as in "In a Gondola ;" or simply human, and possible anywhere and anywhen, as in "The Last Ride Together ;" or in "Dîs aliter Visum," and "James Lee's Wife," which might be classed with them.    I am now using it to mark certain cases, in which the author's imagination has not brought itself to the test of *any* consistent experience, but simply presents us with certain groups of material and mental— of real and ideal possibilities, which we may each interpret for ourselves.    They occur in

---

[1] We have a conspicuous instance of this in "Pippa Passes."

[2] This spontaneous mode of conception may seem incompatible with the systematic adherence to a fixed class of subjects referred to in an earlier chapter.  But it is by no means is so.  With Mr. Browning the spontaneous creative impulse conforms to the fixed rule.

The present remarks properly belong to that earlier chapter.  But it was difficult to divide them from their illustrations.

" Childe Roland to the Dark Tower Came." (" Dramatic Romances." Published in " Men and Women." 1855.)

" The Flight of the Duchess." (" Dramatic Romances."
Published in " Dramatic Romances and Lyrics." 1845.)[1]

The first of these has been taken by some intelligent
critics to be a moralizing allegory ; the second, a moralizing fairy-tale. They are, therefore, a useful type both of
Mr. Browning's poetic genius, and of the misunderstand-
ing, to which its constantly intellectual employment has
exposed him.

"CHILDE ROLAND TO THE DARK TOWER CAME,"
describes a brave knight performing a pilgrimage, in
which hitherto all who attempted it have failed. The
way through which he struggles is unknown to him ;
its features are hideous ; a deadly sense of difficulty
and danger hangs over every step ; and though Childe
Roland's courage is pledged to the undertaking, the
thought of failure at last comes to him as a relief. He
reaches the goal just as failure appears inevitable. The
plain has suddenly closed in ; weird and unsightly
eminences encompass him on every side. In one flash he
perceives that he is in a trap ; in another, that the tower
stands before him ; while round it, against the hill-sides,
are ranged the " lost adventurers " who have preceded
him—their names and story clanging loudly and more
loudly in his ears—their forms revealed with ghastly clear-
ness in the last fires of the setting sun.

So far the picture is consistent ; but if we look below
its surface discrepancies appear. The Tower is much
nearer and more accessible than Childe Roland has
thought ; a sinister-looking man, of whom he asked the
way, and who, as he believed, was deceiving him, has
really put him on the right track ; and as he describes
the country through which he passes, it becomes clear
that half its horrors are created by his own heated imagi-

---

[1] **First** in " Hood's Magazine."

T

nation, or by some undefined influence in the place itself. We are left in doubt whether those who have found failure in this quest, have not done so through the very act of attainment in it ; and when, dauntless, Childe Roland sounds his slughorn and announces that he has come, we should not know, but that he lives to tell the tale, whether in doing this he incurs, or is escaping, the general doom. We can connect no idea of definite pursuit or attainment with a series of facts so dreamlike and so disjointed : still less extract from it a definite moral ; and we are reduced to taking the poem as a simple work of fancy, built up of picturesque impressions which have, separately or collectively, produced themselves in the author's mind.[1]

But these picturesque impressions had, also, their ideal side, which Mr. Browning as spontaneously reproduced ; and we may all recognize under the semblance of the enchanted country and the adventurous knight, a poetic vision of life : with its conflicts, contradictions, and mockeries ; its difficulties which give way when they seem most insuperable ; its successes which look like failures, and its failures which look like success. The thing we may not do is to imagine that an intended lesson is conveyed by it.

" THE FLIGHT OF THE DUCHESS " is the adventure of a young girl, who was brought out of a convent to marry a certain Duke. The Duke was narrow-hearted, pompous, and self-sufficient ; the mother who shared his home, a sickly woman, as ungenial as himself. The young wife, on the other hand, was a bright, stirring creature, who would have been the sunshine of a labourer's home. She pined amidst the dreariness and the formality of her con-

---

[1] I may venture to state that these picturesque materials included a tower which Mr. Browning once saw in the Carrara Mountains, a painting which caught his eye years later in Paris ; and the figure of a horse in the tapestry in his own drawing-room—welded together in the remembrance of the line from " King Lear," which forms the heading of the poem.

jugal existence, and seized the first opportunity of escape
from it. A retainer of the Duke's, whose chivalry her
position had aroused, connived at her escape, and tells the
story of it.

The Duke had decreed a hunt. Custom prescribed that
his wife should attend it. She had excused herself on
the plea of her ill-health ; and he was riding forth in no
amiable mood, when an old gipsy woman, well known in
the neighbourhood, accosted him with the usual prayer
for alms. He was curtly dismissing her, when she mentioned her desire to pay her respects to the young
Duchess. It then occurred to him that the sight of this
ragged crone, and the chronicle of her woes, might be an
excellent medicine for his " froward," ungrateful wife, and
teach her to know when she was well off ; and after speaking in confidence with the old woman, he bade him who
recounts the adventure escort her into the lady's presence.
The interview took place. The Duchess accompanied
her visitor to the castle gate, ordered her palfrey to
be saddled, mounted it with the gipsy behind her, and
bounded away, never to return. The attendant had watched
and obeyed her as in a dream. She left in his hand, in
gratitude for what she knew he felt for her, a little plait of
hair.

These are the real facts of the story. But we have also
its ideal possibilities, as reflected by the imagination of the
narrator. He had seen the gipsy metamorphosed as she
received the Duke's command, from a ragged, decrepit
crone into a stately woman, whose clothing bore the appearance of wealth ; and as he mounted guard on the balcony which commanded the Duchess's room, he saw the
wonder grow. A sound as of music first attracted his
attention ; and as he looked in at the window he saw the
Duchess sitting at the feet of a real gipsy-queen : her head
upturned—her whole being expanding—as the gipsy's
hands waved over her, and the gipsy's eyes, preternaturally

dilated, poured their floods of life into her own. Then the music broke up into words, and he knew what hope and promise that fainting spirit was drinking in : for he heard what the gipsy said. She was telling the young Duchess that she was one of themselves—that she bore their mystic mark in the two veins which met and parted on her brow—that after fiery trial she should return to her tribe, and be shielded by their devotion for evermore. She was telling her how good a thing is love—how strong and beautiful the double existence of those whom love has welded together—how full of restful memories the old age of those who have lived in and for it—how sure and gentle their awakening into the better world. . . . . . Here the words again lost themselves in music, and he understood no more. When the two appeared at the castle gate, the gipsy had shrunk back into her original character ; but the Duchess remained transformed. She had become, in her turn, a queen.

The suggestion of her gipsy origin forms a connecting link between the real and the ideal aspects of the Duchess's flight. We might imagine her fervid nature as being affected by the message of deliverance precisely in the manner described : while the beautified image of her deliverer transferred itself through some magnetic influence to the spectator's mind from her own. He does not, however, present himself as a probable subject for such impressions. He is a jovial, matter-of-fact person, in spite of the vein of sentiment which runs through him ; and the imaginative part of his narrative was more probably the result of a huntsman's breakfast which had found its way into his brain. As in the case of Childe Roland, the poetic truth of the Duchess's romance is incompatible with rational explanation, and independent of it. Various dramatic details complete the story.

## SATIRICAL OR HUMOROUS **POEMS.**

Humour **is** a constant characteristic of Mr. Browning's work,[1] and it sometimes takes the **form** of **direct** and intentional satire ; but his sympathy with human beings and his hopeful view **of** their future destiny, **are** opposed to any development **of** the satirical mood. The impression of sympathy will even neutralize the satire, in poems in which **the** latter is directly and conciously conveyed : as, for instance, **in** " Caliban upon Setebos," and " The Bishop orders his Tomb **at** Saint Praxed's Church." Of grim **or** serious satire, there **is,** I think, only one specimen among his works **: the** first **part** of

" Holy-Cross **Day."** (" Dramatic Romances." **Pub**-lished in " Men **and** Women," 1855.)

**We** may class **as** playful satires (which **I give in the** order of their importance) :

" Pacchiarotto, and how **he worked in Distemper."** (1876.)

" Filippo Baldinucci on the Privilege of Burial." ("Pacchiarotto, and other Poems." 1876.)

" Up at a Villa—Down in the City." (" Dramatic Lyrics." Published in " Men and Women." 1855.)

" Another Way of Love." (" Dramatic Lyrics." Published in " Men and Women." 1855.)

We have a purely humorous picture in

" Garden Fancies, II. Sibrandus Schafnaburgensis." (" Dramatic Lyrics." Published in " Dramatic Romances and Lyrics." 1845.)

" HOLY-CROSS DAY " was the occasion of an " Annual

---

[1] Instances of it occur in the " Dramatic Idyls " and " Jocoseria ;" and will be noticed later.

Christian Sermon," which the Jews in Rome were forced
to attend ; and the poem which bears this title is prefaced
by an extract from an imaginary "Diary by a Bishop's
Secretary," dated 1600 ; and expatiating on the merciful
purpose, and regenerating effect of this sermon. What the
assembled Jews may have really felt about it, Mr. Browning sets forth in the words of one of the congregation.

This man describes the hustling and bustling, the crowding and packing—the suppressed stir as of human vermin
imprisoned in a small space ; the sham groans, and sham
conversions which follow in their due course ; and as he
thus dwells on his national and personal degradation, his
tone has the bitter irony of one who has both realized and
accepted it. But the irony recoils on those who have inflicted the degradation—on the so-called Christians who
would throttle the Jew's creed while they " gut " his purse,
and make him the instrument of their own sins ; and
is soon lost in the emotion of a pathetic and solemn
prayer ; the supposed death-bed utterance of Rabbi Ben
Ezra.

The prayer is an invocation to the justice, and to the
sympathy of Christ. It claims His help against the
enemies who are also His own. It concedes, as possible,
that He was in truth the Messiah, crucified by the nation
of which He claimed a crown. But it points to His
Christian followers as inflicting on Him a still deeper
outrage : a belief which the lips profess, and which the
life derides and discredits. It urges, in the Jew's behalf,
the ignorance, the fear, in which the deed was done ; the
bitter sufferings by which it has been expiated. It pleads
his long endurance, as testimony to the fact, that he with-
stands Barabbas now, as he withstood Christ "then ; "
that he strives to wrest Christ's name from the " Devil's
crew," though the shadow of His face be upon him. The
invocation concludes with an expression of joyful confidence in God and the future.

(Giacomo) "PACCHIAROTTO" was a painter of Siena.[1] His story is told in the "Commentary on the Life of Sodoma" by the editors of Vasari ; Florence, 1855 ; and this contains all, or nearly all, the incidents of Mr. Browning's "Pacchiarotto," as well as others of a similar kind but of later occurrence, which are not mentioned in it.

This painter was a restless, aggressive personage, with a craze for reform ; and a conspicuous member of the "Bardotti : " a society of uncommissioned reformers, whose occupation was to cry down abuses, and prescribe wholesale theoretical measures for removing them. (Hence their title ; which signifies "spare" horses or "freed" ones : they walk by the side of the waggon while others drudge at, and drag it along). But he discovered that men would not be reformed ; and bethought himself, after a time, of a new manner of testifying to the truth. He selected a room in his own house, whitewashed it (we conclude) ; and, working in "distemper" or fresco, painted it with men and women of every condition and kind. He then harangued these on their various shortcomings. They answered him, as he imagined, in a humble and apologetic manner ; and he then proceeded to denounce their excuses, and strip the mask from their sophistries and hypocrisies —doing so with every appearance of success.

But he presumed too much on his victory. A famine had broken out in Siena. The magistrates were, of course, held responsible for it. The Bardotti assembled, and prescribed the fitting remedies. Everything would come right if only the existing social order was turned topsy-turvy, and men were released from every tie. Pacchiarotto was conspicuous by his eloquence. But when he denounced the chief of the municipal force, and hinted that if the right man were in the right place, that officer would

---

[1] Generally confounded with his contemporary and fellow-citizen, Girolamo del Pacchia.

be he, all the other "spare horses" rushed upon him, and he was obliged to run for his life. The first hiding-place which presented itself was a sepulchre, in which a corpse had just been laid. He squeezed himself into this, and crawled forth from it at at the end of two days, starving, covered with vermin, and thoroughly converted to the policy of living and letting live. The authentic part of the narrative concludes with his admission into a neighbouring convent (the Osservanza) where he was cleansed and fed. But Mr. Browning allows Fancy the just employment of telling how the Superior improved the occasion, and how his lesson was received.

"It is a great mistake," this reverend person assures his guest—though one from which his own youth has not been free—" to imagine that any one man can preach another out of his folly. If such endeavours could succeed, heaven would have begun on earth. Whereas, every man's task is to leaven earth with heaven, by working towards the end to which his Master points, without dreaming that he can ever attain it. Man, in short, is to be not the ' spare horse,' but the ' mill-horse ' plodding patiently round and round on the same spot."

And Pacchiarotto replies that his monitor's arguments are, by his own account, doomed to be ineffectual : but that he is addressing himself to one already convinced. He (Pacchiarotto) never was so by living man ; but he has been convinced by a dead one. That corpse has seemed to ask him by its grin, why he should join it before his time because men are not all made on the same pattern : " Because, above, one's Jack and one—John." And the same grin has reminded him that this life is the rehearsal, not the real performance : just an hour's trial of who is fit, and who isn't, to play his part ; that the parts are distributed by the author, whose purpose will be explained in proper time; and that when his brother has been cast for a fool's part, he is no sage who would persuade him to give it up. He is now going back to his paint-pot, and will mind his own business in future.

By an easy transition, Mr. Browning turns the laugh against his own critics, whom he professes to recognize on this May morning, as flocking into his garden in the guise of sweeps. He does not, he says, grudge them their fun or their one holiday of the year, the less so that their rattling and drumming may give him some inkling how music sounds; and he flings them, by way of a gift, the story he has just told, bidding them dance, and "dust" his "jacket" for a little while. But that done, he bids them clear off, lest his housemaid should compel them to do so. He has her authority for suspecting that in their professional character they bring more dirt into the house than they remove from it.[1]

"FILIPPO BALDINUCCI" was the author of a history of art ("Notizie dei Professori del Disegno da Cimabue in qua"); and the incident which Mr. Browning relates as "a reminiscence of A.D. 1670," appears there in a notice of the life of the painter Buti. (Vol. iii. p. 422.)

The Jewish burial-ground in Florence was a small field at the foot of the Monte Oliveto. A path ascending the hill skirted its upper end, and at an angle of this stood a shrine with one side blank, the other adorned by a painting of the Virgin Mary. The painting was intended to catch the eye of all believers who approached from the neighbouring city-gate (Porta San Friano or Frediano); and was therefore so turned that it overlooked the Jewish cemetery at the same time. The Jews, objecting to this, negotiated for its removal with the owner of the ground; and his steward, acting in his name, received a hundred

---

[1] The (Baron) Kirkup mentioned at vol. xiv. page 5 was a Florence friend of Mr. Browning's, and a connoisseur in literature and art. He was ennobled by the King of Italy for his liberal views and for his services to Italian literature. It was he who discovered the portrait of Dante in the Bargello at Florence.

ducats as the price of his promise that the Virgin should be transferred to the opposite side of the shrine. The task was undertaken by Buti, but carried on in the privacy of a curtained scaffolding; and when the curtains were withdrawn, it was seen that the picture *had* been transferred; but that a painting of the Crucifixion occupied its original place. Four Rabbis, the "sourest and ugliest" of the lot, were deputed to remonstrate with the steward; but this person coolly replied that they had no ground of complaint whatever. "His master had amply fulfilled his bond. Did they fancy their 'sordid' money had bought his freedom to do afterwards what he thought fit?" And he advised them to remove themselves before worse befell them. The Jews retired discomfited; and, as the writer hopes, took warning by what had happened, never again to tempt with their ill-earned wealth "the religious piety of good Christians."

Mr. Browning gives this story, with unimportant variations, in the manner of Baldinucci himself; and does full justice to the hostile and contemptuous spirit in which the attitude of the Jews is described by him. But he also heightens the unconscious self-satire of the narrative by infusing into this attitude a genuine dignity and pathos. He enlists all our sympathy by the Chief Rabbi's prayer that his people, so sorely tried in life, may be allowed rest from persecution in their graves; and he concludes with an imaginary incident which leaves them masters of the situation. On the day after what the historian calls this "pleasing occurrence," the son of the High Priest presented himself at Buti's shop, where he and the so-called "farmer" were still laughing over the event; and in tones of ominous mildness begged to purchase that pretty thing—the picture in oils, from which the fresco painting of the Virgin had been made. He was a Herculean young man, and Buti, who white and trembling had tried to slip out of his way, was so bewildered by the offer, that he asked only the proper price for his work. The farmer, however, broke forth in expressions of pious delight, "Mary had surely wrought a miracle, and *converted* the Jew!"

The Jew turned like a trodden worm. "Truly," he replied, "a miracle has been wrought, by a power which no canvas yet possessed, in that I have resisted the desire to throttle you. But my purchase of your picture is not due to a miracle. It means simply that I have been cured of my prejudices in respect to art. Christians hang up pictures of heathen gods. Their 'Titians' paint them. A cardinal will value his Leda or his Ganymede beyond everything else which he possesses. If I express wonder at this sacrifice of the truth, I am told that the truth of a picture is in its drawing and painting, and that these are valued precisely because they *are* true. Why then should not your Mary take her place among my Ledas and the rest; be judged as a picture, and, since—as I fear—Master Buti is not a Titian, laughed at accordingly?"

"So now," the speaker concludes, "Jews buy what pictures they like, and hang them up where they please, and,"—with an inward groan—"no, boy, you must not pelt them." This warning, which is supposed to be addressed by the historian in his old age to a nephew with a turn for throwing stones, reveals the motive of the story: a sudden remembrance of the good old pious time, when Jews *might* be pelted.

"Up at a Villa—Down in the City" is a lively description of the amusements of the city, and the dulness of villa life, as contrasted by an Italian of quality, who is bored to death in his country residence, but cannot afford the town. His account of the former gives a genuine impression of dreariness and monotony, for the villa is stuck on a mountain edge, where the summer is scorching and the winter bleak, where a "lean cypress" is the most conspicuous object in the foreground,

and hills "smoked over" with "faint grey olive trees" fill
in the back ; where on hot days the silence is only broken
by the shrill chirp of the cicala, and the whining of bees
around some adjacent firs.   But the other side of the
picture, though sympathetically drawn, is a perfect parody
of what it is meant to convey.   For the speaker's ideal
" city" might be a big village, with its primitive customs,
and its life all concentrated in the market-place or square ;
and it is precisely in the square that he is ambitious to
live.   There the church-bells sound, and the diligence
. rattles in, and the travelling doctor draws teeth or gives
pills ; there the punch-show or the church procession displays itself, and the last proclamation of duke or archbishop is posted up.   It is never too hot, because of the
fountain always plashing in the centre ; and the bright
white houses, and green blinds, and painted shop-signs
are a perpetual diversion to the eye . . . . But alas ! the
price of food is prohibitive ; and a man must live where
he can.

"ANOTHER WAY OF LOVE" is the complement to
"One Way of Love," and displays the opposite mood.
The one lover patiently gathers June roses in case they
may catch his lady's eye.   The other grows tired of such
patience even when devoted to himself; he tires of June
roses, which are always red and sweet.   His lady-love is
bantering him on this frame of mind.   It is true, she says,
that such monotony is trying to a man's temper : there is
no comfort in anything that can't be quarrelled with ; and
the person she addresses is free to "go."   She reminds
him, however, that June may repair her bower which his
hand has rifled, and the next time "consider" which of
two courses she prefers : to bestow her flowers on one
who will accept their sweetness, or use her lightnings to
kill the spider who is weaving his films about them.

"SIBRANDUS SCHAFNABURGENSIS" is apparently the

name of an old pedant who has **written a tiresome book ;**
and the adventures of **this** book form the subject of **the**
poem. Some wag relates **how he read** it a month ago,
having come into the garden for that purpose ; and then
revenged himself by dropping **it** through **a crevice**
in **a** tree, and enjoying **a** picnic lunch and **a chapter** of
" Rabelais " on **the** grass close by. **To-day,** in a fit of
compunction, he has raked the " treatise " out ; **but mean-**
while it has blistered in the sun, and run **all colours in the**
rain. Toadstools have **grown in it ; and all the creatures**
that creep **have** towzed it and browsed **on it, and devoted**
bits **of** it to their different domestic use. It is altogether
a melancholy sight. **So the** wag thinks his victim **has**
sufficiently suffered, **and** carries it back to his **book-shelf,**
to " **dry-rot** " **there** in **all** the comfort it deserves.

## DESCRIPTIVE **POEMS.**

Mr. Browning's poems abound in descriptive passages,
and his power of word-painting is very vivid, as well as
frequently employed. But we have here another instance
of a quality diffused throughout his work, yet scarcely
ever asserting itself in a distinct form. The reason is,
that he deals with men and women first—with **nature**
afterwards ; and that **the** details of a landscape have
little meaning for him, except in reference **to** the mental
or dramatic situation **of** which they form **a** part. This
is very apparent **in such** lyrics **or** romances **as :** " By
the Fire-side," **" In a** Gondola," **and** " Childe Roland to
the Dark Tower Came." We find three poems only which
might have been written for the sake of the picturesque
impressions which they convey :

"De Gustibus—" ("Dramatic Lyrics." Published in "Men and Women." 1855.)

"Home-Thoughts, from Abroad." ("Dramatic Lyrics." Published in "Dramatic Romances and Lyrics." 1845.)

"The Englishman in Italy." ("Dramatic Romances." Published as "England in Italy" in "Dramatic Romances and Lyrics." 1845.) And even here we receive the picture with a lyric and dramatic colouring, which makes it much less one of facts than of associations. It is also to be remarked that, in these poems, the associations are of two opposite kinds, and Mr. Browning is in equal sympathy with both. He feels English scenery as an Englishman does : Italian, as an Italian might be supposed to, feel it.

"DE GUSTIBUS—" illustrates the difference of tastes by the respective attractions of these two kinds of scenery, and of the ideas and images connected with them. Some one is apostrophizing a friend, whose ghost he is convinced will be found haunting an English lane, with its adjoining corn-field and hazel coppice : where in the early summer the blackbird sings, and the bean-flower scents the air. And he declares at the same time that Italy is the land of his own love, whether his home there be a castle in the Apennine, or some house on its southern shore ; among "wind-grieved" heights, or on the edge of an opaque blue sea : amidst a drought and stillness in which the very cicala dies, and the cypress seems to rust ; and scorpions drop and crawl from the peeling walls . . . . and where "a bare-footed girl tumbles green melons on to the ground before you, as she gives news of the last attack on the Bourbon king."

"HOME-THOUGHTS, FROM ABROAD" is a longing reminiscence of an English April and May, with their young leaves and their blossoms, their sunshine and their dew, their song of the chaffinch, and their rapturous music of

the thrush. Appreciation is heightened by contrast; **and**
the buttercup—England's gift to her little children—is
pronounced far brighter than the "gaudy melon-flower"
which the exiled Englishman has at this moment before
him.

"THE ENGLISHMAN IN ITALY" **is a vivid** picture of
Italian peasant-life on the plain of Sorrento: **the** occasion
being **an** outbreak of the well-known hot wind—the
"scirocco"—which, in this case, has brought with it a storm
**of** rain. A little frightened peasant girl has taken refuge
by the side of the Englishman, **who is** apparently lodging
in her mother's cottage. And he is diverting her attention
by describing his impressions **of the** last twenty-four
hours : how everything looked before **the rain ; how he**
knew while **yet** in bed **that** the rain **had** come, **by the**
rattling down of the quail-nets,[1] which were to **be** tugged
into shelter, while girls ran on **to the housetops to** fetch
**the** drying figs ; how the black churning waters forbade
the fishermen **to** go **to** sea (what strange creatures they
bring home when they **do** go, and how the brown naked
children, who look like so many shrimps, cling screaming
about them at the sight); how all hands are now employed
at the wine-making, and her brother **is** at this moment
dancing bare-legged in a vat half as high as the house ; how
the bigger girls bring baskets of grapes, with eyes closed
to keep out the rain ; and how the smaller ones gather
snails in the wet grass, which will appear with fried pump-
kin **at** the labourer's **supper ;** how, yesterday, he climbed
Mount Calvano—that very brother **of** hers for his guide—
his mule carrying him with dainty steps through the plain—
past the woods—up a path ever wilder and stonier, where

[1] **Nets** spread to catch quails as they fly to or from the other side of the
Mediterranean. They are slung by rings on to poles, and stand sufficiently
high for the quails to fly into them. This, and every other detail of the
poem, are given from personal observation.

sorb and myrtle fall away, but lentisk and rosemary still cling to the face of the rock—the head and shoulders of some new mountain ever coming into view; how he emerged, at last, where there were mountains all around; below, the green sea; above, the crystal solitudes of heaven; and, down in that green sea, the slumbering Siren islands: the three which stand together, and the one which swam to meet them, but has always remained half-way. These, and other reminiscences, beguile the time till the storm has passed, and the sun breaks over the great mountain which the Englishman has just described. He and little "Fortú" can now go into the village, and see the preparations being made for to-morrow's feast—that of the Virgin of the Rosary—which primitive solemnity he also (by anticipation) describes. He concludes with a brief allusion to the political scirocco which is blackening the English sky, and will not vanish so quickly as this has done; and thus hints at a reason, if the reader desires one, for his temporary rustication in a foreign land.

# NON-CLASSIFIED POEMS (CONTINUED).

## MISCELLANEOUS POEMS.

EVEN so imperfect, not to say arbitrary, a classification as I have been able to attempt, excludes a number of Mr. Browning's minor poems ; for its necessary condition was the presence of some distinctive mood of thought or feeling by which the poem could be classed ; and in many, even of the most striking and most characteristic, this condition does not exist. In one group, for instance, the prevailing mood is either too slightly indicated, or too fugitive, or too complex, or even too fantastic, to be designated by any term but "poetic." Others, again, such as songs and legends, depict human emotion in too simple or too general a form, to be thought of as anything but "popular ;" and a third group may be formed of dramatic pictures or episodes, which unite the qualities of the other two.

In the first of these groups we must place—

"The Lost Leader." ("Dramatic Lyrics." Published in "Dramatic Romances and Lyrics." 1845.)

"Nationality in Drinks." ("Dramatic Lyrics." Published as "Claret and Tokay," without 3rd Part, in "Dramatic Romances and Lyrics." 1845.) [1]

"Garden Fancies. I. The Flower's Name." ("Dramatic Lyrics." Published in "Dramatic Romances and Lyrics." 1845.) [1]

[1] Both of these first in " Hood's Magazine."

U

"Earth's Immortalities." ("Dramatic Lyrics." Published in "Dramatic Romances and Lyrics." 1845.)

" Home-Thoughts, from the Sea." ("Dramatic Lyrics." Published in "Bells and Pomegranates." 1842 or 1845.)

"My Star." ("Dramatic Lyrics." Published in "Men and Women." 1855.)

"Misconceptions." ("Dramatic Lyrics." Published in "Men and Women." 1855.)

"A Pretty Woman." ("Dramatic Lyrics." Published in "Men and Women." 1855.)

"In a Year." ("Dramatic Lyrics." Published in "Men and Women." 1855.)

"Women and Roses." ("Dramatic Lyrics." Published in "Men and Women." 1855.)

"Before." ("Dramatic Lyrics." Published in "Men and Women." 1855.)

"After." ("Dramatic Lyrics." Published in "Men and Women." 1855.)

"Memorabilia." ("Dramatic Lyrics." Published in "Men and Women." 1855.)

"The Last Ride Together." ("Dramatic Romances." Published in "Men and Women." 1855.)

"A Grammarian's Funeral." ("Dramatic Romances." Published in "Men and Women." 1855.)

"Johannes Agricola in Meditation." ("Men and Women." Published in "Dramatic Lyrics." 1842.)

"Confessions." ("Dramatis Personæ." 1864.)

"May and Death." ("Dramatis Personæ." 1864.)

"Youth and Art." ("Dramatis Personæ." 1864.)

"A Likeness." ("Dramatis Personæ." 1864.)

"Appearances." ("Pacchiarotto, and other Poems." 1876.)

"St. Martin's Summer." ("Pacchiarotto, and other Poems." 1876.)

"Prologue to 'La Saisiaz.'" 1878.

In the second group :—

"Cavalier Tunes." ("Dramatic Lyrics." 1842.)

"How they brought the Good News from Ghent to Aix." ("Dramatic Lyrics." Published in "Dramatic Romances and Lyrics." 1845.)

"Song." ("Dramatic Lyrics." Published in "Dramatic Romances and Lyrics." 1845.)

"Incident of the French Camp." ("Dramatic Romances." Published as first part of "Camp and Cloister," in "Dramatic Lyrics." 1842.)

"Count Gismond." ("Dramatic Romances." Published as "France" in "Dramatic Lyrics." 1842.)

"The Boy and the Angel." ("Dramatic Romances." Published in "Dramatic Romances and Lyrics." 1845.)[1]

"The Glove." ("Dramatic Romances." Published in "Dramatic Romances and Lyrics." 1845.)

"The Twins." ("Dramatic Romances." Published in "Men and Women." 1855.)

"The Pied Piper of Hamelin; A Child's Story." ("Dramatic Romances." Published in "Dramatic Lyrics." 1842.)

"Gold Hair: A Story of Pornic." ("Dramatis Personæ." 1864.)

"Hervé Riel." ("Pacchiarotto, and other Poems," written at Croisic, 1867. Published in the "Cornhill Magazine." 1871.)

In the third group :—

"Through the Metidja to Abd-el-Kadr." ("Dramatic Lyrics." 1842.)

"Meeting at Night." ("Dramatic Lyrics." Published as "Night" in "Dramatic Romances and Lyrics." 1845.)

"Parting at Morning." ("Dramatic Lyrics." Published as "Morning" in "Dramatic Romances and Lyrics."

"The Patriot. An old Story." ("Dramatic Romances." Published in "Men and Women." 1855.)

---

[1] First in "Hood's Magazine."

"Instans Tyrannus." ("Dramatic Romances." (Published in "Men and Women." 1855.)

"Mesmerism." ("Dramatic Romances." Published in "Men and Women." 1855.)

"Time's Revenges." ("Dramatic Romances." Published in "Dramatic Romances and Lyrics." 1845.)

"The Italian in England." ("Dramatic Romances." Published as "Italy in England" in "Dramatic Romances and Lyrics." 1845.)

"Protus." ("Dramatic Romances." Published in "Men and Women." 1855.)

"Apparent Failure." ("Dramatis Personæ." 1864.)

"Waring." ("Dramatic Romances." Published in "Dramatic Lyrics." 1842.) This poem is a personal effusion of feeling and reminiscence, which can stand for nothing but itself.

### *First Group.*

"THE LOST LEADER" is a lament over the defection of a loved and honoured chief. It breathes a tender regret for the moral injury he has inflicted on himself; and a high courage, saddened by the thought of lost support and lost illusions, but not shaken by it. The language of the poem shows the lost "leader" to have been a poet. It was suggested by Wordsworth, in his abandonment (with Southey and others) of the liberal cause.

"NATIONALITY IN DRINKS." A fantastic little comment on the distinctive national drinks—Claret, Tokay, and Beer. The beer is being drunk off Cape Trafalgar to the health of Nelson, and introduces an authentic and appropriate anecdote of him. But the laughing little claret flask, which the speaker has on another occasion seen plunged for cooling into a black-faced pond, suggests to him the image of **a** "gay French lady," dropped, with straightened limbs, into the **silent ocean** of death ; while the Hungarian Tokay (Tokayer Ausbruch), in **its** concentrated strength, seems to jump on to the table **as a** stout pigmy castle-warder, strutting and swaggering in his historic costume, and ready to defy twenty men **at once** if the occasion requires.

"THE FLOWER'S NAME. Garden Fancies," **I.** A **lover's** reminiscence of a garden in which he and his ladylove have walked together, and of a flower which she has consecrated by her touch and voice : its dreamy Spanish name, which **she** has breathed **upon it,** becoming **part of** the charm.

"EARTH'S IMMORTALITIES." **A sad and** subtle **little** satire on the vaunted permanence of love and fame. **The** poet's grave falls to pieces. The words : "love **me for** ever," appeal **to** us from a tombstone which records **how** Spring garlands are severed by the hand **of** June, **and** June's fever is quenched in winter's snow.

"HOME-THOUGHTS, FROM THE SEA." An utterance of patriotic pride and gratitude, aroused in the mind of an Englishman, by the sudden appearance of Trafalgar in the blood-red glow of the southern setting sun.

"MY STAR" may be taken as a tribute to the personal element in love : the bright peculiar light in which the sympathetic soul reveals itself to the object of its sympathy.

"MISCONCEPTIONS" illustrates the false hopes which may be aroused in the breast of any devoted creature by an incidental and momentary acceptance of its devotion.

"A PRETTY WOMAN" is the picture of a simple, compliant, exquisitely pretty, and hopelessly shallow woman : incapable of love, though a mere nothing will win her liking. And the question is raised, whether such a creature is not perfect in itself, and would not be marred by any attempt to improve it, or extract from it a different use. The author decides in the affirmative. A rose is best "graced," not by reproducing its petals in precious stones for a king to preserve ; not by plucking it to " smell, kiss, wear," and throw away ; but by simply leaving it where it grows. A "pretty" woman is most appropriately treated when nothing is asked of her, but to be so.

"In a Year" is a wondering and sorrowful little comment on a man's shallowness and inconstancy.

"Women and Roses" is the impression of a dream, and both vague and vivid, as such impressions are. The author *dreams* of a "red rose-tree," with three roses upon it : one withered, the second full-blown, the third still in the bud ; and, floating round each, a generation of women : those famed in the past ; the loved and loving of the present ; the "beauties yet unborn." He casts his passion at the feet of the dead ; but they float past him unmoved. He enfolds in it the glowing forms of the living ; but these also elude him. He pours it into the budding life, which may thus respond to his own ; but the procession of maidens drifts past him too. They all circle unceasingly round their own rose.

"Before" and "After" are companion poems, which show how differently an act may present itself in prospect and in remembrance, whether regarded in its abstract justification, or in its actual results. The question is that of a duel ; and "Before" is the utterance of a third person to whom the propriety of fighting it seems beyond a doubt. "A great wrong has been done. The wronged man, who is also the better one, is bound to assert himself in defence of the right. If he **is** killed, he will have gained his heaven. For his slayer, hell will have begun : for he will feel the impending judgment, in the earth which still offers its fruits ; in the sky, which makes no sign ; in the leopard-like conscience[1] which leers in mock obeisance at his side, ready to spring on him whenever the moment comes. There has been enough **of** delay and extenuation. Let the culprit acknowledge his guilt, **or take its** final consequences."

The duel **is** fought, but **it** is the guilty one who falls ; and "AFTER" gives the words of his adversary—his boyhood's friend—struck with bitter remorse for what he has done. **As** the man who wronged him lies wrapped in **the** majesty of death, his offence dwindles into insignificance ; and the survivor can only feel **how** disproportionate has been the punishment, and above all, how unavailing. "Would," he exclaims, "that the past could **be** recalled, and they were boys again together ! It would **be** so easy then to endure !"

" MEMORABILIA " shows the perspective of memory in a tribute to the poet Shelley. His fugitive contact with **a** commonplace life, like the trace of an eagle's passage across the moor, leaves an illumined spot amidst blankness.

"THE LAST RIDE TOGETHER " depicts **the** emotions of **a** ride, which a finally dismissed lover has been allowed to take with his beloved. He has vainly passed his youth in loving her. But as this boon is granted, she lies for a moment on his breast. " She might have loved him more ; she might also have liked him less." As they ride away side by side, a sense **of** resignation comes over

---

[1] I here use the word " conscience " in its intellectual rather than its moral sense ; as signifying that *consciousness* of a wrong done, which may, for a time, be evaded or pushed aside.

him. His life is not alone in its failure. Every one strives. Few or none succeed. The best success proves itself to be shallow. And if it were otherwise—if the goal could be reached on earth—what care would one take for heaven? Then the peace which is in him absorbs the consciousness of reality. He fancies himself riding with the loved one till the end of time ; and he asks himself if his destined heaven may not prove to be this.

"A GRAMMARIAN'S FUNERAL." describes the rendering of the last honours to one whose life has consumed itself in the pursuit of knowledge. The knowledge pursued has been pedantic and minute, but for him it represented a mighty truth ; and he has refused to live, in the world's sense, till he had mastered that truth, co-extensive, as he believed it, with life everlasting. Like Sordello, though in a different way, he would KNOW before he allowed himself to BE. He would realize the Whole ; he would not discount it. His disciples are bearing him to a mountain-top, that the loftiness of his endeavour may be symbolized by his last resting-place. He is to lie

> " where meteors shoot, clouds form,
> Lightnings are loosened." (vol. v. p. 159.)

where the new morning for which he waited will figuratively first break upon him.

" JOHANNES AGRICOLA IN MEDITATION " is a glowing and fantastic description of the privileges of the " elect," cast in the form of a monologue, and illustrated in the person of the speaker. Johannes Agricola was a German reformer of the sixteenth century, and alleged founder of the sect of the Antinomians : a class of Christians who extended the Low Church doctrine of the insufficiency of good works, and declared the children of God to be exempt from the necessity of performing them ; absolved from doing right, because unable to do wrong ; because **no sin** would be accounted to them **as** such. Some authorities contend that he personally rejected only the Mosaic, **not** the moral law ; but Mr. Browning has credited him **with** the full measure of Antinomian belief, and makes **him** specially exult in the Divine assurance that the concen- trated venom of the worst committed **sins can only work** in him for salvation. He also comments wonderingly on the **state** of the virtuous man **and woman, and** of **the** blameless child, "undone," as he was saved, **before the** world began ; whose very striving **is** turned to sin; whose life-long prayer and sacrifice can only end in damnation. But, as he declares, he praises God the **more that he** cannot understand Him ; **that** His ways are inscrutable, that His love may not be bought.

"CONFESSIONS" **is** the answer **of a** dying man **to the** clergyman's question : does he "view the world **as a** vale of tears?" His fancy is living through **a** romance of past days, **of** which the scene comes back to him in **the** arrangement of physic-bottles on **a** table beside him, while the curtain, which **may** be green, but **to** his dying eyes is blue, makes the June weather about it **all.** He is seeing the girl he loved, as watching for him from **a** ter- race near the stopper of that last and tallest bottle in the row ; and he is retracing the path by which he could creep, unseen by any eyes but hers, to the "rose-wreathed" gate which was their trysting-place. " No, reverend sir," is the first and last word of his reply, "the world has been no vale of tears to **me."**

"MAY AND DEATH" expresses a mourner's wish, so natural to the egotism of **a** deep sorrow, that the season which robbed him of his friend's life should bury all its sweetness with him. The speaker retracts this wish, in justice to the many pairs of friends who have each their right to happiness. But there is, he says, one red-streaked plant which their May might spare, since one wood alone would miss it. For its leaf is dashed as with the blood of Spring; and whenever henceforth it grows in that same place, the drop will have been drawn from his heart.[1]

"YOUTH AND ART" is a humorous, but regretful reminiscence of "Bohemian" days, addressed by a great singer to a sculptor, also famous, who once worked in a garret opposite to her own. They were young then, as well as poor and obscure; and they watched and coquetted with each other, though they neither spoke nor met; and perhaps played with the idea of a more serious courtship. Caution and ambition, however, prevailed; and they have reached the summit of their respective professions, and accepted the social honours which the position insures. But she thinks of all that might have been, if they had listened to nature, and cast in their lot with each other; of the sighs and the laughter, the starvation and the feasting, the despairs and the joys of the struggling artist's career; and she feels that in its fullest and freest sense, their artist life has remained incomplete.

"A LIKENESS" describes the feelings which are inspired by the familiar or indifferent handling of any object sacred to our own mind. They are illustrated by the idea of a print or picture, bought for the sake of a resemblance; and which may be hanging against a wall, or stowed away in a portfolio: and, in either case, provoke comment, contemptuous or admiring, which will cause a secret and angry pain to its possessor.

"APPEARANCES," a little poem in two stanzas, illus-

---

[1] This poem was a personal utterance, provoked by the death of a relative whom Mr. Browning dearly loved.

**trates** the power of association. Its contents can only be given in its own words.

"St. Martin's Summer" represents a **lover, with his** beloved, striving to elude the memory **of a** former attachment, and finding himself cheated by it. **As the fires** of a departed summer will glow once more, **in the** countenance of the wintry year, **so** also **has his** past life projected itself into the present, assuming its **features as a** mask. **And** when the ghosts, from whom, figuratively, the young **pair are** hiding, **rise from** their moss-grown graves; **and the lover** would disregard their remonstrant procession **as** only "faint march-music in the **air": he** becomes suddenly conscious **that** the past has withdrawn **its** gifts, **and that the mere** mask **of** love remains **to him.**

The poem would **seem** intended **to deny** that **a** second love can be genuine: were **not its light tone and** fantastic circumstance incompatible with serious intention.

Prologue to "La Saisiaz," **reprinted as** "Pisgah-Sights," III., is a fantastic little vision **of the** body and the soul, as disengaged from each other by death: the soul wandering at will through the realms of air; the body consigned to the

> " Ferns of all feather,
> Mosses and heather," (vol. xiv. p. 156.)

of its native earth.

### Second Group.

"Cavalier Tunes" consists **of** three songs, with chorus, full of rousing enthusiasm for the cause of King Charles, and of contemptuous defiance for the Roundheads who are opposing him: I. "Marching Along." II. "Give a Rouse." III. "Boot and Saddle."

"HOW THEY BROUGHT THE GOOD NEWS FROM GHENT TO AIX" is an imaginary picture, which would gain nothing in force by being true. It is that of three horsemen galloping to save the life of their town ; galloping without rest, from moonset to sunrise, from sunrise into the blaze of noon ; one horse dropping dead on the way, the second, within sight of the goal ; and the third, Roland, urged on by frantic exertions on his rider's part—the blood filling his nostrils, and starting in red circles round his eyes— galloping into the market-place of Aix ; to rest there with his head between his master's knees : while the last measure of wine which the city contains is being poured down his throat.

"SONG" is a lover's assertion of his lady's transcendent charms, which he challenges those even to deny who do not love her.

"INCIDENT OF THE FRENCH CAMP." A boy soldier of the army of Napoleon has received his death wound in planting the Imperial flag within the walls of Ratisbon. He contrives by a supreme effort to gallop out to the Emperor—who has watched the storming of the city from a mound a mile or two away—fling himself from the horse, and, holding himself erect by its mane, announce the victory. No sign of pain escapes him. But when Napoleon suddenly exclaims : "You are wounded," the soldier's pride in him is touched. "I am killed, Sire," he replies ; and, smiling, falls dead at the Emperor's feet. The story is true ; but its actual hero was a man.

"COUNT GISMOND" is an imaginary episode of the days of chivalry. It relates how a young girl had been chosen queen of a tournament ; and how a false knight, instigated by two cousins who where jealous of her beauty, accused her, in the open field, of being unfit to bestow a crown;

how a true knight who loved her, killed the lie by a blow struck at the liar's mouth ; and then, mortally wounding him in single combat, dragged him to retract it at the lady's feet ; how he laid his protecting arm around her, and led her away to the southern home where she is now his proud and happy wife, with sons growing up to resemble him.

The fearless confidence with which she has awaited the result of the duel, as bearing God's testimony to the truth, is very characteristic of the time.

"THE BOY AND THE ANGEL" is an imaginary legend which presents one of Mr. Browning's deepest convictions in a popular form. Theocrite was a poor boy, who worked diligently at his craft, and praised God as he did so. He dearly wished to become Pope, that he might praise Him better, and God granted the wish. Theocrite sickened and seemed to die. And he awoke to find himself a priest, and also, in due time, Pope. But God missed the praise, which had gone up to Him from the boy craftsman's cell ; and the angel Gabriel came down to earth, and took Theocrite's former place. And God was again not satisfied ; for the angelic praise could not replace for Him the human. "The silencing of that one weak voice had stopped the chorus of creation." So Theocrite returned to his old self ; and the angel Gabriel became Pope instead of him.

"THE GLOVE" is the well-known story[1] of a lady of the Court of Francis I., who, in order to test the courage of her suitor, threw her glove into the enclosure in which a captive lion stood ; and describes the suitor—one De Lorge—as calmly rescuing the glove, but only to fling it in the lady's face ; this protest against her heartlessness and

[1] Told by Schiller and Leigh Hunt.

vanity being endorsed by both the King and Court. But at this point Mr. Browning departs from the usual version: for he takes the woman's part. The supposed witness and narrator of the incident, the poet Ronsard, sees a look in her face which seems to say that the experiment, if painful, has been worth making; and he gives her the opportunity of declaring so. She had too long, she explains, been expected to take words for deeds, and to believe on his mere assertion, that her admirer was prepared to die for her; and when the sight of this lion brought before her the men who had risked their lives in capturing it, without royal applause to sustain them, the moment seemed opportune for discovering what this one's courage was worth. She marries a youth, so the poet continues, whose love reveals itself at this moment of her disgrace; and (he is disposed to believe) will live happily, though away from the Court. De Lorge, rendered famous by the incident, woos and wins a beauty who is admired by the King, and acquires practice in seeking her gloves —where he is not meant to find them—at the moments in which his presence is superfluous.

"THE TWINS" is a parable told by Luther in his "Table Talk," to show that charity and prosperity go hand in hand: and that to those who cease to give it will no longer be given. "Dabitur" only flourishes where "Date" is well-fed.

"THE PIED PIPER OF HAMELIN" (Hameln)[1] is the story of a mysterious piper who is said to have appeared at Hameln in the fourteenth century, at a moment when the city was infested by rats. According to the legend, he freed it from this nuisance, by shrill notes of his pipe which lured the rats after him to the edge of the river

[1] Written for and inscribed to a little son of the actor, William Macready.

Weser, where they plunged in and were drowned; and then, to punish the corporation, which had refused him the promised pay, enticed away all its children, by sweet notes from his pipe; and disappeared with them into the Koppelberg, a neighbouring mountain, which opened and then closed on them for ever. The legend also asserts that these facts (to which Mr. Browning has made some imaginative additions), were recorded on a church window, and in the name of a street. But the assertion no longer finds belief.

"GOLD HAIR" is a true "Story of Pornic," which may be read in guide-books to the place. A young girl of good family died there in odour of sanctity; she seemed too pure and fragile for earth. But she had one earthly charm, that of glorious golden hair; and one earthly feeling, which was her apparent pride in it. As she lay on her deathbed, she entreated that it might not be disturbed; and she was buried near the high altar of the church of St. Gilles[1] with the golden tresses closely swathed about her. Years afterwards, the church needed repair. Part of the pavement was taken up. A loose coin drew attention to the spot in which the coffin lay. Its boards had burst, and scattered about, lay thirty double louis, which had been hidden in the golden hair. So the saint-like maiden was a miser.

"HERVÉ RIEL" commemorates the skill, courage, and singleness of heart of a Breton sailor, who saved the French squadron when beaten at Cape la Hogue and flying before the English to St. Malo, by guiding it through the shallows of the river Rance, in a manner declared impracticable by the Maloese themselves; being all the while so unconscious of the service he was rendering, that, when desired

---

[1] A picturesque old church which has since been destroyed.

to name his reward, he begged for a *whole day's holiday*, to run home and see his wife. His home was Le Croisic.

### Third Group.

"THROUGH THE METIDJA TO ABD-EL-KADR" represents a follower of Abd-el-Kadr hastening through the desert to join his chief. Mystic fancies crowd upon him as he "rides" and "rides" : his pulses quickened by the end in view, and by the swift unresting motion of a horse which never needs the spur ; and as he describes his experience in his own excited words, we receive not only the mental picture, but the physical impression of it. This poem is a strong instance of Mr. Browning's power of conveying sense by sound, when he sees occasion for doing so.

"MEETING AT NIGHT" is a glimpse of moonlight and repose ; and of the appropriate seclusion in the company of the one woman loved.

"PARTING AT MORNING" asserts the need of "men" and their "world," which is born again with the sunshine.

"THE PATRIOT" tells, as its second title informs us, "an old story." Only this day year, the "patriot" entered the city as its hero, amidst a frenzy of gratitude and joy. To-day he passes out of it through comparatively silent streets ; for those for whom he has laboured last as first, are waiting for him at the foot of the scaffold. No inflic-tion of physical pain or moral outrage is spared him as he goes. He is "safer so," he declares. The reward men have withheld awaits him at the hand of God.

"INSTANS TYRANNUS"[1] is the confession of a king,

[1] The "Threatening Tyrant." Suggested by some words in Horace : 8th Ode. ii. Book.

who has been possessed by an unreasoning and uncontrolled hatred for one man. This man was **his** subject, but so friendless and obscure that no hatred **could** touch, **so** stupid or so upright that no temptation could lure him into his enemy's power. The King became exasperated by the very smallness of the creature which thus kept him **at** bay ; drew the line of persecution closer and closer ; and at last ran his victim to earth. But, at the critical moment, the man so long passive and cowering threw himself on the protection of God. The King saw, in a sudden revulsion of feeling, an Arm thrown out from **the** sky, **and the** "wretch" he had striven to crush, safely enfolded **in it.** Then he in his turn—was "afraid."

" MESMERISM " **is** a fanciful but **vivid** description of an act of mesmeric power, which draws a woman, alone, in the darkness, and through every natural obstacle, to the presence of the man who loves her.

" TIME'S REVENGES " is also a confession made in **the** form of a soliloquy. The speaker has a friend whose devotion is equal to any test, and whose love he barely repays with liking ; and he has a lady-love by **whom** this friend is avenged ; for he has given up to his passion for her his body and his soul, his peace and his renown, every laudable ambition, every rational aim ; and he knows she would let him roast by a slow fire if this would procure her an invitation to a certain ball.

" THE ITALIAN IN ENGLAND " is the supposed adventure of a leading Italian patriot, told by himself in later years. He tells how he was hiding from **the** Austrians, who had put a price upon his head, and were scouring the country in pursuit of him ; how, impelled by hunger, he disclosed his place of concealment to a peasant girl—the last of a troop of villagers who were passing by ; and how

X

she saved his life at the risk of her own, and when she
would have been paid in gold for betraying him.   He
relates also that his first thought was to guard himself
against betrayal by not telling her who he was ; but that
her loyal eyes, her dignified form and carriage (perhaps
too, the consummate tact with which she had responded to
his signal) in another moment had put the thought to flight,
and he fearlessly placed his own, and his country's destiny
in her hands.   He is an exile in England now.   Friends
and brothers have made terms with the oppressor, and
his home is no longer theirs.   But among the wishes
which still draw him to his native land, is one, less acknowledged than the rest and which perhaps lies deeper, that
he may see that noble woman once more ; talk to her of
the husband who was then her lover, of her children, and
her home ; and, once more, as he did in parting from her,
kiss her hand in gratitude, and lay his own in blessing on
her head.[1]

"PROTUS" is a fragment of an imaginary chronicle : recording in the same page and under the head of the
same year, how the child-Emperor, Protus, descended from
a god, was growing in beauty and in grace, worshipped
by the four quarters of the known world ; and how John,
the Pannonian blacksmith's bastard, came and took the
Empire ; but, as "some think," let Protus live—to be
heard of later as dependent in a foreign court : or perhaps
to become the monk, whom rumour speaks of as bearing
his name, and who died at an advanced age in Thrace.

A fit comment on this Empire lost and won, is supplied
by two busts, also imaginary, one showing a "rough
hammered" coarse-jawed head ; the other, a baby face,
crowned with a wreath of violets.

[1] Mr. Browning is proud to remember that Mazzini informed him he had
read this poem to certain of his fellow-exiles in England to show how an
Englishman could sympathize with them.

"APPARENT FAILURE" is Mr. Browning's verdict on three drowned men, whose bodies he saw exposed at the Morgue[1] in Paris, in the summer of 1856. He justly assumes that the death was suicide; and as he reads in each face its special story of struggle and disappointment,

> "Poor men, God made, and all for that !"  (vol. vii. p. 247.)

the conviction lays hold of him that their doom is not final, that the life God blessed in the beginning cannot end accursed of Him; that even a despair and a death like these, record only a seeming failure.

The poem was professedly written to save the memory of the Morgue, then about to be destroyed.

The friend, to whom "WARING" refers, is a restless, aspiring, sensitive person, who has planned great works, though he has completed none: who feels his powers always in excess of his performance, and who is hurt if those he loves refuse them credit for being so. He is gone now, no one knows whither; and the speaker, who is conscious that his own friendship has often seemed critical or cold, vainly wishes that he could recall him. His fancy travels longingly to those distant lands, in one of which Waring may be playing some new and romantic part; and back again to England, where he tries to think that he is lying concealed, while preparing to surprise the world with some great achievement in literature or art. Then someone solves the problem by saying that he has seen him—for one moment—on the Illyrian coast; seated in a light bark, just bounding away into the sunset. And the speaker rejoins

> "Oh, never star
> Was lost here but it rose afar !"  (vol. v. p. 89.)

and, we conclude, takes comfort from the thought.

---

[1] A small, square building on one of the quays, in which the bodies of drowned persons were placed for identification.

# CONCLUDING GROUP.

## "DRAMATIC IDYLS." "JOCOSERIA."

### "DRAMATIC IDYLS."

THE Dramatic Idyls form, like the Dramas, a natural group; and though, unlike these, they might be distributed under various heads, it would not be desirable to thus disconnect them; for their appearing together at this late period of Mr. Browning's career, constitutes them a landmark in it. They each consist of a nucleus of fact—supplied by history or by romance, as the case may be—and of material, and in most cases, mental circumstance, which Mr. Browning's fancy has engrafted on it; and in both their material and their mental aspect they display a concentrated power, which clearly indicates what I have spoken of as the "crystallizing" process Mr. Browning's genius has undergone. A comparison of these poems with "Pauline," "Paracelsus," or even "Pippa Passes," will be found to justify this assertion.

The Idyls consist of two series, occupying each a volume. The first, published 1879, contains :—

"Martin Relph."
"Pheidippides."
"Halbert and Hob."
"Ivàn Ivànovitch."
"Tray."
"Ned Bratts."

The hero of " MARTIN RELPH " is an old man, whose life is haunted by something which happened to him when little more than a boy. A girl of his own village had been falsely convicted of treason, and the guns were already levelled for her execution, when Martin Relph, who had stolen round on to some rising ground behind the soldiers and villagers who witnessed the scene, saw what no one else could see : a man, about a quarter of mile distant, rushing onwards in staggering haste, and waving a white object over his head. He knew this was Vincent Parkes, Rosamond Page's lover, bearing the expected proofs of her innocence. He knew also that by a shout he might avert her doom. But something paralyzed his tongue, and the girl fell. The man who would have rescued her but for delays and obstacles, which no power of his could overcome, was found dead where Martin Relph had seen him.

The remembrance of these two deaths leaves Martin Relph no rest ; for conscience tells him that his part in them was far worse than it appeared. It tells him that what struck him dumb at that awful moment was not, as others said, the simple cowardice of a boy : he loved in secret the girl whom Vincent Parkes was coming to save ; and if *he* had saved her, it would have been for that other man. But that thought could only flash on him in one second of fiery consciousness ; he had no time to recognize it as a motive ; and he clings madly to the hope that his conscience is mistaken, and it was not that which silenced him. Every year, at the same spot, he re-enacts the scene, striving to convince himself—with those who hear him—that he has been a coward, but not a murderer ; and in the moral and physical reaction from the renewed agony, half-succeeds in doing so.

The story, thus told in Martin Relph's words, is supposed to have been repeated to the present narrator by a grandfather, who heard them. It embodies a vague remembrance of something read by Mr. Browning when he was himself a boy.

The facts related in " PHEIDIPPIDES" belong to Greek legendary history, and are told by Herodotus and other writers. When Athens was threatened by the invading Persians, she sent a running messenger to Sparta, to demand help against the foreign foe. The mission was unsuccessful. But the "runner," Pheidippides, fell in on his return, with the god Pan ; and though alone among Greeks the Athenians had refused to honour him, he promised to fight with them in the coming battle. Pheidippides was present, when this battle—that of Marathon—was fought and won. He "ran" once more, to announce the victory at Athens ; and fell, dead, with the words, " Rejoice, we conquer !" on his lips. This death followed naturally on the excessive physical strain ; but Mr. Browning has used it as a connecting link between the historic and the imaginary parts of the idyl. According to this, Pheidippides himself tells his first adventure, to the assembled rulers of Athens : depicting, in vivid words, the emotions which winged his course, and bore him onwards over mountains and through valleys, with the smooth swiftness of running fire ; and he also relates that Pan promised him a personal reward for his " toil," which was to consist in release from it. This release he interprets as freedom to return home, and to marry the girl he loves. It meant a termination to his labours, more tragic, but far more glorious : to die, proclaiming the victory which they had helped to secure.

Pan is also made to present him with a sprig of fennel —symbol of Marathon, or the " fennel-field "—as pledge of his promised assistance.

" HALBERT AND HOB" is the story of a fierce father and son who lived together in solitude, shunned by their fellow-men. **One** Christmas night they drifted into a quarrel, in the course of which the son seized his father, and was about to turn him out of doors : when the latter, with unaccustomed mildness, bade him stay his hand. Just **so,** he said, in his youth, had he proceeded against **his** own father ; and at just this stage of the proceeding had a voice in his heart bidden him desist . . **And the son** thus appealed to desisted also.

This fact is told by Aristotle[1] as an instance of the hereditary nature of anger. But Mr. Browning sees more in it than that. If, he declares, Nature creates hard hearts, it is a power beyond **hers** which softens them ; and **in** his version **of** " Halbert and Hob " this supernatural power completes the **work** it has begun. The two return **in** silence to their fireside. **The next** morning the **father is** found dead. The son has become a harmless **idiot, to re-** main **so** till the end **of** his life.

" IVAN IVANOVITCH " is the reproduction, with fictitious names and imaginary circumstances, of a popular Russian story, known as " The Judgment of God." A young woman travelling through the forest on a winter's night, is attacked by wolves, and saves her own life by throwing her children to them. But when she reaches her village, and either confesses the deed or stands convicted of it, one of its inhabitants, by trade a carpenter and the Iván Ivánovitch of the idyl, lifts the axe which he is plying, and strikes off her head : this informal retribution being accepted, by those present, as in conformity with the higher law.

Mr. Browning has raised the mother's act out of the sphere of vulgar crime, by the characteristic method of making her tell her story : and show herself, as she may easily have been, not altogether bad ; though a woman of weak maternal instincts, and one whose nature was power-

[1] Ethics, VII. vi. 2.

less against the fear of pain, and the impulse to self-pre-
servation. She describes with appalling vividness the
experiences of the night : the moonlit forest—the snow-
covered ground—the wolves approaching with a whispering tread, which seems at first but the soughing of a gentle
wind—the wedge-like, ever-widening mass, which emerges
from the trees ; then the flight, and the pursuit : the
latter arrested for one moment by the sacrifice of each
victim ; to be renewed the next, till none is left to sacrifice :
one child dragged from the mother's arms ; another shielded
by her whole body, till the wolf's teeth have fastened in
her flesh ; and though she betrays, in the very effort
to conceal it, how little she has done to protect her children's lives, we realize the horror of her situation, and pity
even while we condemn, her. But some words of selfish
rejoicing at her own deliverance precede the fatal stroke,
and in some degree challenge it. And Mr. Browning farther
preserves the spirit of the tradition, by giving to her sentence the sanction of the village priest or "pope," into
whose presence the decapitated body has been conveyed.
The secular authorities are also on the spot, and condemn
the murder as contrary both to justice and to law. But the
pope declares that the act of Ivàn Ivànovitch has been one
of the higher justice which is above law. He himself is
an aged man—so aged, he says, that he has passed through
the clouds of human convention, and stands on the firm
basis of eternal truth. Looking down upon the world
from this vantage-ground, he sees that no gift of God is
equal to that of life ; no privilege so high as that of reproducing its "miracle ;" and that the mother who has cast
away her maternal crown, and given over to destruction
the creatures which she has borne, has sinned an "unex-
ampled sin," for which a "novel punishment" was required. No otherwise than did Moses of old, has Ivàn
Ivànovitch interpreted the will—shown himself the servant
—of God.

How Mr. Browning's Ivàn Ivànovitch himself judges the case, is evidenced by this fact, that after wiping the blood from his axe, he betakes himself to playing with his children ; and that when the lord of the village has—reluctantly—sent a deputation to inform him **that he is free**, the words, " how otherwise ?" are his only **answer**.

" TRAY " describes an instance **of** animal courage **and** devotion which a friend of Mr. Browning's actually **witnessed** in Paris. A little girl had **fallen** into the river. None of the bystanders attempted **to** rescue her. But a dog, bouncing over the balustrade, brought the child **to** land ; dived again, no one could guess why ; and **after** battling **with** a dangerous current, emerged **with the** child's **doll** ; then trotted away **as** if nothing **had** occurred.

This "Tray" is made to illustrate Mr. Browning's ideal of a hero, in opposition to certain showy and conventional human types ; and **the** little narrative contains some scathing reflections on those who talk of such **a** creature as merely led by instinct, or would dissect its brain alive to discover how the " soul " is secreted there.

"NED BRATTS" was suggested **by the** remembrance of a passage in John Bunyan's " Life and Death of Mr. Badman." Bunyan relates there that some twenty years ago, "at a summer assizes holden at Hertford, while the judge was sitting on the Bench," a certain old Tod came into the Court, and declared himself " the veriest rogue that breathes upon the earth "—a thief from childhood, &c., &c. ; that the judge first thought him mad, but after conferring with some of the justices, agreed to indict him " of several felonious actions ;" and that as he heartily confessed to all of these, he was hanged, with his wife, at the same time. Mr. Browning has turned Hertford into Bedford ; made the time of the occurrence coincide with that of Bunyan's imprisonment ; and supposed the evident conversion of this man and woman to be among the many which he effected there. The blind daughter of Bunyan, who plays an important part in " Ned Bratts," is affectingly spoken of in her father's work; and the tag-laces, which have subserved the criminal purposes of Bratts and his wife, represent an industry by which he is known to have supported himself in prison. Mr. Browning, finally, has used the indications Bunyan gives, of the incident taking place on a very hot day, so as to combine the sense of spiritual stirring with one of unwholesome and grotesque physical excitement ; and this, as he describes it, is the genuine key-note of the situation.

The character of Ned Bratts is made a perfect vehicle for these impressions. His " Tab " (Tabitha) has had an interview with John Bunyan, and been really moved by his majestic presence, and warning, yet hope-inspiring words. But he himself has been principally worked upon by the reading of the " Pilgrim's Progress ; " and we see in him throughout, an unregenerate ruffian, whose carnal energies have merely transferred themselves to another field ; and whose blood is fired to this act of martyrdom both by yesterday's potations, and to-day's virtuously endured thirst. " A mug," he cries, in the midst of his confessions ; or, " no (addressing his wife), a prayer ! "

" Dip for one out of the Book !    .    .    . " (vol. xv. p. 67.)

The precarious nature of his conversion is, indeed, vividly present to his own mind. It is borne in upon him that he is " Christmas," and must escape from the City of Destruction. He would like nothing better, in his present mood, than to undertake the whole Pilgrimage, and, as it were, cudgel his way through ; and since it is late in the day for this, he chooses the short cut by the gallows, as the next best thing. But he is, above all, desirous to be taken while the penitent fit is on him : and urgently sets forth those past misdeeds, which constitute his **and** his wife's claim to a speedy despatch, such as will place them beyond the danger of backsliding. Already, he declares, Satan is whispering to him of the pleasures he **is** leaving behind ; and the seductions of to-morrow's brawl and bear-baiting are threatening to turn the scale. Another moment, and instead **of** going up to heaven, like Faithful, in a chariot and pair, he will be **the** Lost **Man in the** Iron Cage !

When the **two** have **had** their wish, and been hanged "out of hand," the bystanders **are** edified **to tears.** But **the** loyalty of **the** Chief Justice forbids any **im-**puting of the act of grace to the influence of John Bunyan. Its cause lies rather, he asserts, in the twelve years' pious reign of the restored Charles.

The second series **of** the "Dramatic Idyls" was **pub-**lished in 1880, and contains :—

"Echetlos."

"Clive."

"Muléykeh."

"Pietro of Abano."

"Doctor —— "

"Pan and Luna."

It has also a little prologue and epilogue : the former satirizing the pretension to understand the Soul, which we cannot see, while we are baffled by the workings of the bodily organs, which we can see ; the latter directed against the popular idea that the more impressible and more quickly responsive natures are the soil of which "song" is born. The true poet, **it** declares, is as **the** pine tree which has grown out of a rock.

"ECHETLOS" (holder of the ploughshare) is another legend of the battle of Marathon. It tells, in Mr. Browning's words, how one with the goat-skin garment, and the broad bare limbs of a "clown," was seen on the battle-field ploughing down the enemy's ranks: the ploughshare flashing now here, now there, wherever the Grecian lines needed strengthening; how he vanished when the battle was won; and how the oracle, of which his name was asked, bade the inquirers not care for it:

> "Say but just this: We praise one helpful whom we call
> The Holder of the Ploughshare.  The great deed ne'er grows small."
>
> (vol. xv. p. 87.)

Miltiades and Themistocles had shown that a great name could do so.[1]

The anecdote which forms the basis of "CLIVE," was told to Mr. Browning in 1846 by Mrs. Jameson, who had shortly before heard it at Lansdowne House, from Macaulay.  It is cursorily mentioned in Macaulay's "Essays."

When Robert Clive was first in India, a boy of fifteen, clerk in a merchant's office at St. David's, he accused an officer with whom he was playing, of cheating at cards, and was challenged by him in consequence.  Clive fired, as it seems, prematurely, and missed his aim.  The officer, at whose mercy he had thus placed himself, advanced to within arm's length, held the muzzle of his pistol to the youth's forehead, and summoned him to repeat his accusation.  Clive did repeat it, and with such defiant courage that his adversary was unnerved.  He threw down the weapon, confessed that he had cheated, and rushed out of the room.  A chorus of indignation then broke forth among those who had witnessed the scene.  They declared that the "wronged civilian" should be righted; and that he who had thus disgraced Her Majesty's Service should be drummed—if needs be, kicked—out of the regiment.  But here Clive interposed.  Not one, he said, of the eleven, whom he addressed by name and title, had raised a finger

---

[1] The story is told in Pausanias.  A painting of Echetlos was to be seen in the Pœcile at Athens.

to save his **life.** He would clear scores with any or **all** among them who breathed a word against the man who had spared it. Nor, **as** the narrative continues, and as the event proved, was such a word ever spoken.

Clive is supposed to relate this experience, a week **be-** fore his self-inflicted death, to a friend **who** is dining **with** him ; and who, struck by his depressed mental state, strives to arouse him from it by the question : which of his past achievements constitutes, in his own judgment, the greatest proof of courage. He gives the moment **in** which the pistol was levelled at his head, as that in which he felt, not most courage, but most **fear. But, as** he explains to his astonished listener, **it was not the** almost certainty of death, which, for one awful minute, **made a** coward of him ; **it was** the bare possibility **of a reprieve,** which would have left **no** appeal from its dishonour. **His** opponent refused **to** fire. He might **have done so with** words like these :

> " Keep your life, calumniator !—worthless life I freely spare :
> Mine you freely would have taken—murdered me and my good fame
> Both at once—and all the better ! Go, and thank **your own** bad aim
> Which permits me to forgive you ! . . " **(vol. xv. p.** 105.)

What course would have remained to him but to seize the pistol, and himself send the bullet into his brain ? This tremendous mental situation is, we need hardly say, Mr. Browning's addition to the episode.

The poem contains also some striking reflections on the risks and responsibilities of power ; and concludes with an expression of reverent pity for the " great unhappy hero " for whom they proved too great.

" MULÉYKEH " is an old Arabian story. The name which heads it is that of a swift, beautiful mare, who was Hóseyn—her owner's, " Pearl." He loved her so dearly, that, though a very poor man, no price would tempt him to sell her ; and in his fear of her being stolen, he slept always with her head-stall thrice wound round his wrist : and Buhéysch, her sister, saddled for instantaneous pursuit. One night she was stolen ; and Duhl, the thief, galloped away on her and felt himself secure : for the Pearl's speed was such that even her sister had never overtaken her. She chafed, however, under the strange rider, and slackened her pace. Buhéysch, bearing Hóseyn, gained fast upon them ; the two mares were already "neck by croup." Then the thought of his darling's humiliation flashed on Hóseyn's mind. He shouted angrily to Duhl in what manner he ought to urge her. And the Pearl, obeying her master's voice, no less than the familiar signal prescribed by him, bounded forward, and was lost to him for ever. Hóseyn returned home, weeping sorely, and the neighbours told him he had been a fool. "Why not have kept silence and got his treasure back?

"'And —— beaten in speed !' wept Hóseyn : 'You never have loved my
Pearl.'"                                        (vol. xv. p. 116.)

The man who gives his name to "PIETRO OF ABANO" was the greatest Italian philosopher and physician of the thirteenth century.[1] He was also an astrologer, pretending to magical knowledge, and persecuted, as Mr. Browning relates. But the special story he tells of him has been told of others also.

Pietro of Abano had the reputation of being a wizard ; and though his skill in curing sickness, as in building, star-reading, and yet other things, conferred invaluable services on his fellow-men, he received only kicks and curses for his reward. His power seemed, nevertheless, so enviable, that he was one day, in the archway of his door, accosted by a young Greek, who humbly and earnestly entreated that the secret of that power might be revealed to him. He promised to repay his master with loving gratitude ; and

---

[1] Petrus Aponensis: author of a work quoted in the Idyl: Conciliator Differentiarum. Abano is a village near Padua.

hinted that the bargain might be worth **the** latter's consideration, since nature, in all else his slave, forbade his
drinking milk (this is told of the **true** Pietro) : **in** other
words, denied him the affection which softens and sweetens
the dry bread of human life. Pietro pretended to consent,
and began, to utter, by way **of** preface, **the word** "bene-
dicite." The young Greek lost consciousness at its second
syllable; and awoke to find himself alone, and with a first
instalment of Peter's secret in his mind. "Good is pro-
duct of evil, and to be effected through **it."** Acting upon
this doctrine, he traded on the weaknesses of his fellow-
creatures wherever the opportunity occurred ; and attained
by this means, first, wealth ; next temporal, **and** then
spiritual, power ; rising finally **to the** dignity of **Pope.**
At each stage of this progress, Peter came to him in apparent destitution, **and** claimed the promised gratitude in an
urgent, but very modest prayer **for** assistance. And each
time Peter's presence infused into him **a** fresh power **of**
unscrupulousness, and sent him a step farther **on his way.**
But each time also **the** pupil postponed **his** obligation, **till**
he at last disclaimed it ; and—enthroned in the **Lateran**
—was dismissing his benefactor with insult : when **the**
closing syllables—"dicite"—sounded in his ear ; and he
became conscious of Peter's countenance smiling back at
him over his shoulder, and Peter's door being banged in
his face. And he then knew that he had lived a lifetime
in the fraction of a minute, and that the magician, by
means of whom he had done so, justly declined to trust
him.

Mr. Browning, however, bids the young Greek per-
severe ; since he might ransack Peter's books, without
discovering a better secret for gaining power over the
masses, than the "cleverness uncurbed by conscience,"
which he perhaps already possesses.[1]

---

[1] Some expressions in this Idyl may require explaining. "Salomo si
nôsset" (novisset) (p. 136). "Had Solomon but known this." "Teneor

"DOCTOR ——" is an old Hebrew legend, founded upon the saying that a bad wife is stronger than death. Satan complains, in his character of Death, that man has the advantage of him : since he may baffle him, whenever he will, by the aid of a bad woman ; and he undertakes to show this in his own person. He comes to earth, marries, and has a son, who in due time must be supplied with a profession. This son is too cowardly to be a soldier, and too lazy to be a lawyer ; Divinity is his father's sphere. So Satan decides that he shall be a doctor; and endows him with a faculty which will enable him to practise Medicine, without any knowledge of it at all. The moment he enters a sick room, he will see his father spiritually present there ; and unless he finds him seated at the sick's man's head, that man is not yet doomed. Thus endowed, Doctor —— can cure a patient who was despaired of, with a dose of penny-royal, and justly predict death for one whose only ailment is a pimple. His success carries all before it. One day, however, he is summoned to the emperor, who lies sick ; and the emperor offers gold, and power, and, lastly, his daughter's hand, as the price of his recovery. But this time Satan sits at the head of the bed, and not even such an appeal to his pride and greed will induce him

vix " (p. 136). " I scarcely contain myself." " Hactēnus " (p. 136). The " e " is purposely made long. " Hitherto." " Peason " (p. 138). The old English plural of " pea." " Pou sto " (p. 138). " Where I may stand :" The alleged saying of Archimedes—" I could move the world had I a place for my *fulcrum*—' where I might stand ' to move it." " Tithon " (p. 141). Tithonus—Aurora's lover: for whom she procured the gift of eternal life. " Apage, Sāthanas !" (p. 142). " Depart Satan." Customary adjuration.

The term " Venus," as employed in the postscript to the Idyl, signified in Roman phraseology, the highest throw of the dice. It signified, therefore the highest promise to him, who, in obedience to the oracle, had tested his fortunes at the fount at Abano, by throwing golden dice into it. The " crystal," to which Mr. Browning refers, is the water of the well or fount, at the bottom of which, as Suetonius declared, the dice thrown by Tiberius, and their numbers, were still visible. The little air which concludes the postscript reflects the careless or " lilting " mood in which Mr. Browning had thrown the " fancy dice " which cast themselves into the form of the poem.

to grant the patient even a temporary reprieve. The son, thus driven to bay, pretends to be struck by a sudden thought. " He will try the efficacy of the mystic Jacob's staff." He whispers to an attendant to bid his mother bring it ; and as Satan's Bad Wife enters the room, Satan vanishes through the ceiling, leaving a smell of sulphur behind him. The Emperor gets well ; but Doctor —— renounces the promised gold : for it was to be the Princess's dowry ; and he is too wise to accept it on the condition of saddling himself with a wife.

" PAN AND LUNA " describes a mythical adventure of Luna—the moon, given by Virgil in the Georgics ; and has for its text a line from them (III. 390) :

" Si credere dignum est." [1]

According to the legend, Luna was one night entrapped by Pan who lay in wait for her in the form of a cloud, soft and snowy as the fleece of a certain breed of sheep ; and, Virgil continues, followed him to the woodland, " by no means spurning him." But Mr. Browning tells the story in a manner more consonant with the traditional modesty of the " Girl-Moon." She was, he says, distressed by the exposure of her full-orbed charms, as she flew bare through the vault of heaven : the protecting darkness ever vanishing before her ; and she took refuge for concealment in the cloud of which the fleecy billows were to close and contract about her, in the limbs of the goat-god. How little she accepted this her first eclipse, may be shown, he thinks, by the fact that she never now lingers within a cloud longer than is necessary to " rip " it through.

[1] " If it is proper to be credited."

V

## "JOCOSERIA."

The volume so christened (grave and gay), published 1883, shows a greater variety of subject and treatment than do the Dramatic Idyls, and its contents might be still more easily broken up ; but they are also best given in their original form.   They are—

"Wanting is—what?"
"Donald."
"Solomon and Balkis."
"Cristina and Monaldeschi."
"Mary Wollstonecraft and Fuseli."
"Adam, Lilith, and Eve."
"Ixion."
"Jochanan Hakkadosh."
"Never the Time and the Place."
"Pambo."

"WANTING IS—WHAT?" is an invocation to Love, as the necessary supplement to whatever is beautiful in life. It may equally be addressed to the spirit of Love, or to its realization in the form of a beloved person.

"DONALD" is a true story, repeated to Mr. Browning by one who had heard it from its hero the so-called Donald, himself.   This man, a fearless sportsman in the flush of youth and strength, found himself one day on a narrow mountain ledge—a wall of rock above, a precipice below, and the way barred by a magnificent **stag** approaching from the opposite side.   Neither could retrace his steps.   There was not space enough for them **to** pass each other.   One expedient alone presented **itself:** that **the man should lie** flat, and the stag (if it would) step over **him.   And so it** might have been.   Donald slipped sideways on to his back. The stag, gently, cautiously, not grazing him with the tip of a hoof, commenced the difficult transit ; the feat was already half accomplished. But the lifted hind legs laid bare the stomach of the stag ; and Donald, who was sportsman first, **and man** long afterwards, raised himself on his elbow, and stabbed it. The two rolled over into the abyss. The stag, for the second time, saved its murderer's life ; for it broke his fall. He came **out** of the hospital into which he had been carried, a crippled, patched-up wretch, but able to crawl on hands and knees **to** wherever his " pluck " might be appreciated, and earn **a** beggar's livelihood by telling how it was last displayed.

These facts are supposed to be related in **a** Scotch bothie, to a group of young men already fired by the attractions of sport ; and **are** the narrator's comment **on the** theory, that moral soundness as well as physical strength, is promoted by it.

" SOLOMON AND BALKIS " **is the** Talmudic version [1] of the dialogue, which took place between Solomon and the Queen of Sheba, on the occasion of **her** visit to the 'wise King. They begin by talking for effect : and when questioned by each other as to the kind of persons they most readily admit to their respective courts, Solomon answers that he welcomes the Wise, whatever be their social condition ; and Balkis declares that her sympathies are all with the Good. But a chance (?) movement on her part jostles the hand of Solomon ; and the ring it bears slips round, so that the truth-compelling Name is turned outwards instead **of** in. Then he confesses that he loves the Wise just so long as he is the object of their appreciation ; she that she loves the Good so long as they bear the form of young and handsome men.

---

[1] This version is more crudely reproduced by the Persian poet Jami.

He acknowledges, with a sigh, that the soul, which will soar in heaven, must crawl while confined to earth ; she owns, with a laugh and a blush, that she has not travelled thus far to hold mental communion with him.[1]

" CRISTINA [2] AND MONALDESCHI " gives the closing scene of the life of Monaldeschi, in what might be Cristina's own words. She is addressing the man whom she has convicted of betraying her, and at whose murder she is about to assist ; and the monologue reflects the outward circumstance of this murder, as well as the queen's deliberate cruelty, and her victim's cowardice. They are in the palace of Fontainebleau. Its internal decorations record the loves of Diane de Poitiers and the French king, in their frequent repetition of the crescent and the salamander,[3] and of the accompanying motto, " Quis separabit ; " and Cristina, with ghastly irony, calls her listener's attention to the appropriateness of these emblems to their own case. Then she plays with the idea that his symbol is the changing moon, hers the fire-fed salamander, dangerous to those only who come too close. Changing the metaphor, she speaks of herself as a peak, which Monaldeschi has chosen to scale, and which he wrongly hoped to descend when he should be weary of the position, by the same ladder by which he climbed ; and her half-playful words assume a still more sinister import, as she depicts the whirling waters, the frightful rocky abyss, into which a moment's giddiness on his part, a touch from her, might precipitate him. She bids him

---

1 The word "conster," which rhymes in the poem with "monster," is Old English for "construe."

2 Daughter of Gustavus Adolphus, and Queen of Sweden.

3 Some confusion has here arisen between Francis I., whose emblem was the salamander, and Henry II., the historic lover of Diane de Poitiers. But Francis was also said to have been, for a short time, attached to her ; and the poetic contrast of the frigid moon and the fiery salamander was perhaps worth the dramatic sacrifice of Cristina's accuracy.

cure the dizziness, **ward** off the danger, by kneeling, even crouching, at her feet ; act the lover, though he no longer is one. And all the while she is drawing him towards the door of that " Gallery of the Deer," where the priest who is to confess, the soldiers who are to slay, are waiting for him.

Cristina's last words are addressed, in vindication **of** her deed, to the priest (Lebel), who **is** aghast **at its** ferocity. He, she says, has received the culprit's confession, and would not divulge it for a crown. The church at Avon [1] must tell how *her* secrets have been guarded by him to whom she had entrusted them.

" MARY WOLLSTONECRAFT AND FUSELI " **is** the mournful yet impassioned expression of an unrequited love.

" ADAM, LILITH, AND EVE " illustrates **the** manner **in** which the typical man and woman will proceed towards each other : the latter committing herself by imprudent disclosures when under the influence of fear, and turning them into a joke as soon as the fear is past ; the former pretending that he never regarded them as serious.

" IXION " is an imaginary protest of this victim **of** the anger of Zeus, wrung from him by his torments, as he whirls on the fiery wheel.[2] He has been sentenced to this punishment for presuming on the privileges which Zeus had conferred upon him, and striving to win Heré's [3] love ; and he declares that the punishment is undeserved : " he was encouraged to claim the love of Heré, together with the friendship of Zeus ; he has erred only in his trust

---

[1] A village close to Fontainebleau, in the church of which Monaldeschi was buried.

[2] " Winged " or " fiery : " fiery from the rapidity of its motion.

[3] Juno.

in their professions. And granting that it were otherwise
—that he had sinned in arrogance—that, befriended by
the gods, he had wrongly fancied himself their equal: one
touch from them of pitying power would have sufficed to
dispel the delusion, born of the false testimony of the
flesh!" He asks, with indignant scorn, what need there
is of accumulated torment, to prove to one who has re-
covered his sight, that he was once blind; and in this
scorn and indignation he denounces the gods, whose
futile vindictiveness would shame the very nature of man;
he denounces them as hollow imitations of him whom
they are supposed to create : as mere phantoms to which
he imparts the light and warmth of his own life. Then
rising from denunciation to prophecy, he bids his fellow-
men take heart. " Let them struggle and fall! Let
them press on the limits of their own existence, to find
only human passions and human pettiness in the sphere
beyond ; let them expiate their striving in hell ! The
end is not yet come. Of his vapourized flesh, of the
' tears, sweat, and blood ' of his agony, is born a rainbow
of hope ; of the whirling wreck of his existence, the pale
light of a coming joy. Beyond the weakness of the god
his tormenter he descries a Power, unobstructed, all-pure.

" Thither I rise, whilst thou—Zeus, keep the godship and sink !"

If any doubt were still possible as to Mr. Browning's
attitude towards the doctrine of eternal punishment, this
poem must dispel it.

"JOCHANAN HAKKADOSH" relates how a certain Rabbi
was enabled to extend his life for a year and three months
beyond its appointed term, and what knowledge came to
him through the extension. Mr. Browning professes to
rest his narrative on a Rabbinical work, of which the title,
given by him in Hebrew, means "Collection of many
lies ; " and he adds, by way of supplement, three sonnets,

supposed to fantastically illustrate the old Hebrew proverb,
" From Moses to Moses [1] never was one like Moses," and
embodying as many fables of wildly increasing audacity.
The main story is nevertheless justified by traditional
Jewish belief ; and Mr. Browning has made it the vehicle
of some poetical imagery and much serious thought.

Jochanan Hakkadosh was at **the** point of death. He
had completed his seventy-ninth year. But his faculties
were unimpaired ; and his pupils had gathered round him
to receive the last lessons of his experience ; and **to know**
with what feelings he regarded the impending change.
Jochanan Hakkadosh had but one answer to give : his life
had been a failure. He had loved, learned, **and** fought ;
and in every case his object had **been** ill-chosen, his
energies ill-bestowed. He had shared **the** common lot,
which gives power into the hand of folly, and places wisdom in command when no power is left to be commanded.
With this desponding utterance he bade his " children"
farewell.

But here a hubbub of protestation arose. " This must
not be the Rabbi's last word. It need not be so ;" for, as
Tsaddik, one of the disciples, reminded his fellows, there
existed a resource against such a case. Their " Targums"
(commentaries) assured them that when one thus com-
bining the Nine Points of perfection was overtaken by
years before the fruits of his knowledge had been matured,
respite might be gained for him by a gift from another
man's life : the giver being rewarded for the wisdom to
which he ministered **by a** corresponding remission of ill-
spent time. The sacrifice was small, viewed side by side
with the martyrdoms endured in Rome for the glory of the
Jewish race. [2] " Who of those present was willing to make
it ?" Again a hubbub arose. The disciples within, the
mixed crowd without, all clamoured for the privilege of

[1] That is, to Moses Maimonides.
[2] The names and instances given are, as well as the main fact, historical.

lengthening the Rabbi's life from their own. Tsaddik de-
precated so extensive a gift. "Their teacher's patience
should not be overtaxed, like that of Perida (whose story
he tells), by too long a spell of existence." He accepted
from the general bounty exactly one year, to be recruited
in equal portions from a married lover, a warrior, a poet,
and a statesman ; and, the matter thus settled, Jochanan
Hakkadosh fell asleep.

Four times the Rabbi awoke, in renewed health and
strength : and four times again he fell asleep : and at the
close of each waking term Tsaddik revisited him as he sat
in his garden—amidst the bloom or the languors, the
threatenings or the chill, of the special period of the year
—and questioned him of what he had learned. And each
time the record was like that of the previous seventy-nine
years, one of disappointment and failure. For the gift had
been drawn in every case from a young life, and been
neutralized by its contact with the old. As a lover, the
Rabbi declares, he has dreamed young dreams, and his
older self has seen through them. He has known beforehand that the special charms of his chosen one would
prove transitory, and that the general attraction of her
womanhood belonged to her sex and not to her. As a
warrior, he has experienced the same process of disen-
chantment. For the young believe that the surest way to
the Right and Good, is that, always, which is cut by the
sword : and that the exercise of the sword is the surest
training for those self-devoting impulses which mark the
moral nature of man. The old have learned that the most
just war involves, in its penalties, the innocent no less than
the guilty ; that violence rights no wrong which time and
patience would not right more fully ; and that for the purposes of self devotion, unassisted love is more effective
than hate. (Picturesque illustrations are made to support
this view.) As poet, he has recalled the glow of youthful
fancy to feel it quenched by the experience of age : to see

those soaring existences whose vital atmosphere is the
future, frozen by their contact with a dead past.  As
statesman, he has looked out upon the forest of life, again
seeing the noble trees by which the young trace their
future path.  And, seeing these, he has known, that the way
leads, not by them, but among the brushwood and briars
which fill the intervening space ; that the statist's work
is among the mindless many who will obstruct him at
every step, not among the intellectual few by whom his
progress would be assisted.

As he completes his testimony another change comes
over him ; and Tsaddik, kissing the closing eyelids, leaves
his master to die.

The rumour of a persecution scatters the Jewish inhabitants of the city.  Not till three months have expired do
they venture to return to it ; and when Tsaddik and the
other disciples seek the cave where their master lies, they
find him, to their astonishment, alive.  Then Tsaddik remembers that even children urged their offering upon him,
and concludes that some urchin or other contrived to
make it "stick ;" and he anxiously disclaims any share in
the "foisting" this crude fragment of existence on the
course of so great a life.  Hereupon the Rabbi opens his
eyes, and turns upon the bystanders a look of such absolute relief, such utter happiness, that, as Tsaddik declares,
only a second miracle can explain it.  It is a case of the
three days' survival of the " Ruach " or spirit, conceded
to those departed saints whose earthly life has anticipated
the heavenly ; who have died, as it were, half in the
better world.[1]

Tsaddik has, however, missed the right solution of the
problem.  Jochanan Hakkadosh can only define his state as
one of *ignorance confirmed by knowledge ;* but he makes it
very clear that it is precisely the gift of the child's con-

[1] A Talmudic doctrine still held among the Jews.  The " Halaphta," with
whom Mr. Browning connects it, was a noted Rabbi.

sciousness, which has produced this ecstatic calm. The child's soul in him has reconciled the differing testimony of youth and manhood : solving their contradictions in its unquestioning faith and hope. It has lifted him into that region of harmonized good and evil, where bliss is greater than the human brain can bear. And this is how he feels himself to be dying ; bearing with him a secret of perfect happiness, which he vainly wishes he could impart.[1]

"NEVER THE TIME AND THE PLACE" is a fanciful expression of love and longing, provoked by the opposition of circumstances.

The name of "PAMBO" or "Pambus" is known to literature,[2] as that of a foolish person, who spent months—Mr. Browning says years—in pondering a simple passage from Psalm xxxix. ; and remained baffled by the difficulty of its application. The passage is an injunction that man look to his ways, so that he do not offend with his tongue. And Pambo finds it easy to practise the first part of this precept, but not at all so the second. Mr. Browning declares himself in the same case. "He also looks to his ways, and is guided along them by the critic's torch. But he offends with his tongue, notwithstanding."

1 The "Bier" and the "three daughters" was a received Jewish name for the Constellation of the Great Bear. Hence the simile derived from this (vol. xv. pp. 217-244).

The "Salem," mentioned at p. 218, is the mystical New Jerusalem to be built of the spirits of the great and good.

2 "Chetw. Hist. Collect.," cent. 1., p. 17. Quoted by Nath. Wanley, "Wonders of the Little World," p. 138.

# SUPPLEMENT.

## "FERISHTAH'S FANCIES."

THE idea of "FERISHTAH'S FANCIES" grew out of a fable by Pilpay, which Mr. Browning read when a boy. He lately put this into verse ; and it then occurred to him to make the poem the beginning of a series, in which the Dervish, who is first introduced as a learner, should reappear in the character of a teacher. Ferishtah's "fancies" are the familiar illustrations, by which his teachings are enforced. Each fancy or fable, with its accompanying dialogue, is followed by a Lyric, in which the same or cognate ideas are expressed in an emotional form ; and the effect produced by this combination of moods is itself illustrated in a Prologue by the blended flavours of a favourite Italian dish, which is fully described there. An introductory passage from " King Lear " seems to tell us what we soon find out for ourselves, that Ferishtah's opinions are in the main Mr. Browning's own.

Fancy I. "THE EAGLE," contains the lesson which determined Ferishtah, not yet a Dervish, to become one. He has learned from the experience which it describes, that it is man's mission to feed those hungry ones who are unable to feed themselves. " The soul often starves as well as the body. He will minister to the hunger of the

soul. And to this end he will leave the solitude of the woods
in which the lesson came to him, and seek the haunts of
men."

The Lyric deprecates the solitude which united souls
may enjoy, by a selfish or fastidious seclusion from the
haunts of men.

2. "THE MELON-SELLER," records an incident referred
to in a letter from the "Times'" correspondent, written
many years ago. It illustrates the text—given by Mr.
Browning in Hebrew—"Shall we receive good at the
hands of God, and shall we not receive evil?" and marks
the second stage in Ferishtah's progress towards Dervish-
hood.

The Lyric bids the loved one be unjust for once if she
will. "The lover's heart preserves so many looks and
words, in which she gave him more than justice."

3. "SHAH ABBAS" shows Ferishtah, now full Dervish,
expounding the relative character of belief. "We wrongly
give the name of belief to the easy acquiescence in those
reported facts, to the truth of which we are indifferent ; or
the name of unbelief to that doubting attitude towards
reported facts, which is born of our anxious desire that
they may be true. It is the assent of the heart, not that
of the head, which is valued by the Creator."

Lyric. Love will guide us smoothly through the recesses
of another's heart. Without it, as in a darkened room, we
stumble at every step, wrongly fancying the objects misplaced, against which we are stumbling.

4. "THE FAMILY" again defends the heart against the
head. It defends the impulse to pray for the health and
safety of those we love, though such prayer may imply
rebellion to the will of God. "He, in whom anxiety for
those he loves cannot for the moment sweep all before it,
will sometimes be more than man, but will much more
often be less."

Lyric. "Let me love, as man may, content with such

perfection as may fill a human heart ; not looking beyond it for that which only an angel's sense can apprehend."

5. " THE SUN " justifies the tendency to think of God as in human form. " Life moves us to many feelings of love and praise. These embrace in an ascending scale all its beneficent agencies, unconscious and conscious, and cannot stop short of the first and greatest of all. This First Cause must be thought of as competent to appreciate our praise and love, and as moved by a beneficent purpose to the acts which have inspired them. The sun is a symbol of this creative power—by many even imagined to be its reality. But that mighty orb is unconscious of the feelings it may inspire ; and the Divine Omnipotence, which it symbolizes, must be no less incompetent to earn them. For purpose is the negation of power, implying something which power has not attained ; and would imply deficiency in an existence which presents itself to our intelligence as complete. Reason therefore tells us that God can have no resemblance with man ; but it tells us, as plainly, that, without a fiction of resemblance, the proper relation between Creator and creature, between God and man, is unattainable.[1] If one exists, for whom the fiction or fancy has been converted into fact—for whom the Unknowable has proved itself to contain the Knowable : the ball of fire to hold within it an earthly substance unconsumed; he deserves credit for the magnitude, not scorn for the extravagance, of his conception.

Lyric. " Fire has been cradled in the flint, though its ethereal splendours may disclaim the association."

6. " MIHRAB SHAH " vindicates the existence of physical suffering as necessary to the consciousness of well-being ; and also, and most especially, as neutralizing the

[1] We must remark that these arguments are not directed against Atheism and its naturalistic philosophy, which supplies, in Mr. Browning's judgment, a consistent, if erroneous, solution of the problem. They only attack the position of those who would retain the belief in a personal God, and yet divest Him of every quality which makes such a Being thinkable.

differences, and thus creating the one complete bond of sympathy, between man and man.

Lyric. " Your soul is weighed down by a feeble body. In me a strong body is allied to a sluggish soul. You would fitly leave me behind. Impeded as you also are, I may yet overtake you."

7. " A CAMEL-DRIVER" declares the injustice of punishment, in regard to all cases in which the offence has been committed in ignorance ; and shows also that, while a timely warning would always have obviated such an offence, it is often sufficiently punished by the culprit's too tardy recognition of it. " God's justice distinguishes itself from that of man in the acknowledgment of this fact."

The Lyric deals specially with the imperfections of human judgment. " You have overrated my small faults, you have failed to detect the greater ones."

8. " TWO CAMELS" is directed against asceticism. " An ill-fed animal breaks down in the fulfilment of its task. A man who deprives himself of natural joys, not for the sake of his fellow-men, but for his own, is also unfitted for the obligations of Life. For he cannot instruct others in its use and abuse. Nor, being thus ignorant of earth, can he conceive of heaven."

The Lyric shows how the Finite may prefigure the Infinite, by illustrations derived from science and from love.

9. " CHERRIES" illustrates the axiom that a gift must be measured, not by itself, but by the faculty of the giver, and by the amount of loving care which he has bestowed upon it. Man's general performance is to be judged from the same point of view.

The Lyric connects itself with the argument less closely and less seriously in this case than in the foregoing ones. The speaker has striven to master the art of poetry, and found life too short for it. " He contents himself with doing little, only because doing nothing is worse. But when he turns from verse-making to making love, or, as the sense implies, seeks to express in love what he has failed to express in poetry, all limitations of time and power are suspended ; every moment's realization is absolute and lasting."

10. "PLOT-CULTURE" is a distinct statement **of the** belief in a purely personal relation between God and man. It justifies every experience which bears moral fruit, **how**ever immoral from human points of view ; and refers both the individual and his critic to the final harvest, on which alone the Divine judgment will be passed.

The Lyric repeats **the** image **in** which **this idea** is clothed, more directly than the idea itself. A lover pleads permission to love with his whole being—with **Sense as** well as with Soul.

11. **"A** PILLAR AT SEBZEVAR" lays down the proposition that the pursuit of knowledge is invariably disappointing : while love is always, and in itself, a gain.

The Lyric modifies this idea into the advocacy of a silent love : one which reveals itself without declaration.

12. "A BEAN-STRIPE : ALSO APPLE-EATING" is a summary of Mr. Browning's religious and practical beliefs. We cannot, it says, determine the prevailing colour of any human life, though we have before us a balanced record of its bright and dark days. For light or darkness is only absolute in so far as the human spirit can isolate or, as it were, stand still within, it. Every living experience, actual or remembered, takes something of its hue from those which precede or follow it: now catching **the** reflection of the adjoining lights and shades ; now brighter or darker by contrast with them. The act of living fuses black and white into grey ; and as we grasp the melting whole in one backward glance, its blackness strikes most on the sense of one man, its whiteness on that of another.

Ferishtah admits that there are lives which seem to be,

perhaps are, stained with a black so deep that no intervening whiteness can affect it ; and he declares that this
possibility of absolute human suffering is a constant
chastener to his own joys.  But when called upon to
reconcile the avowed optimism of his views with the actual
as well as sympathetic experience of such suffering, he
shows that he does not really believe in it.   One race, he
argues, will flourish under conditions which another would
regard as incompatible with life ; and the philosophers
who most cry down the value of life are sometimes the
least willing to renounce it.   He cannot resist the conviction that the same compensating laws are at work
everywhere.

In explanation of the fact, that nothing given in our experience affords a stable truth—that the black or white of
one moment is always the darker or lighter grey of another —
Ferishtah refers his disciples to the will of God.   Our very
scheme of goodness is a fiction, which man the impotent cannot, God the all-powerful does not, convert into reality.  But
it is a fiction created by God within the human mind, that it
may work for truth there ; so also is it with the fictitious
conceptions which blend the qualities of man with those
of God.   To the objection

"A power, confessed past knowledge, nay, past thought,
—Thus thought and known !"   (vol. xvi. p. 84.)

Ferishtah replies that to know the power by its opera-
tion, is all we *need* in the case of a human benefactor or
lord : all we *can* in the case of those natural forces which
we recognize in every act of our life.  And when reminded
that the sense of indebtedness implies a debtor—one ready
to receive his due : and that we need look no farther for
the recipient than the great men who have benefited our
race : his answer is, that such gratitude to his fellow-men
would be gratitude to himself, in whose perception half
their greatness lies.   "He might as well thank the star-

light for the impressions of colour, which have been supplied by his own brain."

The Lyric disclaims, in the name of one of the world's workers, all excessive—*i.e.*, loving recognition of his work. The speaker has not striven for the world's sake, nor sought his ideals there. "Those who have done so may claim its love. For himself he asks only a just judgment on what he has achieved."

Mr. Browning here expresses for the first time his feeling towards the "Religion of Humanity;" and though this was more or less to be inferred from his general religious views, it affords, as now stated, a new, as well as valuable, illustration of them. The Theistic philosophy which makes the individual the centre of the universe, is, perhaps, nowhere in his works, so distinctly set forth as in this latest of them. But nowhere either has he more distinctly declared that the fullest realization of the individual life is self-sacrifice.

> " Renounce joy for my fellows sake? That's joy
> Beyond joy ;"
>
> (*Two Camels,* vol. xvi. p. 50.)

The lyrical supplement to Fancy 12 somewhat obscures the idea on which it turns, by presenting it from a different point of view. But here, as in the remainder of the book, we must regard the Lyric as suggested by the argument, not necessarily as part of it.

The EPILOGUE is a vision of present and future, in which the woe and conflict of our mortal existence are absorbed in the widening glory of an eternal day. The vision comes to one cradled in the happiness of love ; and he is startled from it by a presentiment that it has been an illusion created by his happiness. But we know that from Mr. Browning's point of view, Love, even in its illusions, may be accepted as a messenger of truth.

Index to names and titles in " Ferishtah's Fancies : "—

z

P. 12.  "Shah Abbas."  An historical personage, used fictitiously.

P. 15.  "Story of Tahmasp."  Fictitious.

P. 16.  "Ishak son of Absal."  Fictitious.

P. 20.  "The householder of Shiraz."  Fictitious.

P. 32.  "Mihrab Shah."  Fictitious.

P. 36.  "Simorgh."  A fabulous creature in Persian mythology.

P. 40.  The "Pilgrim's soldier-guide."  Fictitious.

P. 41.  "Raksh." Rustum's horse in the "Shah Nameh." (Firdausi's "Epic of Kings.")

P. 50.  (*Anglicè*), "Does Job serve God for nought?" Hebrew word at p. 51, line 2, "Mē Elōhīm" : "from God."

P. 54.  "Mushtari."  The planet Jupiter.

P. 65.  "Hudhud."  Fabulous bird of Solomon.

P. 68.  "Sitara."  Persian for "a star."

P. 85.  "Shalim Shah."  Persian for "King of kings."

P. 86.  "Rustem," "Gew," "Gudarz," "Sindokht." "Sulayman," "Kawah."  Heroes in the "Shah Nameh."

P. 87.  The "Seven Thrones."  Ursa Major. "Zurah." Venus.  "Parwin."  The Pleiades.  "Mubid."  A kind of mage.

P. 88.  "Zerdusht."  "Zoroaster."

# "PARLEYINGS WITH CERTAIN PEOPLE OF IMPORTANCE IN THEIR DAY."

THIS volume occupies, even more than its predecessor, a distinctive position in **Mr.** Browning's work. It **does** not discard **his** old dramatic methods, but in a manner it inverts them ; **Mr.** Browning has summoned his group of men not for the sake of drawing their portraits, but **that** they might help him **to** draw his **own.** It seems **as if** the accumulated convictions **which** find vent **in** the "parleyings" could **no** longer endure even the form of dramatic disguise ; and they appear in them **in all** the force of direct reiterated statement, and all the freshness of novel points of **view.** And the portrait is in some degree a biography ; **it is** full of reminiscences. The "people" with whom Mr. Browning parleys, important in their day, virtually unknown **in** ours, are with one exception his old familiar friends : men whose works connect themselves with the intellectual sympathies and the imaginative pleasures of his very earliest youth. The parleyings are :

I. "With Bernard de Mandeville."
II. "With Daniel Bartoli."
III. "With Christopher Smart."
IV. "With George Bubb Dodington."
V. "With Francis Furini."
VI. "With Gerard de Lairesse."
VII. "With Charles Avison."

They are enclosed between a Prologue and an Epilogue

both dramatic and fanciful, but scarcely less expressive of the author's mental personality than the body of the work.

"Apollo and the Fates."
"Fust and his Friends."

In "Apollo and the Fates" the fanciful, or rather fantastic element preponderates. It represents Apollo as descending into the realms of darkness and pleading with the Fate Sisters for the life of Admetus, the thread of which Atropos is about to clip; and shows how he obtained for him a conditional reprieve by intoxicating the sisters with wine. The sequel to this incident has been given in Mr. Browning's transcript from "Alkestis"; and the present poem is introduced by references to that work of Euripides, to the "Eumenides" of Æschylus and to Homer's "Hymn to Mercury": the general sense of the passages indicated being this :—

Euripides.—"Admetus—whom, cheating the fates, I saved from death."

Æschylus (to Apollo).—"Aye, such were your feats in the house of Pheres, where you persuaded the fates to make a mortal immortal : you it was destroyed the ancient arrangement and deceived the goddesses with wine."

Homer.—"The Fates are three virgin sisters,—winged and white-haired,—dwelling below Parnassus: they feed on honey, and so get drunk, and readily tell the truth. If deprived of it they delude."

Mr. Browning, however, varies the legend, first by making the Fates find truth in the fumes of wine; and, secondly, by assuming that they never knew an inspiring drunkenness until they tasted it : profoundly intoxicating as their (fermented) honey must have been.

Apollo urges his request that Admetus, now threatened with premature death, may live out the appointed seventy years. The Fates retort on him by exclamations **on** the worthlessness of such a boon. They enumerate the follies and miseries which beset the successive stages of man's earthly career, and maintain that its only brightness **lies** in the delusive sunshine, the glamour of hope, with which he (Apollo) gilds it. Apollo owns that human happiness may rest upon *i/lusion*, but undertakes to show that man holds the magic within himself ; and to that end persuades **the** sisters **to** drain a bowl of wine which he has brought with him. In the moment's intoxication the scales fall from their eyes, and they see that life is good. They see that if its earlier course means conflict, old age is its recorded victory. They see it enriched by the joys which are only remembered as by the good which only might have been. They praise the Actual and still more the Potential—the infinite possibilities to which Man is born and which imagination alone can anticipate ; and joining hands with Apollo in **a** delirious dance, proclaim the discovery of the lost secret : *Fancy compounded with Fact.*

This philosophy is, however, ill-suited to the dark ministers of fate ; and an oracular explosion from the earth's depths startles them back into sobriety; in which condition they repudiate the new knowledge which **has** been born of them, flinging it back on their accomplice with various expressions of disgust. They admit, nevertheless, that the web of human destiny often defeats their spinning : its intended good and evil change places with each other ; the true significance of life is only revealed by death ; and though they still refuse to yield to Apollo's demand, they compromise with it : Admetus shall live, if someone else will voluntarily die for him. It is true they neutralize their concession by deriding the idea of such a devoted person being found ; and Apollo also shows himself a stranger to the decrees of the higher powers by making wrong guesses as to the event ; but the whole episode is conceived in a humorous and very human spirit which especially reveals itself in the attitude of the contending parties towards each other. The Fates display throughout a proper contempt for what they regard as the showy but unsubstantial personality of the young god ; and the natural antagonism of light and darkness, hope and despair, is as amusingly parodied in the mock deference and ill-disguised aversion with which he approaches them. Apollo finally vindicates Mr. Browning's optimistic theism by claiming the gifts of Bacchus, youngest of the gods, for the beneficent purpose and anterior wisdom of Zeus.

The one serious idea which runs through the poem is conveyed in its tribute to the power of wine : in other words, to the value of imagination as supplement to and interpreter of fact. Its partial, tentative, and yet efficient illumining of the dark places of life is vividly illustrated by Apollo : and he only changes his imagery when he speaks of Reason as doing the same work. It is the imaginative, not the scientific "reason" which Mr. Browning invokes as help in the perplexities of experience ;[1] as it is the spiritual, and not scientific "experience" on which, in the subsequent discussions, he will so emphatically take his stand.[2]

In the first "parleying" Mr. Browning invokes the wisdom of BERNARD DE MANDEVILLE on certain problems of life : mainly those of the existence of evil and the limitations of human knowledge ; and the optimistic views in which he believes Dr. Mandeville to concur with him are brought to bear on the more gloomy philosophy of Carlyle, some well-known utterances of whom are brought

---

[1] It has been wrongly inferred from the passage in question that Mr. Browning admits the pretensions of science to solve the problems of the universe.

[2] The "goddess-sent plague" woven by Lachesis into the destiny of Admetus was a vengeance of Artemis which befell him on the day of his marriage. He had slighted her by omitting the usual sacrifice, and in punishment of this she sent a crowd of serpents to meet him in the nuptial chamber ; but Apollo effected a reconciliation between them.

forward for confutation. The chief points of the argument
are as follows :—

Carlyle complains that God never intervenes to check
the tyranny of evil, so that it not only prevails in the **pre-**
sent life, but for any sure indications which exist to **the**
contrary may still do so in the life to come.  It would **be**
something, he thinks, **if even** triumphant wrong were
checked, although (here **we** must read between the lines)
this would be tantamount **to the** condoning **of** evil in all
its less developed **forms ;** better still if **he** who has **the**
power to do so habitually crushed it at the birth.

Mr. Browning (alias Mandeville) replies by the parable
of a garden in which beneficent and noxious plants grow
side **by** side.  " You must either," **he** declares, " admit—
**which** you do not—that both good **and evil were chance**
sown, or refer their joint presence **to** some necessary **or**
pre-ordained connection between them.  In the latter case
you may use your judgment in pruning **away the too great**
exuberance of the noxious plant, but **if** you destroy it once
for all, you have frustrated the intentions **of him who placed**
it there."

Carlyle reminds his opponent **of** that other **parable,**
according to which it was an **enemy** who surreptitiously
sowed the tares of evil, and these grow because **no one**
can pull them out.  Divine power and foresight are, **in**
his opinion, incompatible with either theory, and both of
these mistaken efforts on man's part to "cram" the infinite within the limits of his own mind and understand
what passes understanding.  He deprecates **the** folly of
linking divine and human together on the strength of the
short space which they may tread side by side, and the
anthropomorphic spirit which subjects the one to the other
by presenting the illimitable in human form.

Mr. Browning defends his position by an illustration of
the use (as also abuse) of symbols spiritual and material ; Carlyle retorts somewhat impatiently that in thinking

of God we have no need of symbolism ; we know Him as Immensity, Eternity, and other abstract qualities, and to fancy Him under human attributes is superfluous ; and Mr. Browning dismisses this theology, with the intellectual curiosities and intellectual discontents which he knows in the present case to have accompanied it, in a modification of the Promethean myth—such a one as the more "human" Euripides might have imagined. "When the sun's light first broke upon the earth, and everywhere in and on this there was life, man was the only creature which did not rejoice : for he said, I alone am incomplete in my completeness ; I am subject to a power which I alone have the intellect to recognize, hence the desire to grasp. I do not aspire to penetrate the hidden essence, the underlying mystery of the sun's force ; but I crave possession of one beam of its light wherewith to render palpable to myself its unseen action in the universe. And Prometheus then revealed to him the 'artifice' of the burning-glass, through which henceforward he might enslave the sun's rays to his service while disrobing them of the essential brilliancy which no human sight could endure."

In the material uses of the burning-glass we have a parallel for the value of an intellectual or religious symbol. This too is a gathering point for impressions otherwise too diffuse ; or, inversely conceived, a sign guiding the mental vision through spaces which would otherwise be blank. Its reduced or microcosmic presentment of facts too large for man's mental grasp suggests also an answer to those who bemoan the limitations of human knowledge. Characteristic remarks on this subject occur at the beginning of the poem.

Bernard de Mandeville figures throughout the "parleying" as author of "The Fable of the Bees"; and it is in this work that Mr. Browning discovers their special ground of sympathy. "The Fable of the Bees," also entitled

" Private Vices Public Benefits," and again " The Grumbling Hive, or Knaves turned Honest," is meant **to** show that self-indulgence and self-seeking carried even **to** the extent of vice are required to stimulate the activities and secure the material well-being **of** a community.  The doctrine, as originally set forth, had at least an appearance of cynicism, and is throughout not free from conscious **or** unconscious sophistry ; and though **the** theological condemnation evoked by **it** was nothing short **of** insane, we cannot wonder that the morality of the author's purpose was impugned.  He defends **this,** however, **in** successive additions to the work, asserting and re-asserting, by statement and illustration, that his object has been to expose the vices inherent to human society—in no sense to justify them ; and Mr. Browning fully accepts the vindication and even regards **it as** superfluous.  **He** sees nothing, either in the fable itself or the commentary first attached to it, which may not equally be covered by the Christian doctrine **of** original sin, **or** the philosophic acceptance of evil **as a** necessary concomitant, or condition, of good : and finds fresh guarantees for a sound moral intention in the bright humour and sound practical sense in which the book abounds.  This judgment was formed (as I have already implied) very early in Mr. Browning's life, even before the appearance of "Pauline," and supplies a curious comment on any impression of mental immaturity which his own work of that period may have produced.

Bernard de Mandeville was a Dutch physician, born at Dort in the second half of the last century, but who settled in England after taking his degree.  He published, besides " The Fable of the Bees," some works of a more professional kind.  His name, as we know it, must have been Anglicized.

DANIEL BARTOLI was a Jesuit and historian of his

order. Mr. Browning characterizes him in a footnote as " a learned and ingenious writer," and while acknowledging his blindness in matters of faith would gladly testify to his penetration in those of knowledge ;[1] but the Don's editor, Angelo Cerutti, declares in the same note that his historical work so overflows with superstition and is so crammed with accounts of prodigious miracles as to make the reading it an infliction ; and the saint-worship involved in this kind of narrative is the supposed text of the " parleying." Mr. Browning claims Don Bartoli's allegiance for a secular saint : a woman more divine in her non-miraculous virtues than some at least of those whom the Church has canonized, and whose existence has the merit of not being legendary. The saint in question was Marianne Pajot, daughter of the apothecary of Gaston Duke of Orleans ; and her story, as Mr. Browning relates it, a well-known episode in the lives of Charles IV., Duke of Lorraine, and the Marquis de Lassay.

Charles of Lorraine fell violently in love with Marianne Pajot, whom he met at the " Luxembourg " when visiting Madame d'Orleans, his sister. She was "so fair, so modest, so virtuous, and so witty " that he did not hesitate to offer her his hand ; and they were man and wife so far as legal formalities could make them when the Monarch (Louis XIV.) intervened. Charles had by a recent treaty made Louis his heir. This threatened no obstacle to his union, since a clause in the marriage contract barred all claims to succession on the part of the children who might be born of it. But " Madame " resented the mésalliance ; she joined her persuasions with those of the Minister le Tellier ; and the latter persuaded the young King, not absolutely to prevent the marriage, but to turn it to account. A paper was drawn up pledging the Duke to

---

[1] He had, as a young man, so great an admiration for one of Bartoli's works, "De' Simboli trasportati al Morale," that when he travelled he always carried it with him.

fresh concessions, and the bride was challenged in the King's name to obtain his signature to it. On this condition she was to be recognized as Duchess with all the honours due to her rank ; failing this, she was to be banished to a convent. The alternative was offered to her at the nuptial banquet, at which le Tellier had appeared—a carriage and military escort awaiting him outside. She emphatically declined taking part in so disgraceful a compact :[1] and after doing her best to allay the Duke's wrath (which was for the moment terrible), calmly allowed the Minister to lead her away, leaving all the bystanders in tears. A few days later Marianne returned the jewels which Charles had given her, saying, it was not suitable that she should keep them "since she had not the honour of being his wife." He seems to have resigned her without farther protest.

De Lassay was much impressed by this occurrence, though at the time only ten years old. He too conceived an attachment for Marianne Pajot, and married her, being already a widower, at the age of twenty-three. Their union, dissolved a few years later by her death, was one of unclouded happiness on his part, of unmixed devotion on hers; and the moral dignity by which she had subjugated this somewhat weak and excitable nature was equally attested by the intensity of her husband's sorrow and by its transitoriness. The military and still more amorous adventures of the Marquis de Lassay make him a conspicuous figure in the annals of French Court life. He is indirectly connected with our own through a somewhat pale and artificial passion for Sophia Dorothea, the young

[1] Her reply was that if she possessed any influence over M. de Lorraine she would never use it to make him do anything so contrary to his honour and to his interests ; she already sufficiently reproached herself for the marriage to which his friendship for her had impelled him ; and would rather be " Marianne " to the end of her days than become Duchess on such conditions. The reply has been necessarily modified in Mr. Browning's more poetic rendering of the scene.

Princess of Hanover, whose husband became ultimately George I. Mr. Browning indicates the later as well as earlier stages of de Lassay's career ; he only follows that of the Duke of Lorraine into an imaginary though not impossible development. Charles had shown himself a being of smaller spiritual stature than his intended wife ; and it was only too likely, Mr. Browning thinks, that the diamonds which should have graced her neck soon sparkled on that of some venal beauty whose challenge to his admiration proceeded from the opposite pole of woman- hood. Nevertheless he feels kindly towards him. The nobler love was not dishonoured by the more ignoble fancy, since it could not be touched by it. Duke Charles was still faithful as a man may be.

With CHRISTOPHER SMART is an interrogative comment on the strange mental vicissitudes of this mediocre poet, whose one inspired work, "A Song to David," was produced in a mad-house.[1] Of this "Song" Rossetti has said (I quote the "Athenæum" of Feb. 19, 1887) in a published letter to Mr. Caine, " This wonderful poem of Smart's is the only great *accomplished* poem of the last century. The *un-* accomplished ones are Chatterton's—of course I mean earlier than Blake or Coleridge, and without reckoning so exceptional a genius as Burns. A masterpiece of rich imagery, exhaustive resources, and reverberant sound." How Mr. Browning was impressed by such a work of genius, springing up from the dead level of the author's own and his contemporary life, he describes in a simile.

He is exploring a large house. He goes from room to room, finding everywhere evidence of decent taste and sufficient, but moderate, expenditure : nothing to repel and nothing to attract him in what he sees. He suddenly enters the chapel ; and here all richness is massed, all

---

[1] Indented,—for want of writing materials,—with a key on the wainscot of his cell.

fancy is embodied, art of all styles and periods is blended
to one perfection. He passes from it into another suite
of rooms, half fearful of fresh surprise ; and decent medio-
crity, respectable commonplace again meet him on every
side. Thus, it seems **to** him, **was** the imagination of
Christopher Smart for one moment transfigured **by the**
flames of madness to resume for ever afterwards the prosaic character of its sanity ; and he now asks the author
of " A Song to David" how one who had thus touched the
absolute in art could so decline from it. He assumes that
the madness had but revealed **the poet** : whether **or not**
the fiery outbreak was due to force suppressed or to **par-**
ticles of brain substance disturbed. Why **was** he after **as**
before silent ?

It might **be** urged **in** answer that **the** full glory **of that**
vision did not return—that the strength and beauty of the
**universe** never came **to** him again with so direct **a mes-**
sage **for** the eye **and ear of** his fellow men. But, **Mr.**
Browning continues, impressions of strength **and** beauty
**are** only **the** materials of knowledge. They contain the
lesson **of life.** And that lesson is **not** given in the reiterated vision of what is beautiful, but **in the** patient conversion into knowledge and motive **of** such impressions of
beauty—in other words, of strength **or** power—as Man's
natural existence affords. The poet's privilege, as the
poet's duty, is not merely to impart the pleasure, but to
aid the process of instruction. He only suggests the explanation to disclaim it in Smart's name.

These arguments are very typical of Mr. Browning's
philosophy of Art : of his conviction that Art has no mission, its intuitions have no authority, distinct from moral
and intellectual truth. He concludes the little sermon by
denouncing that impatience of Fancy which would grasp
**the** end of things before the beginning, and scale the
heights of Knowledge, while rejecting Experience, through
which, as by a ladder, we scale them step by step.

The lines in "Paracelsus," vol. ii., p. 36, which are in this view so appropriate to the case of Christopher Smart, bore reference to him. The main facts of his life may be found in any biographical dictionary.

With GEORGE BUBB DODINGTON is a lesson in the philosophy of intrigue, or the art of imposing on our fellow men. It is addressed to Bubb Dodington [1] as to an ambitious, obsequious, unscrupulous, and only partially successful courtier ; and undertakes to show that, being (more or less) a knave, his conduct also proclaimed him a fool, and lost him the rewards of knavery. Mr. Browning does not concern himself with the moralities of the case ; these, for the time being, are put out of court. He assumes, for the purposes of the discussion, that everyone is selfish and no one need be sincere, and that "George" was justified in labouring for his own advancement and cheating others, if possible, into subservience to it ; but he argues that the aim being right, the means employed were wrong, and could only result in failure.

The argument begins and ends in the proposition, in itself a truism but which receives here a novel significance, that nothing in creation obeys its like, and that he who would mount by the backs of his fellow men must show some reason why they should lend them. In the olden time, we are reminded, such reasons were supplied by physical force ; later, force was superseded by intelligence, *i.e.*, wit or cunning ; and this must now be supplemented by something deeper, because it has become the property

---

1 Created Lord Melcombe a year before his death : sufficiently known by his diary from March, 1748, to Feb., 1761. See its character in the Preface to the original edition by his relation, Henry Penruddocke Wyndham, 1784. Other notices will be found in "Edgeworth on Education," Belsham's "George II.," and Hawkins' "Life of Johnson."

of so many persons as to place no one person at an advantage. Bubb Dodington's methods have **been** those of simple cunning, and therefore they have not availed him. The multitude whom he cajoled have seen through his cajoleries, and have resented in these both the attempt to deceive them and the pretension—unfounded as it proved —to exalt himself at their expense.

How then can the multitude be **deceived into** subservience?—By the pretence of indifference **to** them. An impostor is always supposed to **be** in earnest. The commonplace impostor is so : **he has** staked everything on the appearance of being sincere. He, on the **other** hand, who is reckless in mendacity, **who** cheats with **a** laughing eye ; who, while silently strenuous in **a** given cause, appears **to** take seriously neither it, himself, nor those on whom both depend, irresistibly **strikes the** vulgar **as moved** by something greater than himself **or** they. A **"quack"** he may be, but like the spiritualistic quack, he invokes **the** belief in the Supernatural, and perhaps shares it. He has the secret which Bubb Dodington had **not.**

It may be wondered why **Mr.** Browning treats the shallower political cunning as merely a foil **to** the deeper, instead of opposing to it something better than both : but he finds the natural contrast **to** the half-successful schemer in the wholly triumphant one : and the second picture, like the first, has been drawn from life. It is that of the late Lord Beaconsfield—as Mr. Browning sees him.

With FRANCIS FURINI is a defence of the study of the nude, based on the life and work of this Florentine painter (born 1600), who at the age of forty also became a priest. According to his biographer, Filippo Baldinucci,[1] Furini

---

[1] Furini is also honourably mentioned in Pilkington's "Dictionary of

was not only a skilful artist, but a conscientious priest, and a good man. No reproach attached to him but that he attained a special charm of colouring through the practice of painting very young women undraped ; and we may infer that he repented this from the current report that when he felt himself dying he entreated those about him to have his pictures burnt. But Baldinucci also relates that he had a specious answer ready for whoever remonstrated with him on thus endangering his soul. The answer, which he frankly quotes, is by no means "specious" in the sense in which it is made ; and Mr. Browning cannot believe that a man so inspired by the true artistic passion as those words imply, could in any circumstances become ashamed of the acts to which they refer. " If," Furini says, " those scrupulous persons only knew what is the agony of endeavour with which the artist strives at faithfully imitating what he sees, they would also know how little room this leaves in him for the intrusion of alien " (immoral) "thoughts." Mr. Browning goes farther still. He asserts not only the innocence, but the religiousness, of the painter's art when directed towards the marvels of the female form. He declares its exercise, so directed, to be a subject, not of shame in the sight of the Creator, but of thanksgiving to Him, and also the best form in which human thanks can be conveyed ; and he employs all the vividness of his illustration and all the force of his invective against the so-called artist who sees in the Divineness of female beauty only incitement to low desires ; in the art which seeks to reproduce it only a cloak for their indulgence. His argument is very strong, and would be unanswerable, but for the touch of speciousness which Baldinucci by

Painters," revised by Fuseli, and till the middle of the present century the authoritative work on the subject. It is stated in the edition of 1805 that " many of his paintings are in Florence, which are deemed to add honour to the valuable collections of the nobility of that city."

anticipation detects in it : Mr. Browning—as did Furini
—regards the breach of formal chastity exclusively from
the artist's point of view.  But he may also argue that
this will in the long run determine that of the spectator
and that the model herself is from the first amenable
to it.

Mr. Browning lays stress upon the technical skill which
results from the close copying of nature, and by virtue of
which Furini must be styled a good painter, whether or
not a great one : and though he has never underrated
the positive value of technical skill, we do not feel that in
this third page of the "parleyings" he gives to the inspiring
thought as high a relative place as in his earlier works.
The old convictions reappear at pages 182-3 of vol. xvi.,
when he asserts the danger in which the skilled hand may
involve the artistic soul, by stifling its insight into the
spiritual essence of fleshly things or silencing its testimony
to it ; when, too, he admits that not the least worthy of
the "sacred" ones have been thus betrayed.  He still,
however, maintains that the true offender against Art will
ever be the mock artist—the Philistine—who sees cause of
offence in it.

After proclaiming the religiousness of Art, Furini is
called upon to unfold his theology : and he then passes to
a confession of faith in which Mr. Browning's known personal Theism is contrasted with the scientific doctrines of
Evolution.  The Scientist and the Believer would as he
distinguishes them join issue on the value of the artistic
study of man, since man is for both of them the one essential object of knowledge ; but the study (artistic or scientific) is, Mr. Browning considers, unrepaying in the one
case, while it yields all necessary results in the other.
According to the scientist, Man reigns supreme by his
intelligence ; according to the Believer, he is subject to

all the helplessness of his ignorance. In reasoning, therefore, each from his own consciousness, the one finds his starting point at the summit of creation, the other virtually at the bottom of it. The Scientist acknowledges no mind beyond that of man ; he seeks the impulse to life within itself, and can therefore only track it through the descending scale of being into the region of inorganic atoms and blind force. The *believer* refers that impulse to a conscious external First Cause, and is content to live surrounded by its mystery, entrenched within the facts of his own existence, guided (i.e., drawn upwards) by the progressive revelations which these convey to him.

It is so that Furini has lived and learned. He has found his lesson in the study of the human frame. There, as on a rock of experience, he has planted his foot, finding confusion and instability wherever he projected this beyond it ; striking out sparks of knowledge at every stamp on the firm ground. He has learned that the Cause of Life is external, because he has seen how the soul permeates and impels the body, how it makes it an instrument of its own raptures and a sharer in them ; and he believes that that which caused the soul and thus gifted it will ultimately silence the spiritual conflict with Evil and perfect Its own creation. He believes this because Evil has revealed itself to him as the necessary complement of Good—the antitype through which alone the type defines itself ; as a condition of knowledge ; as a test of what is right ; as a motive to life and virtue so indispensable that it must exist as illusion if it did not exist as fact ; because, therefore, its existence cannot detract from the goodness of the First Cause or the promise which that contains.

This constant assertion of the necessity of evil would land Mr. Browning in a dilemma, if the axiom were presented by him in any character of dogmatic truth : since it claims priority for certain laws of thought over a Being which, if Omnipotent, must have created them. But the anomaly disappears in the more floating outlines of a poetic personal experience ; and Mr. Browning (alias Furini) once more assures us that what he "knows" of the nature and mode of action of the First Cause he knows for himself only. How it operates for others is of the essence of the mystery which enfolds him. Whether even the means of his own instruction is reality or illusion, fiction or fact, is beyond his ken ; he is satisfied that it should be so.

Mr. Browning reverts to his defence of the nude in the description of a picture—exhibited last year at the Grosvenor Gallery—the subject of which he offers to Furini for treatment in the manner described.[1]

With GERARD DE LAIRESSE is a critical reminiscence of the unreal and mythological in art, and its immediate subject a Belgian painter, born at Liege, but who flourished at Amsterdam in the second half of the seventeenth century. De Lairesse was a man of varied artistic culture as well as versatile skill ; but he was saturated with the pseudo-classical spirit of the later period of the renaissance ; and landscape itself scarcely existed for him but as a setting for mythological incident or a subject for embellishment by it. This is curiously apparent in a treatise on the Art of Painting, which he composed, and, by a form of dictation, also illustrated, when at the age of fifty he had lost his sight. An English version of this fell into Mr. Browning's hands while he was yet a child, and the deep and, at the time, delightful impression which it made upon him is the motive of the present poem. Foremost in his memory is an imaginary

[1] The allusion in vol. xvi. p. 195, to the old artificer who could make men "believe" instead of merely "fancy" that what he presented to them was real, refers especially to the Greek painter Zeuxis ; but it is suggested by the generally realistic character of Greek art.

"Walk,"[1] in which the exercise of fancy which the author practises and, Mr. Browning tells us, enjoins, is strikingly displayed by his "conjecturing" Phaeton's tomb from the evidence of a carved thunderbolt in an empty sepulchre, and the remains of the "Chariot of the Sun" from a piece of broken wheel and some similar fragment buried in the adjoining ground.

The remembrance converts itself into a question : the poet's fancy no longer peoples the earth with gods and goddesses ; has his insight become less vivid ? has the poetic spirit gone back ? The answer is unwavering ; retrogression is not in the creative plan. The poet does not go back. He is still as of yore a seer ; he has only changed in this, that his chosen visions are of the soul ; their objects are no longer visible unrealities, but the realities which are unseen. He can still, if he pleases, evoke those as these, and Mr. Browning proceeds to show it by calling up a series of dissolving views representing another " walk."

A majestic and varied landscape unfolds before us in the changing lights of a long summer's day ; and at each appropriate artistic moment becomes the background of a mythological, idyllic, or semi-mythical scene. In the early dawn we see Prometheus amidst departing thunders chained to his rock :[2] the glutted, yet still hungering vulture cowering beside him ; in the dews of morning, Artemis triumphant in her double character of huntress-queen and goddess of sudden death ; in the heats of noon, Lyda and the Satyr, enacting the pathetic story of his passion and her indifference ;[3] in the lengthening shadows, the approaching shock of the armies of Darius and Alex-

---

[1] Described at p. 253 and onwards under the heading "Painter-like Beauty in the Open Air."

[2] The last line and a half of the eighth stanza was directly suggested by the tragedy of Æschylus ; the thunderstorm by another version of the Promethean myth.

[3] See Shelley's translation from Moschus.

ander ;[1]—in **the** falling night, a **dim,** silent, deprecating
figure : in other words, a ghost.

And here Mr. Browning bids the "fooling" stop ; for
he has touched the point of extreme divergence **between**
the classic spirit and **his** own. The pallid vision which
he repels speaks dumbly of pagan regret for **what** is past,
of pagan hopelessness of the to-come. *His* religion, as
we **are** again reminded, **is** one of hope. **Let** us, he says,
do and not dream, look **forward and not** back ; ascend
the tree of existence into **its** ripening **glory,** not hastening
**over** leaf or blossom, not dallying with them ; leave Greek
lore buried in its own ashes, and accept the evidence of
life itself that extinction is impossible; that death—mystery
though it is, calamity though it may be—ends nothing
which has **once** begun. **We** may **then** greet **the** spring
which we **do** not live to **see** in other **words than** those of
the Greek bard ; and the words suggested are those of a
dainty lyric, in which the note of gladness seems to break
with **a** little sob, and rings, perhaps, on **that** account the
truer.[2]

With CHARLES AVISON might be called a reverie on
music and musicians, but for the extraordinary vividness
of the images and emotions which it conveys. It was induced, Mr. Browning tells us, by a picturesque little incident which set his thoughts vibrating to the impressions
of the word "March": and supplies a parable for their
instinctive flight into a discredited and forgotten past.
They have been feeling for a piece of march-music ; they
have bridged the gulf which separates the school of Wagner
and Brahms from that of Handel or Buononcini ; they
alight on Charles Avison's "Grand March."[3] It is a simple

[1] Battle of Arbela.
[2] These lines were published in 1886 in the little volume entitled "The New Amphion."
[3] Organist of Newcastle about 1750; author of "An Essay on Musical Expression" and other works.

continuous air, such as hearts could beat to in the olden time, though flat and somewhat thin, and unrelieved by those caprices of modulation which are essential to modern ears ; and as it repeats itself in Mr. Browning's brain, the persistent melody gains force from its very persistence . till it fills with the sound, as it were glows with the aërial clashings, of many martial instruments, till it strides in the lengthening, drum-accentuated motion of many marching feet. He ponders the fact that such melody has lost its power, and asks himself why this must be : since the once perfected can never be surpassed, and the music of Charles Avison was in its own day as inspiring and inspired—in other words, as perfect—as that for which it has been cast aside.

He finds his answer in the special relation of this art to the life of man. Music resembles painting and poetry in the essential characteristic that her province is not Mind but Soul—the swaying sea of emotion which underlies the firm ground of attainable, if often recondite, fact. All three have this in common with the activities of Mind that they strive for the same result ; they aim at recording feeling as science registers facts. The two latter in some measure attain this end, because they deal with those definite moments of the soul's experience which share the nature of fact. But music dredges deeper in the emotional sea. She draws forth and embodies the more mysterious, more evanescent, more fluid realities of the soul's life ; and so, effecting more than the sister arts, she yet succeeds less. Her forms remain ; the spirit ebbs away from them. As, however, Mr. Browning's own experience has shown, the departed spirit may return :—

> ". . . . Off they steal—
> How gently, dawn-doomed phantoms ! back come they
> Full-blooded with new crimson of broad day—
> Passion made palpable once more."          (P. 232.)

The revived passion may breathe under the name of

another man ; it may stir again in the utterance of one
dead and forgotten ; and Mr. Browning, borrowing the
language of chemistry, invokes the reactive processes
through which its many-coloured flamelets may spring to
life.[1] He then passes by an insensible—because to him
very natural—transition from the realities of feeling to
those of thought, and to the underlying truth from which
both series derive : and combats the idea that in thought,
any more than in feeling, the present can disprove the
past, the once true reveal itself as delusion. Time—otherwise growth—widens the range as it complicates the
necessities of musical, *i.e.* emotional expression. It
destroys the enfolding fictions which shield without concealing the earlier stages of intellectual truth. But the
emotions were in existence before music began ; and
Truth was potentially "at full" within us when as it were
reborn to grow and bud and blossom for the mind of man.[2]
Therefore, he has said, addressing Avison's March,
" Blare it forth, bold C Major !" and " Therefore," he continues, in a swift return of fancy :—

> " . . . Bang the drums,
> Blow the trumps, Avison ! March motive ? That s
> Truth which endures resetting. Sharps and flats,
> Lavish at need, shall dance athwart thy score
> When ophicleide and bombardon's uproar
> Mate the approaching trample, even now
> Big in the distance—or my ears deceive—
> Of federated England, fitly weave
> March-music for the future ! "                    (P. 137.)

The musical transformation is for a moment followed back
to the days of Elizabethan plain-song, and then arrested
at those of Avison, where he may be imagined as joining
chorus with Bach in celebrating the struggle for English

---

[1] The "Relfe" spoken of in this connection was Mr. Browning's music-
master : a learned contrapuntist.

[2] In interpreting this passage I have somewhat exceeded the letter, but
only to emphasize the spirit of Mr. Browning's words.

liberty. The closing stanzas are written to the music of Avison's March, which is also given [1] at the end of the poem, and throws a helpful light on its more technical parts.

Fust and His Friends is based on a version of the Faust legend which identifies the inventor of printing with Dr. Faust, and contains allusions to some of the incidents of Goethe's double poem : the magical drinking bout of the first part, and the appearance of the Grecian Helen in the second ; but whereas the popular tradition makes Fust's great discovery the fruit of his alliance with the powers of Evil, Mr. Browning represents it as an act of atonement for the figurative devil-worship which was involved in a disorderly and ostentatious life. Fust has by his own admission sinned to this extent.[2] He has obeyed the father of lies. He has also accepted with thankfulness the chance of redeeming his soul by a signal service rendered to the cause of Truth. The process of engraving on gold, furtively witnessed in a Tuscan workshop, has suggested to him the manufacture of metallic types, and he has been for years secluded with the conception of his printing-press, and glowing visions of that winged word which should one day fly forth at his command. Complacent ignorance and stupidity have buzzed freely about him as he sat unaided and alone in what Mr. Browning poetically depicts as the prolonged travail of a portentous mental birth ; and, as we are led to imagine, much well-meant remonstrance and advice rebounded from his closed door. But at the moment in question the door is open, for the work of Fust is complete. Seven " Friends " present themselves prepared to lecture him for his good and for that of their city (Mayence) which is endangered by

---

[1] From an MS. copy formerly in the possession of Mr. Browning's father.

[2] The wealth to which he alludes was justly imputed to him, as the real Fust was a goldsmith's son.

his compact with the Devil ; and **the** ensuing intensely humorous colloquy supplies him with **the** fitting occasion for distributing specimens of his new **art** and **displaying** the mechanism through which its apparent magic is achieved.   He then pours forth his soul in an impassioned utterance, half soliloquy, half prayer, **in** which gratitude for his own redemption tempers the sense of triumph in the world-wide intellectual deliverance he has been privileged to effect, and becomes **a** tribute of **adoration** to that Absolute of Creative Knowledge, **the law of** which he has obeyed ; which stirs **in** the unconsciousness of the ore and plant, and impels man to **Its** realization step by step in the ever-receding, ever-present vision of his **own** ignorance.

**He owns,** however, when the talk **is** resumed, **that** his happiness is not free from cloud : **since the** wings which he has given to truth will also **aid** the diffusion of falsehood ; and the note of humour returns **to** the situation when this contingency asserts itself in **the** mind of some of **the** "friends."   These worthies **have** passed through **the** descending scale of feeling proper to such persons on such an occasion.   They have received Fust's invention as diabolical—as wonderful—as **very** simple after all ; and now the fact stares them in the face that, printing being so simple, the Hussite may publish his heresies as well as the Churchman his truth, and the old sure remedy of burning him and his talk together will no longer avail. One of the two Divines on whom this impresses itself had indeed " been struck by it from the first."

The poem concludes with a joke on the name of Huss, which (I am told) is the Bohemian equivalent for " goose," and his reported prophecy of the advent and the triumph of Luther : which prophecy Fust re-echoes.[1]

1 The relation of John Fust to the popular legend is pleasantly set forth in Mr. Sutherland Edwards' little book, " The Faust Legend : Its Origin and Development."

# NOTE.

The following note shows Mr. Browning in **a more pronounced** attitude towards the opponents of the new Greek
spelling than does that which, by his **desire, I inserted** in
**my first** edition ; but the last mood was **in** this **case** only
a natural development of the first :—

"I have just noticed in this month's 'Nineteenth **Cen-**
tury' that it is inquired by **a** humorous objector **to the**
practice of spelling (under exceptional conditions) Greek
proper names as they are spelt **in Greek literature,** why
the same principle **should not be** adopted by 'Ægyptolo-
gists, Hebraists, Sanscrittists, Accadians, Moabites, **Hit-**
tites, and Cuneiformists ?' Adopt it, **by** all means, when-
**ever the** particular language enjoyed **by any** fortunate
possessor **of** these shall, like Greek, have been for **about**
three hundred years insisted upon in England as an acqui-
sition of paramount importance, **at school and** college, **for**
every aspirant to distinction **in** learning, even at the cost
of six or seven years' study—a **sacrifice** considered well
worth making for even an imperfect acquaintance with
'the most perfect language in the world.' Further, **it** will
**be** adopted whenever the letters substituted **for** those in
ordinary English use shall do no more than represent to
the unscholarly what the scholar accepts without scruple
when, for the hundredth time, he reads the word which,
for once, he has occasion to write in English, and which
**be** concludes must be as euphonic as the rest of a language renowned for euphony. And, finally, the practice
will be adopted whenever the substituted letters effect no
sort of organic change so as to jostle the word from its
pride of place in English verse or prose. 'Themistokles'

fits in quietly everywhere, with or without the *k* : but in a certain poetical translation I remember, by a young friend, of the Anabasis, beginning thus felicitously, '*Cyrus the Great and Artaxerxes (Whose temper bloodier than a Turk's is) Were children both of the mild, pious, And happy monarch, King Darius,*'—who fails to see that, although a correct 'Kuraush ' may pass, yet 'Daraya-vush ' disturbs the metre as well as the rhyme ? It seems, however, that 'Themistokles' may be winked at : not so the 'harsh and subversive Kirke.' But let the objector ask somebody with no knowledge to subvert, how he supposes 'Circe' is spelt in Greek, and the answer will be ' with a soft *c*.' Inform him that no such letter exists, and he guesses, 'Then with *s*, if there be anything like it.' Tell him that, to eye and ear equally, his own *k* answers the purpose, and you have, at all events, taught him that much, if little enough—and why does he live unless to learn a little?"　　　　　　　　　　　　" R. B."

*Jun.* 4, 1866.

# A CHRONOLOGICAL BIBLIOGRAPHY
# OF BROWNING'S WORKS.

1833. PAULINE; A FRAGMENT OF A CONFESSION. 8vo. Saunders and Otley, 1833. Dated at the end "Richmond, Oct. 22, 1832." Reprinted in the six vol. editions of the *Poetical Works*, 1868, and later. Also reprinted from the original edition and edited by T. J. Wise, 1886.

1834. SONNET, "Eyes calm beside thee (Lady couldst thou know!") Dated Aug. 17, 1834, and signed "Z." *Monthly Repository*, vol. viii., N.S., 1834, p. 712. Not reprinted by Mr. Browning.

1835. PARACELSUS. By Robert Browning. 8vo. Effingham Wilson, 1835. Reprinted in *Poems*, 2 vols. 1849, and in *Poetical Works* later, but without Preface, dated 15th March, 1835.

1835. THE KING. "A king lived long ago." 54 lines signed "Z," in the *Monthly Repository*, vol. ix., N.S., 1835, pp. 707-8. Afterwards given in *Pippa Passes* (sc. 1, act iii.) with six additional lines.

1836. PORPHYRIA. "The rain set early in to-night." Sixty lines signed "Z," in *Monthly Repository*,

vol. x., N.S., 1836, pp. 43-4.  Afterwards appeared
in *Bells and Pomegranates* under the heading
" Madhouse Cells II."  Was called " Porphyria's
Lover" in the *Works*, 1863 and after.

1836.  JOHANNES AGRICOLA.  "There's Heaven above;
and night by night."  Sixty lines signed " Z," in
*Monthly Repository*, vol. x., N.S., 1836, pp. 45-6.
Reprinted in *Bells and Pomegranates* under the
heading "Madhouse Cells I."

1836.  LINES.  " Still ailing, wind ? wilt be appeased or
no ?"  Six stanzas signed " Z," in the *Monthly
Repository*, vol. x., N.S., 1836, pp. 270-71.  Reappeared in *Dramatis Personæ* (1864) as the first
six stanzas of section vi. of " James Lee."

1837.  STRAFFORD : AN HISTORICAL TRAGEDY.  By
Robert Browning. 8vo. Longmans, 1837.  Acted
at Covent Garden Theatre, May 1, 1837.  Reprinted without preface in *Poetical Works*, 1863,
and later.  Acting edition, for the North London
Collegiate School for Girls, 1882, 8vo.  An edition
(including preface of 1837) with notes and preface
by Miss E. H. Hickey, and introduction by S. R.
Gardiner, LL.D., 1884, 8vo.

1840.  SORDELLO.  By Robert Browning.  8vo.  E.
Moxon, 1840.  Revised edition with prefatory
letter to J. Milsand, in *Poetical Works*, 3 vols.
1863, and later.

1841-6. BELLS AND POMEGRANATES.  Eight numbers in
wrappers, Rl. 8vo., 1841-46, as follows :—

1841.  No. 1.  PIPPA PASSES.  By Robert Browning.
London, E. Moxon, 1841.

1842.  No. 2.  KING VICTOR AND KING CHARLES.  By
Robert Browning.  London, E. Moxon, 1842.

1842.  No. 3.  DRAMATIC LYRICS.  By Robert Browning,
London, E. Moxon, 1842.

Contents :

Contents :

*Italy in England.* [Called "The Italian in England" in the *Poems*, 1849], p. 4.

*England in Italy.* [Called "The Englishman in Italy" in *Poems*, 1849], p. 5.

*The Lost Leader*, p. 8.

*The Lost Mistress*, p. 8.

*Home Thoughts from Abroad.* I. "Oh, to be in England."—II. "Here's to Nelson's Memory." [Put after *Claret and Tokay*, in *Poet. Works*, 1863, under "Nationality in Drinks."]—III. "Nobly, nobly Cape St. Vincent," p. 8. ["Home Thoughts from the Sea."]

*The Tomb at St. Praxed's*, p. 9.

*Garden Fancies.* I. *The Flower's Name.*—II. *Sibrandus Schafnaburgensis*, p. 10.

*France and Spain.* I. *The Laboratory (Ancien Régime).*—II. *The Confessional*, p. 11.

*The Flight of the Duchess*, p. 12.

*Earth's Immortalities.* I. "See, as the prettiest graves."—II. "So the year's done with," p. 19.

*Song.* "Nay, but you, who do not love her," p. 19.

*The Boy and the Angel.* [A fresh couplet added on republication in *Poet. Works*, 1868,] p. 19.

*Night and Morning.* I. *Night.*—II. *Morning.* [Called "Meeting at Night" and "Parting at Morning" in 1863], p. 20.

*Claret and Tokay.* I. "My heart sunk with our Claret-flask." II. "Up jumped Tokay on our table." [These grouped together, with "Here's to Nelson's Memory," as "Nationality in Drinks," No. 37 in *Poet. Works*, 1863,] p. 20.

*Saul* [Part the First, only; completed in *Men and Women*, 1855,] p. 21.

*Time's Revenges*, p. 22.

*The Glove.* (Peter Ronsard *loquitur*), p. 23.

1846. No. 8, and Last. LURIA; and A SOUL'S TRAGEDY. By Robert Browning. London, E. Moxon, 1846.

*Luria.* A Tragedy in five acts, p. 2.

*A Soul's Tragedy.* Part First, being what was called the Poetry of Chiappino's Life; and Part Second, its Prose. [With Preface to *A Soul's Tragedy* not reprinted], p. 21.

1844. THE LABORATORY (Ancien Régime). By Robert Browning, in *Hood's Magazine*, vol. i., 1844, pp. 513-14. Reprinted in *Dramatic Romances and Lyrics* (*Bells and Pomegranates*, No. 7), 1845, as the first of two poems called *France and Spain.*

1844. CLARET AND TOKAY. By Robert Browning. ["My heart sunk with our Claret-flask," and "Up jumped Tokay on our table"], in *Hood's Magazine*, vol. i., 1844, p. 525. Reprinted in *Dramatic Romances and Lyrics* (*Bells and Pomegranates*, No. 7), 1845.

1844. GARDEN FANCIES. By Robert Browning. I. *The Flower's Name.*—II. *Sibrandus Schafnaburgensis.* In *Hood's Magazine*, vol. ii., pp. 140-42, 1844. Revised and enlarged in *Dramatic Romances and Lyrics* (*Bells and Pom.*, No. 7), 1845.

1844. THE BOY AND THE ANGEL. By Robert Browning. In *Hood's Magazine*, vol. ii., pp. 140-2. Enlarged in *Dramatic Romances and Lyrics* (*Bells and Pomegranates*, No. 7), 1845.

1845. THE TOMB AT ST. PRAXED'S (ROME 15—). By Robert Browning. In *Hood's Magazine*, vol. iii., pp. 237-9, 1845. Enlarged in *Dramatic Romances and Lyrics* (*Bells and Pomegranates*, No. 7) in same year. Reappeared in *Works*, 1863, and after, with the title "The Bishop Orders his Tomb in St. Praxed's Church."

1845. THE FLIGHT OF THE DUCHESS. By Robert
      Browning. Part the first, in *Hood's Magazine*,
      vol. iii., pp. 313-18, 1845. Part II. appeared
      when the first part was reprinted in *Bells and
      Pomegranates*, No. 7, in the same year,
      *Dramatic Romances and Lyrics*.

1849. POEMS BY ROBERT BROWNING. A New Edition
      [but the first collection under a collective title].
      2 vols., 8vo. Chapman and Hall, 1849.
          *Contents:* vol. i. Paracelsus, p. 1. Pippa
      Passes, a Drama, p. 163. King Victor and King
      Charles, a Tragedy, p. 231. Colombe's Birthday,
      a Play, p. 302.
          Vol. ii. A Blot in the 'Scutcheon, a Tragedy,
      p. 1. The Return of the Druses, a Tragedy, p. 61.
      Luria, a Tragedy, p. 139. A Soul's Tragedy,
      p. 211. Dramatic Romances and Lyrics, p. 253;
      38 of the 41 pieces in *Bells and Pomegranates*,
      Nos. 3 and 7, the three omitted being *Claret*,
      *Tokay*, and *Here's to Nelson's Memory*.

1850. CHRISTMAS-EVE AND EASTER-DAY. A Poem.
      By Robert Browning. 8vo. Chapman and Hall,
      1850. Reprinted in *Works*, 1863, and after.

1852. Letters of Percy Bysshe Shelley. With an Intro-
      ductory ESSAY BY ROBERT BROWNING. London,
      E. Moxon, 1852. 8vo. [The Essay is on Shelley
      —not on the " Letters," which were afterwards
      discovered to be spurious, with one exception.]
      The Essay was reprinted in the *Browning
      Society's Papers*, Part I., 1881. Edited by Dr.
      F. J. Furnivall. Another reprint, edited by W.
      Tyas Harden, appeared in 1888, 8vo.

1854. TWO POEMS. By Elizabeth Barrett and Robert
      Browning. 8vo. London, Chapman and Hall,
      1854. Price Sixpence. The poem by Robert

Browning here is "The Twins," and is dated
"Rome, March 30th, 1854." Reprinted in *Men
and Women*, 1855, and in *Works*, 1863 and after.
The "Two Poems" were printed by Miss
Arabella Barrett for sale at a bazaar in aid of a
"Refuge for Young Destitute Girls." Mrs.
Browning's contribution was "A Plea for the
Ragged Schools of London."

1855 MEN AND WOMEN. By Robert Browning. In
   two vols. 8vo. London, Chapman and Hall.

Contents : Vol. I.—

*Life in a Love*, p. 175.
*How it Strikes a Contemporary*, p. 177.
*The Last Ride together*, p. 184.
*The Patriot.* An Old Story, p. 191.
*Master Hugues of Saxe-Gotha*, p. 194.
*Bishop Blougram's Apology*, p. 205.
*Memorabilia*, p. 259.

Contents of Vol. II. :

*Andrea del Sarto*, p. 1.
*Before*, p. 15.
*After*, p. 19.
*In Three Days*, p. 21.
*In a Year*, p. 24.
*Old Pictures in Florence*, p. 30.
*In a Balcony*, p. 49.
*Saul*, p. 111.
" *De Gustibus*," p. 147.
*Women and Roses*, p. 150.
*Protus*, p. 154.
*Holy-Cross Day*, p. 158.
*The Guardian Angel*, p. 167.
*Cleon*, p. 171.
*The Twins*, p. 190.
*Popularity*, p. 193.
*The Heretic's Tragedy*, p. 198.
*Two in the Campagna*, p. 205.
*A Grammarian's Funeral*, p. 210.
*One Way of Love*, p. 218.
*Another Way of Love*, p. 220.
" *Transcendentalism*," p. 223.
*Misconceptions*, p. 227.
*One Word More.* To E. B. B., p. 229.

1856. BEN KARSHOOK'S WISDOM. By Robert Browning.
Twenty lines in *The Keepsake* for 1856, edited by

Miss Power. Never reprinted by Mr. Browning. **The** poem seems to be alluded to in "One Word More."

1857. MAY AND DEATH. By Robert Browning. **In** *The Keepsake* for 1857. Reprinted in *Dramatis Personæ*, 1864, and in *Works* 1868, and after.

1863. THE POETICAL WORKS OF ROBERT BROWNING. ; Third edition. Three vols., 8vo. London, Chapman and Hall, 1863. No new poems in this collection. It was re-issued as "Fourth Edition" in 1865.

Contents : **Vol. I.**

LYRICS.

### ROMANCES.

### Contents of Vol. II.

<small>TRAGEDIES AND OTHER PLAYS.</small>
*Pippa Passes—A Drama*, p. 1.
*King Victor and King Charles—A Tragedy*,
   p. 68.
*The Return of the Druses—A Tragedy*, p. 140.
*A Blot in the 'Scutcheon—A Tragedy*, p. 216.
*Colombe's Birthday—A Play*, p. 275.
*Luria—A Tragedy*, p. 357.
*A Soul's Tragedy*, p. 428.
*In a Balcony—A Scene*, p. 468.
*Strafford—A Tragedy*, p. 503.

### Contents of Vol. III.

*Paracelsus*, p. 1.
*Christmas-Eve and Easter-Day*, p. 163.
*Sordello*, p. 252.

1863. SELECTIONS FROM THE POETICAL WORKS OF ROBERT BROWNING. 8vo. London, Chapman and Hall, 1863. The editors of this first selection were John Foster and B. W. Procter ("Barry Cornwall"). The volume was re-issued in 1869 with the imprint of Smith, Elder & Co.

1864. DRAMATIS PERSONÆ. By Robert Browning. 8vo. London, Chapman and Hall, 1864. Second edition published same year.

### Contents.

*James Lee*, p. 3. [This appears as "James Lee's Wife" in the *Poetical Works*, 1868 and after.]
*Gold Hair: a Legend of Pornic*, p. 27.
*The Worst of it*, p. 37.
*Dis aliter visum; or, Le Byron de nos Jours*,
   p. 47.

*Too Late*, p. 57.

***Abt** Vogler*, p. 67.

*Rabbi ben Ezra*, p. 77.

*A Death in the Desert*, p. 91.

*Caliban upon Setebos ;* **or,** *Natural Theology in the Island*, p. 123.

*Confessions*, p. 139.

*May and Death*, p. **145.**

*Prospice*, p. **149.**

*Youth and **Art**,* p. 153.

***A** Face*, **p. 161.**

***A** Likeness*, p. 165.

***Mr.** Sludge, "the Medium,"* **p. 171.**

*Apparent Failure*, **p. 239.**

*Epilogue*, **p. 245.**

Three of the **above** poems were reprinted from advance sheets in the *Atlantic Monthly* (Boston, U.S.), vol. xiii., 1864, viz., *Gold **Hair**,* May, pp. 596-599 ; *Prospice*, May, p. 694 ; ***Under the** Cliff* (part of *James Lee*), May, pp. 737-8.

1864. ORPHEUS AND EURYDICE. Eight lines in the Royal Academy Catalogue for 1864, in F. Leighton's (now P.R.A.) picture so named. First collected in *Poetical Works*, 1868, under the title of "Eurydice to Orpheus, a Picture by Fred. Leighton, A.R.A."

1864. POETICAL WORKS OF ROBERT BROWNING. Fourth edition. A reprint of the Third edition (which see under "1863").

1865. A SELECTION FROM THE WORKS OF ROBERT BROWNING. Square post 8vo. "Moxon's Miniature Poets," E. Moxon & Co., 1865. With Dedication to Alfred Tennyson ; and a photographic portrait of Robert Browning.

1866. A Selection from the Poetry of Elizabeth Barrett

Browning. 8vo. London, Chapman and Hall, 1866. EDITED by Robert Browning, and has a PREFACE signed " R. B.," and dated "London, November, 1865."

1866. Last Poems by Elizabeth Barrett Browning. 8vo. London, Chapman & Hall, 1862. THE DEDICATION ("To Grateful Florence," etc.), and "ADVERTISEMENT" (dated "London, February, 1862"), written by Robert Browning. See *Browning Soc. Papers* [additions to Bibliography], Parts I. and II., 1881, pp. 111, 162.

1868. THE POETICAL WORKS OF ROBERT BROWNING. Six vols. London, Smith, Elder and Co., 1868. There is only one new piece in this collection, viz., *Deaf and Dumb;* written for a marble group of two children by T. Woolner in the International Exhibition of 1862.

### Contents of Vol. I.

*Pauline*, p. 1.
*Paracelsus*, p. 43.
*Strafford*, p. 207.

### Contents of Vol. II.

*Sordello*, p. 1.
*Pippa Passes*, p. 219.

### Contents of Vol. III.

*King Victor and King Charles*, p. 1.
*Dramatic Lyrics* :—
    *Cavalier Tunes*, p. 75.
    *The Lost Leader*, p. 78.
    *How they brought the Good News from Ghent to Aix*, p. 80.
    *Through the Metidja to Abd-el-Kadr*, p. 83.
    *Nationality in Drinks*, p. 85.

*Too Late*, p. 85.

*Abt Vogler*, p. 92.

*Rabbi ben Ezra*, p. 99.

*A Death in the Desert*, p. 110.

*Caliban upon Setebos*, p. 136.

*Confessions*, p. 148.

*May and Death*, p. 150.

*Deaf and Dumb: a group by Woolner*, p. 151.

*Prospice*, p. 152.

*Eurydice to Orpheus; a Picture by Leighton*,
    p. 153.

*Youth and Art*, p. 154.

*A Face*, p. 158.

*A Likeness*, p. 159.

*Mr. Sludge, "the Medium,"* p. 162.

*Apparent Failure*, p. 219.

*Epilogue* (Three Speakers) p. 222.

1868-9. THE RING AND THE BOOK. By Robert Browning. In four vols., 8vo. London, Smith, Elder & Co., vols. i., ii., 1868; vols. iii., iv., 1869. The volumes were issued one by one, between November 1868 and February 1869. A "second edition," four volumes, appeared 1869.

1871. HERVÉ RIEL. In the *Cornhill Magazine*, March, 1871, pp. 257-60. Is dated "Croisic, Sept. 30th, 1867." Reprinted in *Pacchiarotto*, &c., 1876.

1871. BALAUSTION'S ADVENTURE: INCLUDING A TRANSCRIPT FROM EURIPIDES. By Robert Browning. 8vo. London, Smith, Elder & Co., 1871. With dedication to the Countess Cowper dated July 22, 1871. A third edition appeared in 1881. *The Last Adventure of Balaustion*, in *Aristophanes' Apology*, &c., 1875, is a sequel to this work.

1871. **PRINCE** HOHENSTIEL-SCHWANGAU : SAVIOUR OF SOCIETY. By Robert Browning. **8vo.** London, Smith, Elder & Co., 1871.

1872. FIFINE AT THE FAIR. By Robert Browning. **8vo.** London, Smith, Elder & Co.. 1872.

1872. SELECTIONS FROM THE POETICAL WORKS **OF** ROBERT BROWNING. London, Smith, Elder **&** Co., 1872. With a preface dated "London, May 14th, 1872." "Dedicated to Alfred Tennyson."

1872. THE POETICAL WORKS OF ROBERT BROWNING. (The Tauchnitz selection). **Two** vols., 8vo. Leipzig ; "Collection **of** British Authors." **As** this is a "copyright edition," **the** selection must **have** been either made **or** sanctioned **by Mr. Browning.**

1872-4. COMPLETE **WORKS OF** ROBERT BROWNING. **A** reprint from **the latest** English edition. 8vo. Chicago. Nos. 1-19 of **the "**Official **Guide of the** Chicago and Alton **R.R. and** Monthly Reprint and Advertiser." Edited by the manager **of** the railway, Mr. James Charlton. **A copy is** in the British Museum.

1873. RED COTTON NIGHT-CAP COUNTRY, **OR** TURF AND TOWERS. By Robert Browning. 8vo. London, Smith, Elder & Co., 1873. Dated **at** the end "January 23, 1873." Dedicated "To Miss Thackeray."

1875. ARISTOPHANES' APOLOGY, INCLUDING **A** TRANSCRIPT FROM EURIPIDES, BEING THE LAST ADVENTURE OF BALAUSTION. By Robert Browning. 8vo. London, Smith, Elder & Co., 1875. The "Transcript" is "Herakles."

1875. THE INN ALBUM. By Robert Browning. 8vo. London, Smith, Elder & Co., 1875.

A translation of this work into German by E. Leo: "Das Fremdenbuch," Hamburg, 1877.

1876. PACCHIAROTTO AND HOW HE WORKED IN DIS-
TEMPER: WITH OTHER POEMS.  By Robert
Browning.  8vo.  London, Smith, Elder & Co.,
1876.

Contents.

*Prologue.* ("O the old wall here.") [Called
"A Wall" in the selection of 1880], p. 1.

*Of Pacchiarotto and how he worked in Dis-
temper,* p. 4.

*At the "Mermaid,"* p. 47.

*House,* p. 60.

*Shop,* p. 64.

*Pisgah-Sights,* I., p. 75.

*Pisgah-Sights,* II., p. 78.

*Fears and Scruples,* p. 83.

*Natural Magic,* p. 88.

*Magical Nature,* p. 90.

*Bifurcation,* p. 91.

*Numpholeptos,* p. 95.

*Appearances,* p. 106.

*St. Martin's Summer,* p. 108.

*Hervé Riel,* p. 117.

*A Forgiveness,* p. 131.

*Cenciaja,* p. 162.

*Filippo Baldinucci on the Privilege of Burial,*
p. 184

*Epilogue* ["'The Poets pour us wine,'"] p. 223.

1877. THE AGAMEMNON OF ÆSCHYLUS, transcribed by
ROBERT BROWNING.  8vo., Smith, Elder & Co.,
1877, with preface dated London, October 1st,
1877.

1877. FAVOURITE POEMS.  By Robert Browning.  [A
selection].  Illustrated, pp. 96, 16mo.  Boston,

James R. Osgood & Co., 1877. [The Vest-Pocket Series of Standard and Popular Authors].

1878. LA SAISIAZ : THE TWO POETS OF CROISIC. By Robert Browning. 8vo. Smith, Elder & Co., 1878. "Dedicated to Mrs. Sutherland Orr." *La Saisiaz* is dated "November 9th, 1877," and *The Two Poets of Croisic,* "January 15th, 1878." The Proem to the *Two Poets of Croisic* was named "Apparitions" in the *Selections* of 1880.

1879. "OH LOVE, LOVE." *Two Stanzas—eighteen lines translated from the Hippolytus of Euripides,* contributed to Mr. J. P. Mahaffy's **Euripides,** p. 115, Macmillan, 1879. Not included in any collection of Robert Browning's Poems. Reprinted in *Browning Soc. (Bibliography) Papers,* pt. I, 1881, p. 69.

1879. DRAMATIC IDYLS. By Robert Browning. **Post** 8vo. London, Smith, Elder & Co., **1879.**

### Contents.

*Martin Relph,* p. 1.
*Pheidippides,* p. 27.
*Halbert and Hob,* p. **45.**
*Ivàn Ivànovitch,* p. 57.
*Tray,* p. 101.
*Ned Bratts,* p. 107.

1879. "THE BLIND MAN TO THE MAIDEN SAID." Poem, twenty lines, in "The Hour Will Come," by Wilhelmine von Hillern, translated from the German by Mrs. Clara Bell (vol. ii., p. 174). London, 8vo. Quoted in *Whitehall Review,* March 1, 1883, with statement that the English version of the poem is by Mr. Browning. Reprinted with some particulars in the *Browning Society's Papers,* pt. ii., p. 410, 1883.

1880. DRAMATIC IDYLS. Second Series. By Robert
    Browning. Post 8vo. London, Smith, Elder &
    Co., 1880.

> Contents.
>
> [*Proem*] ("You are sick, that's sure"), p. vii.
> *Echetlos*, p. 1.
> *Clive*, p. 9.
> *Muléykeh*, p. 43.
> *Pietro of Abano*, p. 61.
> *Doctor* ——, p. 113.
> *Pan and Luna*, p. 137.
> [*Epilogue*], ("Touch him ne'er so lightly"), p.
>     149.

> Ten additional· lines to this epilogue have
> been published—"Thus I wrote in London,
> musing," &c.   These lines appeared in the
> *Century Magazine* (Scribner's), vol. 25, 1882,
> pp. 159, 160, and were there said to have been
> written in an autograph album, October 14th,
> 1880.   They were reprinted in the *Browning
> Society's Papers*, pt. iii., p. 48*, November, 1882,
> but have been withdrawn from the Society's
> later issues.

1880. SELECTIONS FROM THE POETICAL WORKS OF
    ROBERT BROWNING. Second Series. 8vo.
    London, Smith, Elder & Co., 1880.   The First
    Series appeared in 1872.   Both were reprinted
    in 1884.

1882. A SELECTION FROM THE WORKS OF ROBERT
    BROWNING.   With a Memoir of the Author, and
    explanatory notes, by F. H. Ahn, 8vo.   Berlin,
    1882.   This is vol. viii. of Ahn's *Collection of
    British and American Standard Authors.*

1883. JOCOSERIA. By Robert Browning. 8vo. London,
    Smith, Elder & Co., 1883.

Contents.

1883. LYRICAL AND DRAMATIC POEMS SELECTED FROM **THE** WORKS OF ROBERT BROWNING. Edited by E. T. Mason. 8vo. New York, 1883.

[1883.] SELECTIONS FROM THE POETRY OF ROBERT BROWNING. With **an** Introduction **by R.** G. White, 8vo. New York.

1883. SONNET ON GOLDONI. Dated " Venice, **Nov. 27,** 1883," and written for the Album **of** the Committee of the Goldoni Monument at Venice, where it appears upon the first page. Printed in the *Pall Mall Gazette,* Dec. 8, 1883, and in the *Browning Society's Papers,* pt. **v., p.** 98*, 1884.

1883. PARAPHRASE FROM HORACE. (On Singers). [Horace's " *Omnibus hoc vitium est cantoribus,*" etc.] Four lines written impromptu for Mr. Felix Moscheles. Published in the *Pall Mall Gazette,* Dec. 12, 1883, and in the *Browning Society's Papers,* pt. v. p. 99*, 1884.

1884. SONNET ON RAWDON BROWN. Dated Nov. 28, 1883, and published in **the** *Century Magazine,* vol. 27, Feb. 1884, p. **640.** Reprinted in the *Browning Society's Papers,* pt. v., p. 132 *, 1884.

1884. THE FOUNDER OF THE FEAST.—A Sonnet. Inscribed by Mr. Browning in the Album presented to Mr. Arthur Chappell, director of the St. James's Hall Popular Concerts, etc. (*The World*, April 16, 1884). Reprinted in the *Browning Society's Papers*, pt. vii., p. 18 *, 1884. The sonnet is dated "April 5th, 1884."

1884. THE NAMES. Sonnet on Shakspeare. On page 1 of the "Shaksperian Show Book" of the Shaksperian Show held at the Albert Hall, May 29-31, 1884. The poem is dated "March 12, '84," and was published in the *Pall Mall Gazette*, May 29, 1884, and in the *Browning Society's Papers*, pt v., p. 105 *.

1884. "The Divine Order, and other Sermons and Addresses. By the late Thomas Jones." Edited by Brynmor Jones; with a short INTRODUCTION by Robert Browning. London, 1884, 8vo.

1884. FERISHTAH'S FANCIES. By Robert Browning. 8vo. Smith, Elder & Co., 1884.

Contents :

*Prologue* ("Pray Reader"), p. 1.
1. *The Eagle*, p. 5.
2. *The Melon-Seller*, p. 9.
3. *Shah Abbas*, p. 13.
4. *The Family*, p. 25.
5. *The Sun*, p. 33.
6. *Mihrab Shah*, p. 46.
7. *A Camel-Driver*, p. 59.
8. *Two Camels*, p. 69.
9. *Cherries*, p. 78.
10. *Plot-Culture*, p. 87.
11. *A Pillar at Sebzevah*, p. 93.
12. *A Bean-Stripe ; also Apple-eating*, p. 105.
    *Epilogue* ["Oh, Love—no Love !"] p. 140.

1884. SELECTIONS FROM THE POETICAL WORKS OF ROBERT BROWNING. Two series. 2 vols. 8vo. London, Smith, Elder & Co., 1884. A reprint of the two series, which appeared respectively in 1872 and 1880.

**1884.** THE PIED PIPER OF HAMELIN. By Robert Browning. London, Robert Dunthorne, 1884. Small 4to. Not published for **sale,** but printed by Mr. Browning's permission "**to** accompany Mr. Macbeth's Etchings, after the late G. J. Pinwell's drawings illustrating its subject."

1885. POMEGRANATES **FROM AN** ENGLISH GARDEN : A SELECTION FROM **THE** POEMS OF ROBERT BROWNING. With Introduction and **Notes** by John Munro Gibson. **New** York, 1885, **8vo.**

1885. WHY I **AM** A LIBERAL. Sonnet contributed **to** "Why I **am** a Liberal," edited by Andrew Reid. London, Cassell & Co., n.d. [1885]. Not collected **by** Mr. Browning, but reprinted **in** *Browning Society's Papers,* October, 1885, p. 89 *, **and in** "Sonnets of the Century," edited by W. Sharp, 1886.

1886. Spring Song ("Dance, yellows and whites and reds !") contributed to *The New Amphion : being the Book of the* Edinburgh University Union *Fancy Fair.* Edinburgh University Press, 1886, p. 1. (Reappeared in *Lairesse* in *Parleyings,* &c., p. 189).

1886. SELECT POEMS OF ROBERT BROWNING, with notes by W. **J.** Rolfe and H. E. Hersey. New York, 1886, 8vo.

1887. PARLEYINGS WITH CERTAIN PEOPLE OF IMPORTANCE IN THEIR DAY ; to wit :
*Bernard de Mandeville,*
*Daniel Bartoli,*

*Christopher Smart,*
*George Bubb Dodington,*
*Francis Furini,*
*Gerard de Lairesse,* and
*Charles Avison.*

Introduced by *A Dialogue between Apollo and The Fates;* concluded by another between *John Fust and his Friends.* By Robert Browning. London, Smith, Elder & Co., 1887, 8vo. Dedicated "In Memoriam J. Milsand, obit. iv. Sept. MDCCCLXXXVI. *Absens absentem auditque videtque.*"

1888-9. THE POETICAL WORKS OF ROBERT BROWNING. Sixteen vols. 8vo. Smith, Elder & Co., 1888-9. All the works collected by the author, excepting only *Asolando.*

Contents.

*Pauline,* vol. i., p. 1.
*Sordello,* vol. i., p. 47.
*Paracelsus,* vol. ii., p. 1.
*Strafford,* vol. ii. p. 187.
*Pippa Passes,* vol. iii., p. 1.
*King Victor and King Charles,* vol. iii., p. 81.
*Return of the Druses,* vol. iii., p. 167.
*A Soul's Tragedy,* vol. iii., p. 257.
*A Blot in the 'Scutcheon,* vol. iv., p. 1.
*Colombe's Birthday,* vol. iv., p. 71.
*Men and Women,* vol. iv., p. 171.
*Dramatic Romances,* vol. v., p. 1.
*Christmas-Eve and Easter-Day,* vol. v., p. 209.
*Dramatic Lyrics,* vol. vi., p. 1.
*Luria,* vol. vi., p. 209.
*In a Balcony,* vol. vii., p. 1.
*Dramatis Personæ,* vol. vii., p. 45.

*The Ring and the Book.* Books 1 to 4, **vol.** viii., p. 1.

     „    „    Books 5 to 8, vol. ix., **p. 1.**

     „    „    Books 9 to 12, vol. **x., p. 1.**

*Balaustion's Adventure,* **vol** xi., p. **1.**

*Prince Hohenstiel-Schwangau,* vol. xi., **p. 123.**

*Fifine at the Fair,* **vol.** xi., **p. 211.**

*Red Cotton Night-Cap Country,* vol. xii., p. 1.

*The Inn Album,* **vol.** xii., p. 179.

*Aristophanes' Apology,* including **a** Transcript **from** Euripides, being the *Last Adventure of Balaustion,* vol. xiii., p. **1.**

*The Agamemnon of Æschylus,* vol. xiii., p. 259.

*Pacchiarotto, and how he worked in Distemper;* with **other** Poems, **vol. xiv.,** p. **1.**

*La Saisiaz:* and *The Two Poets of Croisic,* vol. **xiv.,** p. **153.**

*Dramatic Idyls.* First series, vol. **xv., p. 1.**

     „    „    Second series, vol. xv., p. 85.

*Jocoseria,* vol. xv., **p.** 165.

*Ferishtah's Fancies,* vol. xvi., p. 1.

*Parleyings with Certain People of Importance in their Day,* vol. xvi., **p.** 93.

[1889]. THE PIED PIPER OF HAMELIN. By Robert Browning. With 35 illustrations by Kate Greenaway. Pp. 64, Routledge & Sons, 4to.

1889. FIVE LINES (beginning "Wind wafted from the sunset"), on a picture by Mr. Felix Moscheles, "The Isle's Enchantress." Printed in the *Pall Mall Gazette* for March 26, 1889.

1889-90. The Poetical Works of Elizabeth Barrett Browning. In six volumes. London, Smith, Elder & Co., 1889-90. 8vo. Vol. i. contains a PREFATORY NOTE signed "R. B.," and dated "29, De Vere Gardens, W., December 10, 1887" ["1887" must

be a misprint for 1888, as the " Prefatory Note"
mentions a Memoir of E. B. Browning by John
H. Ingram, which was published in September,
1888].

1890. ASOLANDO: FANCIES AND FACTS.   By Robert
Browning.   8vo.   Smith, Elder & Co., 1890.
With dedication "To Mrs. Arthur Bronson."
Now (1891) in its eighth edition.   The dedication
is dated "Asolo, October 15, 1889."   The volume
was published on the day of the poet's death,
December 12, 1889.

Contents.

*Prologue* ("The Poet's age is sad ; for why?")
p. 1.

*Rosny*, p. 5.

*Dubiety*, p. 8.

*Now*, p. 10.

*Humility*, p. 11.

*Poetics*, p. 12.

*Summum Bonum*, p. 13.

*A Pearl, a Girl*, p. 14.

*Speculative*, p. 15.

*White Witchcraft*, p. 17.

*Bad Dreams*, I., II., III., IV., p. 19.

*Inapprehensiveness*, p. 34.

*Which?* p. 37.

*The Cardinal and the Dog*, p. 40.

*The Pope and the Net*, p. 42.

*The Bean-Feast*, p. 46.

*Muckle-Mouth Meg*, p. 52.

*Arcades ambo*, p. 56.

*The Lady and the Painter*, p. 58.

*Ponte dell' Angelo, Venice*, p. 61.

*Beatrice Signorini*, p. 76.

*Flute Music, with an Accompaniment*, p. 99.

"*Imperante Augusto natus est ——,*" p. 112.

*Development*, **p. 123.**

*Rephan*, p. 131.

*Reverie*, p. 141.

*Epilogue* ("At the midnight, in the silence of the sleep-time"), p. 156.

1890. Poems by Elizabeth Barrett Browning. With PRE-FATORY NOTE by R. B. 16mo. London, Smith Elder & Co., 1890.

1890. POCKET VOLUME OF SELECTIONS FROM THE POETICAL WORKS OF ROBERT BROWNING. **London,** Smith, Elder & Co., 1890, **16mo.**

*\*\** **In the** "Bibliography" attached to Mr. William Sharp's "Life of Robert Browning" (London, W. Scott, 1890), under Section **II.,** "Single Works," appear the following entries :—

(1) "Cleon. Moxon : London, 1855. 8vo. Reprinted in *Men and Women.*"

(2) "Gold Hair : a Legend **of** Pornic. [London], 1864. **8vo.** Reprinted in *Dramatis Personæ.*"

(3) "The Statue and the Bust. Moxon : London, 1855. 8vo. Reprinted in *Men and Women.*"

(4) Mr. Sharp also (p. 173) mentions a leaflet containing "Prospice."

Pamphlets bearing the titles of the first and third certainly exist, and this may also be the case with regard to the second and fourth ; but as nothing is known of the history of any one of the four, all are excluded from the foregoing Bibliography.

# AN ALPHABETICAL LIST OF ROBERT BROWNING'S WORKS,

## BEING AN INDEX TO THE FOREGOING BIBLIOGRAPHY AND TO THE COLLECTED EDITIONS OF 1868 AND 1889-90.

# INDEX TO FIRST LINES OF SHORTER POEMS.

## NEW UNIFORM EDITION.

# INDEX.

420     *Index.*

CHISWICK PRESS:—C. WHITTINGHAM AND CO., TOOKS COURT, CHANCERY LANE.